NATO ASI Series

Advanced Science Institutes Series

A series presenting the results of activities sponsored by the NATO Science Committee, which aims at the dissemination of advanced scientific and technological knowledge, with a view to strengthening links between scientific communities.

The Series is published by an international board of publishers in conjunction with the NATO Scientific Affairs Division

A	Life Sciences	Plenum Publishing Corporation
B	Physics	London and New York
C	Mathematical and Physical Sciences	Kluwer Academic Publishers Dordrecht, Boston and London
D	Behavioural and Social Sciences	
E	Applied Sciences	
F	Computer and Systems Sciences	Springer-Verlag Berlin Heidelberg New York
G	Ecological Sciences	London Paris Tokyo Hong Kong
H	Cell Biology	Barcelona Budapest
I	Global Environmental Change	

NATO-PCO DATABASE

The electronic index to the NATO ASI Series provides full bibliographical references (with keywords and/or abstracts) to more than 30 000 contributions from international scientists published in all sections of the NATO ASI Series. Access to the NATO-PCO DATABASE compiled by the NATO Publication Coordination Office is possible in two ways:

- via online FILE 128 (NATO-PCO DATABASE) hosted by ESRIN, Via Galileo Galilei, I-00044 Frascati, Italy.

- via CD-ROM "NATO Science & Technology Disk" with user-friendly retrieval software in English, French and German (© WTV GmbH and DATAWARE Technologies Inc. 1992).

The CD-ROM can be ordered through any member of the Board of Publishers or through NATO-PCO, Overijse, Belgium.

Series F: Computer and Systems Sciences Vol. 129

The ASI Series F Books Published as a Result of
Activities of the Special Programme on
ADVANCED EDUCATIONAL TECHNOLOGY

This book contains the proceedings of a NATO Advanced Research Work-
shop held within the activities of the NATO Special Programme on Advanced
Educational Technology, running from 1988 to 1993 under the auspices of the
NATO Science Committee.

The volumes published so far in the Special Programme are as follows (further
details are given at the end of this volume):

Human-Machine Communication for Educational Systems Design

Edited by

Maddy D. Brouwer-Janse

Institute for Perception Research/IPO
P. O. Box 513, 5600 MB Eindhoven, The Netherlands

Thomas L. Harrington

Fast Motion Perception
4715 Mayberry Drive, Reno, NV 89509, USA

Springer-Verlag
Berlin Heidelberg New York London Paris Tokyo
Hong Kong Barcelona Budapest
Published in cooperation with NATO Scientific Affairs Division

Proceedings of the NATO Advanced Study Institute on Basics of Man-Machine
Communication for the Design of Educational Systems, held in Eindhoven, The
Netherlands, August 16–26, 1993

LB
1028.38
.H86
1994

CR Subject Classification (1991): K.3, H.5.1-2, I.2-4, J.7

ISBN 3-540-57748-3 Springer-Verlag Berlin Heidelberg New York
ISBN 0-387-57748-3 Springer-Verlag New York Berlin Heidelberg

CIP data applied for

© Springer-Verlag Berlin Heidelberg 1994
Printed in Germany

Typesetting: Camera-ready by authors/editors
SPIN: 10130718   45/3140 – 5 4 3 2 1 0 – Printed on acid-free paper

Preface

This book contains the papers presented at the NATO Advanced Study Institute (ASI) on the Basics of Man-Machine Communication for the Design of Educational Systems, held August 16–26, 1993 in Eindhoven, The Netherlands.

The ASI addressed the state of the art in the design of educational systems with respect to theories, enabling technologies and advanced applications and implementation issues. The topics discussed are grouped into four main subject areas: 1) Fundamentals of human perception and reasoning, 2) New media: enabling technologies, 3) Artificial Intelligence; software and design techniques, and 4) Advanced applications. This interdisciplinary approach, with a clear focus on the application domain of learning environments, provided the platform for interdisciplinary exchange and communication between the participants.

The role of human perception and reasoning was presented in the context of design requirements. The construction of usable human-machine interfaces requires designers to be aware of the inherent competence of the human user. That is, a designer needs to understand the resources that the user brings to the interaction. This includes the general nature of human and world interactions; the nature of the human perceptual system; the natural learning processes by which the information given by the senses is transformed into knowledge of the world; the reasoning processes that allow humans to make inferences from that knowledge once acquired; and the ways in which acquired knowledge may be communicated to others through language.

New media that support human-machine communication and the enabling technologies upon which they depend were presented and discussed. Topics included: new and novel types of human-computer interaction techniques; the use of sound effects in educational software; electronic books for interactive learning; three-dimensional view setting; the use of animated icons to promote the learning of the functions that they represent; and the use of generated natural language within an immersive language learning system. A fundamental goal of human-machine communication research is to increase the useful bandwidth across the interface. Since the user of this path is difficult to modify, it is the computer side that provides fertile ground for research in human-machine communication. Ideally this research should start with studies of the characteristics of human communication channels and skills and then work toward developing devices and techniques that communicate effectively to and from those channels.

Three themes dominated the Artificial Intelligence, software and design sessions. They are: the role of social interaction between agents, the role of dialogue in learning and problem solving, and the use of visual display in programming and knowledge elicitation. Two ways of achieving the interaction between agents were discussed: by distributed AI using blackboard architectures and contract net protocols and by treating cooperation and other social issues in the framework of situated agents. The role of dialogue was presented in the context of providing users with intelligent assistance from a learning companion or from an expert system.

The program emphasized the application of research in actual working educational systems and promoted the two-way transfer of technology between the research community and the engineering and design communities. Examples of advanced applications were presented and discussed during the ASI, among others, multimedia information access based on cohesion as an alternative for browsing via menus and keywords, handwriting for non-Roman languages, and interactive multimedia for foreign language learning. Demonstrations of applications for a variety of educational tasks were given, for example, learning fundamental concepts in science and engineering, learning foreign languages, and training on simulators.

This book was conceived, designed and produced during the ASI as a joint effort of all participants of the ASI. A major objective was to give researchers from different disciplines the opportunity to communicate about their different approaches to the theoretical and applied problems that dominate the domain of educational technology. These opportunities for interdisciplinary communication are rare and the transfer of knowledge across disciplinary borders is difficult, i.e., differences in scientific language, in scientific cultures, and in available tools affect the synergy needed to design educational systems for a wide variety of application domains and different communities of end users. This book is a compendium of the finalized and refined ideas, and contributions of knowledge and methodology that each individual participant submitted after the experience of the ASI. The material is organized into four sections, each with an introduction by one of the participants.

Many people contributed to the organization of the ASI. A very special mention needs to be made of the efforts of the main lecturers and the organizing committee members. Without their support and dedication it is doubtful that this ASI could have been accomplished. The organizing committee included Dominique Béroule, Robbert-Jan Beun and Tom Bösser. The ASI was organized by the Institute for Perception Research/IPO, Eindhoven. We are very grateful for all the facilitating support of the administrative and technical staff of IPO. We are especialy indebted to Ilse van Kuijck, our production editor, who before, during and after the ASI was largely responsible for keeping us all on track. Final thanks are to be extended to the NATO Committee on the Special Programme on Advanced Educational Technology who made the ASI possible.

January 1994

Maddy D. Brouwer-Janse
Thomas L. Harrington

Table of Contents

Part 1: Fundamentals of Human Perception and Reasoning

Part 2: New Media: Enabling Technologies

Part 3: Artificial Intelligence, Software and Design Techniques

Part 4: Advanced Applications

Part 1

Fundamentals of Human Perception and Reasoning

Fundamentals of Human Perception and Reasoning

Introduction

The role of human perception and reasoning is presented in the context of design requirements. The construction of usable human-machine interfaces requires designers to be aware of the inherent competences of human users in at least two different ways. First, a designer needs to understand the resources that the user brings to the interaction. This includes the general nature of human and world interactions; the nature of the human perceptual system; the natural learning processes by which the information given by the senses is transformed into knowledge of the world; the reasoning processes that allow to make inferences from that knowledge once acquired; and the ways in which acquired knowledge may be communicated to others through language.

The contributions in this section address all of these fundamental issues for human-machine communication. Kaptelinin introduces a framework for understanding human-world and hence human-machine interactions in terms of "activity theory", a psychological approach recently receiving much attention in the area of human-computer interaction. Harrington & Bidyuk and Van Nes address visual perception and the consequences of the principles discovered for the presentation of information by computer. Munro introduces the fundamental neural principles underlying human learning that are being uncovered by neural network research. Oaksford introduces some of the reasoning biases to which people are apparently prone and suggests that these are natural consequences of peoples' probabilistic reasoning strategies. Van Hoe discusses the cognitive load theory and provides experimental evidence of its role in the acquisition of problem-solving skills. In the area of language, Cremers addresses issues of reference in a shared environment and Beun investigates a tractable approach to model cooperative behaviour in dialogues.

Second, peoples' natural competences may be revealed in the way that they manipulate tools (computational or otherwise). Psychological evaluation and analysis of such interactions can serve to bring practices into line with those natural competences. Bösser discusses how models of human-computer interaction can be used to measure the usability of systems. Three papers in this section seek to understand how people naturally cope with some traditional tasks, like constraint management in computer mediated design (Day); the acquisition of troubleshooting skills (Schaafstal & Schraagen); and macro use in using menus (Saariluoma & Miettinen).

Activity Theory: Implications for Human Computer Interaction

Victor Kaptelinin

Psychological Institute, Russian Academy of Education,
9 "V" Mokhovaja Str., 103009 Moscow, Russia

Abstract. Recently interest has grown in applying activity theory, the leading theoretical approach in Russian psychology, to issues of human computer interaction. This paper analyzes the reasons why the experts in the field are looking for an alternative to the currently dominant cognitive approach. The basic principles of activity theory are presented and their implications for human computer interaction are discussed. The paper concludes with an outline of the potential impact of activity theory on studies and design of computer use in real-life settings.

Keywords. Activity theory, models of human computer interaction, psychology of computer use

1 The Current Need For a Theory of Human Computer Interaction

It is generally accepted that the lack of an adequate theory of human computer interaction (HCI) is one of the most important reasons why progress in the field of HCI is relatively modest, compared with the rate of the technological development. People coming to the field of HCI from different disciplines--psychology, computer science, graphics design, etc.--have serious problems in coordinating and combining their efforts. This can be illustrated by the HCI curricula for undergraduate and graduate students. Typically, these curricula present a mixture of knowledge from various disciplines, rather than an integrated perspective.

Traditional conceptual approaches cannot provide an appropriate basis for addressing many important aspects of HCI, including Computer Supported Cooperative Work (CSCW) and cross-cultural aspects of computer use. In consequence the impact of HCI studies on current design practice is limited--user interface design being based mainly on intuition and expensive trial-and-error.

The form of a suitable HCI theory has been subjected to much debate recently (see Carroll, et al., 1991). A major trend in the debate has been the growing dissatisfaction with the dominant cognitive approach (Bannon, 1991; Wood, 1992; Monk, et. al., 1993). In contrast to the general agreement that current attempts to apply cognitive psychology to HCI are not very successful, there is little agreement on the most promising theoretical alternatives. Proposals vary from an enrichment of the traditional cognitive scheme (Barnard, 1991) to a radical shift in paradigms, e.g., from scientific experimental studies to ethnographic methodology (see Monk, et al., 1993).

In this period of theoretical uncertainty there has been a growing interest in "activity theory". This interest was greatly stimulated by S. Bødker's works (1989, 1991). She was the first western researcher who presented the basic ideas and potential benefits of activity theory to the HCI community. Recently, a number of papers discussing the activity theory approach to HCI appeared in major international journals and conference proceedings (Bannon, Bødker, 1991; Draper, 1993; Kaptelinin, 1992-a; Kuutti, 1992; Kuutti & Bannon, 1993; Nardi, 1992; Norman, 1991; Raeithel, 1992; Wood, 1992).

The aim of the present paper is to summarize current work and the implications of activity theory for the field of human computer interaction. The rest of the paper discusses the main differences between activity theory and cognitive psychology, reviews recent attempts to apply activity theory to HCI, and outlines some directions for further development.

2 From Cognitive Psychology to Contextual Analysis of HCI

According to cognitive psychology, the human mind is a specific type of an information processing unit. Various architectures of human cognition have been proposed, all of which differentiate between three basic modules, or subsystems: 1) sensory input subsystem; 2) central information processing subsystem; 3) motor output subsystem. Another fundamental idea underlying most cognitive models is that of levels of processing. Essentially, this is the dimension of concreteness/abstractness. Input and output represent low levels of human information processing, since they deal with the "raw" data of external reality. Higher level processing provides identification and classification of these data, as well as their assimilation into mental representations, understanding, analysis, decision making, etc. For a specific action to be made, abstract goals and strategies must be formulated in a concrete form. In other words, the information is processed in both directions: from reality to models and from models to reality.

The theoretical constructs of cognitive psychology have direct analogies in computer science, and the difference in terminology used in these two disciplines is minimal, which was the major factor behind the dominant role of cognitive psychology in HCI.

From the traditional cognitive point of view, the HCI system is composed of two information processing units--the human being and the computer--so that the output of one unit enters the other's input, and *vice versa*. In other words, human computer interaction can be described as an "information processing loop" (see Fig. 1). The advantages of this scheme are rather obvious. First, it provides a coherent description of the whole system of human computer interaction within the information processing framework. Second, it structures the problem space of HCI in a useful way. Aspects of human computer interaction, such as presentation of the information to the user, user's perceptions, mental models, user's control of the system, input devices, user interface vs functionality of the system, can be easily located within this scheme.

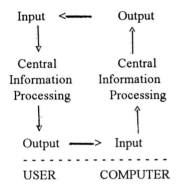

Fig. 1. The "information processing loop" of human computer interaction.

The idea of levels of processing has also influenced studies of HCI. For instance, many researchers were influenced by the hierarchical structure of human computer interfaces proposed by Moran (1981). He identified five levels, namely: the task level, the semantic level, the syntactic level, the level of interaction, and the level of physical devices. This structure is explicitly design-oriented: it is supposed to support an analogy with top-down programming in user interface design.

So, it appears that cognitive psychology can be successfully applied to a number of problems of human computer interaction. However, this approach has some limitations. Namely, the "ecological validity" of cognitive psychology is questionable (see Neisser, 1976).

The information processing loop mentioned above is closed. It is difficult to take into consideration the phenomena that exist outside this loop. It is obvious, however, that human computer interaction can only be understood within a wider context. People use computers to create documents, to communicate with others, etc., i.e., to achieve some goals that are meaningful beyond actual computer use. Essentially, the "task level," according to the hierarchy proposed by Moran (see above), is supposed to put computer use into the right global context. Yet the relevant concepts and procedures were not articulated by Moran specifically enough, and the models of human computer interaction based on his ideas (see Nielsen, 1986; Clarke, 1986) are just the models of the closed information processing loop (or a hierarchy of virtual loops).

There is an emerging consensus that the cognitive approach to HCI may be limited. It does not provide an appropriate conceptual basis for studies of computer use in its social, organizational, and cultural context, in relation to the goals, plans and values of the user, in the context of development. In consequence, current studies of HCI, that concentrate not only on the low level events of computer use but on the higher level events as well (Grudin, 1990), require an appropriate theoretical framework in which to analyze the context of computer use.

There are several candidate approaches, including situated actions, distributed cognition, and activity theory (see Nardi, 1992). The next section presents the basic principles of activity theory outlining its conceptual potential for studies of human computer interaction.

3 Basic Principles of Activity Theory

The general philosophy of activity theory can be characterized as an attempt to integrate three perspectives: 1) the objective; 2) the ecological; 3) the socio-cultural. Like cognitive psychology, and unlike some other approaches in psychology, activity theory tends to be a "real," i.e. a "natural-science-like" theory. Like J. Piaget's (Piaget, 1950) and J. J. Gibson's (Gibson, 1979) approaches and unlike traditional cognitive psychology, it analyzes human beings in their natural environment. Moreover, activity theory takes into account cultural factors and developmental aspects of human mental life. These statements can be clarified as follows (see also Bødker, 1991; Leontiev, 1978,1981; Wertsch, 1981).

The most fundamental principle of activity theory is the principle of the "unity of consciousness and activity." "Consciousness" in this expression means the human mind as a whole. "Activity" means human interaction with the objective reality. This principle states, therefore, that the human mind emerges and exists as a special component of human interaction with the environment. Mind is a special "organ" that appears in the process of evolution to help organisms to survive. So, it can be analyzed and understood only within the context of activity.

The next principle is "object-orientedness". This principle specifies the activity theory approach to the environment with which human beings are interacting. Unlike Piaget and Gibson, activity theory considers social/cultural properties of the environment to be as objective as physical, chemical, or biological ones. These properties exist regardless of our feelings about them. "The object is a book," is no less an objective property of a thing than "the surface of object mostly reflects the light of the red spectrum," (i.e., that the object is "red").

So, human beings live in an environment that is meaningful in itself. This environment consists of entities that combine all kinds of objective features, including the culturally determined ones, which, in turn, determine the way people act on these entities. The principle of object-orientedness is an obvious contrast to the assumption behind the cognitive approach that the human mind contacts reality only through low level input/output processes.

The third basic principle of activity theory is the "hierarchical structure of activity." Activity theory differentiates between processes at various levels (or, rather, groups of levels) taking into consideration the objects to which these processes are oriented. Activities are oriented to motives, i.e. the objects that are impelling by themselves. Each motive is an object, material or ideal, that satisfies a need. Actions are the processes functionally subordinated to activities, they are directed at specific conscious goals. According to activity theory, the dissociation between objects that motivate human activity and the objects to which this activity is immediately directed, is of fundamental significance. Actions are realized through operations that are determined by the actual conditions of activity.

The importance of these distinctions is determined by the ecological attitude of activity theory. In a real-life situation it is often necessary to predict human behavior. For this purpose it is of critical importance to differentiate between motives, goals, and conditions. In particular, people behave differently in different situations of frustration. When operations are frustrated, i.e. when familiar conditions are changed, often people do not even notice and automatically adapt themselves to the new situation. When a goal is frustrated, it is necessary to realize what to do next and to set a new goal. But this is often done without much effort and without any negative emotion. Also, it is possible to predict what the new goal will be, provided that the motive remains the same. When a motive is frustrated, people are upset and behavior is most unpredictable.

In consequence, to understand and to predict the changes of people's behavior in different situations, it is necessary to take into account the "status" of the behavior in question, that is, is it oriented to a motive, a goal, or actual conditions? This is why activity theory differentiates between activities, actions, and operations. The criteria for separating these processes are: 1) whether the object to which the given process is oriented is impelling in itself or is auxiliary (this criterion differentiates between activities and actions); 2) whether the given process is automatized (this criterion differentiates between actions and operations).

The fourth principle of activity theory is the principle of internalization/externalization (Vygotsky, 1978). This principle describes the mechanisms underlying the originating of mental processes. It states that mental processes are derived from external actions through the course of internalization.

The concept of internalization was also introduced by J. Piaget, but the meaning of this concept within activity theory is somewhat different. According to L. Vygotsky (1978), internalization is social by its very nature. The range of actions that can be performed by a person in cooperation with others comprises the so called "zone of proximal development." In other words, the way human beings acquire new abilities can be characterized as "from inter-subjective mental actions to intra-subjective ones." The process opposite to internalization is externalization. Mental processes manifest themselves in external actions performed by a person. So, they can be verified and corrected, if necessary.

The fifth principle is "mediation." Human activity is mediated by a number of tools, either external (like a hammer or scissors) or internal (like concepts or heuristics). These tools specify their modes of operation, i.e., those developed over the history of society. The use of these culture-specific tools shapes the way people act and, through the process of internalization, greatly influences the nature of mental development. So, tools are the carriers of cultural knowledge and social experience. Tool mediation is no less an important source of socialization than formal education is.

The mechanism underlying tool mediation is the formation of "functional organs." The latter are the combination of natural human abilities with the capacities of external components -- tools -- to perform a new function or to perform an existing one in a more efficient way. For example, human eyes equipped with glasses compose a functional organ that provides better vision.

The last (but not least!) principle is the principle of development. According to activity theory, to understand a phenomenon means to know how it developed into its existing form. It is the principle of development that gives an opportunity to conduct thorough scientific analysis of complex phenomena while avoiding mechanistic oversimplifications.

The principles described above are not isolated ideas. They are closely interrelated; the nature of activity theory is manifested in this set of principles taken as an integrated whole.

4 Activity Theory and Human Computer Interaction

According to activity theory, the computer is just another tool that mediates the interaction of human beings with their environment. The only way to come to an adequate understanding of human computer interaction is to reconstruct the overall activity of computer use. As Kuutti (1992) argued, activity provides a "minimal meaningful context" for human computer interaction. The questions that arise when computer use is considered from the point of view of activity theory, are: What is the hierarchical level of human computer interaction within the structure of activity? Does computer use correspond to the level of particular activities, to the level of actions, or to the level of operations? Which tools, other than computerized tools, are available to the user? What is the structure of social interactions surrounding computer use? What are the objectives of computer use by the user and how are they related to the objectives of other people and the group/organization as a whole?

These questions may seem to be too global and loosely related to the practice of user interface evaluation and design. However, when these questions are ignored undesirable consequences may follow, including low software usability (Grudin, 1991-a, 1991-b) and the choice of software not suited to a specific culture (Borgman, 1992).

Another general idea directly relevant to the field of human/computer interaction is that of development. The importance of analyzing computer use within a developmental context is relevant to both the individual level and the group/organizational level. An assimilation of new technologies causes emerging of new tasks (the so called "task-artifact cycle," see Carroll, et. al., 1991). A possible way to cope with unpredictable structural changes on a users' activity is to support users in customizing the system according to their current needs (Henderson, Kyng, 1991). Yet this is not a universal solution because users often need substantial assistance even in formulating their own needs. So, a conceptual analysis of the basic factors and regularities of organizational development is needed to predict this development and to provide an efficient use of information technologies.

The development of individual expertise is also an important factor that is not adequately addressed by the cognitive approach. Cognitive models of skill acquisition, based on ideas of procedural knowledge compilation or chunking, have troubles with accounting for the qualitative changes that cognitive skills undergo in the process of development (see, e.g., Kaptelinin, 1992-b). Yet these very transformations can be studied and predicted from the standpoint of N. Bernstein's theory (Bernstein, 1967) which is usually closely associated with activity theory.

The tool mediation perspective suggests a structure for human computer interaction that is radically different from the information processing loop. The components of the structure should not only be the user and the computer but also the object the user is operating on through the computer application, and the other people with whom the user is communicating (Bødker, 1991).

The tool mediation perspective means that there are actually two interfaces that should be considered in any study of computer use: the human/computer interface and the computer/environment interface (see Fig. 2)

```
   |                    |
   | USER <——> COMPUTER | <——> ENVIRONMENT
   |                    |
```

Fig.2. Two interfaces in human computer interaction

Interface in the traditional sense is not only a border separating two entities but also a link which provides the integration of a computer tool into the structure of human activity. The mechanisms underlying this integration can be understood from the point of view of activity theory as the formation of a functional organ. It means, therefore, that computer applications are the extensions of some natural (pre-computer) human abilities. One of the most important functions of computer tools in the structure of human activity seems to be the extension of the cognitive structure referred to within activity theory as the "internal plane of actions" (IPA). The equivalent of the IPA within the cognitive tradition is the mental space where mental models are located. Its function is to simulate potential outcomes of possible events before making actions in reality.

In sum, activity theory provides a wider theoretical basis for studies of human computer interaction, than cognitive psychology. It can account for social interactions and for cultural factors, for the developmental aspects and for higher level goals and values. At the same time this conceptual framework does not reject the experimental results and techniques accumulated within the cognitive tradition. According to M. Cole, "... US standard cognitive psychology is a reduced subset of a cultural-historical activity approach -- without realizing it." (Cole, personal communication, October 1992). Actually, if we compare the information processing loop (see Fig. 1) and the tool mediation scheme (see Fig. 2), we can see that the former can easily be placed in the context of the latter.

5 Prospects for the Future Development of Activity-oriented Approaches to Human Computer Interaction

One fundamental difficulty related to building up a theory of human computer interaction is the changing nature of the subject matter of the study. In contrast to physical laws, the laws of human computer interaction are not necessarily invariant over time. When the current methods, styles, standards, etc., of human computer interaction are used, the results are inevitably obsolete soon after they are formulated. Activity theory puts human computer interaction into the context of basic, invariant principles underlying human activity, so it provides a better chance for creating a theoretical framework that has a predictive potential.

Attempts to apply activity theory to the field of HCI have only been made recently. Most papers, including the present one, are intended just to describe the basics of activity theory and to discuss its general plausibility. However, there are also some cases of the "real" use of activity theory as a conceptual tool in approaching actual problems. These efforts include the analysis of some conceptual problems related to the meaning of the term "interface" (Kuutti, Bannon, 1993), the "mapping" technique that makes it possible to construct a structured two-dimensional representation of the process of computer use and to identify the critical events that take place over this process (Bødker, 1993), and the development of the "cognitive - cultural" approach to collaborative writing (Wood, 1992).

In my view, there are good reasons to expect more tangible results from activity theory in the coming years. First, I believe a new model of human computer interaction will replace the information processing loop underlying the cognitive approach. This model will identify and present in a thorough way the most important aspects of computer use by individuals and groups/organizations. This model will hopefully provide various parties involved in the study and design of human computer interaction with a framework that can make their mutual understanding and cooperation more efficient.

Activity theory can influence the methodology, analysis and evaluation of human computer interaction. The results obtained by Bødker (1993) can be considered as a first step toward the development of methods that provide the opportunity to organize appropriate field observations or laboratory studies and to obtain valid and reliable data that would be relevant in real-life contexts.

Finally, activity theory can make an important impact on the development of design support tools. The design of a new interactive system involves the design of a new activity -- individual or organizational. However, even the perfect design of an ideal activity does not guarantee the success of a system. The transformation of an activity from an initial to a target state can be difficult and even painful. Activity theory may be used as a basis for the development of a representational framework that would help designers to capture current practice, as well as to build predictive models of activity dynamics. Such conceptual tools would enable designers to achieve at appropriate design solutions, especially during the early phases of design.

Acknowledgments

I would like to thank Mike Oaksford, Donald Day, and Kirsten Foot for valuable comments on an earlier draft of this paper.

References

Bannon L. (1991) From human factors to human actors: The role of psychology and human computer interaction studies in system design. In: J.Greenbaum, M. Kyng (eds.) Design at Work: Cooperative Design of Computer Systems. Hillsdale, NJ: Lawrence Erlbaum.

Bannon L., Bødker S. (1991) Beyond the interface: Encountering artifacts in use. In: J. Carroll (ed.) Designing Interaction: Psychology at the Human-Computer Interface. Cambridge: Cambridge University Press.

Barnard P. (1991) Bridging between basic theories and the artifacts of human computer interaction. In: J. Carroll (ed.) Designing Interaction: Psychology at the Human-Computer Interface. Cambridge: Cambridge University Press.

Bernstein N. (1967) The Co-ordination and Regulation of Movements. Oxford: Pergamon Press.

Bødker S. (1989) A human activity approach to user interfaces. Human Computer Interaction, 4.

Bødker S. (1991) Through the Interface: A Human Activity Approach to User Interface Design. Hillsdale, NJ: Lawrence Erlbaum.

Bødker S. (1993) Reframing the human computer interaction from the activity theory point of view. The Journal of Psychology (Psikhologicheski Zhurnal), 14(4) (in Russian).

Borgman C.L. (1992) Cultural diversity in interface design. SIGCHI Bulletin, October.

Carroll J.M., Kellogg W.A., Rosson M.B. (1991) The task-artifact cycle. In: J. Carroll (ed.) Designing Interaction: Psychology at the Human-Computer Interface. Cambridge: Cambridge University Press.

Clarke A.A. (1986) A three-level human-computer interface model. International Journal of Man-Machine Studies, 24.

Draper S. (1993) Activity theory: The new direction for HCI? International Journal of Man-Machine Studies, 38.

Gibson J.J. (1979) The Ecological Approach to Visual Perception. Boston: Houghton Mifflin.

Grudin J. (1990) The computer reaches out: the historical continuity of interface design. In: Proceedings of CHI'90. Seattle, WA.

Grudin J. (1991a) Interactive systems: Bridging the gaps between developers and users. Computer, April 1991.

Grudin J. (1991b) Utility and usability: Research issues and development contexts. In: Proceedings of the 1st International Moscow HCI'91 Workshop. Moscow: ICSTI.

Henderson A., Kyng M. (1991)There's no place like home: Continuing design in use. In: J. Greenbaum, M. Kyng (eds.) Design at Work: Cooperative Design of Computer Systems. Hillsdale, NJ: Lawrence Erlbaum.

Kaptelinin V. (1992a) Human computer interaction in context: The activity theory perspective. In: J. Gornostaev (ed.) Proceedings of EWCHI'92 Conference. Moscow: ICSTI.

Kaptelinin V.N. (1992b) Can mental models be considered harmful? In: Proceedings of CHI'92. Short talks and posters. Monterey, CA: ACM.

Kuutti K. (1992) HCI research debate and activity theory position. In: J. Gornostaev (ed.) Proceedings of the EWCHI'92 Conference. Moscow: ICSTI.

Kuutti K., Bannon L. (1993) Searching for unity among diversity. In: INTERCHI'93 Conference Proceedings. Amsterdam: ACM.

Leontiev A.N. (1981) Problems of the Development of Mind. Moscow: Progress.

Leontiev A.N. (1978) Activity. Consciousness. Personality. Englewood Cliffs, NJ: Prentice Hall.

MacLean A., Young R.M., Belotti V., Moran T. (1991) Questions, options, and criteria: Elements of design space analysis. Human-Computer Interaction, 6.

Monk A., Nardi B., Gilbert N., Mantei M., McCarthy J. (1993) Mixing oil and water? Ethnography versus experimental psychology in the study of computer-mediated communication. In: INTERCHI'93 Conference Proceedings. Amsterdam: ACM.

Moran T. (1981) The Command Language Grammar: A representation for the user interface of interactive computer systems. International Journal of Man-Machine Studies, 15, 1981.

Nardi B. (1992) Studying context: A comparison of activity theory, situated action models, and distributed cognition. In: J. Gornostaev (ed.) Proceedings of EWCHI'92 Conference. Moscow: ICSTI.

Nielsen J. (1986) A virtual protocol model for computer-human interaction. International Journal of Man-Machine Studies, 24.

Nielsen J. (1990) International user interfaces: An exercise. SIGCHI Bulletin, April.

Norman D. (1988) The Psychology of Everyday Things. NY: Basic Books.

Norman D. (1991) Cognitive Artifacts. In: J. Carroll (ed.) Designing Interaction: Psychology at the Human-Computer Interface. Cambridge, UK: Cambridge University Press.

Piaget J. (1950) The Psychology of Intelligence. London: L. Routledge and Paul. Raeithel A. (1992) Activity theory as a foundation for design. In: C. Floyd et al. (eds.) Software Development and Reality Construction. Berlin: Springer.

Shneiderman B. (1992) Human values and the future of technology. The Journal of Psychology (Psikhologicheski Zhurnal), 13 (3) (in Russian).

Vygotsky L.S. (1978) Mind and Society. Cambridge, MA: Harvard University Press.

Wertsch J. (1981) The concept of activity in Soviet psychology: An introduction. In: J. Wertsch (ed.).The Concept of Activity in Soviet Psychology. Armonk, NY: M.E. Sharpe.

Wood C.C. (1992) A cultural-cognitive approach to collaborative writing. In: Human Computer Interaction: Tasks and Organizations. ECCE 6 Conference Proceedings. Balatonfured, Hungary: EACE.

Motion as a Variable of Visual Communication

Thomas L. Harrington[1], Peter I. Bidyuk[2] and Marcia K. Harrington[1]

[1]Fast Motion Perception, 4715 Mayberry Drive, Reno, Nevada 89509 USA
[2]Department of Mathematical Analysis, Kiev Polytechnical Institute, 37 Pobedy Avenue
  Kiev, Ukraine, e-mail:>internet: pbidyuk@sovamsu.sovusa.com

Abstract. The increasing power of modern computers now allows the use of sophisticated nuances of visual motion. Ways of transforming information into visual motion and some new varieties of visual motion are presented.

Keywords. visual motion, perception, vision, education, scientific visualization

1 Transforming the Perceptual Task

Often, information that the human brain processes poorly can be transformed into the world of visual motion where it is processed well. Our technological advancement and education have profited many times from such transformations in other realms. For example, humans have difficulty seeing, judging, and remembering quantities such as temperature, torque and weight. So we have transformed the tasks of perceiving these into tasks where instead we process visual forms, numbers, and assess relative visual location: is the pointer to the left, to the right or directly above the mark on the dial? We are good at perceiving form and relative location.

In addition to facilitating the perception of "invisible" or difficult information, the intensity of information flowing through the interface often can be increased by a perceptual transformation--more information can be perceived in less time.

In the design of interfaces for education faster pacing can be important beyond simply getting the student through the material more quickly. Many systems, such as the brain, change modes completely when certain configurations of their parameters reach critical levels. Speed boats hydroplane, kettles suddenly boil and jugglers can juggle. A slight change will virtually destroy the process. Similarly, the brain has dynamic properties that can often be coaxed into synergy: new information comes in and is assimilated and associated before the electro-chemical remnants of the older material can die out, and again, a slight delay can destroy the process--attention crumbles and information that is essential to continuing the process evaporates.

Until recently much of the educational process has been transformed to verbalisms anchored to the turning of paper pages and to laborious visual search. With the slower computers of old, transforming to visual motion would have drained too much processing power from the interface. Now however, computers are fast enough to deal with at least simple kinds of motion. Thus it is feasible to synchronize the interface with higher faster modes of operation of the learning system, perception, cognition, memory and motivation.

2 The Perceptual Power of Motion

Each perceptual facility has its own unique profile of utility, of power and weakness. In the case of the visual systems that deal with motion, first there is the power to process vast amounts of information in parallel. For example, one can immediately apprehend the complex changing patterns etched on fields of wheat or on the ocean by the wind. We easily process the complex motions of individual bees in a swarm. We guide our own locomotion using complicated patterns of flowing motion.

In addition to simply carrying large amounts of information, visual motion can serve operational needs of the interface. Motion is a very powerful visual grouping agent that can cement multitudes of diverse elements into perceptible units. The swarm of bees stands out from the forest behind. And elements of perceptual groups can readily be regrouped by motion into new configurations.

Motion is a powerful attractor of attention which can allow quick and flexible cueing of what to perceive next, of what to react to and when to react. It is a purveyor of timing and an excellent teacher and historian of sequences of events and actions.

Visual motion is processed in many cases better in the periphery of vision than are other variables. This often allows redistributions of much of a task's information over a broader visual area, leaving the fovea free to perform the many tasks that only it can do. The periphery of vision can hold rosters of entities or of information that can direct awareness without requiring eye movements.

Motion can convey information about hidden variables such as relative mass that can be readily perceived when translated into motion, for example into a collision of two objects on the screen in which the lighter of the two rebounds more vigorously or is deflected more, or into the erratic wobbling of a ball that is heavy on one side.

Motion can be an aid to motivation in that it is often seductively addictive. Humans and other animals spontaneously watch moving configurations such as screen savers and goldfish, and they may interact almost compulsively with moving targets, as in video games or with animated cursors.

3 Transforming Educational Variables to Visual Motion

In general, any nuance of human perceptual experience can be transformed into any other. Accordingly, in the educational milieu, information can be transformed into nuances of the motions of single elements, into motion of fields of elements, and into modulations of the relative motions of the visual elements that make up the fields.

The initial difficulty is in discovering which aspects of the educational task should be transformed to which perceptual variables. The most certain path to a useful solution is to simply try out the sensory re-mappings from the educational setting to the world of motion that look promising. Consider a few examples of variables in education, then a few variables of motion, and finally some illustrative examples.

Table 1:

VARIABLES OF EDUCATION	THE WORLD OF MOTION
Configuration	The Basic Parameters
Static Quantities	The Type of Motion
Control Information	Fields of Motion
Sequencing	The Timing of Motion
Complex Quantities	Personality of Motion
Complex Arrays	Naturalistic Motion
Hidden Quantities	

The left-hand column of Table 1 shows one possible breakdown of hypothetical material to be taught. Each of these variables can be transformed into the types of visual motion at the right of the table. The task being taught could be medical: the management of a diabetic or other patient. It might be a skill such as the piloting of an airliner, or the batting of a ball; or it could be a set of concepts from the calculus.

Configurational information is often of the utmost importance in education. Items in an educational context often should be grouped into specific configurations to facilitate understanding or memorization. But these groupings may change throughout a process so grouping them simply by "proximity," putting members of each group together on the screen, may not be practical. Situations such as this may occur for example when dealing with groups of symbols or numbers such as in the analysis of variance or in the multiplication of two matrices. Also, often items that must be grouped together perceptually are widely separated in space, for instance in the cockpit of an airliner, and ways are needed to make them be seen as grouped.

Proceeding through the table, *static quantities* appear in nearly every education setting, which must be accounted for or portrayed, for example, mass, velocity, intensity, force, amounts of various kinds and geometrical dimensions.

In many types of education, especially the *control of systems*, information for teaching appropriate control needs to be portrayed in terms of the dynamic actions and interactions, and of the effects of the control maneuvers in causing a need for further control. In education there is often difficulty in portraying these complex networks, states and their feedback loops.

In a similar vein, information about *sequencing*, information about *complex quantities*, about *complex arrays* of quantities, and *hidden features* often is required. Each of these can be transformed into a type or a combination of the types of motion that occur in the table.

In the right-hand side of the table, first are the *basic parameters* of motion which include the motion's *direction*, its *location*, its *velocity* and *acceleration*. These simple variables alone can represent most types of perceptual information.

The *type of motion* itself can represent perceptual quantities, for instance the way that the motion is constrained: e.g. it may be circular as opposed to triangular, regular vs irregular, periodic, idiosyncratic.

Motion of visual elements in *concert* and in *depth*, perhaps as seen when viewing a flock of birds, or fish "schooling," appeals very strongly to the visual system and can be used to portray many types of complex sets of data, such as that obtained in fluid flow.

Motion in time, for instance, the *relative times* at which two motions begin, or their phase, is powerful visually, and can be used to code other perceptual information.

The *personality* of motion in many cases resonates strongly with our perceptual mechanisms. For example, a motion can be energetic, calm, gentle, and in general of any sort that can be ascribed to a living organism.

Certain motions seem more "natural" than others, subjectively speaking, and can entrain the perceptual mechanisms forcefully. One striking example is the movement of people. Information about human activity can often be conveyed with minimal stimulation; for example, the perceptual nuances of two people dancing can be shown quite precisely by small lights attached to a few of the joints, viewed in the dark. Accordingly, much information from the educational setting can be represented to perception as *dynamic naturalistic dot-caricatures*.

4 Examples

As noted it is possible to transform any of the kinds of information related to the educational setting, shown in the left of Table 1 into any of the types and nuances of motion appearing on the right. A subset of these transformations, the ones related to grouping, will be illustrated. it will be left as an exercise to finish transforming each member of the column on the left to each aspect of motion on the right.

4.1 Using *Basic Parameters* of Motion to Create Perceived Groups

If the members of one group of elements, for example, icons, points on a display or cells in a vector or matrix, move and other members move differently, or are stationary, perceptual grouping will usually occur which labels or identifies the members of the group, even though they may be widely separated spatially. Perception of the shape of the group of elements is also generated.

For example, in a dynamic two-dimensional scatter plot, sub-groups will be seen if selected elements simply have different velocities, directions of motion or accelerate differently.

4.2 Using *Type-of-Motion* for Perceptual Labelling

In complex problems of perceptual grouping it is possible to indicate overlapping or nested groups, for example in a medical school to show epidemiology as related to a number of variables, or to portray risks to health or intellect in aging or diabetes.

Imagine a complex two-dimensional scatter plot of age vs some aspect of life history such as amount of smoking. *Type-of-motion* can provide sub-grouping. First, suppose it is desired to indicate gender. Points representing the scores on a test of females oscillate sinusoidally, those of males oscillate with a saw-tooth function.

Next, the back-and-forth motions indicating gender are modulated with fast oval motions, as in penmanship's "English ovals" to indicate those who drink alcohol; a nervous jitter superimposed on the motion signifies those who use caffeine, and so forth.

4.3 Grouping in Three-dimensional Fields of Motion

Certain types of moving two-dimensional patterns produce perceived motion in depth. Groups of elements, such as data points or icons, can be forced into different perceived planes of motion, or into clouds, or into arbitrary complex shapes in the third dimension by making the movement more and more complex. Also, hidden forms and clusters can be discovered in data by producing motion in depth that segregates groups that had appeared unitary. Adding a new dimension of space to a display "unsticks" local areas that may previously have been occluded or have appeared to belong grouped with elements that can now be seen to be in fact in front of or behind them.

There are several forms of three-dimensional data structures. Among these are: Data on three-dimensional *surfaces, tangles* and *clouds.*

Movement in perfect concert gives perceptual impressions of plane surfaces. If the points representing data undergo certain transformations then these planes appear to rotate, or to be rotated, in space. Variables of the educational setting can in fact be represented the orientations of these surfaces.

If the visual points move in other ways relative to one another then the plane surfaces appear to bend and information can be represented as parameters of this bending.

If points on a two-dimensional visual plane move in still more complex ways with relation to one another, then they are not perceived as being on surfaces any more, but break apart perceptually into *clouds* of data and again, variables of the educational setting can be cast as variables associated with the perceptions of these changing clouds.

Tangles, which can be viewed as clouds stretched out in time and space, also are easy for the visual system to process if they are moved. For example, imagine that complex data from a medical patient, or a group of them, is plotted in a three-dimensional representation as a cloud--appearing rather like a stationary swarm of bees. Further imagine that the situation, and thus the data, change over time so the swarm begins to move. Next suppose that this plot of the data is given "memory," by using blur patterning (Harrington and Harrington, 1989): each bee's trajectory (perhaps the "movement" of a patient in a three-dimensional space of blood pressure, heart rate and blood sugar) now becomes like a curving string in space, and the conglomerate of data is like a tangle of string. Now if this tangle is "rotated" slowly the visual system will sort out these tangled trajectories perfectly.

4.4 Mapping Information onto Variables that Normally Change Together: Modulating Perceptual Mechanisms of Surface Formation

Some transformations of information to motion in depth are especially compelling in their production of visual groups because they appear to tap basic mechanisms of perception that are very specialized for specific natural tasks, such as guiding locomotion or monitoring the movements of another person. Following are two example employing natural groupings from which *"data creatures"* can be made.

Suppose that it is necessary to monitor and analyze three related variables and all of their interactions: Blood sugar, level of insulin and blood pressure.

These can be mathematically woven into some natural visual entity--here a moving visual surface, in such a way that their values and their interactions will warp the surface in unique ways that are easily-perceived. To do this we transform the variables respectively to three of the variables that dictate the sizes, locations, velocities, and accelerations of the textural elements that make up the surface. These three variables are:

Divergence. As textural elements in the world, such as those on floors or ceilings, move toward us, or we move toward them, they diverge apart optically, as the rails of a railroad do.

Change in Size. As we approach textural elements on a surface they become optically larger.

Change in Velocity. As we approach and pass objects their angular velocities increase--objects on the horizon barely seem to move, then when abreast they go past quickly.

These three variables working in normal synchrony preserve the shapes of objects we move among, floors, ceilings, etc. and we see a normal world with normal surfaces. We are very finely tuned to any aberrations in this world, however. When their complex natural relationships are disrupted the shapes the brain derives are perceptually disrupted too.

Not only changes in the individual variables, but also changes in the complex forms of their mutual high-order interactions become immediately visible. When a visual array such as this is set in motion and warped by changing one of the parameters the perceptual impact is as strong as if one were witnessing a travelling wave in the side of a building or in the pavement. Perceptual leverage is high in that small changes of the variables can cause large changes of the percepts.

4.5 Motion, Stereopsis and Self-Stereopsis in Perceptual Grouping

Just as elements that move together also group together in a two-dimensional perceptual space, in three dimensions groups can be formed, even though their members may be densely interspersed and, it would appear, hopelessly snarled. Consider the following illustration, which employs a new method of presenting certain types of interwoven clouds of data, a *blended self-stereoptic display* (Harrington and Quon, 1989).

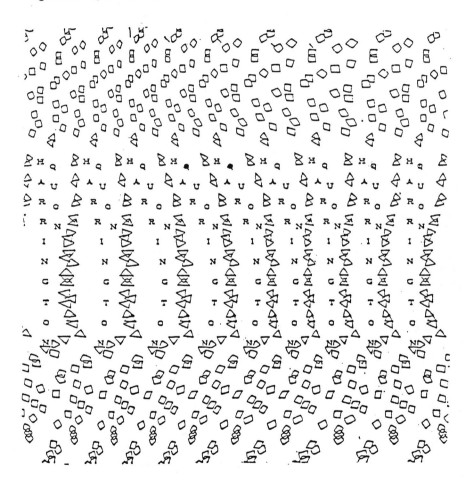

Figure 1.

Grouping of subsets of data can be forced by motion in self-stereopsis. Fig. 1 is a self-stereoptic display. Crossing, or diverging the eyes in such a manner that the two solid 'Q's fuse into three will cause most observers to see the paper disappear and in its place will be seen a three-dimensional surface, completely convincing, not distinguishable from a real three-dimensional surface, unlike the usual three-dimensional surfaces drawn for example by programs for data analysis.

If Fig. 1 is xeroxed onto a transparency which is then registered perfectly over the original figure, or over a paper xerox copy of it, and is then moved, two surfaces will be perceived in depth one cutting through the other.

Using this method, groups of data can be segregated. In addition, although it is not possible to illustrate without a computerized display or other moving media, the visual elements that make up Fig. 1 can be made to "flow" over the respective intersecting surfaces, and the surfaces themselves can be made to undulate as "hills" flow under them, like cats walking under textured blankets. Information then can be transformed into subtleties of the flowing. This *blended confluent auto-stereogram* is a complex combination of grouping-by-motion, discussed in Section 4.3, and the blended auto-stereogram just discussed.

5 Conclusion

Hopefully, these examples provide the seeds of creativity for the reader to freely explore the multitude of visual transformations from educational settings to the world of perceptual motion. These are but a few examples where sensory data that the brain does not deal with well can be transformed to sensory realms where it is highly effective. The best perceptual re-mapping, of course, depends on the specific situation, on the medium, and on other aspects of the specific context. Which mapping is chosen will depend primarily on the intuition of the designer, based on preliminary experimentation, hardware, esthetic considerations and on the many trade-offs that every educational setting has.

Acknowledgements

We are indebted to Robert Cairns for visual animations, research and computerization.We appreciate the programs for graphics supplied by THE FREE MASTERS GROUP of Kiev, Ukraine. Segments of the work were done on MATHCAD, MATHEMATICA, COREL DRAW 4, and PSPLOT.

References

Harrington, T.L., & Quon, D. (1989) A method of stereoptically simulating manifolds of three-dimensional objects using only a single display pattern: A shape-depth-texture invariance. *Perceptual and Motor Skills, 68*, 1163-1175.

Harrington, T.L., & Harrington, M.K. (1981) Visual orientation by motion-produced blur patterns: Detection of curvature change and divergence change. *Acta Psychologica, 48*, 227-237.

Laws of Visual Perception and Their Consequences for the User Interface

Floris L. van Nes

Institute for Perception Research/IPO
P.O. Box 513, 5600 MB Eindhoven, The Netherlands

Abstract. Knowledge of visual perception is needed to display text and graphics in an effective and efficient way. This paper therefore describes the visual processes involved in reading and the effects of typography, spatial layout and text colours on legibility. Some information is given on graphics, as an alternative for text and as the main constituent of graphical user interfaces.

Keywords. Visual displays, legibility, typography, font design, layout, text colours, graphics, graphical user interfaces, reading

1 Introduction

The dominant role of vision in daily life also applies in information technology: the visual display of output from computers and other information processing equipment far outweighs the use of other modalities. The user interface generally comprises a visual display, and perceiving the information presented there is an important part of any task of the user. Good user interfaces therefore must possess good visual displays, i.e. ones that are effective and can be used efficiently, also in the long run. The designer of such effective and efficient visual displays, be it for use by professionals or the general public, therefore needs to know the laws of visual perception. This paper aims to provide a start for the acquisition of that knowledge, as well as guidance for further study, to result in the proper presentation of alphanumerical as well as pictorial material on visual displays.

2 Alphanumeric Text

2.1 Reading Symbols, Words and Codes

The majority of the information on visual displays consists of letters, digits, punctuation marks and some special symbols, that all need to be read by the user. The laws that govern the reading process partly have to do with visual factors, partly with linguistic factors and partly with cognitive ones. We will confine ourselves here mainly to the visual factors because they are the ones influenced by the display.

2.2 Reading and Visual Search

Reading starts with searching. In most reading tasks, the reader does not want to read all symbols that are presented; in fact he or she often wants to read as little as possible, for instance when a dictionary or a telephone directory are consulted. So the reader's eyes hunt for the information of interest - a hunt that may be facilitated or hindered by the way the text is put on the display - by its layout, its contrast and colours and its typography. Headings as are also used in this book, for example, are a very effective means of organizing a text and thus helping the visual search process - provided that the headings stand out from the other text through the use of capitals or bold face, and/or through surrounding a heading with empty space. By such measures, the heading is given a certain degree of conspicuity (Engel, 1980).

2.3 The Visual Reading Process

During normal reading of continuous text the eyes do not move along the lines smoothly, but in a series of rapid movements, the so-called saccades, alternated with fixation pauses in which the eyes are focussed on successive points of the text lines. The saccades in the forward direction are typically 8 × 4 letter positions long and the fixation pauses last about 250 ms (Roufs and Bouma, 1980). In these pauses the text characters are imaged on the central parts of the retinas of both eyes. Then recognition of the text takes place in the visual reading field, being 10-20 letter positions (Bouma, 1980). Both letter recognition and word contour recognition occur simultaneously, leading to word recognition (Bouwhuis, 1979). Word contour recognition is aided by the presence of ascenders and descenders in lower-case letters, since these lend a characteristic contour to a word - therefore, text made up of mixed lower- and upper case is easier to read than text in upper case (capitals) only. If the overall legibility of a text is low, for instance because the luminance contrast between the characters and their background is low, readers may confuse a word with another one which has the same contour, but one or more different letters (Bouma, 1973). This tendency may be reduced by choosing character configurations that are distinct; for instance a /c/ that has a large opening, to avoid confusion with /o/ or /e/ (Bouma and Van Rens, 1971).

Legibility has been defined by Tinker (1964) and refers to the visual properties of a text. This in distinction to a text's *readability*, which has been defined by Klare (1969) as referring to its linguistic properties, and determining the comprehension of a text after it has been visually recognized. Linguistic properties include stylistic factors such as sentence length, type of vocabulary used, etc.

At the end of a line the eyes have to go to the beginning of the next line, and fixate approximately there. Such eye movements are backward saccades; the ones just described may be called normal backward saccades. Other backward saccades, with a much smaller size, may occur within a text line if something there is not recognized or understood properly, because of a legibility or readability that is too low. Such small backward saccades cannot be called abnormal, but should occur only rarely. The normal, or regular backward saccades have to be directed rather accurately, to prevent a fixation at the beginning of a too low or too high text line. This required accuracy is relatively more important for small angles between backward saccades and the direction of the text lines. This is the reason for the reduced legibility of tightly-packed text, which has short inter-line distances compared with the line lengths.

2.4 Legibility and Typography

In the two previous sections, 2.2 and 2.3, several aspects of typography were already mentioned: upper or lower case, different type faces such as bold or italics, and different character configurations i.e. type fonts. In principle there is no difference between the requirements on typography for paper or for visual displays. Indeed high-resolution displays have typographic capabilities comparable to paper and the corresponding possibilities to use different fonts of high legibility, in normal, bold or italics type and of course with both upper and lower case. However, medium- or low-resolution displays have a more limited typographic repertory, with rather coarse characters, typically in a 5 × 7 dot matrix. The design of character sets with optimal legibility within such severe constraints requires an analysis of the relevant character aspects. Such an analysis was done by Bouma and Leopold (1969) leading to requirements for three such aspects:
1. Acceptability. Configurations of characters should be chosen so as to yield a high acceptability, i.e. high degree of correspondence between the dot matrix configuration of, for instance, a letter and the internal image of this letter that people have.
2. Detail identifiability. The details of characters should stand out from their background clearly. This is especially important for inner details, such as the horizontal stroke of the lower case /e/.
3. Individuality, or discriminability. The chosen configurations for similar symbols, such as /c/ and /o/, or /n/ and /h/ should yield a high discriminability of these symbols, especially if they need to be recognized on their own strength, as in codes, without the support of the redundancy of normal language.

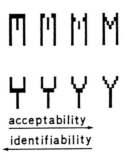

Fig. 1. Two examples of a conflict between acceptability and identifiability (from Bouma and Leopold, 1969).

One of the challenges of designing these coarse characters is that the requirements for acceptability and individuality may be in conflict with each other. This is shown in Fig. 1 for the upper case characters /M/ and /Y/ from Bouma and Leopold's research (1969). Not too many graphical designers have taken up this challenge; in fact the very requirement of individuality is somewhat in conflict with a basic principle for the design of a particular font as applied by most graphical designers: a certain degree of commonality between the configurations for the letters from a particular alphabet, so as to carry its specificity. Still, in some instances graphical designers already in the early days of matrix characters for displays created those fonts (Crouwel and Dirken, 1973; Unger, 1977), but by and large the field was long left to engineers. Ergonomists then pointed out the necessity to evaluate the legibility of matrix characters, in order to choose the best configurations (Vartabedian, 1973; Huddleston, 1974; Maddox, Burnett and Gutmann, 1977; Snyder and Maddox, 1980).

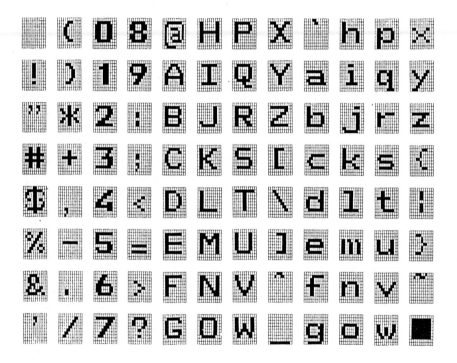

Fig. 2. The basic set of IPO-Normal 12 × 10 dot matrix characters (copyrighted). The complete IPO-Normal set is protected under the rules of the International Design Registration effected under the Geneva Protocol of 1975.

Indeed visual displays may be used in conditions where legibility is especially critical. The affected legibility factor is luminance contrast: it typically is lower for visual displays than for printed paper, because of reflection on the glass front of the display. Another affected legibility factor is viewing distance: in videotex applications such as Teletext it commonly is twice as large, or more, as the viewing distance recommended for the character size applied (Van Cott and Kinkade, 1972). A special character set was therefore designed for Teletext decoders, and extensively tested as to its discriminability (Van Nes, 1986b). This set, shown in Fig. 2, was designed within a matrix of 12×10 elements (horizontal $\times$ vertical, including inter-character and inter-line gaps). One of the features of this IPO-Normal character set is that the vertical numeral strokes are 1.5 times as wide as the vertical letter strokes, to facilitate the distinction between similar numeral-capital pairs such as /5/ and /S, /8/ and /B/, and, especially, /0/ and /O/.

2.5 Legibility and Layout

2.5.1 Line Length and Line Spacing

As was explained in section 2.3, legibility is reduced if the space between successive lines is small compared to their length, because of the then required small angle, with a small tolerance, between backward saccades and text lines. A minimum value of 0.033 has been recommended for the inter-line space/line length ratio (Bouma, 1980). If this ratio is computed for consecutive text lines in videotex systems such as Teletext, a value of 0.035 is found. In other words, the legibility of a regular videotex page is only moderate - as indeed may be observed in practice. Possible measures to increase this legibility are an increase of the inter-line spaces, which may be achieved by only filling alternate videotex lines with characters, or a reduction of the actual text line length, for instance by only putting 20 characters on one line, instead of the maximum 40. Both measures will of course halve the text-carrying capacity of the page; but if two narrow columns of text are employed, as in a newspaper, the original capacity is almost reached again (Van Nes, 1986a).

2.5.2 Spatial Text Grouping

Even with long text lines at a short distance legibility may be influenced positively by the editor of the text: through spatial text grouping by the insertion of empty lines, as in Fig. 3, where the whole text is split up in two paragraphs. This figure also shows that lines which are only partially filled, such as the fourth one, tend to improve legibility, because then it is easier for the eyes, i.e. the direction of gaze, to find the start of the next text line, in this case the fifth one.

Spatial grouping is especially important in tables, where it may facilitate search for the desired items. Tables are, therefore, generally organized in vertical columns, separated by quite a bit of empty space, or by thin vertical lines. But a horizontal organization also helps to guide the eye. Good tables should have an empty line between groups of about five filled lines. Figs. 4 and 5 also may be called tables, with a horizontal organization. The information that is grouped here refers to programmes broadcasted by three radio stations, Hilversum 1, Hilversum 2 and Hilversum 3. The font used in Fig. 4 is the old-fashioned 6×10 dot matrix Teletext font, whereas the font used in Fig. 5 is the current 'IPO-Normal' 12×10 dot matrix font (see section 2.4).

Fig. 3. The division of this text in two paragraphs as well as the only partial filling of the fourth text line improve legibility. The font used here is IPO-Bold: the bold variation of IPO-Normal.

2.6 Legibility and Colour

The application of colour in the display of text and graphics has increased very much over the last 20 years. This is primarily caused by progress in colour display technology, but also by the inherent attraction of coloured images in general. Unfortunately, the growth in numbers of colour displays has not been paralleled by a similar growth of insight in the effects on perception, both of text and graphics (De Weert, 1988). Yet the rules for an advantageous use of colour are fairly simple.

2.6.1 Recognition of Coloured Text

First of all a coloured text should be seen at all, i.e. be recognized. This recognition mainly depends on the luminous contrast between text characters and background, both for bright and dark backgrounds. Colour contrast plays only a small role (Bruce and Foster, 1982). This is of importance in systems such as videotex, that do not compensate for the luminous efficiency differences between the red, green and blue phosphors. It means that the eight available 'colours': white, yellow, cyan, green, magenta, red, blue and black differ in luminosity and brightness; from high to low in this order. On a dark or 'black' background the brighter colours should be used for the characters whereas on a bright background the darker colours should be used, to provide sufficient luminance contrast.

2.6.2 Accentuation by Colour Difference

If some characters from a text have another colour than the surrounding characters they will be conspicuous (Engel, 1980) and thus may be perceived as being accentuated. On low-resolution displays that do not permit the use of different type faces such as bold or italics, colour is one of the few remaining means to accentuate a text part. However, colour is so powerful in this respect that an overemphasis easily occurs (Van Nes, 1991). In the coloured version of Figs. 4 and 5, a moderate emphasis has been lent to the headings 'Hilversum 1, 2 and 3' by their cyan colour, among otherwise differently coloured characters.

Fig. 4. A table with a horizontal organization; the empty lines above 'Hilversum 2' and 'Hilversum 3' clearly distinguish the programmes of the radio stations Hilversum 1, Hilversum 2 and Hilversum 3. The font used here is the old-fashioned 6 × 10 dot matrix Teletext font. In order to distinguish the digit zero from the capital O, a diamond shape was chosen.

2.6.3 Coding Text by Colours

Parts of a text may be coded by giving them a specific colour. Such a code then attaches a particular meaning to those text parts, in addition to their normal semantic meaning. As with all codes, this code must be known to be useful for the reader. Its usefulness is diminished if it is not employed consistently in the whole text concerned. A (somewhat inconsistent) application of such a code in Teletext systems can be seen in The Netherlands and, to a limited extent, in Belgium: cyan, or light blue text in a programme guide refers to programmes that are at the moment *not* available - so it makes no sense to try and select them.

2.6.4 Associating Text Parts by Colour Grouping

Text parts or figure fragments with the same colour are perceptually grouped, i.e. seen as belonging together. This association mechanism operates more or less autonomously - at least as long as not too many different colours are present in the text or figure, typically three or four, according to Reynolds (1979). The association, or grouping effect has been attributed to the formation of a 'Gestalt' by equally coloured image parts. These Gestalts are assumed not to be formed or to break down, if too many colours are present in the image (Cahill and Carter, 1976). An inverse effect may be observed fairly often in practice: parts of a text (or figure) that have a different colour are difficult to be seen as related. This may actually hamper the understanding of a sentence that is displayed in two colours because it is basically perceived as two unrelated parts (Van Nes, 1991).

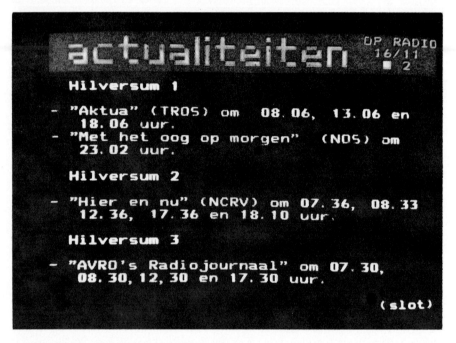

Fig. 5. The same table as shown in Fig. 4, but now with the current IPO-Normal 12 × 10 dot matrix font. In this font all numerals are bold compared to the letters, to facilitate the distinction between, e.g., the digit zero and the capital O.

3 Graphics

3.1 The Choice between Pictures and Words

Whether to use a picture or text to render visually displayed information depends on a variety of issues, from unspecific but very real factors such as avoiding an impression of monotony or dullness to specific ones, for instance the well-documented superiority of a graph over a table for interpreting the relationship between two sets of numbers (Oborne, 1987). Tullis (1988) mentions a number of instances that support the well-known Chinese proverb: "A picture is worth a thousand words". However, the choice certainly also depends on the context of the reader's task. A recent study of how engineers use either graphical representations or text for electronics suggests that either graphics or text may be preferred, depending on the accessibility of information needed while the engineers perform their tasks (Petre and Green, 1990).

3.2 Graphical User Interfaces

Just as is the case with text, nowadays electronic displays can represent graphics (almost) as well as printed paper. In fact such displays, together with the underlying computing power, may give an extra dimension to graphics, for example animation (Tiritoglu and Juola, elsewhere in this volume). In general, the advent and success of Graphical User Interfaces has spurred an interactive use of graphics and therefore, created an increased importance of the perceptual laws governing the recognition and interpretation of graphical images such as 'icons', the small representations of 'windows' when they are in their closed state. In their open or visible state 'windows' are bordered screen areas with a specific content. A considerable development in the use of graphics may still be expected, possibly through a joint effort of various professionals such as cartographers, graphic designers, visual perception experts and cognitive scientists. Such a development is needed because presently the abundant use of graphics is known to sometimes distract the user (Billingsley, 1988, p. 421). One should not forget that the graphical ingenuity as described by Verplank (1988), having resulted in the generally praised user interface of the Xerox Star (Johnson et al., 1989) may be contrasted by lists of common errors in graphical design as compiled by Wainer (1980) and by the many cases of 'deceptive graphics' collected by Tufte (1983, p. 53). Although many practical guidelines exist for the design of good graphics (Tufte, 1983, pp. 91-190) there as yet is no graphical counterpart of the theoretical foundation for alphanumeric legibility research and knowledge (Twyman, 1979).

4 Conclusion

For the best visual displays electronic text may now have nearly the same quality as printed text. Consequently, the legibility of electronic text will soon be the same as that of printed text. This does not imply, however, that reading *multipage* printed text such as books can be done with equal ease and speed in the case of multipage electronic text (Wright, 1989). On the other hand electronic books can be equipped with indexing systems that are superior to the passive indexes from books; and indeed information retrieval from such 'electronic books' has been shown to be superior to information retrieval from a printed book of similar content (Egan et al., 1989; Leventhal et al., 1993).

References

Billingsley, P.A. (1988) Taking panes: issues in the design of windowing systems. In: M. Helander (ed.) Handbook of Human-Computer Interaction, 413-436. Amsterdam: Elsevier Science Publishers (North-Holland)

Bouma, H. (1973) Visual interference in the parafoveal recognition of initial and final letters of words. Vision Research 13, 767-782

Bouma, H. (1980) Visual reading processes and the quality of text displays. E. Grandjean, E. Vigliani (eds).) Ergonomic Aspects of Visual Display Terminals, 101-114. London: Taylor & Francis

Bouma, H., Leopold, F.F. (1969) A set of matrix characters in a special 7×8 array. IPO Annual Progress Report 4, 115-119

Bouma, H., Rens, A.L.M. van (1971) Completion of an alphanumeric matrix display with lower-case letters. IPO Annual Progress Report 6, 91-94

Bouwhuis, D.G. (1979) Visual Recognition of Words. Catholic University of Nijmegen. Ph.D. dissertation

Bruce, M., Foster, J.J. (1982) The visibility of colored characters on colored backgrounds in viewdata displays. Visible Language 16, 382-390

Cahill, M.C., Carter Jr., R.C. (1976) Color code size for searching displays of different density. Human Factors 18, 273-280

Cott, H.P. van, Kinkade, R.G. (eds.) (1972) Human Engineering Guide to Equipment Design. Revised ed., 107. Washington DC: American Institutes for Research

Crouwel, W.H., Dirksen, J.M. (1973) Alphanumeric symbols for mosaic printers and display tubes. Icographic 6, 12-14

Egan, D.E., Remde, J.R., Landauer, T.K., Lochbaum, C.C., Gomez, L.M. (1989) Behavioral evaluation and analysis of a hypertext browser. In: Proceedings CHI '89 Human Factors in Computing Systems, 205-210. New York: ACM

Engel, F.L. (1980) Information selection from visual display units. In: E. Grandjean, E. Vigliani (eds.) Ergonomic Aspects of Visual Display Terminals, 121-125. London: Taylor & Francis

Huddleston, H.F. (1974) A comparison of two 7×9 matrix alphanumeric designs for TV displays. Applied Ergonomics 5 (2), 81-83

Johnson, J., Roberts, T.L., Verplank, W., Smith, D.C., Irby, C.H., Beard, M., Mackey, K. (1989) The Xerox Star: A retrospective. Computer 22 (9), 11-29

Klare, G.R. (1969) The Measurement of Readability, 1-2. Ames, Iowa: The Iowa State University Press

Leventhal, L.M., Teasley, B.M., Instone, K., Rohlman, D.S., Farhat, J. (1983) Sleuthing in HyperHolmes (TM): an evaluation of using hypertext vs. a book to answer questions. Behaviour and Information Technology 12 (3), 149-164

Maddox, M.E., Burnett, J.T., Gutmann, J.G. (1977) Font comparisons for 5×7 dot matrix characters. Human Factors 19, 89-93

Nes, F.L. van (1986a) Space, colour and typography on visual display terminals. Behaviour and Information Technology 5 (2), 99-118

Nes, F.L. van (1986b) A new Teletext character set with enhanced legibility. IEEE Trans. Electron Devices (ED-33) 8, 1222-1225

Nes, F.L. van (1991) Visual Ergonomics of Displays. Chapter 6 of The Man-Machine Interface (J.A.J. Roufs, ed.), Volume 15 of Vision and Visual Dysfunction. London: Macmillan Press

Oborne, D.J. (1987) Man-machine communication: words and symbols. In: Ergonomics at Work, 2nd ed., 32. Chichester: John Wiley & Sons

Petre, M., Green, T.R.G. (1990) Where to draw the line with text: Some claims by logic designers about graphics in notation. In: D. Diaper, D. Gilmore, G. Cockton, B. Shackel (eds.) Proceedings of Human-Computer Interaction - INTERACT '90, 463-468. Amsterdam: Elsevier Science Publishers (North-Holland)

Reynolds, L. (1979) Teletext and viewdata - a new challenge for the designer. Information Design Journal 1, 2-14

Roufs, J.A.J., Bouma, H. (1980) Towards linking perception research and image quality. Proceedings Soc. Information Display 21 (3), 247-270

Snyder, H.L., Maddox, M.E. (1980) On the image quality of dot-matrix displays. Proceedings Soc. Information Display 21 (1), 3-7

Tinker, M.A. (1964) Legibility of Print. Ames, Iowa: The Iowa State University Press

Tiritoglu, A., Juola, J.F. (1993) Animated icons promote learning of their functions. This volume

Tufte, E.R. (1983) The Visual Display of Quantitative Information. Cheshire, Connecticut: Graphics Press

Tullis, T.S. (1988) Screen design. In: M. Helander (ed.) Handbook of Human-Computer Interaction, 377-411. Amsterdam: Elsevier Science Publishers (North-Holland)

Twyman, M. (1979) A scheme for the study of graphic language. In: P.A. Kolers, M.E. Wrolstad, H. Bouma (eds.) Processing of Visible Language (1), 117-150. New York: Plenum Press

Unger, G. (1977) Telefoongidsen: nieuwe typografie. Compres 2 (8)

Vartabedian, A.G. (1973) Developing a graphic set for cathode ray tube display using a 7×9 dot pattern. Applied Ergonomics 4 (1), 11-16

Verplank, W.L. (1988) Graphic challenges in designing object-oriented user interfaces. In: M. Helander (ed.) Handbook of Human-Computer Interaction, 365-376. Amsterdam: Elsevier Science Publishers (North-Holland)

Wainer, H. (1980) Making newspaper graphs fit to print. In: P.A. Kolers, M.E. Wrolstad, H. Bouma (eds.) Processing of Visible Language (2), 125-142. New York: Plenum Press

Weert, C.C.M. de (1988) The use of colour in visual displays. In: G.C. van der Veer, G. Mulder (eds.) Human-Computer Interaction: Psychonomic Aspects, 26-40. Berlin: Springer-Verlag

Wright, P. (1989) The need for theories of NOT reading: some psychological aspects of the human-computer interface. In: B.A.G. Elsendoorn, H. Bouma (eds.) Working Models of Human Perception, 319-340. London: Academic Press

Learning in Neural Networks

Paul Munro

Department of Information Science, University of Pittsburgh, Pittsburgh PA 15260 USA

Abstract. Until recently, the overwhelmingly dominant mode of machine computation has been absolutely deterministic. Neural networks provide an alternative approach to computation that is inspired by neurobiological principles. These systems can learn categories from examples, and generalize their learning, such that
novel examples can be classified. Correct classification depends on a variety of factors, including the goodness of the sample used for training and the consistency of
the test item with the statistics of the training set. Neural network training procedures are more closely related to statistical regression techniques than they are to
mainstream AI. Analyses of the networks both during and after training show remarkable similarities to human learning, and may give insight to the principles underlying human information processing.

1 Background

The biological principles that enable higher level cognition are just beginning to be
understood. While the neural components that make up our brain are so much
slower than the electronic devices found in computers, they are much more numerous, and thus process information in parallel; this massive parallelism gives rise to
forms of computation that are very different than those performed on electronic
computers, which process instructions one at a time in sequence. Parallel distributed processing has been found to account for several cognitive phenomena (see
Rumelhart and McClelland; 1986) from perception (e.g., optical illusions) to higher
levels (e.g., language and problem solving).

1.1 Neural Network Fundamentals

The theory behind parallel distributed processing borrows its essential concepts
from neurobiology, but a host of aspects considered vital by neurobiologists are ignored (to the chagrin of many). Of course, no singular description describes all neural network models, and so the following description should not be interpreted as a
strict definition. A neural network is defined as a structure consisting of nodes
joined by "one-way" connections (i.e., a directed graph). Each node receives signals
along connections that terminate on it, and transmits a signal on connections that it
originates. The transmitted signal is a function of the received signals and some internal parameters. A small network is shown on the left of Figure 1.1, and a general node is shown on the right, where the output is a function of the inputs, s, t, u,
etc., and some internal parameters, A, B, C, etc.

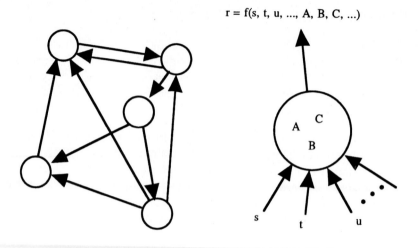

$$r = f(s, t, u, ..., A, B, C, ...)$$

Fig. 1.1. A small neural network (left) and a schematic of one node (right).

The internal parameters of the nodes are typically weight factors assigned to the node's input signals. So in Figure 1.1, the unit might have a response like $r=As+Bt+Cu$. More typically, this weighted sum would be computed and then passed into a threshold-like function, like $r=0$ if $(As+Bt+Cu)<0$, and $r=1$ otherwise. Hence each node produces an output value (r) in response to a "stimulus pattern" of input values (s, t, u). Information is presented to the network and read from it by specifying two subsets of nodes, respectively known as the input and output layers. For a given network architecture, the output is ultimately a function of the input values (to which the input nodes are assigned), and the weight parameters of all the nodes. Thus, proper functioning of a network requires appropriate parameter values.

Neural network models can be partitioned into those that are trainable (modifiable weights), and those that are not (fixed weights). Fixed weights are generally assigned according to principles that relate to presumed correlations between nodes. In these models, each node represents a hypothesis; consistent hypotheses are connected by positively weighted connections and inconsistent nodes have negative connections, with the weight magnitudes reflecting the degree of correlation (or anti-correlation). The notion of correlation motivated an early principle for how the strengths of the synapses (the biological "connections" between neurons) are modified. Hebb's (1949) "neurobiological postulate" has inspired many mathematical approaches to learning in neural networks (e.g., Hopfield, 1982):

> "When an axon of cell A is near enough to excite a cell B and repeatedly or persistently takes part in firing it, some growth process or metabolic change takes place in one or both cells such that A's efficiency, as one of the cells firing B is increased."

The ability to train networks by example has captured the attention of the research community. Consider a classification task, for example, in which a population of input nodes corresponds to various measurements or observations, like light intensities on the retina, or phoneme sequences, and several output nodes that represent potential categories to which the input stimulus might belong, like "images of trees", or "the word, 'appetite'". Training generally involves the following notion: given a set of known data pairs, the weight parameters are initialized to random values, and then iteratively modified such that each stimulus in the set produces the appropriate response. After this learning procedure, the network has hopefully abstracted the relevant features of the input that are used in the classification task. If so, the network will respond appropriately to novel stimuli (i.e. data not in the training set). Thus the procedure is related to the idea of estimating a function from a finite collection of sampled data. Regression, the statistical tool for fitting functions to data, is reviewed below; as we will see, neural network training is fundamentally a kind of regression.

1.2 Regression

Since the dawn of modern science, researchers dealing with data have recognized the need for procedures that can generalize from examples. Regression techniques are the most common for this kind of analysis. In broad overview, regression requires two steps: [1] Assumption of a (parametrized) functional form that the data will be assumed to follow, and [2] optimization of the parameters for the given data. The neural network training approach described in this article is a kind of iterative regression technique, in which the class of functions is inspired by ideas of neuronal processing and architecture.

The example of linear regression is most commonly used, in which we have a set of data pairs that are assumed to be be related in a way that is reasonably approximated by a linear relationship. Given the data pairs, the regression technique can be used to find the straight line, that comes closest to passing through the data points. Simple mathematical relationships (linear, exponential, etc.) between measurable quantities are very rarely followed exactly, but under appropriate conditions, they are often close approximations.

Of course, many data sets can be more closely approximated by functions that are nonlinear. In general, the more parameters used to specify a function, the more powerful the regression; that is, the space of possible functions is more extensive. However, too many parameters leads to "overfitting" the data, a situation in which the known data is precisely fit by a high order function, while a lower order function would generalize better even though it performs imperfectly on the training data. This is particularly a problem when the data is imperfect due to errors or imprecise measurements (generally unavoidable). Figure 1.2 shows how a high-order function can be fit *precisely* to data that is roughly linear, but generalize in ways that are absurd. Linear regression is predicated on the assumption that the variables *x* and *y* are linearly related and stipulates a formula for the finding parameters *a* and *b* to fit the general linear relation $y = ax + b$ that most closely approximates the data. However, if there are more than two data points, the regression line will not exactly intersect the data points exactly, in general. A function with more parameters can fit the data precisely. For example, a polynomial function of order *n* can generally be found to precisely fit *n* +1 data points. The quality of generalization tends to diminish as *n* increases (see the dotted lines and arrows in Figure 1.2).

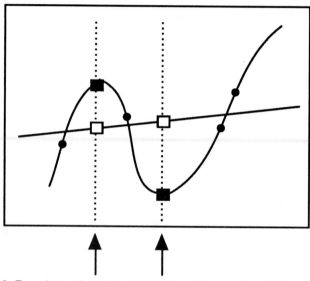

Fig 1.2. Four data points (filled circles) are fit approximately by a straight line and exectly by a third order polynomial. Subsequent approximations to two test values (arrows) by the linear fit (open squares) and the cubic curve (filled squares) are not in agreement.

In certain cases, like linear functions, the function parameters can be computed directly from the training data. In the absence of a direct formula (which is generally the case), an iterative process can be used. The strategy is to start with random values for the parameters, which will give a poor fit (barring extreme good fortune). Then, a single item (x,y) from the training set is checked against the random curve, by computing the "error", $y - f(x; a,b,...)$, and the parameters *a*, *b*, etc. are altered to reduce this difference. After repeating this process many times for the entire training set, the function will hopefully reach an acceptable approximation to the data, and the further hope is, of course, that the function will generalize well. This general approach of *error correction* has been found to be broadly applicable in neural networks and other adaptive systems. However, error correction schemes do not always lead to the optimal set of parameters. The problem stems from the gradual nature of changing the parameters. Since only small changes are permitted, the procedure can get stuck in a region of the parameter space where a locally optimal point is "surrounded" by a neighborhood that gives higher errors for every small change in the parameters, so the parameters cannot change to a more distant region where the error may be lower. This effect, known as a "local minimum", is illustrated in Figure 1.3.

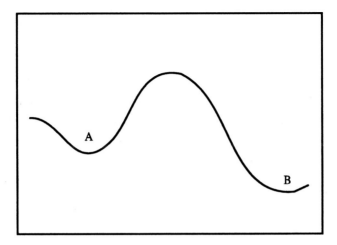

Fig. 1.3. An error function for a hypothetical one-parameter system. An error-correction procedure could get stuck at point A, a local minimum, since small changes in x do not reduce the error. Hence better parameter values, like B, will never be found. Note that the success of this procedure depends on the choice of the initial parameter value.

2 The Perceptron and Learning

Several techniques for training neural networks have been put forward, most based on either regression techniques, or Hebb's postulate, or both. Of these, one has emerged as the dominant candidate. The idea was first sketched by Rosenblatt (1961), but he was not able to implement it. The impasse was not overcome until the work of Werbos (1974), whose contribution remained unrecognized for over a decade, when three papers were independently published that showed how Rosenblatt's idea could be implemented and gave hints as to its implications for machine learning and cognitive science (Le Cun, 1986; Parker, 1985; Rumelhart, Hinton, and Williams, 1986).

2.1 Rosenblatt's Perceptron

A simple procedure, the "Perceptron Learning Procedure", to build a neuron-like classification device was devised by Rosenblatt (1961). Using this scheme, a linear threshold unit is trained to learn a categorization task by example. Here, we assume that there are two kinds of stimulus patterns, those in the category (A), and those outside (B). A perceptron unit responds with either a 0 or a 1; optimal performance on the task corresponds to responding with a 1 to all the patterns in A, and with a 0 to those in B. The perceptron can only form *linear* boundaries between categories (a straight line in a 2 dimensional space, a flat plane in 3-D, etc.), hence they can only form categories that are *linearly separable* (see Figure 2.1).

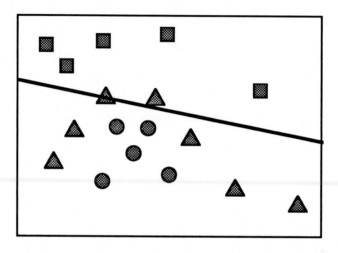

Fig. 2.1. Linear separability is a necessary condition for the success of perceptron learning. The axes represent input activations on the two input lines, each point corresponds to a possible input pattern. The shapes connote category membership. Here, the circle category is separable from the set of squares, but not from the triangles.

The Perceptron Learning Procedure is an error correction procedure applied to a linear threshold unit; that is, unit which responds $r=0$ if $x<\theta$, and $r=1$ if $r\geq\theta$, where x is the weighted sum of the inputs. The weights and the threshold θ are parameters initialized to random values and subsequently optimized by the learning procedure. The algorithm can be conceptualized visually since the weights and thresholds determine a boundary in the pattern space. The error is reduced by selecting data points randomly and checking the correct class against the unit's response. If the point is classified correctly, there is no error and hence no change to the parameters; however, if the unit has misclassified the point, the parameters are changed such that the line moves a fixed distance in a direction towards the point. Thus if the line was sufficiently close to the point, it will cross, and become correctly classified; otherwise, it just moves closer to the correct category (see Figure 2.2). Note that when a particular pattern induces change it never moves from a correct category to an incorrect category, however this fate may befall another pattern in the training set. In spite of this, after many repetitions of the entire training set, the unit is guaranteed to settle in the solution state (assuming the categories were linearly separable).

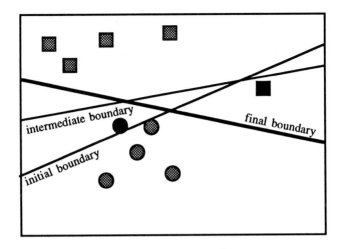

Fig. 2.2. The perceptron learning procedure is visualized at three stages. Initially, two items are misclassified. Presentation of one misclassified item, the dark circle, induces a change in the parameters, such that it is correctly classified (intermediate boundary). The second misclassified item (the dark square) changes the parameters such that all points are correctly classified, so the algorithm stops.

2.2 The Multilayered Perceptron

Unfortunately, linear separability is a very harsh restriction, since it does not include most tasks of interest. Rosenblatt proposed using multiple layers, since such a network can handle problems of arbitrary complexity (see Figure 2.3). All units in the network are linear threshold units (in the figure, all information flow is upward). He showed that there exists a mapping from the input to the hidden layer that will render any classification task linearly separable in the hidden unit space, at least if the original inputs are binary valued. However, the solution may require the introduction of extra parameters (in this case, extra hidden units), and can have an adverse effect on generalization.

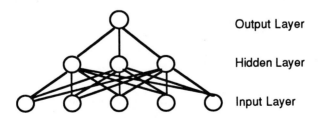

Fig 2.3. A multilayered perceptron consists of at least two layers of weights. So-called "hidden" units lie between the input and output layers.

The effectiveness of the intermediate layer is nicely illustrated by exclusive or (XOR), the simplest boolean task that is not linearly separable (see Figure 2.4). A multilayered perceptron can compute XOR using two hidden units, where one hidden unit computes X OR Y, and the other computes X AND Y (see Figure 2.5).

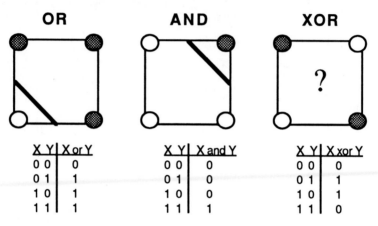

X Y	X or Y
0 0	0
0 1	1
1 0	1
1 1	1

X Y	X and Y
0 0	0
0 1	0
1 0	0
1 1	1

X Y	X xor Y
0 0	0
0 1	1
1 0	1
1 1	0

Fig 2.4. Boolean tasks are shown with standard truth tables and plotted on the X-Y plane. Each combination of X and Y is a corner of the unit square. Gray indicates a truth value of 1, and white corresponds to 0. The diagonal lines indicate where a linear category boundary could be placed.

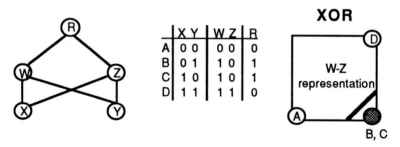

	X Y	W Z	R
A	0 0	0 0	0
B	0 1	1 0	1
C	1 0	1 0	1
D	1 1	1 1	0

Fig 2.5. A network with linear threshold units can compute functions that the individual units cannot compute. The input representation (X-Y) is, *not* linearly separable, whereas, the intermediate representation (W-Z) is.

While Rosenblatt was on the right track, he was unable to devise a method by which such a network could be trained by example. The impasse was finally breached with the work of Werbos (1974), and was rediscovered about 12 years later by three research groups working independently (Le Cun, 1986; Parker, 1985; Rumelhart, Hinton, and Williams, 1986). By using units that were not quite threshold units, they were able to derive an error-correction procedure for training multilayered perceptrons, that has generally come to be known as the technique of backward propagation of error, or "backprop".

3 Discussion

Most cognitive models that use neural networks, especially those using backprop, make a loud disclaimer that the units do not correspond to biological neurons, and emphasize that they do *not* mean to assert that backprop is neurally plausible. Neurobiologists agree that these models are a far cry from the real brain. Nevertheless, these models feel much closer to the biological substrate than previous models, and have given successful accounts of many cognitive phenomena, with unprecedented detail.

But certain aspects of neural computation captured by network models provide psychologists with new tools for describing and conceptualizing cognitive phenomena. For example, the following lesson of the multilayer perceptron may give new insight to the nature of biological computation: neural systems compute functions far more complex than is possible for individual neurons, by gradually transforming the representation space, layer by layer, reducing the complexity of the computation to be performed with each step; then, at the penultimate stage, there is a representation that renders the task computable for the individual neurons at the output level.

Studies of neuronal response at the intermediate stages of the systems of animals have shown correspondences with model systems trained by backpropagation (e.g. Zipser and Andersen, 1988). Zipser and Andersen stress that in their simulation of posterior parietal neurons in monkey cortex, they are making claims about the computations performed by the system *after* training, but expressly *not* about the training procedure itself (backprop): "That the back-propagation method appears to discover the same algorithm that is used by the brain in no way implies that back propagation (sic) is actually used by the brain".

Analyses of intermediate representations across several stages may have implications for processes involving manipulation of concepts, such as analogical reasoning, and may shed light on controversies involving competing theories for mental representations, including the symbolic vs. subsymbolic debate in AI, the imagery vs. propositional debate in cognitive neuroscience, and the temporal vs. spatial debate in spatial knowledge acquisition.

Over the last 10 years or so, neural network models have had an increasingly pervasive impact on our understanding of human information processing, and hold the hope (if not the promise) of explaining cognitive processes in a biological (or pseudobiological) framework. One of the most compelling features of this approach is its intrinsic capacity to describe and simulate learning phenomena, which in turn reveal more about the end product of the learning process: the mind.

References

Hebb, D. O. (1949) The Organization of Behavior. New York: Wiley

Hopfield, J. J. (1982) Neural networks and physical systems with emergent collective computational properties. Proceedings of the National Academy of Sciences 79, 2554-2558

Le Cun, Y. (1986) Learning processes in an asymmetric threshold network. In: E. Bienenstock, F. Fogelman Souli, G. Weisbuch (eds.), Disordered systems and biological organization. Berlin: Springer

Parker, D. (1985) Learning Logic, MIT Center for Computational Research in Economics and Management Science Technical Report TR-87. Cambridge MA

Werbos, P. J. (1974) Beyond regression: new tools for prediction and analysis in the behavioral sciences., Ph.D. thesis, Harvard University, Cambridge MA.

Rumelhart, D. E., Hinton, G. E., and Williams, R. J. (1986) Learning internal representations by error propagation. In: D. E. Rumelhart, J. L. McClelland (eds.) Parallel distributed processing: Explorations in the microstructure of cognition. Cambridge: MIT Press

Rumelhart, D. E., McClelland J. L. (1986) Parallel distributed processing: Explorations in the microstructure of cognition. Cambridge: MIT Press

Zipser, D. and Andersen, R. A. (1988) A back-propagation programmed network that simulates response properties of a subset of posterior parietal neurons. Nature, 331, 679-684

The Probabilistic Retreat From Biases: Implications for Man-Machine Communication?

Mike Oaksford[1] and Nick Chater[2]

[1]Department of Psychology, University of Wales at Bangor, Bangor, Gwynedd, LL57 2DG, UK. (E-mail: PSS Ø27@bangor.ac.uk OR mike@cogsci.ed.ac.uk)
[2]Department of Psychology, University of Edinburgh, 7, George Square, Edinburgh, EH8 9JZ, UK. (E-mail: nicholas@cogsci.ed.ac.uk)

Abstract A recent trend within cognitive psychology has been the move away from the depiction of human reasoning as errorful and prone to bias and towards more appropriate probabilistic models of the behavioural data. This paper reviews this trend in three areas - probabilistic reasoning, causal reasoning and hypothesis testing - and discusses some possible implications for user modelling in man-machine communication.

Key Words: Reasoning, psychology, probabilistic reasoning, causal reasoning, hypothesis testing, heuristics, biases, man-machine communication

1 Introduction

Until recently the psychological study of reasoning has been interpreted to reveal that untutored human reasoners fall far short of the standards of rationality provided by normative theories. In laboratory tasks normal adults appear to reveal a variety of apparently irrational and systematic biases from the prescriptions of logic and mathematics (see, Evans, 1989, or Evans, Newstead & Byrne, 1993, for overviews). Theoretical responses to these findings have included appeal to short cut processing strategies, i.e., heuristics, and the use of special representational formats, i.e., mental models. Over the last few years, however, it has become clear that many of the tasks taken to reveal biases are susceptible to more rational interpretations. It seems that the wrong logico-mathematical frameworks may have been taken to define rational behaviour in these tasks and that subjects may use probabilistic strategies that are wholly consistent with mathematical probability theory.

An awareness of these developments may be important to user modelling in man-machine communication. According to Norman and Draper (1986), in designing profitable human-computer interactions it is important that a task be "presented so that it matches human skills." The skills to be matched invariably involve some element of reasoning. Hence in constructing methodologies for interacting with computers a minimal requirement may be an understanding of how people reason. Moreover, on briefly scanning the contents of some recent edited collections in this area we were struck by how many made appeal to the theoretical constructs - such as heuristics and mental models - that have become popular as a result of work on biases in human reasoning. To the extent that the invocation of such constructs is being re-thought in the cognitive psychology of reasoning, a similar re-evaluation may be necessary in the area of man-machine communication.

In this chapter we discuss three areas where a probabilistic re-interpretation has been successful: probabilistic reasoning, causal reasoning, and hypothesis testing. We first introduce each area, outlining the principle tasks used. We then discuss the new probabilistic accounts of these data due, in the case of probabilistic reasoning, to Birnbaum (1983) and Gigerenzer and Murray (1987), in the case of causal reasoning, to Cheng and Novick (1990), and in the case of hypothesis testing, to Oaksford and Chater (Oaksford & Chater, 1993).

2 Biases in Human Reasoning

2.1 Probabilistic Reasoning and Base Rate Neglect

Perhaps one of the most well known examples of bias in the reasoning literature concerns Kahneman and Tversky's (1972) demonstration that subjects tend to ignore base rate information. We illustrate this using Tversky and Kahneman's (1980) cabs problem. Subjects were provided with the following information:

> A cab was involved in a hit-and-run accident at night. Two cab companies, the Green and the Blue, operate in the city. You are give the following data:
> (i) 85% of the cabs in the city are Green and 15% are Blue
> (ii) A witness identified the cab as a Blue cab. The court tested his ability to identify cabs under appropriate visibility conditions. When presented with a sample of cabs (half of which were Blue and half of which were Green) the witness made correct identifications in 80% of the cases and erred in 20% of the cases.
> *Question*: What is the probability that the cab involved in the accident was Blue rather than Green.

In terms of Bayes' theorem the probability of the cab being blue given the witnesses testimony ($P(Blue|"Blue")$) is,

$$P(Blue|"Blue") = \frac{P("Blue"|Blue)P(Blue)}{P("Blue")}$$

That is the likelihood that the witness correctly identifies the cab

($P("Blue"|Blue)$) times the ratio of the base rates of Blue cabs in the city and the witness giving the evidence "Blue." The probability $P("Blue")$ can be calculated by conditioning on the probabilities of the cab being Green or Blue (since these are exhaustive and mutually exclusive events), so,

$$P("Blue") = P("Blue"|Blue)P(Blue) + P("Blue"|Green)P(Green)$$

The Cabs problem therefore provides all the information needed to deploy Bayes' theorem to calculate the probability that it was indeed a Blue cab that was involved in the hit-and-run accident:

$$P(Blue|"Blue") = \frac{0.80 \times 0.15}{0.80 \times 0.15 + 0.20 \times 0.85} = 0.41$$

However, most undergraduate student subjects report the probability of the cab being Blue as around 0.80 (this was the median response and the most frequent response). This concurs with the likelihood that the witness correctly identifies the cab, i.e., 0.80. Tversky and Kahneman therefore concluded that their subjects neglect base rate information in calculating posterior probabilities.

2.2 Bias in Causal Attributions

Another area where bias has been commonly observed is causal attribution in social psychology. We illustrate these biases by reference to Kelley's (1967) ANOVA model which represents the attribution process as relying on the principle of co-variation embodied in the analysis of variance. The analysis of variance is of course typically regarded as a normative inductive procedure.

The co-variation principle states that for an event C to be viewed as the cause of event E, E must occur when C does and when C does not occur neither should E. Kelley proposed three dimensions in the attribution of the cause of an event. The cause could be due to persons (P), stimuli (S) or times (T). Three informational variables contribute to "who, what or when" gets the blame, these are:

Consensus between P's response to S and other's response to S at T.
Distinctiveness of P's response to S from P's response to other stimuli at T.
Consistency of P's response to S at T with P's responses to S at other Ts.

Only distinctiveness is directly proportional to covariation. So *high* distinctiveness corresponds to a *high* covariation between S and the response, i.e., high distinctiveness means the response rarely occurs in the absence of S. This contrasts with, for example, consensus information, where *high* consensus corresponds to a *low* covariation between P and the response, i.e., lots of other people also make this response. It is then a trivial corollary of the model that the

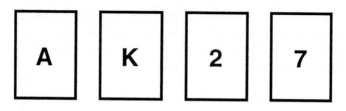

Figure 1: The four cards in the abstract version of Wason's selection task.

following patterns of high or low consensus, distinctiveness or consistency information (in that order) should lead to the indicated attributions: **LLH** = Person, **HHH** = Stimulus, **HLL** = Time. However, while there has been some good general agreement between model and data, some systematic biases have also been observed.

I concentrate on two of these biases. First, it has been found that consensus information is underused particularly in determining person (P) attributions. Recall that low consensus means that there is a high covariation between that person and the response, i.e., the response is rarely observed without this person being involved. Consensus information should therefore be important in determining person attributions. However, McArthur (1972) found that consensus information accounts for only 6% of the variance in person attributions and only 3% of the total variance in causal attributions. Second, there would appear to be a strong bias towards person attributions as opposed to stimulus or time attributions. In McArthur's (1972) results (noted by Jaspars *et al.*, 1983), 82% of subjects made person attributions when P covaried with the response, as opposed to 62% who made stimulus attributions when S covaried with the response, and 33% who made time attributions when T covaried with the response.

2.3 Hypothesis Testing

Perhaps the most notorious area where biases have emerged in the reasoning literature concerns human hypothesis testing and in particular work carried out using Wason's (1966, 1968) selection task. Wason's task, which is probably the most replicated task in cognitive psychology, requires subjects to assess whether some evidence is relevant to the truth or falsity of a conditional rule of the form *if p then q*, where by convention "*p*" stands for the antecedent clause of the conditional and "*q*" for the consequent clause. Subjects are presented with four cards each having a number on one side and a letter on the other (see Figure 1). The subjects are also given a rule, e.g., *if there is a vowel on one side (p), then there is an even number on the other side (q)*. The four cards show an "A"(*p* card), a "K"(*not-p* card), a "2"(*q* card) and a "7"(*not-q* card). By convention these are labelled the *p* card, the *not-p* card, the *q* card, and the *not-q* card respectively. Subjects have to select those cards they must turn over to determine whether the rule is true or false. Typical results were: p and q cards (46%); p card only (33%), p, q and *not-q* cards (7%), p and *not-q* cards (4%) (Johnson-Laird & Wason, 1970).

The normative theory of the selection task was derived from standard logic and Popper's (1959) account of falsification. Popper argued that a scientific law can not be shown to be true because it is always possible that the next instance of the law observed will be falsifying. However, one can be logically certain that a law is false by uncovering a single counter-example. Furthermore, this means that scientific reasoning is fundamentally deductive in character - what must be established is a logical contradiction between putative laws and observation. Hence looking for false (p and *not-q*) instances should be the goal of scientific inquiry. However, in the selection task subjects typically select cards that could *confirm* the rule, i.e., the p and q cards.

Confirmation bias, however, does not adequately account for the data on the selection task. Evans and Lynch (1973) showed that when negations are varied between antecedent and consequent of a rule subjects reveal a bias towards selecting those cards that are named in the rules, ignoring the negations. For example, take the rule "if there is not an A on one side, then there is not a 2 on the other side", and the four cards showing an "A", a "K", a "2" and a "7". The matching response would be to select the A and the 2 cards. In contrast according to confirmation the K and the 7 card should be selected and for falsification the K and the 2 card should be selected. Evans and Lynch (1973) refer to this phenomenon as *matching bias*. Matching could also account for the data from the standard affirmative selection task (see above) where no negations are employed in the task rules. This is because the matching and confirmation strategies coincide on the selections they predict for the affirmative rule, i.e., the A and the 2 cards. Thus subjects behaviour on the selection task may not reveal any hypothesis testing strategy at all!

3 Interlude

Having summarised three areas where biases have typically been observed in human reasoning we now turn to how these "biases" are being reconciled with normative theory by the adoption of more appropriate normative models based largely on probability theory. It is interesting to first note that there were always three possible reactions to the observation of biases (Thagard, 1988, p. 123):

1. *People are dumb*. They simply fail to follow the normatively appropriate inferential rules.
2. *Psychologists are dumb*. They have failed to take into account all the variables affecting human inferences, and once all the factors are taken in to account it should be possible to show that people are in fact following appropriate rules.
3. *Logicians [Mathematicians, my insertion] are dumb*. They are assessing the inferential behaviour of human thinkers against the wrong set of normative standards.

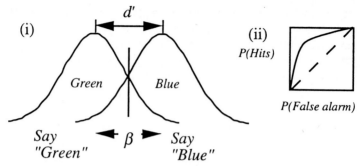

Figure 2: Signal detection theory. (i) Area in "Blue" distribution to the right of β = *P(hit)*; area in the "Green" distribution to the right of β = *P(false alarm)*. (ii) The Receiver Operating Curve (ROC)

Psychologists seem to have largely opted for 1 and explained why in terms of cognitive limitations. Our preference is go after 2 and 3 However, our target in this paper is mainly 3 and we will only briefly touch on work pursuing 2 when we discuss Cheng and Novick's account of biases in causal attribution. (For work pursuing 2, see, e.g., Beyth-Marom, 1982; Gigerenzer, Hell & Blank, 1988; Oaksford & Stenning, 1992.)[1]

4 The Probabilistic Retreat from Biases

4.1 Probabilistic Reasoning and Base Rate Neglect

Birnbaum (1983) has shown that the cabs problem of Tversky and Kahneman (1980) can be recast in the language of Signal Detection Theory (SDT) which is based on Neyman and Pearson's statistics. He shows that when this is done the resulting model concurs with Tversky and Kahneman's (1980) data.

SDT represents the discrimination problem in terms of two partially overlapping normal distributions along which a decision boundary or criterion (β) may be specified (see Figure 2(i)). The discriminability of the two distributions is determined by the separation between their mean (peak) values, this is *d'* which is measured in z-score units. In the case of the cabs problem one of the distributions corresponds to Green and the other to Blue. The eye witnesses testimony defines a hit rate (80%) and a false alarm r[1] ate (20%) from which *d'* can be calculated. In this case it equals 1.68. Given one point, a whole ROC curve is defined which corresponds to a plot of pairs of false alarm rates and hit rates for a single *d'* as the criterion β is varied (see Figure 2(ii)). The

---

[1] It is worth noting that logicians/mathematicians do not always see their work as directly applicable to these data in the ways that psychologists would wish. Hence often it is simply the wrong theory that psychologists have "adopted."

standard psychophysical procedure for plotting an ROC curve is to vary the base rates of the distributions (Green and Blue) thereby moving the criterion to obtain another false alarm rate/hit rate pair. The critical observation in accounting for the cabs problem is that the base rates in the court's test (50%-50%) were different from the night when the witness saw the accident (85%-15%). Hence the witnesses criterion will have been set differently on the night of the accident in comparison to when the test was conducted. However, the lighting conditions were carefully mimicked in the test so it can be assumed that d' remains the same.

What is the effect of altering the base rates? The problem is that SDT does not specify where the criterion is to be placed when the base rates change. However, Birnbaum assumes that witnesses set their criterion to minimise incorrect testimony in the knowledge that there are 15% Blue cabs. This leads to a hit rate of 0.302 and a false alarm rate of 0.698. If these values are then translated back in to likelihoods and used in Bayes' theorem, a value of 0.82 is returned for the posterior probability that the cab was indeed blue given the witnesses testimony. This is remarkably close to the 0.80 actually observed in Tversky and Kahneman (1980).

As Gigerenzer and Murray (1987) point out this analysis depends on *attending* to bases rates not *neglecting* them. They also observe that just by taking Tversky and Kahneman's own proposals seriously with respect to which base rates should be used can lead to the observed data. Subjects may regard the base rates *in the city* as irrelevant seeking instead base rates of cabs *in accidents*. In the absence of relevant information to the contrary, they may assume that the Green and Blue cabs are equally likely to be involved in an accident, i.e., the relevant base rates are 50%-50%. Assuming these base rates, the posterior probability that the cab was indeed blue given the witnesses testimony is 0.80! In sum, it seems that the conclusion of a bias towards base rate neglect may have been premature.

This account of the cabs problem has probably not been influential because (i) of its isolation in a sea of data apparently supporting the existence of biases and (ii) the corresponding lack of promising normative analyses of these data. However, such analyses are now increasing in number as the next two more recent examples demonstrate.

4.2 Bias in Causal Attributions

Cheng and Novick (1990) argue that the problem of causal attribution can be framed in terms of their normative probabilistic contrast model. They show that their model predicts the detailed pattern of results on causal attribution when subjects are provided with complete information.

Cheng and Novick (1990) note that only incomplete information is provided by consensus, distinctiveness and consistency. If we cast the persons, stimuli and times dimensions into Kelley's famous ANOVA cube then each of

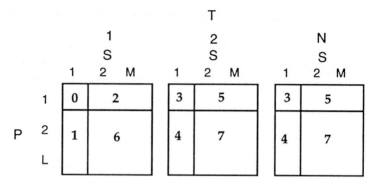

Figure 3. Kelley's ANOVA cube for persons (P), stimuli (S) and times (T), showing the eight regions of information.

these informational sources can be treated as specifying information about specific regions of the cube (see Figure 3).

Figure 3 shows the eight regions of the cube. Consensus information provides information about the agreement between person 1's response to stimulus 1 at time 1, i.e., it provides information about region 1 of the cube (distinctiveness provides information about region 2 and consistency about region 3). Consensus does not provide information about the agreement between person 1's response and others' responses to the other stimuli $S_M - S_1$ at other times $T_N - T_1$, i.e., it fails to provide information about regions 4 and 5 of the cube. Cheng and Novick (1990) note that the ANOVA uses information in all regions to determine main effects and interactions. Hence biases in causal attribution may be due to incomplete information. They therefore used materials that provide the missing information. For example, the following materials were used for an **LLH** problem (see above).

> *Jane had fun washing the dishes on this occasion.*
> 1. In fact, Jane always has fun doing all chores.
> 2. But nobody else ever has fun doing any chores.

The first sentence provides information about region 0, i.e., there is a positive relationship between this person (Jane) on this occasion for this stimulus (washing the dishes) and having fun (the response). Clause 2 provides information about regions 2, 3 and 5 (+ relationship) and clause 2 provides information about regions 1, 4, 6 and 7 (- relationship).

Cheng and Novick (1990) derive predictions for the detailed patterns of attributions (including interactions) using their probabilistic contrast model (for details of this approach, see, Cheng & Novick, 1990). They show that their model predicts the detailed pattern of results on causal attribution when complete information is specified (like the ANOVA complete information is required for their model). Moreover, their data reveal that with complete information all signs of bias evaporate. Taking the bias against using consensus information, Cheng and Novick (1990) found that consensus accounted for 31% of the variance in their data, distinctiveness 33%, and consistency 24%, i.e., no indication of bias was observed. Similarly, for the bias towards person attributions they found that for the problems where only persons (**LLH**), stimuli (**HHH**), or times (**HLL**) covaried with the response the proportion of subjects making the appropriate attribution were 75%, 80% and 85%, i.e., no indication of bias was observed.

Again conclusions of bias have proved to be premature, when complete information is provided subjects show no bias against using consensus information or towards making person attributions. Moreover, their behaviour is predicted by a normative probabilistic model.[2]

4.3 Hypothesis Testing

Oaksford and Chater (1993) show that Wason's selection task can be recast as a problem of optimal data selection that is susceptible to a Bayesian analysis. When this is done they show that all the main results on the selection task can be derived from their normative model.

Any problem of deciding what experiment to perform next, or which observation is worth making, is a problem of optimal data selection. Consider assessing the truth of a mundane regularity, such as that eating tripe makes people feel sick: to collect evidence should we ask people who complain that they feel sick, or perhaps those who do not feel sick, whether they have eaten tripe; should we investigate people who are known tripe eaters or tripe avoiders. This case is analogous to the selection task: the rule *if tripe then feeling sick* is of the form *if p then q*, and the various populations which may be investigated correspond to the various visible card options, *p*, *not-p*, *q* and *not-q*. The subject must judge which of these people should be questioned concerning either how they feel or what they have eaten.

Oaksford and Chater (1993) suggest that those data points expected to provide the greatest information gain should be selected. The information gain given some data is the difference between the uncertainty *before* receiving the data and the uncertainty *after* receiving the data. Uncertainty is measured using the Shannon-Wiener information measure and hence the information gain of a data point D may be defined as follows:

$$I_g(D) = -\sum_{i=1}^{n} P(H_i)\log_2 P(H_i) + \sum_{i=1}^{n} P(H_i|D)\log_2 P(H_i|D) \qquad (3)$$

---

[2] It could be argued that Cheng and Novick's probabilistic contrast model is redundant if it makes the same predictions as the ANOVA. However, (i) their model also accounts for other areas of causal reasoning where bias had been observed, (ii) the computations involved in their model are far simpler and therefore more psychologically plausible, (iii) a direct indication of facilitatory or inhibitory causation is provided.

That is the difference between the information contained in the *prior* probability of a hypothesis (*H_i*) and the information contained in the *posterior* probability of that hypothesis given some data *D*. In calculating the posterior probability Oaksford and Chater assume that the hypothesis under test, which indicates a dependence between *p* and *q*, is compared to an alternative hypothesis which indicates that *p* and *q* are independent (the principle of indifference between these hypotheses is assumed, so they are both taken to be equally probable, i.e., the *priors* for both are 0.5).

In the selection task, however, when choosing which data point to examine further (that is, which card to turn), the subject does not know what that data point will be (that is, what will be the value of the hidden face). However, what can be calculated is the *expected* information gain. If we assume that there are two possible data points that might be observed (in the case of the *not-q* card, for example, corresponding to the hidden face being, say, *p* or *not-p*), then the expected information gain of the *not-q* card is:

$$E(I_g(\neg q)) = \sum_{jk} P(H_j)P(p_k | \neg q, H_j)I_g(p_k, \neg q) \qquad (4)$$

Oaksford and Chater then show that arriving at appropriate probability models for the dependence and independence hypotheses only involves specifying the frequency in the population of the properties described by *p* and *q*. They label these parameters *a* and *b* respectively. With *a* and *b* specified all the values needed to compute (4) for each card are available.

In accounting for the selection task Oaksford and Chater (1993) carried out an extensive meta-analysis of the data which revealed that over some 34 studies involving almost 900 subjects the frequency of card selections was ordered such that *p* > *q* > *not-q* > *not-p*. To model this data they calculated the expected information gain of each card with *a* = *b* = 0.1. That is, they assumed that the properties described in *p* and *q* are rare in the population. A similar assumption was made by Klayman and Ha (1987) in accounting for related data on Wason's (1960) 2-4-6 task. On this assumption the order in expected information gain is:

$$E(I_g(p)) > E(I_g(q)) > E(I_g(not-q)) > E(I_g(not-p))$$

That is, if subjects base their card selections on the expected information gain of the cards then the observed order in the frequency of card selections is exactly as Oaksford and Chater's (1993) model of optimal data selection predicts. Oaksford and Chater (1993) also show how their model generalises to all the main patterns of results in the selection task, including the manipulation described above of introducing negations into the task rules.

In sum, if the selection task is regarded as a problem of probabilistic optimal data selection then the putative biases observed in this task disappear.

5 Conclusions and Some Possible Implications for Man-Machine Communication

5.1 Summary

We began this chapter by claiming that much of the bias literature needs to be re-interpreted in the light of the growing number of normative probabilistic re-analyses of the data upon which claims of bias have been based. These analyses, as the first example of Birnbaum (1983) reveals, were often contemporaneous with the heyday of the "heuristic and biases" tradition. However, these analyses were largely set aside in the rush to explain these biases in process terms. Of course these accounts simply ignored the fact that they were now assigning apparently irrational functions to the processes they invoked. Recently, however, there has been a re-emergence of concern with rationality and rational analysis (see, e.g., Anderson, 1991; and the collection edited by Manktelow & Over, 1993) and with it we suspect that we are witnessing a degenerative problem shift (Lakatos, 1970) for work in the area of heuristics and biases. Lopes (1991) has observed that the rhetorical emphasis of the heuristics and biases tradition was on Thagard's 1 above, i.e., on human dumbness. She points out that this de-emphasised the importance of rationality in cognitive explanation. In witnessing a problem shift back towards rational function we should be wary that the psychological insights of the heuristics and biases account are not similarly abandoned. As Gigerenzer and Murray (1987, see also, Gigerenzer, Hoffrage & Kleinbölting, 1991) observe there has always been an essential subjective, psychological aspect to probability theory. As we have seen assumptions about which *priors* to employ or their effects on the decision criterion, for example, are not decideable within probability theory. In arriving at psychological theories of reasoning in any domain there will be a need for essentially psychological accounts of how these values are arrived at and how people tractably implement their probabilistic competence.[3] Nevertheless, following Marr (1982), first identifying the rational functions that the human cognitive system needs to compute is again being seen as a feasible and necessary first step in specifying an adequate cognitive theory.

---

[3] For further discsussion of the computational tractability of reasoning theories, see Chater & Oaksford, 1990, 1993; Oaksford, 1993; Oaksford & Chater, 1991, 1992, 1993; Oaksford, Chater & Stenning, 1990, 1992.

5.2 Man Machine Communication

We now outline an area where these considerations may be relevant to man-machine communication: the apparent success of graphics interfaces like the highly usable Macintosh interface. We make the assumption that all interfaces are deterministic systems. That is, the actual rules that determine what happens given user input are deterministic, i.e., as long as the system is functioning normally, a given input, key press sequence, mouse click in a menu location etc., yields a single specific action with probability 1. Now at some metaphysical level of description the world may be a deterministic system. Certainly classical mechanics which for the bulk of our everyday macroscopic needs is all we need to predict the physical world, regards the world deterministically. However, this does not mean that in acquiring knowledge of the macroscopic world human beings model it deterministically. Irremediable ignorance of the disposition of a complex system whose next state we wish to predict often precludes deterministic prediction. Instead scientists must settle for probabilistic theories in order to make adequate predictions. Similarly, when confronted with a complex user interface novice users may model the system not deterministically but probabilistically.

This provides a possible explanation for the success of interfaces like the Macintosh. Deterministic command line interfaces are all or nothing affairs, either you know the appropriate command or you don't. The organisation of access is also very flat in that if you don't know the specific command there are no higher level exploratory actions you can perform in order to find out. This kind of organisation is only suited to rote learning of the appropriate command language and rules. This contrasts with the Macintosh interface, where there are often many ways of performing the same action. Moreover, there are a set of high level actions, like pulling down menus, clicking on *labelled* buttons, scrolling etc. that enable the user to interact with the computer in an exploratory manner. This is analogous to our normal inductive interactions with the world. In acquiring practical skills the ability to manipulate and explore bits of our world permits us to learn much faster. It seems possible, therefore, that these interfaces succeed because they exploit the same abilities that allow us to learn so effectively about the world in order to inductively explore the interface. In sum, novices may model their interactions probabilistically in accordance with their natural competences; the very competences that are now being revealed in the probabilistic retreat from bias.

References

Anderson, J. R. (1991). Is human cognition adaptive? *Behavioral and Brain Sciences*, **14**, 471-517.

Beyth-Marom, R. (1982). Perception of correlation reexamined. *Memory & Cognition*, **10**, 511-519.

Birnbaum, M. H. (1983). Base rates in Bayesian inference: Signal detection analysis of the cab problem. *American Journal of Psychology*, **96**, 85-94.

Chater, N. & Oaksford, M. (1990). Autonomy, implementation and cognitive architecture: A reply to Fodor and Pylyshyn. *Cognition*, **34**, 93-107.

Chater, N. & Oaksford, M. (1993). Logicism, mental models and everyday reasoning: Reply to Garnham. *Mind & Language*. **8**, 72-89.

Cheng, P. W., & Novick, L. R. (1990). A probabilistic contrast model of causal induction. *Journal of Personality and Social Psychology*, **58**, 545-567.

Evans, J. St. B. T. (1989). *Bias in human reasoning: Causes and consequences*. Hillsdale, NJ: Erlbaum.

Evans, J. St. B. T., & Lynch, J. S. (1973). Matching bias in the selection task. *British Journal of Psychology*, **64**, 391-397.

Evans, J. St. B. T., Newstead, S. E., & Byrne, R. M. J. (1993). *Human Reasoning*. Hillsdale, N.J.: Lawrence Erlbaum Associates.

Gigerenzer, G., Hell, W., & Blank, H. (1988). Presentation and content: The use of base rates as a continuous variable. *Journal of Experimental Psychology: Human Perception and Performance*, **14**, 513-525.

Gigerenzer, G., Hoffrage, U., & Kleinbölting, H. (1991). Probabilisitic mental models: A Brunswickian theory of confidence. *Psychological Review*, **98**, 506-528.

Gigerenzer, G., & Murray, D. J. (1987). *Cognition as intuitive statistics*. Hillsdale, N.J.: Lawrence Eerlbaum Associates.

Jaspars, J. M. F., Hewstone, M. R. C., & Fincham, F. D. (1983). Attribution theory and research: The state of the art. In J. M. F. Jaspars, F. D. Fincham, & M. R. C. Hewstone (Eds.), *Attribution theory: Essays and experiments*, (pp. 3-36). Orlando, FL: Academic Press.

Johnson-Laird, P. N., & Wason, P. C. (1970). A theoretical analysis of insight into a reasoning task. *Cognitive Psychology*, **1**, 134-148.

Kahneman, D., & Tversky, A. (1972). On prediction and judgement. *ORI Research Monograph*, **12**.

Kahneman, D., & Tversky, A. (1982). The simulation heuristic. In D. Kahneman, P. Slovic, & A. Tversky (Eds.), *Judgement under uncertainty: Heuristics and biases*, Cambridge: Cambridge University Press.

Kelley, H. H. (1967). Attribution theory in social psychology. In Levine D. (Ed.), *Nebraska Symposium on Motivation* Vol. 15, (pp. 192-238). Lincoln: University of Nebraska Press.

Klayman, J., & Ha, Y. (1987). Confirmation, disconfirmation and information in hypothesis testing. *Psychological Review*, **94**, 211-228.

Lakatos, I. (1970). Falsification and the methodology of scientific research programmes. In I. Lakatos, & A. Musgrave (eds.), *Criticism and the growth of knowledge*, (pp. 91-196). Cambridge: Cambridge University Press.

Lopes, L. L. (1991). The rhetoric of irrationality. *Theory & Psychology*, **1**, 65-82.

Manktelow, K. I., & Over D. E. (Eds.) (1993). *Rationality*, London: Routledge.

Marr, D. (1982). *Vision*. San Fransisco, CA: W. H. Freeman & Co.

McArthur, L. Z. (1972). The how and what of why: Some determinants and consequecnces of caual attribution. *Journal of Personality and Social Psychology*, **22**, 171-193.

Norman, D. A., & Draper, S. W. (1986). *User-centred System Design*. Hillsdale, N.J.: Lawrence Erlbaum Associates.

Oaksford, M. (1993). Mental models and the tractability of everyday reasoning. *Behavioural & Brain Sciences*. **16**, 360-361.

Oaksford, M. & Chater, N. (1991). Against logicist cognitive science. *Mind & Language*. **6**, 1-38.

Oaksford, M. & Chater, N. (1992). Bounded rationality in taking risks and drawing inferences. *Theory & Psychology*. **2**, 225-230.

Oaksford, M., & Chater, N. (1993). Reasoning theories and bounded rationality. In K. I. Manktelow & D. E. Over (Eds.) *Rationality.* pp. 31-60, London: Routledge.

Oaksford M, & Chater N. (1993). A rational analysis of the selection task as optimal data selection. Technical Report No. CCN-UWB-93-05: Centre for Cognitive Neuroscience, University of Wales, Bangor. (In submission).

Oaksford, M., Chater, N. & Stenning, K. (1990). Connectionism, classical cognitive science and experimental psychology. *AI & Society*, **4**, 73-90.

Oaksford, M., Chater, N., & Stenning, K. (1992). Connectionism, classical cognitive science and experimental psychology. In Clark, A. & Lutz, R. (Eds.) *Connectionism in Context.* pp. 57-74, Berlin: Springer-Verlag.

Oaksford, M., & Stenning, K. (1992). Reasoning with conditionals containing negated constituents. *Journal of Experimental Psychology: Learning, Memory & Cognition*, **18**, 835-854.

Popper, K. R. (1959). *The logic of scientific discovery.* London: Hutchinson.

Thagard, P. (1988). *Computational philosophy of science.* Cambridge, MA: MIT Press.

Tversky, A., & Kahneman, D. (1980). Causal schemas in judgements under uncertainty. In Fishbein M (Ed.), *Progress in social psychology*, Hillsdale, N.J.: Lawrence Erlbaum Associates.

Wason, P. C. (1960). On the failure to elminate hypotheses in a conceptual task. *Quarterly Journal of Experimental Psychology*, **12**, 129-140.

Wason, P. C. (1966). Reasoning. In B. Foss (ed.), *New horizons in psychology*, Harmondsworth, Middlesex: Penguin.

Wason, P. C. (1968). Reasoning about a rule. *Quarterly Journal of Experimental Psychology*, **20**, 273-281.

Cognitive Load and the Acquisition of a Problem Solving Skill

Rudy R.G. Van Hoe

Institute for Perception Research/IPO, PO Box 513, 5600 MB Eindhoven, The Netherlands

Abstract. Current theories of learning consider the restructuring of the components of a weak problem solving sequence into a domain-specific procedure to be the fundamental learning mechanism in complex knowledge domains. Within the context of cognitive load theory, there is growing evidence that applying weak methods such as means-ends analysis, do not necessarily result in learning, but can in fact induce a high mental load which prevents the problem solver inducing domain-specific rules. The major goal of this article is to provide a direct test of the cognitive load theory. Experimental evidence was found that the cognitive load imposed by a weak problem solving activity can retard the acquisition of a problem-solving skill.

Keywords. learning, problem solving, experimental research

1 Cognitive Load Theory

In the eighties there was much research interest in the study of expert and novice performance in complex knowledge domains. It is now generally accepted that experts use strong, domain-specific methods and novices weak, domain-independent problem solving methods (Anderson, 1989). Taking this major finding into account, the central problem of learning theories is to describe the transition process from novice performance based on weak methods to expert performance based on domain-specific procedures. Current theories of learning consider restructuring as the fundamental learning mechanism in semantically rich domains (Carlson, Sullivan, & Schneider, 1989).

There is very little research on the relation between problem solving and learning. One can say that a synergetic view of the relation between problem solving and learning (restructuring) dominates in the literature. This view consists basically of two assumptions. First that learning is a process driven by problem solving: learning takes place in a problem solving context (Holland, Holyoak, Nisbett, & Thagard, 1986). Second that problem solving is an effective context for learning: the weak problem solving process does not interfere with the learning process.

An exception to the synergetic view is the research program of John Sweller and his colleagues which resulted in what now is known as the cognitive load theory (Sweller, 1988; Chandler & Sweller, 1991). Cognitive load theory belongs to the class of limited capacity theories. According to this class of theories, the resources of a cognitive system are limited and when this processing capacity is reached, performance decrements occur. Cognitive load theory deals in particular with the manner in which cognitive resources are focused and used during learning and problem solving. The central idea of the theory is that a problem solving context can impose a high level of cognitive load which interferes with learning, and consequently impedes schema acquisition.

The cognitive load theory and related experimental results have some interesting consequences for current theories of learning and problem solving. In the first place, it is clear that the definition of learning as the restructuring of a weak problem solving sequence is too general and needs refinement. Applying weak methods such as means-ends analysis on novel problems does not necessarily result in schema acquisition, but can in fact prevent the problem solver from inducing domain-specific rules. This is in sharp contrast with, for example, the general ACT* learning theory of John Anderson which predicts a significant learning performance improvement on the basis of one problem solving trial (Anderson, 1987). In the second place, cognitive load theory defines problem solving and learning explicitly as two distinct processes which are executed in parallel and which can compete for the same limited amount of cognitive processing capacity. This point of view has two major implications. First, the interference of problem solving with learning, does not exclude learning in the context of problem solving, but results in a graceful degradation of the learning performance, i.e., the restructuring process is retarded and incomplete. Second, if a clear distinction is made between problem solving and learning as two independent processes, then it is necessary to evaluate separately the effects of each process on performance (see also: Logan, 1992). In a problem solving or concept learning experiment, the decrease in errors and solution time over learning blocks is usually interpreted as evidence for the effect of learning.

Although Sweller and his colleagues used the cognitive load theory to generate several experiments (Chandler & Sweller, 1991), they found only indirect evidence that, for example, means-ends analysis demands a high processing capacity and consequently constrains the relation between problem solving and learning. The major goal of this article is to provide a more direct test of the cognitive load theory.

2 The Nature of the Experimental Domain

The experimental domain was restricted in terms of required knowledge and number of problem tasks by using an artificial diagnosis task. The design of the experiment is based on the experimental paradigm used in concept learning research and the dual-task methodology (cf., Fig. 2.1.). This implies that in the experiment a distinction is made between a learning and a transfer phase. In the learning phase the same number of problem exemplars of two alternative problem schemata were presented randomly over several learning blocks. After each learning trial, subjects received feedback. In the transfer phase subjects had to solve old and new diagnosis problems as quickly as possible, without receiving feedback.

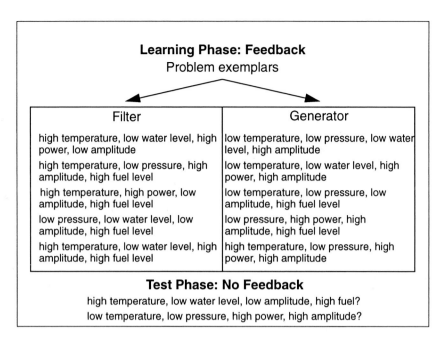

Fig. 2.1. Experimental procedure

Since artificial tasks were used, the problem domain was new for all subjects. In the initial instructions subjects were asked to act as an operator of an hypothetical machine. Thereafter, subjects received a manual with general information about the structure and functioning of machines, how machines can become defective and how to diagnose the malfunctioning of machines. In the manual no information was provided about the machine which was used in the experiment itself. That was done just before the start of the learning phase of the experiment. In the learning phase subjects were informed, over problem solving trials, about the malfunctioning of this machine by means of abnormal values of machine state parameters (e.g., temperature, pressure, water level, and power) on a simulated control display. For each trial, it was the task of the subjects to decide which of the two components of the machine (filter or generator) was responsible for the abnormal machine state (cf., Fig. 2.1.). In order to do this, the subjects could consult a graphical representation of the machine.

3 Experiment

In the experiment two main factors, completeness and type of knowledge, were introduced (cf., Fig. 3.1.). As already mentioned, the information to which the subjects had access, described how two machine components determined the value of each state parameter. The machine had six parameters. On each trial subjects received information about the abnormal values of four machine state parameters. The completeness factor had three levels: (1) no information on the influence of the components of the machine on each of the six machine state parameters, (2)

Completeness of Knowledge	Type of Knowledge	
	Relevant	Not-Relevant
No Knowledge	*Control Group*	
Incomplete Knowledge		
Complete Knowledge		

Fig. 3.1. Design of experiment 1

incomplete knowledge, i.e., information on the influence of the machine components on three of the six state parameters, and (3) complete knowledge, i.e., information for all six machine parameters. The variable type of knowledge had two levels: relevant and not-relevant machine knowledge. In the relevant knowledge conditions subjects could infer for each state parameter, by interpreting the graphical display of the machine, which of the two components caused the abnormal value of the parameter. In other words, there was a semantic correlation between symptoms (abnormal value) and diagnosis (machine component). The relevant machine knowledge was also consistent with most of the values of the problem exemplars. This means that the subjects could infer for the majority of the problem exemplars that three of the four symptoms of an exemplar were caused by one and the same component. In the not-relevant knowledge condition on the other hand, the subjects could not infer which component caused the malfunctioning of the machine. The machine knowledge was devised in such a way that the subjects were "forced" to conclude that the abnormal value of a state parameter could be caused by component A (e.g., filter), as well as by component B (e.g., generator). Hence, in the not-relevant conditions, the subjects could not make a knowledge-based distinction between the two alternative problem categories (components).

As can be seen from Fig. 3.1., the no-knowledge—relevant condition and the no-knowledge—not-relevant condition are integrated into one condition, called the control group, because both conditions are equivalent. Fig. 3.1. also illustrates how the experiment can be interpreted as an operationalization of five different problem solving or knowledge contexts. The control group is comparable with a standard concept learning task, i.e., the subjects have no access to prior knowledge and their only task is to learn which problem exemplars belong to which problem category, using feedback information. The four other groups are each an instantiation of a specific problem solving context.

In order to derive the cognitive load predictions, the experiment is interpreted as a dual-task design. The dual-task methodology is frequently used to study the processing requirements of cognitive processes. According to the dual-task technique, the performance on a primary task in single task conditions (only one process is executed) is compared with the performance on the same task in dual task conditions (simultaneously executing the primary and a secondary task) and/or the performance on a primary task executed in different dual-task conditions is compared. It is assumed that in a dual-task situation the primary and secondary process access the same limited amount of processing capacity. When the cognitive resources limit is reached, interference between the processes takes place resulting in a graceful degradation of the secondary task. For instance, Fisk and Schneider (1984) found that an increase of controlled attention for a primary task, resulted in a decrease of the storage rate of items in long term memory. Hence, the performance on the secondary task is an measurement of the level of interference between the primary and secondary process in a dual-task context.

According to cognitive load theory, problem solving and learning can be considered as two independent processes which are executed in parallel and compete for the same limited amount of processing capacity. In the learning phase of the experiment, increasing the amount of machine knowledge increases the extent in which subjects are involved in a problem solving activity (i.e., interpretation of the available machine knowledge) and hence increases the degree of interference between the primary task, i.e., problem solving, and the secondary task, i.e., learning. The test phase of the experiment is an evaluation of the learning performance of the subjects. This implies that the performance on the secondary task in the test phase is an measurement of the level of interference between problem solving and learning in the learning phase of the experiment. Therefore it is predicted that increasing the amount of machine knowledge (i.e., problem solving) will result in a decrement of the learning performance as evaluated in the test phase of the experiment.

In section 1 we emphasized that as an immediate implication of the cognitive load theory, it is necessary to evaluate separately the effects of problem solving and learning on the subjects' performance. Consequently, for the error performance in the learning phase of the experiment, it is predicted that the performance will be in the first place the result of the problem solving activity of the subjects, i.e., the subjects interpreting the machine knowledge. In other words, the error performance will be a function of the relevancy of the machine information.

The experimental method was described in section 2. It suffices to mention that 55 first-year students of the Psychology Faculty of the University of Ghent (Belgium) participated in the experiment. They were randomly assigned to one of the five conditions of the experiment. For a more detailed description of the experimental method, we refer to Van Hoe (in press).

3.1 Results

The main results are discussed briefly. For a more extended discussion see Van Hoe (in press). The data were analyzed using the MANOVA-approach of repeated measures designs (McCall & Appelbaum, 1973).

Table 3.1. contains the mean number of errors per learning block per condition. There were no significant differences between the two relevant knowledge groups and between the two not-relevant conditions. The control subjects made significantly more errors than the subjects in the incomplete relevant knowledge condition: $F(1,50) = 9.03$, $p < 0.01$, and the subjects in the complete relevant condition: $F(1,50) = 19.32$, $p < 0.001$. Subjects in the not-relevant conditions made significantly more errors than the control subjects: $F(1,50) = 21.49$, $p < 0.001$, and the relevant knowledge subjects: $F(1,50) = 53.17$, $p < 0.001$. These error performance differences could not be attributed to reaction time differences since

Table 3.1. Mean number of errors per learning block

Completeness of Knowledge	Type of Knowledge	
	Relevant	Not-Relevant
Incomplete Knowledge	2.79	4.04
Complete Knowledge	2.40	5.12
Control	3.68	

Note: the maximum number of errors per learning block is 10.

no significant differences between corresponding (i.e., complete relevant versus complete not-relevant, and incomplete relevant versus incomplete not-relevant) knowledge groups were found.

In the learning phase, 10 different tasks were used. In the case of the complete relevant knowledge condition, 7 out of the 10 tasks could be correctly solved using the graphical representation of the machine. These tasks are called *G2*-tasks. For the three remaining tasks, no knowledge-based distinction was possible. These tasks are called *G1*-tasks. If it is true that the error performance is a function of the relevancy of knowledge and the subjects used the diagnosis strategy as described in the manual, it can be predicted that the subjects in the complete relevant condition will make significantly less errors on the *G2*-tasks than on the *G1*-tasks. Furthermore, performance differences between the complete relevant condition and the other groups are to be found on the *G2*-tasks rather than on the *G1*-tasks. For the incomplete-relevant group, a similar distinction between type of tasks can be made, and hence similar predictions can be formulated. For that condition, the *G3*-tasks refer to the tasks for which no knowledge-based decision was possible, and the *G4*-tasks are the tasks for which the incomplete relevant knowledge was sufficient to correctly solve them. Table 3.2. contains the mean number of errors per block per task type. The complete-relevant subjects made significantly less errors on the *G2*-tasks than on the *G1*-tasks: $F(1,50) = 74.13$, $p < 0.001$. Compared

Table 3.2. Mean number of errors per block per task type

Condition	Task type			
	G1	G2	G3	G4
Control	0.45	0.33	0.43	0.32
Incomplete - Relevant	0.39	0.23	0.50	0.13
Complete - Relevant	0.51	0.12	0.34	0.17
Incomplete - Not-relevant	0.46	0.38	0.44	0.38
Complete - Not-relevant	0.54	0.50	0.53	0.50

Note: the maximum number of errors per block per task type is 1.00.

with the other conditions, subjects in the complete-relevant condition made significantly less errors on the $G2$-tasks: compared with the control group: $F(1,50)$ = 31.29, $p < 0.001$; compared with the complete not-relevant group: $F(1,50)$ = 60.59, $p < 0.001$; compared with the incomplete not-relevant group: $F(1,50)$ = 27.96, $p < 0.001$; and compared with the incomplete relevant group: $F(1,50)$ = 5.11, $p < 0.05$. The incomplete relevant group made significantly less errors on the $G4$-tasks in comparison with the $G3$-tasks: $F(1,50) = 77.85$, $p < 0.001$. On the $G4$-tasks the incomplete-relevant subjects performed significantly better than the control group: $F(1,50) = 24.79$, $p < 0.001$, the incomplete not-relevant group: $F(1,50) = 25.33$, $p < 0.001$, and the complete relevant group: $F(1,50) = 54.99$, $p < 0.001$.

For the retention tasks, no differences were found between the knowledge groups. The control group (mean proportion incorrect: 0.16) made significantly less errors in comparison with the relevant conditions (mean proportion incorrect: 0.38): $F(1,50) = 5.54$, $p < 0.05$, and the not-relevant conditions (mean proportion incorrect: 0.41): $F(1,50) = 8.88$, $p < 0.01$. The data-analysis of the retention task

Table 3.3. Mean number errors per retention task type

Condition	Task type			
	G1	G2	G3	G4
Control	0.24	0.13	0.30	0.08
Incomplete - Relevant	0.48	0.33	0.64	0.21
Complete - Relevant	0.39	0.38	0.43	0.34
Incomplete - Not-relevant	0.36	0.34	0.39	0.32
Complete - Not-relevant	0.52	0.46	0.52	0.44

Note: the maximum number of errors per retention task type is 1.00.

types (cf., Table 3.3.) showed no significant difference between the $G1$ and $G2$-task type for the complete relevant subjects. On the $G2$-task types, the complete relevant condition performed significantly worse than the control group: $F(1,50)$ = 5.19, $p < 0.05$. No differences were found between the complete relevant condition and the not-relevant knowledge groups. The incomplete relevant group made significantly less errors on the $G4$-tasks than on the $G3$-tasks: $F(1,50)= 24.46$, $p < 0.001$.

For the transfer tasks as a whole the control group (mean proportion incorrect: 0.36) performed significantly better than the complete not-relevant group (mean proportion incorrect: 0.46): $F(1,50) = 4.02$, $p < 0.05$. For the prototypical transfer items however, it was found that the complete relevant group (mean proportion incorrect: 0.91) performed significantly worse than the control group (mean proportion incorrect: 0.30): $F(1,50) = 6.26$, $p < 0.05$, and the incomplete relevant group (mean proportion incorrect: 0.27): $F(1,50) = 6.52$, $p < 0.05$. No differences were found between the complete relevant group and the not-relevant groups.

3.2 Discussion and Conclusion

For the learning phase it was predicted that error performance would be in the first place a function of the relevancy of knowledge. That was indeed what happened: an increase in relevancy of knowledge (not-relevant -> control -> relevant) resulted in an significant decrease in number of errors. It is interesting in this respect that the subjects in the complete relevant condition performed significantly better on the problem tasks for which a knowledge-based decision was possible, the so-called *G2*-tasks, compared with the so-called *G1*-tasks, tasks for which no knowledge-based solution was possible. It was also on the *G2*-tasks that the significant differences between the complete relevant group and the other groups were found.

For the test phase it was predicted that an increase in the amount of knowledge would result in a corresponding significant increase in errors on the test items as a consequence of the higher degree of interference between learning and problem solving. That is what the data reveal, certainly for the complete relevant group. As the control subjects executed the task in single-task conditions they made significantly less errors than the knowledge subjects who performed in dual-task conditions. As described in the previous paragraph, the subjects in the complete relevant group performed quite well in the learning phase, however that was not the case in the test phase. More specifically, for the complete relevant condition:

1. In contradistinction from the learning phase, no retention performance differences were found between *G1* and *G2*-tasks;
2. On the *G2*-tasks, the subjects performed significantly worse than the control subjects. No differences were found with the not-relevant groups. In other words, the performance pattern on the *G1* and *G2*-tasks was completely reversed in the test phase;
3. On the prototypical transfer items, subjects performed significantly worse than the control subjects. Again, no differences were found with the not-relevant groups. This result is surprising, since the subjects more or less constantly induced the prototypical exemplar of each problem category during the learning phase.

Summarized, the overall data pattern of the complete relevant knowledge condition corresponds with the cognitive load predictions. The data pattern also illustrates a striking implication of cognitive load theory: apparently the relevancy of knowledge had no significant impact on the test performance, i.e., there were no test performance differences between the complete relevant group and the not-relevant conditions.

The data picture for the not-relevant groups is more complicated. At first glance, the data pattern for these conditions also fit within the cognitive load theory. However, an alternative explanation for the overall bad performance of the not-relevant conditions is that the fact of trying to use not-relevant information for solving the problem tasks had on itself an effect on performance, independent of a high degree of interference. This and other questions are addressed in van Hoe (in press).

The major goal of this article was to provide a direct test of the cognitive load theory. Experimental evidence was found that the cognitive load imposed by a weak problem solving activity can retard the acquisition of a problem-solving skill.

However, the experiment also illustrates that the major drawback of the cognitive load theory is the central concept of the theory itself. The term "cognitive load" is a rather vague and abstract concept which stands for a set of variables (attention, effort, storage capacity) which can constrain the interaction between processes, and because the cognitive load imposed by a process is not directly measurable, it is not always clear whether a variable or which variable constrains the relation between problem solving and learning.

References

Anderson, J.R. (1987). Skill acquisition: Compilation of weak-method problem solutions. Psychological Review, 94, 192-210.

Anderson, J.R. (1989). Practice, working memory, and the ACT* theory of skill acquisition: A comment on Carlson, Sullivan, and Schneider (1989). Journal of Experimental Psychology: Learning, Memory, and Cognition, 15, 527-530.

Carlson, R.A., Sullivan, M., & Schneider, W. (1989). Practice and working memory effects in building a procedural skill. Journal of Experimental Psychology: Learning, Memory, and Cognition, 15, 517-526.

Chandler, P., & Sweller, J. (1991). Cognitive load theory and the format of instruction. Cognition and Instruction, 8, 293-332.

Fisk, A.D., & Schneider, W. (1984). Memory as a function of attention, level of processing, and automatization. Journal of Experimental Psychology: Learning, Memory, and Cognition, 10, 181-197.

Holland, J.H., Holyoak, K., Nisbett, R.E., & Thagard, P. (1986). Induction: Processes of inference, learning, and discovery. Cambridge, MA: Bradford Books.

Kotovsky, K., Hayes, J.R., & Simon, H.A. (1985). Why are some problems hard? Evidence from Tower of Hanoi. Cognitive Psychology, 17, 248-294.

Logan, G. (1992). Shapes of reaction-time distributions and shapes of learning curves: A test of the instance theory of automaticity. Journal of Experimental Psychology: Learning, Memory, and Cognition, 18, 883-914.

McCall, R.B., & Appelbaum, M.I. (1973). Bias in the analysis of repeated-measures designs: Some alternative approaches. Child Development, 44, 401-415.

Rosenbloom, P., & Newell, A. (1987). An integrated computational model of stimulus-response compatibility and practice. The Psychology of Learning and Motivation, 21, 1-52.

Schooler, J.W., Ohlsson, S., & Brooks, K. (1993). Thoughts beyond words: When language overshadows insight. Journal of Experimental Psychology: General, 122, 166-183.

Sweller, J. (1988). Cognitive load during problem solving: Effects on learning. Cognitive Science, 12, 257-285.

Sweller, J., Mawer, R., & Ward, M. (1983). Development of expertise in mathematical problem solving. Journal of Experimental Psychology: General, 112, 639-661.

van Hoe, R.R.G. (in preparation). An experimental test of cognitive load theory.

Referring in a Shared Workspace

Anita H.M. Cremers

Institute for Perception Research, P.O. Box 513, 5600 MB Eindhoven, The Netherlands[1]

Abstract. Effective cooperation of humans with other humans and with intelligent machines requires a language of words and gestures that is accurate and efficient in making reference to objects. In the present investigation, expressions and gestures that were used by subjects to direct partners' attentions to building blocks during a collaborative construction task were analyzed and classified into four main categories. In addition, the influence of mutual knowledge of the participants (either knowledge about the dialogue or about the domain of conversation) on the referential acts used was studied. The focus of attention, both within the dialogue and within the domain, plays an important role in the use of references. In particular, the effect of focus within the domain of conversation on the use of referential acts needs to be investigated further.

Keywords. Referential expressions, referential gestures, dialogues, mutual knowledge, focus of attention

1 Introduction

When two people discuss a task they are to perform together, they must indicate which of the available materials and/or tools each person is going to use. Ordinarily, each will use *referential acts*, verbal and non-verbal signals to single out each object in space, so that the partner will be able to locate it.

Research into the means of referring to objects or places in the extra-linguistic context has focused mainly on the linguistic part of referential acts uttered in isolation. It is reported that the decision of a speaker to use a particular expression to refer to an object largely depends on the type of coordinate system that is used, the place of the origin of this system and, possibly, the chosen *relatum*, i.e. the object or person that is chosen as a reference point with respect to which this object is located (Levelt 1989). However, in face-to-face dialogues, these utterances are in many cases accompanied by non-verbal communicative acts, such as gestures, facial expressions and/or bodily postures. In addition, the form (the information that is included in the expression) and content (the object the

---

1. The research presented here is financed by the Tilburg-Eindhoven Organisation for Inter-University Cooperation.

expression refers to) of referential acts largely depend on the mutual knowledge of speaker and hearer; the *common ground*, as Clark and Wilkes-Gibbs call it (Clark and Wilkes-Gibbs 1986). Mutual knowledge can either be general knowledge about the domain of discourse (e.g. properties of objects in the domain), knowledge about the actual state and history of the domain of discourse (e.g. the past or the present location of a certain object) or knowledge about the preceding utterances in the dialogue (e.g. a name that has been given to a certain object).

The goal of the present research is to provide an overview of types of referential expressions and gestures, and to investigate how a speaker's assumption about the hearer's knowledge influences the information that is included in subsequent references. In the following, the methodology of one dialogue experiment that was carried out to study referential expressions relating to objects in a relatively restricted domain will first be described. Then, a classification will be given of the types and amounts of referential expressions and gestures that were used in the dialogues. Finally, the influence of the speakers' and the hearers' mutual knowledge on the type of referential act used will be outlined.

2 Methodology

A dialogue experiment was carried out in which 10 pairs of Dutch subjects participated. The experimental set-up and task were designed so as to evoke as many varied referential acts as possible. One of the participants (the instructor) was told to instruct the other (the builder) in rebuilding a block-building on a toy foundation plate in accordance with an example that was provided. The building consisted of blocks of one of four different colours, three sizes and four shapes. The partners were seated side by side at a table, but were separated by a screen. Only their hands were visible to one another, and only when placed on top of the table in the vicinity of the foundation plate. Both subjects were allowed to observe the building domain, to talk about it, and to gesticulate in it, but only the respective builders were allowed to manipulate blocks. The experimental configuration is depicted in Figure 1. The 10 building sessions, the dialogues of which were similar to Grosz's task dialogues (Grosz 1977), were recorded on videotape.

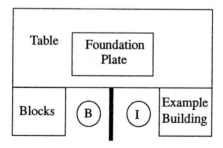

Figure 1. Experimental configuration (top view)
B = Builder, I = Instructor

3 Referential Expressions in the Dialogues

In the dialogues four main categories of reference were distinguished: reference to physical features of the object; reference to the location of the object in the domain; reference to the orientation of the object in the building domain and, finally, reference to the history which was developed in the course of actions that were carried out in the domain and the topics that were discussed in the dialogue. In the dialogues a total amount of 665 referential expressions occurred, of which 59.5% (396) actually contained information out of one or more of the four categories mentioned above. These expressions either acted as direct references to objects in the domain (62.4%, 247) or as anaphora, which means reference to objects that had already been introduced previously in the dialogue (37.6%, 149). The remaining 40.5% (269) consisted of pronominals or demonstratives.

3.1 Reference to Physical Features of an Object

By far the majority of the referential expressions that were used included information about physical features of the object. Specifically, 92.2% (365) of the referential expressions included this type of information, and 77.5% (307) of the expressions consisted of physical information only. The features that were used in the dialogues were colour (e.g. *red*[2]), size (e.g. *large*) and shape (e.g. *square*) of the blocks, which were the three distinguishing physical features in the set of blocks. There was a preference for the feature colour. This was used in 97.3% (355) of the references that contained information about physical features, whereas size and shape were mentioned in only 25.2% (92) and 17.8% (65) of the cases, respectively.

3.2 Reference to the Location of an Object

Reference to the location of an object was mainly used by participants who did not use pointing gestures at all. This is not surprising, because both referential means seem to accomplish the same effect, one by means of language, the other through gesturing.

3.2.1 Location in General

Participants in dialogues sometimes used general expressions referring to objects in the domain, e.g. *here* and *there*. In 3.8% (15) of the information-containing expressions this was done, and in 1.8% (7) of the cases this reference type was used in isolation. When these references were used to refer directly (non-anaphorically) to

---

2. Since the examples of referential expressions provided in this paper are merely abstractions of the Dutch expressions that were used in the dialogues, they are only given in English.

objects in the domain, pointing gestures were always added. Most of the occurrences of this type of reference were uttered at points where the speaker shifted his or her attention to another region of the domain, for instance to give instructions about building a new part of the block-building. We shall call this kind of shift a transition of the *focus of attention*.

3.2.2 Location with Respect to the Participants

The location of an object was sometimes indicated by stating its relative position with respect to both participants, e.g. *the blue one on the right*. This type of information was used in 6.1% of the references, and in 1.5% of the cases it was the only type used. These expressions were hardly ever accompanied by pointing gestures, probably because they already contained enough information to identify the intended object. Referencing by indicating the location of an object with respect to the participants was again mainly used to install a new focus of attention in the domain.

3.2.3 Location with Respect to Other Objects

The locations of objects were also indicated as a position with respect to other objects in the domain, e.g. *the blue block behind the yellow one*. In these expressions the position of the participants should also be taken into account. They were used in 3.5% (14) of the cases, and in 0.8% (3) of the cases this was the only type of information supplied. This type of reference was used mainly when the current block was located in the neighbourhood of the block referred to previously; in fact this happened in 71.4% (10) of the cases. In these cases the previous block was used as relatum for the current one. No transition of focus occurred, because the location was already more or less clear. This could also be reason why no pointing gestures were being used to accompany this type of expression.

3.2.4 Location with Respect to the Hand of a Participant Within the Domain

The occurrence of referential expressions using the hand of a participant as a relatum was probably a consequence of the specific set-up of the task. In this set-up the participants shared the same perspective, and the only difference between each other's body positions they could actually observe was the position of the hands, which changed constantly. Instances of this type of expression occurred in 1.3% (5) of the cases, and in 0.8% (3) of the cases it was the only disambiguating information offered. No gestures accompanied these expressions.

The position of the partner's hand was used in two ways. In the first, the speaker informed the partner about where a block was located with respect to the location of his hand at the moment of the utterance, e.g. *the blue block to your right (to the right of your hand)*. In the second, the speaker told the partner in what direction his hand should move in order to reach the intended object. So, in this case, the location of the hand was presupposed, and instead of informing the partner about the location of the object, the action he or she had to carry out was supplied. This action could either be a default-action or an explicitly indicated one. In the case of a default action the partner was already moving in the right direction and only needed to be encouraged to continue doing so, e.g. *a bit further.* In the latter case, the explicit direction had to be provided, e.g. *go to the left.*

3.3 Reference to the Orientation of an Object

The different ways in which an object can be positioned in the domain all result in different object orientations. Speakers can make use of an object's orientation to distinguish it from other (identical) objects, e.g. *the horizontal yellow block.* In 1.0% (4) of the referential expressions participants made use of this disambiguating device, but the information was always accompanied by other types of information. No accompanying gestures were used.

3.4 Reference to the History of an Object

Finally, an object could be disambiguated by means of reference to earlier events in which the object had been involved, e.g. *the red one you have just put down.* Also, when one of the participants had already talked about the object earlier in the dialogue, this could be used for disambiguation, e.g. *the red one you just mentioned.*

In 7.1% (28) of the expressions participants made use of historical aspects, and in 2.8% (11) of the cases this was the only information they provided. References to the history of the domain and the history of the dialogue occurred equally often. Hardly any accompanying gestures were used. The ones that were used referred to objects that had been talked about before and were still located in the domain.

4 Influence of Mutual Knowledge on Referential Expressions

During the course of a dialogue and of events in the domain of conversation, knowledge is built up about these issues. Later in the dialogue and in the building process, a partner may make use of the knowledge he or she assumes the other has available. In fact, the assumption of the presence of this knowledge may to some extent determine the type of information that is being used in the current expression, although it may be fully disambiguating in its own right.

4.1 Mutual Knowledge About the Dialogue

Assumed knowledge about the dialogue on the part of the partner was reflected in the use of pronominal anaphora and ellipsis in the referential expressions. Anaphora can be used when the speaker assumes that the object referred to is in the focus of attention of both participants (Grosz 1977), in which case a pronominal reference suffices for making clear which object is meant (e.g. *take a small red block, put it on top of the large green one*). Ellipsis occurred when the referential expression in an utterance was omitted altogether, or when parts of the utterance were omitted. Total omissions took place when both participants had already agreed upon which object was being referred to, and only some predicate of the object was left to express, for example the destination of a particular block on which the action had already been carried out (e.g. *take a small red block, put it on top of the large green one, (...) the green one on the right*). Partial omissions occurred when information in the current expression partially coincided with information in the preceding expression, e.g. *place a small yellow block, put a blue one on top of it*. In this example the 'blue one' was taken to be a small block as well, although the explicit information was omitted.

4.2 Mutual Knowledge About the Domain: Focus of Attention

Knowledge about the domain of discourse and about the manipulations that are being or have been carried out in it may be reflected in referential expressions. Triggers for this type of reference that were observed in the experiment are a participant's awareness of the existence of either a spatial or a functional focus of attention.

4.2.1 Spatial Focus

The spatial focus of the domain is the part of the domain that is being attended to most closely. For objects that are located in areas closely attended to, the speaker does not have to provide fully disambiguating information when referring. In these cases, the disambiguation should only concern the part of the domain that is being attended to. The spatial focus can be created either explicitly by verbal means, or implicitly, or by means of gestures.

Explicit. Speakers sometimes announced explicitly that objects that were located in a particular sub-domain should be attended to more closely, e.g. *let's move to the upper right part*. In this way the speaker made sure that the hearer focused his or her attention on the indicated sub-domain, so that he or she could use less information in expressions referring to objects that were located there. In the dialogues, 6.1% of the referential expressions contained this type of information, and 1.5% of these consisted exclusively of this type of information.

Implicit. Speakers also implicitly made use of the assumed focus of attention of the partner. The speaker could have well-founded reasons for believing that the partner's focus was actually directed at this particular sub-domain, for example when he or she had just referred to an object that was located there. In this case, the speaker argued that the partner was inclined to consider the next reduced expression as a reference to an object in the neighbourhood of the one just mentioned. For example, in *please remove these blocks (points at a green, a yellow and a blue block), the red one can remain seated there*, the speaker referred to a red block without fully disambiguating it. However, it was clear to the listener that the speaker was referring to the red block in the vicinity of the three blocks that had been pointed at earlier.

Gestures. The partners used their hands to point at objects, to indicate their orientation in the domain, to touch them, to pick them up or to hold them. Both the instructor and the builder were allowed to point at blocks and to touch them, but the latter could in addition pick up the blocks and hold them in his or her hand. Both partners could also make use of the fact that the other was (incidentally) pointing at or touching a block. In those cases, the speaker could refer orally to that particular block by means of a minimally informative expression, like *that one*. The instructor could also use this mechanism when the builder was picking up a block or holding it. In all of these cases the speaker could use less information than he would have needed if there had not been some involvement of a hand. In the dialogues, participants used some kind of accompanying gesture in 16.8% of the referential expressions. However, three out of ten instructors did not use any gestures at all during the dialogues. Since the participants had been instructed to act as spontaneously as possible, this can be considered a matter of preference. This lack of gesturing did not have a notable effect on the percentage, because in these dialogues the builders had to use more gestures in order to verify whether they had correctly identified a particular block. This was less necessary for builders who had a pointing instructor as a partner.

4.2.2 Functional Focus

In addition to the assumed knowledge about spatial focus, the speakers made use of the partners' assumed knowledge about the current functional focus. Functional focus is related to the actions that have to be carried out in the domain. The concept of functional focus applies when the action that should be carried out more or less restricts the number of blocks that can reasonably be involved in the action. In that case, reduced information is possible, based on the assumed acquaintance of the partner with the pre- or post-conditions of the action.

Preconditions. A partner could make use of the preconditions of an action when an object had to be removed. In that case, the object referred to was most likely the one that was located at a position that was easily reachable, e.g. *remove the little yellow one*, which was taken to be the small yellow block on top of the building, although there were many other small yellow blocks available at positions that were not so easy to reach.

Post-conditions. Post-conditions of an action could be used when an object was to be (re-)placed. Then the object referred to was most likely the one that fitted best at the indicated location. For example, when there was an opening between two yellow blocks that could only contain a small block, the 'green block' in the utterance *place a green block between the yellow ones* was taken to be a small one.

In total, the dialogues contain about 30 cases of the implicit spatial focusing and the functional focus mechanism together. In these cases, it can be demonstrated that the partner was actually making use of one or both of these mechanisms, because the information provided did not fully distinguish the referent object from the surrounding ones, and no pointing gestures were used. Actually, it was not always possible to distinguish between the use of implicit focusing and functional focusing, because these mechanisms coincided many times. For example, when a speaker had just been talking about a yellow block, and subsequently said that a large red block should be placed on top of a small green one, he or she probably meant the green block that was placed in the neighbourhood of the yellow block, and was suitable for having a large block placed on top of it.

5 Summary and Conclusions

In this paper, an analysis has been presented of verbal and gestural references to objects that occurred in 10 task dialogues, in Dutch, and of the influence of mutual knowledge on the usage of these acts. In the dialogues, four main categories of references to objects occurred, namely reference to physical features, to the orientation or the location of objects, and to the history of objects in a domain or in the dialogue. It could be demonstrated that the participants made use of mutual knowledge about the contents of the preceding dialogue, as well as the state and history of the domain of conversation when uttering a particular referential expression.

The focus of attention appeared to be a central notion in the use and interpretation of referential expressions. At focus transitions participants tended to use more expressions referring to the location of objects in general and to locations with respect to the participants. Reference to the location of an object with respect to other objects tended to be used when the focus did not shift. Moreover, the focus of attention played an important role in the production and comprehension of references when speakers made use of mutual knowledge. The effects of the focus of dialogues on the possible use of pronouns and ellipsis are well-known (Grosz 1977, Grosz 1981). However, further research is needed to establish the effects of the focus of the domain of conversation on the use of references.

References

Clark, H.H., Schreuder, R., Buttrick, S. (1983) Common ground and the understanding of demonstrative reference. J. of Verbal Learning and Verbal Behavior 22, 245-258

Clark, H.H., Wilkes-Gibbs, D. (1986) Referring as a collaborative process. Cognition 22, 1-39

Grosz, B.J. (1977) The representation and use of focus in dialogue understanding. Technical Note 151. Menlo Park: SRI International

Grosz, B.J. (1981) Focusing and description in natural language dialogues. In: A. Joshi, B. Webber, I. Sag (eds.) Elements of discourse understanding. New York: Cambridge University Press

Levelt, W.J.M. (1989) Speaking: from intention to articulation. Cambridge: MIT Press

Rules in Dialogue

Robbert-Jan Beun

Institute for Perception Research/IPO, P.O.Box 513, 5600 MB Eindhoven, The Netherlands. Email: rjbeun@prl.philips.nl

Abstract. In this paper a model is presented that describes the cooperative behaviour of two participants in a dialogue. A dialogue is considered as a set of moves (or speech acts) in a game. Each move has a certain function and propositional content and changes the cognitive state of the participants. Two types of rules are considered: *generative* rules that determine the type of speech act that will be performed in the next turn and *update* rules that determine the change in the cognitive state. Goal of the dialogue is to exchange information in a collaborative manner so that, if the information is available, in the final state both participants believe the answer to an initial question. The resulting structure of the information exchange may be complex, because knowledge to find the answer may be distributed among the participants.

Keywords. Dialogue games, speech act generation, cognitive state change, cooperativity, distributed knowledge

1 Introduction

In intelligent tutoring systems a sophisticated dialogue module is crucial for the didactic qualities of the system. This module determines communicative strategies and types of communicative actions that should be provided in the interaction with the apprentice, for example, appropriate feedback questions to answers. Precisely what type of information should be transferred at what time in the interaction and how the beliefs and intentions of the tutor and the apprentice are involved in this process is an open question.

From what is observed in cooperative dialogues, we know, for example, that the information provided by a communicative system should at least be in agreement with the Gricean maxims for cooperation, such as quantity and relevance; i.e. 'say enough', 'do not say too much' and 'be relevant' (Grice 1975). These Gricean maxims may sound obvious; however, when it comes to implementation, it is extremely difficult to formalise these maxims into concrete rules for the generation of adequate communicative behaviour.

In this paper, I would like to discuss a theoretical framework to describe adequate communicative behaviour of participants (human or machine) in a cooperative dialogue. The communicative strategy for utterance generation in this framework is based on a (simple) representation of the beliefs and intentions of the dialogue participants. The main goal of the dialogue is to exchange information in a collaborative manner so that, if the information is available, in the final state both participants believe the answer to an initial question. The resulting structure of the information exchange can be complex, since the knowledge to find the answer to the initial question may be distributed among the participants. This reflects a situation in which a system behaves as a fellow student and tries to solve a problem in cooperation with the dialogue partner (see e.g., Baker 1994).

First, I will briefly discuss two theoretical models for speech act generation, the *dialogue grammar* approach and what I will call the *context-change* approach. Next, I will introduce the basic aspects of the dialogue model presented in this paper and demonstrate an example of a dialogue that can be generated by using the rules of this model.

Dialogue grammar

In the dialogue grammar approach (see for example, Levinson 1983), coherence in the dialogue is described at the level of *speech acts* or interactional *moves* that are made by the utterance in the dialogue. Conversational sequences are primarily regulated by a set of sequencing rules stated over speech act types. For example, questions are followed by answers, offers are followed by acceptances or rejections and greetings are followed by counter-greetings. In this view a model of dialogue can be build on primitive notions from speech act theory and adequate interactive behaviour can be generated from the sequencing rules.

Levinson points out, however, that this analysis is incomplete since the first move can, depending on the situation, be followed by almost any speech act type. A question, for example, can be followed by a partial answer, a rejection, a denial of relevance of the question. Moreover, depending on the propositional content of the utterance, the same sequence of speech acts can be well-formed or ill-formed. For example, in the following pairs of utterances is the illocutionary force of the first utterance a statement and the second one is an excuse and an expression of gratitude:

A1: Mary is in the kitchen
B1: I am sorry, thanks

A2: You are in front of the overhead projector
B2: I am sorry, thanks

In the first case, the sequence sounds ill-formed, whereas in the second case we do not seem to have any problems in judging the utterance sequence as well-formed.[1]

It is not my intention to restate all of Levinson's arguments against the dialogue grammar approach. His criticism can be summarized in one argument, i.e., coherence in dialogue is simply not on the level of speech acts, it is on the level

---

[1] Note that adding the word *thanks* to the second utterance, prevents us to think that B did not understand A's utterance.

of the overall beliefs and intentions, both communicative and non-communicative, of the dialogue participants. Speech acts are only a partial surface representation of the relevant beliefs and intentions of the participants (see also Airenti, Bruno & Colombetti 1993).

Context-change and speech act generation

In the context-change approach, speech acts are characterized in terms of their context-changing effects. In this approach (e.g., Gazdar (1981), Bunt (1989), Perrault (1990) and Beun (1994)) context is limited to cognitive states of the participants in terms of wants, desires, beliefs, intentions, etc., and a speech act is taken as a function that changes one context into another. For example, a statement can cause, under the appropriate circumstances, a change in the listener's cognitive state, from a cognitive state in which the listener does not believe the proposition expressed in the utterance, to one in which it is believed so. In this approach, communicative acts are considered as 'normal' actions, i.e. they are intentionally performed to change certain aspects of the 'cognitive world' of the participants, and they have pre- and postconditions in terms of the participants' beliefs and intentions. Beliefs and intentions are introduced as modal operators and their formal properties are expressed in axiom schemes. Successful communication is accomplished if the preconditions of the act are recognized by the recipient and if the conditions become so-called mutual belief.

The context-change approach for utterance *generation* can be summarized as follows. Suppose someone starts with an initial utterance in the dialogue, for example, a question. The listener recognizes the preconditions of the question (for example, that the speaker intends the listener to believe that the speaker has the intention to know whether p), which in turn may form the new preconditions for the next speech act.

This approach sounds attractive, but it suffers from an enormous computational complexity, because there is no direct connection between the previous speech act and the next one. The preconditions to generate, for example, an answer to a question are determined by the set of formulas that follow from the closure of general axioms on rationality and cooperativity, by the previous cognitive state of the listener, and by the communicated cognitive state that results from the question. This set includes an infinite set of, possibly irrelevant, formulas like 'the listener beliefs that the speaker has the intention that the listener beliefs that the speaker has the intention that the speaker beliefs whether p', etc. The closure of the set may also contain preconditions for different types of speech acts; i.e., which one is the next speaker supposed to choose? And, more dramatically, how is the next speaker going to pick out the correct set of preconditions from the infinite set of formulas for the next turn?

In the following section, I will show how the two approaches – 'dialogue grammar' and 'context-change' – can be combined. In the presented framework, sequences of speech acts will be connected more closely than in the context-change approach, but the idea of grammar rules in terms of speech act concatenation will be discarded.

2   Modelling cooperative behaviour in dialogues

A dialogue will be considered as a set of *moves* in a game, the so-called 'speech acts' (see Carlson 1985). Each move has a function (or goal) and (propositional) content, and changes the cognitive state of the participants. For that reason, we define an *update* function that yields a new cognitive state depending on the old state and the just performed speech act. Vice versa, the new cognitive state of a dialogue partner contains the preconditions for the next move. In other words, a move is completely determined by the cognitive state of one of the participants at a certain time. This implies that the next move is not only based on the previous one, as would be the case with a dialogue grammar based on speech acts, but that the next move is based on both the previous move of one of the participants and the previous cognitive state of the partner.

Questions are answered if the information is available. This may take more than one turn, because the knowledge to answer the question may be distributed among the participants. At the end of the dialogue, all questions should be answered or a reason should be given why a particular question could not be answered.

First, we introduce the types of belief and intention that define the cognitive state of the dialogue participants and the types of speech acts that the participants can perform in the dialogue. Next, the rules for generation and update are introduced. In section 3, a dialogue example is discussed where two dialogue partners generate speech acts according to the rules of the dialogue game. The example is presented in both an abstract schema to reveal the underlying context-changes of the participants and in natural language to show the consequences of the framework for real dialogue.

Participants' belief, intentions and speech acts
Two types of propositions about the domain of discourse will be distinguished: a. simple propositions (p, q, r, ...) and b. compound propositions consisting of a simple proposition, an arrow and a simple proposition ($p \rightarrow q$, ...).

We will model that the two participants in the dialogue have three types of cognitive states:

a. belief about a certain domain of discourse, $B_X p$ (X Believes that p)
b. belief about what the dialogue partner wants to know, $B_X W K_Y(\ldots, p)$ (X Believes that Y Wants to Know whether p)
c. belief about what the dialogue partner does not believe, $B_X \neg B_Y p$ (X Believes that Y does not Believe that p).

Communicative intentions should be worked out in a certain order. Here $W K_Y(\ldots, p)$ means that the dialogue partner Y has the communicative intention to know the truth value of several different propositions, of which p is the last one. $W K_Y(\ldots, p, \ldots)$ means that p is part of the list of communcative intentions, but not necessarily the last one. The list may be empty, indicated by $W K_Y(\emptyset)$, meaning that Y has no communicative intentions. p, $B_X p$, $B_X W K_Y(\ldots, p)$ and $B_X \neg B_Y p$ are all of type 'proposition'. X and Y are universally quantified variables of type 'agent'.

We will assume that, if a participant believes that his or her partner has the intention to know whether p, then he or she also believes that the partner does not believe that p (R1). Moreover, we assume that if agent X believes that p and he or she believes that p → q, then he or she believes that q (R2).

R1. $B_X W K_Y(\ldots, p, \ldots) \rightarrow B_X \neg B_Y p$

R2. $B_X p \& B_X(p \rightarrow q) \rightarrow B_X q$

Belief about the domain of discourse can be incorrect, but the dialogue partners will never know this, since they have no access to a domain of discourse. Only by asking questions to their partner, the knowledge may come available. The belief state B_X is monotonic, i.e. everything that can be inferred from previous belief states, can also be inferred from new belief states. Information about the intention state $B_X W K_Y$ and about the non-belief of the other $B_X \neg B_Y$ can be changed after certain moves. For example, if a question 'whether p' has been answered, the intention to answer this question will be dropped.

Participants may use four types of speech acts: questions ($p?_X$), statements ($p!_X$), an indication that certain knowledge is not available ($p?!_X$) and a closure of the dialogue ($\$_X$). Speech acts are of type 'action'.

The rules of the dialogue

The participants' communicative strategy is determined by the rules of the dialogue game. Two types of rules will be considered: a. *generative* rules that determine which speech act will be performed depending on a certain cognitive state of one of the participants, and b. *update* rules that determine how a cognitive state will be changed depending on a certain speech act.

An explicit link between the preconditions of the act and the act itself is established by the double arrow '⇒'. Left side of the arrow is of type proposition, the right side is of type action. On the left side we introduce the preconditions in terms of the cognitive state of the participant, on the right side the generated speech act as a result of the precondition.

In generation rule G1 it is expressed that if q is the last item on the intention list of participant Y and q is believed by X, then q will be answered by X.[2] If X does not believe q, however, but believes that there is a solution to solve q by knowing the answer to p, then X will ask for the truth of p (G2). If X does not even know a solution to solve p, then X has to admit that he does not know the answer (G3). Finally, a closure speech act is generated if the intention list is empty (G4).

GENERATION

G1. $B_X W K_Y(\ldots, q) \& B_X q \Rightarrow q!_X$

G2. $B_X W K_Y(\ldots, q) \& \neg B_X q \& B_X(p \rightarrow q) \& \neg B_X \neg B_Y p \Rightarrow p?_X$

G3. $B_X W K_Y(\ldots, q) \& \neg B_X q \& \neg B_X(p \rightarrow q) \Rightarrow q?!_X$

---

[2] In fact, we should add in all cases that it is X's turn to speak. We have left this out for reasons of legibility.

G4. $B_X W K_Y(\emptyset) \Rightarrow \$_X$

To represent the consequences (or postconditions) of a particular speech act, the twisted arrow '$\rightsquigarrow$' is introduced. Left side of the arrow is of type action, the right side is of type proposition. On the left side of the arrow we introduce the just performed speech act of a participant, on the right side the new cognitive state as a result of that speech act. We will assume that the respective old belief and intention state will be updated in consistence with the rules R1 and R2. Below, $(\not{p})$ means that, if p exists in a particular belief or intention list, p will be removed from that particular list.

In update rule U1 it is expressed that if X utters a statement with content p, afterwards the recipient, Y, believes that p and X does not believe anymore that Y does not believe that p.[3] If X utters a question with content p, afterwards Y believes that p is a communicative intention of X and p is added at the end of the intention list (U2). If X indicates that he does not know that q, afterwards Y believes that X does not believe that p and p is removed from X's intention list of Y (U3). In U4 it is expressed that the cognitive states do not change after a closing of the dialogue.

UPDATE
U1. $p!_X \rightsquigarrow B_Y p \& B_X \neg B_Y(\not{p})$
U2. $p?_X \rightsquigarrow B_Y W K_X(\ldots, p)$
U3. $p?!_X \rightsquigarrow B_Y \neg B_X p \& B_X W K_Y(\ldots \not{p})$
U4. $\$_X \rightsquigarrow \emptyset$

Closing of the dialogue should only give the turn to the next speaker. To avoid an infinite sequence of closing speech acts, a meta-rule has been defined to close the dialogue:

Closing
Both dialogue partners stop generating speech acts iff two successive closing speech acts are performed (i.e. the sequence $\$_X$ & $\$_Y$).

3 An example

Let us turn to an example where we have the dialogue partners A and B (Table 1). In Table 1, we have indicated the respective cognitive states of A and B and the speech acts (MOVE) that occur as a result of the dialogue rules. Parts of the cognitive states that represent the preconditions for the next move are indicated in bold.

In the initial situation, A believes that $p \rightarrow q$ and believes that $r \rightarrow q$. B believes that $s \rightarrow p$ and believes r. B starts with the initial question $q?_B$. A does not know the answer to the question directly. However, if A comes to know either p or r, then A can solve the problem by rule R2. So, according to rule G3 A has to generate the

---

[3] Note that, in correspondence with rule R1, p will also be removed from $B_X W K_Y(\ldots, p)$.

	B_A	$B_A W K_B$	$B_A \neg B_B$	MOVE	B_B	$B_B W K_A$	$B_B \neg B_A$
	$p \to q$ $r \to q$				$s \to p$ r		
1				$q?_B$			
	$\mathbf{p \to q}$ $r \to q$	$<\mathbf{q}>$	q		$s \to p$ r		
2				$p?_A$			
	$p \to q$ $r \to q$	$<q>$	q		$\mathbf{s \to p}$ r	$<\mathbf{p}>$	p
3				$s?_B$			
	$p \to q$ $r \to q$	$<q, s>$	q, s		$s \to p$ r	$<p>$	p
4				$s?!_A$			
	$p \to q$ $r \to q$	$<q, \not{s}>$	q, s		$\mathbf{s \to p}$ r	$<\mathbf{p}>$	p, s
5				$p?!_B$			
	$\mathbf{p \to q}$ $\mathbf{r \to q}$	$<\mathbf{q}>$	$q, s, \mathbf{p}$		$s \to p$ r	$<\not{p}>$	p, s
6				$r?_A$			
	$p \to q$ $r \to q$	$<q>$	q, s, p		$s \to p$ $\mathbf{r}$	$<\mathbf{r}>$	p, s, r
7				$r!_B$			
	$p \to q, r$ $r \to q, \mathbf{q}$	$<q>$	q, s, p		$s \to p$ r	$<\not{r}>$	$p, s, \not{r}$
8				$q!_A$			
	$p \to q, r$ $r \to q, q$	$<\not{q}>$	$\not{q}, s, p$		$s \to p$ r, q		p, s
9				$\$_B$			
	$p \to q, r$ $r \to q, q$		s, p		$s \to p$ r, q		p, s
10				$\$_A$			
	$p \to q, r$ $r \to q, q$		s, p		$s \to p$ r, q		p, s

Table 1. A and B try to solve the problem whether q is true. Initially, the information about q is distributed; in the final state, both A and B believe that q is true.

question whether p or the question whether r. In Table 1, A starts with the first one. B can solve this problem by asking for s, but A has to inform B that he has no information about s. A was on the wrong track and the goal s has been dropped (rule U3). The goal q is still not solved and p cannot be asked for, since A believes that B does not know anything about p. Now, r can be asked by A, and, since B has direct information about r, B can answer the question. In turn, A can answer B's original question and finally, the dialogue can be closed since all communicative intentions are removed.

Below, the same example has been presented in natural language. The propositions that were used in Table 1 have the following meaning:

p: 'Olga smokes cigars'
q: 'Olga is happy'
r: 'Olga works at IPO'
s: 'Olga is a manager'

In correspondence with Table 1, John ('A') initially believes that 'if Olga smokes cigars, then she is happy' and believes that 'if Olga works at IPO, then she is happy'. Peter ('B') initially believes that 'if Olga is a manager, then she smokes cigars' and believes that 'Olga works at IPO'. For some reason, Peter is interested to know the answer to the question whether Olga is happy.

In order to obtain a more natural dialogue, we have added utterances that are not generated by the rules that were defined in the model, such as opening of the dialogue, indirect questioning, thanks and particles on the level of processing ('Aha', 'Well', 'Eh'). The basic structure, however, is isomorphic to the structure presented in Table 1.

Peter: Hello John, I have a question. Can you tell me whether Olga is happy?
John: Well, let me see, does she smoke cigars?
Peter: Eh... That depends, is she a manager?
John: Sorry, I don't know.
Peter: Then I don't know whether she smokes cigars.
John: Aha, wait... does she work at IPO?
Peter: Yes, she does.
John: Well in that case, don't worry, she's happy.
Peter: Great, thanks a lot, bye.
John: O.K., bye.

4 Discussion

The model presented in this paper for the generation of appropriate speech acts in a cooperative dialogue has several important advantages compared to the dialogue grammar and the context-change approach that were discussed in section 1.

In all approaches, utterance generation is based on the goal-directed behaviour of individuals in conversational settings. In the dialogue grammar approach, sequences of utterances are generated from the concatenation rules for speech acts. This implies that utterance generation is based only on the functional aspects of previous utterances in the dialogue. In our and the context-change approach, however, utterances are not only generated on the basis of functional properties of the utterance, but also on the basis of the content of the utterance and the previous belief of the participants. Moreover, depending on the speech act type, utterances may change the belief of the participants.

The model presented here differs in an important way from the context-change approach as well. As a result of the closure of the axioms, in the context-change approach an infinite number of cognitive states is modelled. In our model, only those cognitive states (6 in total, 3 per participant) are modelled that are needed

able manner. The basic unit of a SANe device model is the operation, defined as

```
Operation :=
CommandState (defined by the set of applicable commands),
Command (entered by the user),
            Conditions (enabling or disabling state transitions)
            Actions (state changes occurring as sideeffects of an operation)
            TaskActions (sideeffects which modify the state of the work object)
            Costs (total cost of performing te operation)
Next CommandState
```

A behaviour space is defined by the states of the device and the possible transitions between states, and is represented as an ATN (Augmented Transition Network), representing the syntax of the device. Often specifications of interactive HW/SW systems include this information, and several specification languages can be translated into a SANe device model, including statecharts, SDL and partly UIL, GIL and Hypertalk. In human-machine interaction the behaviour space of the user, different from natural domains of behaviour, can be described precisely by a system description.

4 Tasks and Procedures in the Behaviour Space

When planning his course of action, the user of a device selects from a set of possible paths a preferred path in the behaviour space. A model requires an adequate definition of the tasks of the user in terms of his goals states, and of the criteria and conditions which dictate his preferences. We represent these aspects firstly by the tasks of the user, and secondly by the notion of the *cost* of performing an operation.

What is a task? The term *task* is used with variable meaning in scientific discourse as well as in everyday language. We argue that it makes best sense to define as task what is to be achieved, i.e. the goal states, and not how the goal is achieved: Tasks exist independently of the procedures by which they are solved, and even if they cannot be solved. The procedural description as a sequence of actions, including conditions and branchings, describes the solution, but also implies the goal.

Both types of task descriptions have their applications: Whilst the declarative description in terms of goal states is the more general one, the vector of statevariables and the trade-offs to be described can easily become too large to be practically manageable. A procedural description may imply the task incorrectly when an alternative, preferable course of action exists. The state variables referenced in a task model define a state space, called the task space. The states of this space are ordered according to their preference, and the super-goal is to attain the most preferred state. This has also been called the motivational space, but its dimensions are in practice difficult to identify for more than two or three independent motivational dimensions (see McFarland & Bösser, 1993).

Tasks at a global level are often described by a hierarchy of subgoals, based on the assumption that there are no alternative courses of actions. For simplicity it is often assumed that skilled behaviour is constituted by fixed sequences. This is strictly not true, behaviour can always be interrupted for a different, more important goal. The nature of this time-sharing mechanism is discussed by McFarland & Bösser (1993).

We conclude that human behaviour is not the activity of a system which tries to attain goals, but of a system which strives for optimality. An important consequence is that this is not a conscious problem solving process - it would be highly inefficient to solve routine tasks by conscious planning. Rather, pre-processed routines are applied most of the time cheaply and without planning - i.e. skills - and these are modelled in the SANe language.

In a SANe task model, task sets and task lists model tasks at a global level. Hierarchic task models of any depth can be described, which always terminate in a declarative task description (in terms of goal states), which should be at a level as high as possible. The following example compares declarative and procedural task models:

The task is *Obtain Milk*, motivated by visitors imminent for the tea hour.
The declarative task description defines the goal state and the optional initial state description.

TASK: OBTAIN MILK   (Declarative task description)

Initial state:	Milk supply:	0 liters.
	Time: Sunday	16.30 hours.
	Milk budget:	3 ECU.
	Location:	Home.
End state:	Milk supply:	> 0.3 liters.
	Time:	Sunday 17.00 hours.
	Milk budget:	>= 0 ECU.
	Location:	Home.

TASK: OBTAIN MILK   (Procedural task description)

IF sunday tea hour is coming up
    AND visitors are expected
    AND visitors may prefer milk in their tea
    AND milk supply is below 0.1 liters
THEN to obtain milk DO
    IF neighbours are likely to have oversupply of milk
        AND friendly relations exist with neighbours
        THEN obtain milk from neighbours
    ELSE IF shop in town center is open
        THEN use bicycle to travel to town center and purchase milk
    ELSE IF motorway filling station stocks UHT milk
        THEN drive to motorway and buy milk at petrol station
ELSE terminate task

When tasks are defined procedurally, inconsistencies do arise when realistic alternative courses of action or the conditions for choice are not considered. As an example consider sending a message: If this task is described as a procedure (write letter > print > stamp > send) this does not take into account that the facsimile machine allows an alternative course of action. In addition, the criteria and conditions for choice among the two means to send the message - fax or letter - must be known to predict the behaviour of the user. The choice may be based on criteria such as confidentiality, legal aspects, or cost in terms of money and time.

A procedure is an instantiation of a solution for a task in a defined context, i.e. one trajectory from home to shop and return with milk. A major function of the simulation module of the SANe toolkit is the automatic search for user procedures which solve defined tasks according to defined criteria - shortest or cheapest solution. A requirement is that the criteria for the choice of a preferred solution are known, which are defined by the cost.

5 The Notion of *Cost* - The Economics of Behaviour

Two other aspects must be considered when modelling behaviour, the context in which behaviour occurs, and cost:

The context, i.e. the environment in which tasks are solved, includes the state of the physical environment (road map, traffic situation, user interface), but also social factors, i.e. the strategy of other agents. The context defines constraints for possible solutions to the task.

Costs are incurred by the use of resources when performing procedures, i.e. time, money, energy, or cognitive effort, and are described in SANe as a cost vector attached to each operation. Costs define preferred solutions, and require a quantitative estimate of the costs for a given solution, and also a rule for combining the cost factors in such a way that a unique order of preference of solutions can be defined.

In order to describe the basis of choice among alternative courses of action, the notion of cost has to be introduced. Costs represent the use of resources when executing behaviour. Choice of the preferred procedure to solve a task is based on an estimate of the cost of the procedure, and the benefits derived from its execution. Leaving aside how the total benefit of procedures is estimated in unpredictable domains, we have to define the criteria according to which the choice is made.

Extensive arguments have been raised in Psychology, Philosophy and Economics about the rationality of human behaviour. The discussion of this topic by McFarland & Bösser (1993) concludes that behaviour is rational, given an adequate consideration of the cost of information processing. This is in line with the view of researchers in AI (Russell & Wefald 1991) or economics (Becker 1976). The main implication for models of human behaviour is that they require an understanding of the notion of cost, i.e. the cost/benefit conditions which govern the choice of a preferred course of action. Psychological experiments appear to show that behaviour is not rational in the sense that the optimal behaviour is often not choosen. The main argument against this view is that these studies do not appropriately consider the cost of cognitive processing, and the effect of learning. The SANe model of skilled behaviour represents human behaviour realistically and adequate for simulation and quantitative evaluation.

6 Learning Mechanisms in SANe

Skilled behaviour is the result of learning, which suggests that learning processes should be included in SANe. The learning mechanisms in SANe include knowledge compilation and practice learning, and are not central for the concept, but show that they can be readily defined as extensions to the SANe model.

Knowledge compilation is an important factor in making the SANe toolkit usable and efficient. Search, the mechanism for problem solving, is costly. It was recognised early that it is advantageous to reuse solutions and partial solutions found (at a cost) previously. A function was included in the SANe simulation module which sorts, stores, and retrieves previously found procedures efficiently when required for the solution of a task. This natural mechanism of knowledge compilation demonstrates its value and raison d'être immediately.

Skill learning is defined as an operation on the cost for performing skills. Costs are not constant, but decrease as a function of repetition. This has two consequences: Firstly practice learning is simulated quantitatively (and it was demonstrated that functions which generate realistic practice curves can be defined in a number of ways) and secondly other effects of practice learning became apparent: As practice occurs more frequently for some operations than for others, in future search these will be cheaper, and therefore may suggest a different preferred solution for a task. One consequence of practice learning is the differentiation between cheap and expensive operations, which, when compared to a mechanism with fixed cost, gives an advantage to the frequently used operations and is thus adaptive.

7 SANe Models, Agents and Robots

Could agents (or robots) such as those described by David Connah (this volume) have a SANe type behaviour model? Yes, but the agent needs an additional component which generates the next goal for the agent: Motivation. Agents must have rules which define what to do next in all states (sometimes even to do nothing). A simple robot could live with a few simple rules, but a more developed robot needs a more complex motivational system where the rules are adapted according to the internal and external state. Sometimes safety is more important than food, or vice versa. Given a desperate depletion of resources, higher risks may have to be accepted.

A more developed agent with some problem solving ability (allowing the solution of new problems) and motivation would do much better under varying environmental conditions than an agent with fixed behaviour rules - such as a SANe. A SANe model is a model of behaviour in a constant, predictable environment, allowing some adaptation, but excludes the ability for problem solving.

A strength of the SANe model is that it represents cost as a basis for choosing the preferable course of actions. Any cost factor may be represented in the cost vector, for models of human-machine interaction the most relevant ones are time, use of sensory, motor and cognitive resources: Vision, decision making, motor responses. An important aspect is the estimation of the cost of learning, which is possible from the model parameters.

8 Application of the Model of User Behaviour

In comparison with similar modelling approaches such as those by Card, Moran & Newell (1983, the GOMS model) or Kieras & Polson (1985 Cognitive Complexity Theory), SANe advances in two respects:
- the SANe toolkit makes the development of models and the calculation of measures efficient, at last one order of magnitude more efficient than other methods, and allows efficient integration with CASE tools and interface builders.
- a set of well defined measures exist, based on the theory of computational complexity and on psychological theory, which describe aspects of human-computer interaction. These measures can be used to evaluate the usability of interactive HW/SW systems.

In the remainder of this paper the measures which we have defined on the basis of the SANe model and their use are described.

9 The Quality of Interactive Systems

Quality is the total cost of using a system over the lifetime of the product. This includes the operating cost, but also the investment into learning of the users and transfer of knowledge, and must consider the total benefit derived from using the system. Quality is the sum of all properties which the user wants to see in a product. The objective of building SANe models is to derive measures from the model which indicate this quality.

User-centered design, to be effective, must be integrated efficiently into the system development process. Model based approaches offer the specific advantage that some evaluation is possible at a stage when specifications, but not a fully developed system, are available. Alternative methods offer other advantages and disadvantages, the most important evaluation methods are:

Performance measurement: Experiments and tests under controlled conditions are most valid but are very expensive and also subject to measurement error. Cognitive workload can not be measured directly, and most indicators are prone to large measurement error. Subjective ratings by users do not indicate causes for ratings. Guidelines and style guides enforce uniformity, but may prevent innovative solutions.

Model-based, analytic measures of the quality of usage of interactive systems are intended to offer specific evaluation capabilities, to be exploited in conjunction with other evaluation and test methods.

10 Measures of Usability

A set of measures - so far over 30 in total - were defined based on considerations of what a SANe model represents. The measures are combined into the factors:
- *performance*, based on sums of the (empirically determined) cost for single operations.
- *learning cost*, a function of the number of elements (operations, commands) which must be learned in a defined task domain.
- *cognitive workload* (decision complexity and memory load), based on branching and intermediate results which are required in procedures
- *robustness*, the cost for error recovery
- *adaptedness* of a HW/SW device to a set of tasks, relating task complexity and procedural complexity.

Because cognitive processes are not directly observable, correlational validation of analytic measures is rarely possible, but predictions relating model parameters and expected performance of human subjects can be made. A number of experiments were performed to test the validity of SANe models, and it was shown that:
- performance at complex tasks can be predicted well on the basis of a model and short and economical tests with single operations
- decision complexity and memory load were shown in experiments (with secondary tasks) to represent valid aspects of interaction quality perceived by users
- learning cost is very well predicted by the number of command states, commands and operations in a set of procedures.

A comparison of SANe models with models developed by use of the most precise methods of protocol analysis showed that the analytic SANe model is a much more precise model of knowledge than the results of protocol analysis.

Whilst some analytical measures can be correlated with empirical measures, others have no empirical equivalent. Our conclusion is that the analytical measures of usability defined on the basis of SANe models do compete favourably in predictive power and cost effectivenes with empirical studies.

	reference	new product X	relative
learning effort	15.1	8.3	0.55
performance	7.6	10.2	1.34
robustness	0.5	0.32	0.64
cognitive workload	0.64	0.43	0.67
adaptedness	0.53	0.76	1.43

The example summarizes the result of the evaluation of an innovative electronic mail program. The measures show that, in comparison to a set of reference products, the innovative system has specific advantages and shortcomings. It is less efficient to use, but easy to learn and well adapted to the specific set of tasks for which it is intended. This information can be analysed in further detail, showing the causes for specific deviations. Reference values exist for IT applications, consumer products, telekom applications, and aerospace and in-car systems.

11 Display Evaluation and Knowledge Model

A SANe model allows a specific form of display evaluation: The display is not represented in a SANe model, and obviously can not be evaluated, but the model can be used to check whether all required elements of information are displayed. Tools for this purpose have been developed and can be efficiently applied.

The SANe model is a detailed model of a skill, including the sequence of operations, conditions and actions to be considered during execution of a skill. Effectively it is a complete description of the procedural knowledge required in a task domain.

We have used SANe models for the documentation of SW tools: The simulation output (procedures) define the structure for the users guide and documentation. The obvious advantage is that development of documentation can be partly automated, resulting in improved quality.

12 Conclusion

Our main argument is that in the well defined behaviour space of human-computer interaction a quantitative dynamic model of human behaviour can be efficiently developed and valid parameters can be identified. This approach is highly effective for the evaluation of the quality of usage of interactive systems.

Acknowledgements

The work reported here was partly supported by the ESPRIT program (project 5429 MUSiC) of the CEC. Dirk Gunsthövel, Daniel Goulet and Elke Melchior have contributed to the work mentioned.

References

Becker, G. (1976) The Economic Approach to Human Behaviour. Chicago: Univ. of Chicago Press.

Bösser, T., & Melchior, E.M. (1992). The SANE toolkit for Cognitive Modeling and User-centered design. In: Galer, M.D., Harker, S.D.P. & Ziegler, J. (Eds.) Methods and Tools in User-Centred Design for Information Technology. (pp. 93 - 126). Amsterdam: North Holland.

Card, S.K., Moran, T. & Newell, A. (1983) The Psychology of Human-Computer Interaction. Hillsdale, N.J.: Lawrence Erlbaum.

Kieras, D. & Polson, P. (1985) An approach to the formal analysis of user complexity. Int. J. of Man-Machine Studies, 20, 201-213.

McFarland, D.J. & Bösser, T. (1993) Intelligent behaviour of artificial and natural systems. Cambridge, Mass: MIT Press.

Russell, S. & Wefald, E. (1991) Do the Right Thing. Cambridge, Mass: MIT Press.

Behavioral and Perceptual Responses to the Constraints of Computer-Mediated Design

Donald L. Day

School of Information Studies, Syracuse University, Syracuse, NY 13244-4100, USA
(Donald_Day.chi@xerox.com)

Abstract. This paper describes an ongoing study of user responses to constraints implemented in software design tools -- constraints which communicate mental models from tool developers to tool users.

Keywords. Constraint management, decision support, automated design, cognitive fit, computer-aided software engineering, process engineering

1 Introduction[1]

This study seeks to improve our understanding of user behavior and perceptions, decision support, and the communication of mental models between design tool users and developers, so as to facilitate design creativity while ensuring reasonable adherence to product and process standards.

Decision support in the context of this study includes the transfer of design and process rules from developers to users, via computer-mediated design tools. The tools in effect sponsor developers' process models as appropriate and efficient means to develop high quality software.

It is a premise of this study that user responses to design tools may be affected substantially by the tools' constraint management subsystems and by the degree of match between the mental models of tool developers and tool users. Such models map developers' desirable processes, functions, tasks and constraints, and are applied by users in the context of their domain knowledge, motivation and understanding of process.

Conflicts sometimes occur between users' sense of design creativity and the need to protect product and process standards (via constraints). These conflicts are due in part to a mismatch (lack of cognitive fit) between values and procedures preferred by tool developers versus tool users.

This misalignment of cognitive fit may be envisioned as a Venn diagram, featuring two overlapping circles representing the user and the developer. The area of overlap (the Congruence Region) marks the extent of agreement between users

---

[1] Portions of this paper appeared originally as "Precis of Behavioral and Perceptual Responses to Constraint Management in Computer-Mediated Design Activities", in the *Electronic Journal of Communication/La Revue Electronique de Communication*, Vol. 3, No. 2, April 1993.

and developers regarding appropriate process engineering (i.e., design procedure). The areas within the circles but outside the area of overlap (the Constraint Regions) represent the extent of disagreement between user and developer. This study seeks to increase the size of the Congruence Region by facilitating compromise between user and developer preferences.

This work also suggests that spreading activation within semantic networks be used to characterize the decision-making process, and investigates user perceptions of relationships among constraints and design task options.

2 Related Disciplines

This study lies at the intersection of several disciplines in the humanities and applied sciences. Included are information science, psychology, computer science, engineering and management science. Information science addresses man-machine systems (e.g., human-computer interaction); psychology contributes cognition (e.g., mental modeling); computer science offers software engineering; management science provides decision support, and engineering adds process design and control (e.g., constraint management).

3 Domain

3.1 Domain Selection

Although the domain featured in this study is software engineering, the conceptual framework, analytic approach, and understanding of user responses developed here may facilitate attempts to refine computer-mediated design tools used in other domains (e.g., publication design, mechanical engineering, architecture, and educational systems).

Software engineering is an appropriate first domain for the study of such tools. Computer-aided software engineering (CASE) tools are used to create software packages, including other tools. The creation of tools for other domains makes it possible for CASE tools to influence design activities in a number of professions and industries.

The software engineering domain is characterized by individuals who are especially capable critics of the tools which they use. Since they themselves are software developers, users in this domain have the experience and knowledge to evaluate CASE tools in detail. Design tool users in other domains are like typical motorists, who may know how their cars should perform, but would not be capable of critiquing the internal (engineering) features of automobile engines.

3.2 Domain Activities

Software engineering proscribes a series of stages in the development of reliable and robust computer software. Key among these are the systematic definition of requirements, the specification of processes necessary to satisfy requirements, the designation of program modules to execute tasks, program generation, test and evaluation, documentation, and maintenance.

In the instance of CASE tools, requirements are levied by various authorities upon developers, who create tools under the supervision of management. Constraints are included in tools according to the software design methodology being employed by a developer. Users then apply the tools to create software application packages. Users are guided or restrained by the constraints which developers wrote into the tools. Finally, applications written by tool users are delivered to their customer or sold on the open market.

Design activities in this domain take place amidst a host of sometimes conflicting priorities, sponsored by a number of major actors. Stakeholders include customers, developer management, developers, user management and users. In the context of this study, "developers" are individuals who design and construct CASE tools for others to use. "Users" are individuals who apply CASE tools to design and construct software for end-user applications. "End-users" are individuals who make use of the applications generated by CASE tool users. This study focuses on users and developers.

Although developers often are not the ultimate authority for requirements which they implement as constraints, the details of implementation emphasis *are* their responsibility. Developers define the processes, functions, tasks and constraints incorporated within a CASE toolset; users select and manipulate functions and tasks in a process sequence to create products (software applications).

Developers' perceptions are influenced by risk assessment, resource management, process control, quality assurance, style preferences, and user satisfaction. User's perceptions are affected by project requirements, training and design experience, the work environment, style preferences, cost and time-on-task (schedule), and satisfaction with CASE tools.

3.3 CASE Tools

CASE tools facilitate the creation and implementation of design elements and the generation of executable software. They do so in part by implementing constraints made necessary by a variety of economic, quality, schedule and maintainability concerns.

These tools make it possible for system analysts, software engineers and programmers to access a common repository of design and implementation information, thereby facilitating cooperation essential to the creation of quality software on large, complex projects. They also embody software development methodologies, ensure consistency, enforce standards, automate the progression of complex systems through the various stages of development, protect end-product quality, and save time.

CASE tools range from single-purpose "programmer's workbench" modules to intertwined toolsets which address most stages in software development. These may include planning, analysis and design; user interface development; code generation; reverse engineering; maintenance; configuration management, and documentation.

4   Constraint Issues

The constraint management subsystem (CMS) within a CASE tool attempts to enforce the weighted process and product quality requirements associated with each stage in the software development life cycle. A properly implemented CMS can be a valuable decision support feature, guiding users in the selection of design options which are consistent with requirements.

In order to study constraint management systematically and rigorously, a typology of constraints is necessary. A carefully constructed typology reduces ambiguity, facilitates the creation of appropriate measurement instruments, and helps to validate the analytic framework. The typology devised for this study consists of four discontinuous axes. It attempts characterization of the key attributes of any constraint implemented by a developer in a tool.

The first axis includes the *authority* whose role, position or recognized expertise underlies the need for a constraint (e.g., customer requirements, management direction or professional standards). The second axis consists of the *style* chosen by a developer to implement the constraint (e.g., functional specificity, transparency to the user, extent of logging). The third axis is the balance of user versus system *control* (the degree to which the system determines the design process, allows user intervention, and provides notice of decisions taken). The final axis is the *weight* of the constraint (the importance of the constraint in terms of the values it seeks to protect, the severity assigned to each potential negotiation strategy, and the mission criticality of the portion of the system associated with the constraint).

All user restrictions addressed in this study are intentional process constraints. These are limitations imposed by the developer to guide the user and protect principles of software engineering (or to protect style preferences of the developer). In fact, these preferences could be implemented more flexibly without sacrificing end-product quality. For example, as changes are made to a program by one tool user, other tool users may be prohibited from making changes to the same program, to avoid chaos due to the simultaneous existence of many versions of the program. However, such configuration control might be protected as well by matching archival (control) copies of a program to the current standard version, at any time. Unrealized or unauthorized changes would be apparent immediately. Resource constraints (limitations imposed by unintentional aspects of hardware or software -- such as a poor interface or inadequate memory), and operative constraints (e.g., limitations imposed by a user's management to ensure a uniform visual appearance to display screens) are excluded from the study.

Constraint satisfaction does not necessarily require the application of inflexible rules; it only mandates that a series of decisions taken as a whole meets necessary and sufficient standards. It is end-product quality, not the constraints intended to ensure that quality, that is important. Therefore, constraint flexibility does not necessarily result in product degradation. Without an appreciation of this aspect of process control, constraints implemented by developers in design tools can be unnecessarily restrictive. (Developer attitudes toward constraint adherence can vary from convictions that constraints should be followed with few exceptions to feelings that exceptions should be permitted for all except the most important constraints.)

An analogy from elsewhere within software engineering might be that of critical path method (CPM) scheduling. Under CPM, project milestones are plotted sequentially in a chronological graph. Some of the activities represented are performed concurrently by several individuals on the programming project. Some tasks take longer than others; certain (antecedent) tasks must be completed before (dependent) others can be started. If it were to take longer than scheduled to complete an antecedent task, the delay would ripple through following dependent tasks and place final delivery off schedule. Antecedent-dependent tasks are on the "critical path". Other tasks not on the critical path can take longer than anticipated without serious repercussion, just as constraints which are not intrinsically vital to product quality, cost or schedule can be relaxed.

In many instances, a user may be involved in only a few stages of product development. Since the CMS addresses all stages in development, it can help improve product quality and reduce error by evaluating user actions in the context of the project as a whole, compensating for the inherently narrow view of a user involved in only a few stages. From the user perspective, however, constraints can be frustrating precisely because they protect concerns from outside of the immediate task environment.

Users may engage in five key constraint negotiation strategies.

In *avoidance*, the user modifies his task approach because he knows that to do otherwise would trigger a constraint condition. In *compliance*, the user modifies his task approach to suit the limitations imposed by a constraint condition that has been encountered. In *deferral*, the user declines to modify his task approach, with the knowledge that subsequent system or human review may either reverse or accept the decision to override the constraint. In *subversion*, the user modifies his task approach to take advantage of known weaknesses in the tool, overriding the spirit but not the mechanism by which the constraint is implemented. Finally, in *negation*, the user declines to modify his task approach, unconditionally overriding the constraint.

5   Research Questions

1. How are characteristics of constraint management within CASE tools (e.g., flexibility) associated with user behavior and perceptions in response to such tools?
2. To what extent are factors such as cognitive fit, trust, mental workload, complexity and users' and developers' mental models associated with user behavior and perceptions in response to CASE tools?
3. How might potential work place confounds confuse apparent relationships among constraint management, cognitive factors, and user behavior and perceptions?
4. How does interaction with a design decision support system educate users regarding principles of software development, and equip them to negotiate constraints?

6   Data Collection and Analysis

6.1 Data Collection

The first of three stages planned for the study is underway: Interviews of key stakeholders, and a task analysis of user work. In Stage 2, tool users and corresponding software engineers and programmers who do *not* use CASE tools (a control group) will be asked to complete a survey questionnaire about their behavior and perceptions; in Stage 3, several users will be observed directly as they execute a standard script of design tasks using a CASE tool.

A structured interview guideline (12 questions) has been drafted, based upon a conceptual analysis of the problem area and a fully defined and operationalized list of variables for the study as a whole. Data are being collected in private interviews with user managers, team leaders, software engineers and programmers at two Fortune 500 firms, and developers at the software engineering unit of a national information systems company (all in the U.S.). Interviews are being audio recorded and transcribed, for verification and analysis.

6.2 Analysis

Transcripts are being separated into sections corresponding to the structure of the interview outline. Next, responses to similar questions will be compared and aggregated. Common and contrasting themes will be identified and matched to the research questions. Later, users' responses to the questionnaire will be contrasted to actual behavior and perceptions reported during direct observation.

7 Future Research and Development

Findings of this and other studies may be helpful in specifying constraint management subsystems that apply knowledge bases. In such subsystems, automatically recorded transaction data describing user constraint negotiation behavior and design task execution sequences (known as "automated discovery") could be used to create customized user-process profiles.

Sufficient understanding of the interplay between constraint implementation and user behavior also may help to develop intelligent assistants which could calibrate constraint flexibility dynamically (within task context), plus project the impact of current decisions upon future choices and end-product quality. The result may be design tools that are as flexible as possible without degrading product quality unacceptably.

The implementation of automated discovery and intelligent assistants might be based upon a network model of decision-making. In this model, constraints would be represented as nodes in conceptual graphs (semantic networks). Each node in such decision networks would include a series of attributes, represented as slots in a node-frame. The network diagrams would depict the nodes, types of links and valences between nodes, inheritance, and levels of abstraction. Spreading activation would be the mechanism by which decision-making behavior would progress through the networks.

In combination with more detailed knowledge about constraints and user responses, such an intelligent system might make possible the more flexible implementation of constraints sought in this study.

References

1. Ackermann, D., Tauber, M. (eds.). Mental Models and Human-Computer Interaction. Amsterdam: North-Holland 1990.

2. Baeker, R., Buxton, W. (eds.): Readings in Human-Computer Interaction, 2d ed. Los Altos, Calif.: Morgan Kaufman 1993

3. Bloomfield, B.: Understanding the social practices of systems developers. J of Info Systems 2, 189-206 (1992).

4. Browne, D., Norman, M.: Adaptive User Interfaces. London: Academic Press 1992.

5. Carey, J.: The issue of cognitive style in MIS/DSS Research. In: J. Carey (ed.) Human Factors in Information Systems: An Organizational Perspective, 337-348. Norwood, N.J.: Ablex 1991

6. Cohen, B.: Psychosocial environments created by computer use for managers and systems analysts. Human-Computer Interaction, 379-384. Amsterdam: Elsevier 1984

7. Curtis, B., Kellner, M., Over, J.: Process modeling. CACM 35, 75-90 (1992).

8. Darses, F.: The constraint satisfaction approach to design: A psychological investigation. Acta Psychologica 78, 307-325 (1991).

9. Darses, F.: Constraints in design: Towards a method of psychological analysis. In: Diaper, D., Gilmore, D., et al, Human-Computer Interaction 135-139. Proceedings, INTERACT'90. Amsterdam: North-Holland 1990

10. Davies, S.: Characterizing the program design activity. Beh & Info Tech 10, 173-190 (1991).

11. Day, D.: Contextual aspects of CASE tool use in information system design and development. Proceedings, Fifth Symposium on Human Factors in Information Systems (Cleveland, October 1993). Norwood, N.J.: Ablex.

12. Day, D. (ed.): Computerized Tools As Intermediaries in the Communication of Mental Maps. Special issue of the Electronic J on Virtual Culture, Spring 1994. Anonymous FTP byrd.mu.wvnet.edu, /pub/ejvc.

13. Egan, D.: Individual differences in human computer interaction. In: M. Helander (ed.), Handbook of Human Computer Interaction, 543-568. Amsterdam: Elsevier 1988.

14. Elam, J.: Can software influence creativity. Information Systems Research 1, 1-22 (1990)

15. Ettema, J.: Studies in creativity and constraint. ERIC ED 259 367 (1985)

16. Fishbein, M.: Attitude and the prediction of behavior. In: Fishbein, M. (ed.), Readings in Attitude Theory and Measurement. New York: Wiley 1967.

17. Fisher, A.: CASE: Using Software Development Tools. New York: Wiley 1991.

18. Gibson, D., Salvendy, G.: Knowledge representation in human problem solving. Beh & Info Tech 9, 191-200 (1990)

19. Guindon, R., Curtis, B.: Control of cognitive processes during software design: What tools are needed? In: Human Factors in Computing Systems CHI'88, 263-268. Proceedings 1988. New York: ACM.

20. Hockey, R.: Styles, skills and strategies: Cognitive variability and its implications for the role of mental models in HCI. In: D. Ackermann, M. Tauber (eds.) Mental Models and Human-Computer Interaction 1, 113-129. Amsterdam: Elsevier 1990

21. Kaiser, G., Feiler, P., Popovich, S.: Intelligent assistance for software development and maintenance. IEEE Software 5, 40-49 (1988)

22. Karake, Z.: Information Technology and Management Control: An Agency Theory Perspective. New York: Praeger 1992

23. Kemerer, C.: How the learning curve affects CASE tool adoption. IEEE Software 9, 23-28 (1992)

24. Kling, R., Scacchi, W.: The web of computing: Computer technology as social organization. Advances in Computers 21, 1-90 (1982)

25. Knauth, P., Joseph, J., Gemunden, H.: User acceptance of computer aided design (CAD). In: H.-J. Bullinger (ed.), Human Aspects in Computing, 1070 1074. Amsterdam: Elsevier 1991

26. Laurel, B.: Constraints. In: B. Laurel, Computers As Theatre, 99-112. Reading, Mass.: Addison-Wesley 1991.
27. Liker, J., Fleisher, M., et al: Designers and their machines: CAD use and support in the U.S. CACM 35, 77-95 (1992)
28. Mackay, J., Barr, S., Kletke, M.: An empirical investigation of the effects of decision aids on problem-solving processes. Decision Sciences 23, 648-672 (1992).
29. Majchrzak, A., Collins, P., Mandeville, D.: A quantitative assessment of changes in work activities resulting from computer-aided design. Beh & Info Tech 5, 259-271 (1986).
30. Muir, B.: Trust between humans and machines, and the design of decision aids. Intl J of Man-Mach Studies (1987)
31. Norman, R., Nunamaker, J.: CASE productivity perceptions of software engineering professionals. CACM 32, 1102-1108 (1989).
32. Orlikowlski, W.: Social implications of CASE tools for systems developers. Proceedings, Boston 1989, 199-210. 10th Intl Conf on Info Systems 1989.
33. Potosnak, K.: Mental models: Helping users understand software. IEEE Software 6, 85-88 (1989)
34. Peckham, J., Maryanski, F.: Semantic data models. ACM Computing Surveys 20, 153-189 (1988)
35. Rasmussen, J.: A cognitive engineering approach to the modeling of decision making. In: Rouse, W. (ed.), Advances in Man-Machine Systems Research 4, 165-243. Greenwich, Conn.: JAI Press 1988.
36. Rosson, M., Maass, S.: The designer as user: Building requirements for design tools from design practice. CACM 31, 1288-1298 (1988)
37. Rouse, W.: Adaptive aiding for human/computer control. Human Factors 30, 431-443 (1988)
38. Savolainen, T.: Expanding human-computer interaction by computer-aided creativity. Interacting with Computers 2, 161-174 (1990).
39. Sheridan, T.: Computer control and human alienation. Tech Rev 83:1 (October), 65-67, 71-73 (1980).
40. Silver, M.: Systems That Support Decision Makers. Chichester, UK: Wiley 1991.
41. Springer, J., Langner, T., et al: Experimental comparison of CAD systems by stressor variables. Intl J of Human-Computer Interaction 3, 375-405 (1991)
42. Tan, B., Lo, T.: The impact of interface customization on the effect of cognitive style on information system success. Beh & Into Tech 10, 297-310 (1991)
43. Todd, P., Benbasat, I.: An experimental investigation of the impact of computer based decision aids on decision making strategies. Info Systems Res 2, 87-115 (1991).
44. Vessey, I., Galletta, D.: Cognitive fit: An empirical study of information acquisition. Info Systems Res 2, 63-84 (1991).
45. Waern, Y.: Cognitive Aspects of Computer Supported Tasks. Chichester, UK: Wiley 1989.
46. Webster, D.: Mapping the design information representation terrain. IEEE Computer 21, 8-23 (1988)
47. Winograd, T., Flores, F.: Understanding Computers and Cognition. Wokingham, UK: Addison-Wesley 1986.
48. Woods, D.: Cognitive Engineering: Human problem solving with tools. Human Factors 30, 415-430 (1988).
49. Woods, D.: Coping with complexity. In: Goodstein, L., Andersen, H., and Olsen, S. (eds.) Mental Models, Tasks and Errors. London: Taylor & Francis 1988
50. Zuboff, S.: In the Age of the Smart Machine. New York: Basic Books 1988.

The Acquisition of Troubleshooting Skill Implications for Tools for Learning

Alma Schaafstal and Jan Maarten Schraagen

TNO Institute for Human Factors, P.O. Box 23, 3769 ZG Soesterberg,
The Netherlands. E-mail: alma@izf.tno.nl

Abstract. A theoretical framework for diagnosis is presented which is used to interpret findings in the literature. Implications of this framework for the development of training and training tools are discussed.

Keywords. troubleshooting, knowledge, strategies, training, training tools

1 Introduction

Troubleshooting may be described rather simply. Given that a system is not functioning properly, the troubleshooter must attempt to locate the reason for the malfunction and must then repair or replace the faulty component. Quite a lot of research has been carried out characterizing diagnostic behavior and diagnostic skill, resulting in models aimed at describing and explaining diagnostic behavior and skill. In this chapter, a theoretical framework for the interpretation of results obtained on the acquisition of troubleshooting skill wil be discussed.

The terms 'diagnosis' and 'troubleshooting' are sometimes used differently in the literature. Diagnosis is often only defined as the process of identification of the symptom to the determination of the fault. In other cases, especially when one speaks about troubleshooting, the whole process of symptom identification, fault determination, and compensatory actions is taken into consideration. In this chapter, diagnosis is used in the wider sense: meaning the complete process from the identification of symptoms to the taking of appropriate corrective actions.

This chapter takes the following structure. First, a theoretical framework is defined to enable the interpretation of results described in the literature. This is followed by a discussion of results obtained in two domains: the paper industry and troubleshooting on board of naval ships. Finally, the implications of these findings for the development of tools for training is discussed.

2 Diagnosis: A Theoretical Framework

Many researchers make a distinction between declarative and procedural knowledge (e.g., Anderson, 1983, 1987). Declarative knowledge is a collection of stored facts also called 'system knowledge' or 'device knowledge' in the domain of technical systems. Examples are knowledge about normal values of certain parameters, or knowledge about the function of the system. Procedural knowledge (knowledge about how-to-do-it) can be regarded as a collection of actions or procedures that an intelligent system can carry out. It also contains knowledge of the procedures with which one investigates a device to make diagnoses about its dysfunctioning, for example the use of the oscilloscope to test certain functions of a system. Procedural knowledge is content-specific and thus only applicable in a limited domain.

In addition to the declarative-procedural distinction, a further distinction can be made between domain-specific knowledge and domain-independent strategic knowledge. This strategic knowledge is applicable across specific content domains, but remains geared towards one task (e.g., diagnosis). For example, in diagnosis, regardless of the domain, one would first *identify and interpret symptoms*, followed by *an investigation of possible reasons*, which will be *tested*, before one will apply a certain *repair or remedy*. At a very general level, problem-solving strategies may be identified which have to do with very general thinking and reasoning skills, such as means-ends analysis, reasoning by analogy, or working backwards (e.g., Newell & Simon, 1972). These general problem-solving strategies, or *weak methods* as they are sometimes called, are applicable across specific domains and across specific tasks.

Thus, if these results are put together, the following framework emerges. At the top level, strategic knowledge is employed, consisting of several goals that have to be fullfilled during task execution. These goals may also be viewed as various subtasks of the diagnostic task. This layer of knowledge is the *task structure*, or the *global strategy*. The order in which those goals are fullfilled is often flexible, and depends on the specific task-situation at hand. Each goal, however, only defines *what* intermediate conclusion has to be deduced, not *how* the intermediate conclusion has to be deduced. The knowledge about how to perform a (sub)task is called the *local strategy*, and may consist of either procedures with a fixed order (how to test a certain part), or may consist of a more flexible sequence of steps: a strategy. The local strategy of a subtask cooperates with the *domain knowledge* necessary to achieve the goal of the task.

The question is what these different reasoning steps, the global strategy, the local strategies, and the underlying domain knowledge, entail in diagnosis in technical environments. The following sections will discuss data pertaining to these issues.

3 Diagnosis in Technical Environments: The Task Structure

Based on experience with the development of knowledge-based systems aimed at diagnosis, Schaafstal (1991) proposes a model for the task structure of diagnosis consisting of a number of goals. The following goals may be distinguished:

Identification of symptoms. Symptoms are the first indication that there is something wrong. This does not necessarily have to lead to an alarm situation, but it may be just a process value that is moving towards the defined limits. 'Being tired' is not necessarily a symptom for a certain disease, but when you think that you are now more tired than you were before, you should start wondering about possible causes. 'The machine is slightly more noisy than yesterday'. In this example 'being noisy' is not the symptom, but 'being more noisy' may possibly be. One needs expertise to interpret a certain signal as a symptom. Symptoms can be hard to describe, especially when they have a large perceptual component. In technical environments it happens quite often that operators or maintainers debate about the appearance of symptoms, or have very idiosyncratic names for symptoms, which makes uniform communication about them rather difficult.

Judgment: How serious is the problem. Depending on a judgment about the seriousness of the problem, the whole line of reasoning and action-taking may change. If a problem is serious, it is important to take some action right away, for example to save someone's life or to prevent that any other unsafe situations will appear. It may also include a prevention of halting of the installation. When the necessary actions have been taken, the normal diagnostic routine may still take over, but that depends on the situation. A correct judgment in this sense is very important in many domains, especially when human safety is at risk, but also in process control situations.

Determination of possible faults. For a certain symptom or set of symptoms there is often more than one possible underlying fault. For example for quality problems in paper and board manufacturing, it is not unusual that there are more than thirty possible faults that may result in the symptom to diagnose. Morris and Rouse (1985) describe that people often have difficulty in generating complete sets of hypotheses. In real-life situations, especially when 'tunnel vision' appears in situations of stress, it is likely that people 'forget' to take some of these possible faults into account. Especially with shift work it occurs quite often that not all operators are aware of all possible faults, due to the fact that they have not been exposed to all of them.

Ordering of faults according to likelihood. The ordering of possible faults according to likelihood is a process in which certain probabilities are 'assigned' to each possible fault. In this way, an ordering of the list of possible faults appears, with the most likely candidates on top. This 'mental list' is the input to the process of testing.

Testing. Testing has the function of selecting the 'right' fault out of many, by ruling out as many of the other candidates as possible. Testing often takes place by collecting additional evidence, and may, especially in humans, be more like 'finding extra arguments for what you already thought it would be', than 'find ways to rule out this possibility' ('confirmation bias').

Determination of repairs or remedies. Repairs can take several forms. Local repairs apply to the exact fault at hand, and are meant to alleviate a specific problem. This is an example of compensation for faults (Bainbridge, 1984). Global repairs, on the other hand, seem to work in many situations, and can sometimes be applied without a full diagnosis of the problem. A local repair in the paper industry would be for example cleaning a dirty element. A more global repair would be slowing the speed of the paper machine down, since that seems to remedy many problems, but is in general not highly recommended. A global remedy in medicine may be 'staying home for a day'. This is an example of compensation for symptoms (Bainbridge, 1984).

Determination of the consequences of the application of repairs. In many domains it is important to realize what consequences the application of a repair might have. For example, what side-effects do certain medications have, or in a paper mill, does application of this repair imply that the installation has to be halted. The outcome of this reasoning process may have an influence on the choice of repair, if there is more than one possibility.

Evaluation: has the situation improved? The final step in diagnosis would be an evaluation of actions undertaken in terms of improvement upon the situation. Has the problem been solved or are other actions necessary? Based on a study of expert and novice operators in the paper industry Schaafstal (1991) concluded that the strategy used by expert and novice operators is rather different. Figure 1 gives an overview of the different global strategies an expert operator may follow.

If the problem is judged to be serious, the operator will immediately continue with the application of a (global) repair, followed by an evaluation whether the problem has been solved. This process may be followed by a more complete diagnosis in which the fault causing the alarm is diagnosed in order to determine the correct local repair, ensuring a solution 'once and for all'. If the problem is not a very serious one, the subject will consider possible faults one by one and test them, until a likely one is found. This is then followed by a determination of repairs, their consequences, an ordering of repairs (if necessary), application of repairs and an evaluation whether the problem has been solved. If not, the expert might do two things: either try another repair, or back up higher in the tree: he may realize that he has not yet spotted the actual fault, and therefore the problem has not been solved. In case no possible faults are left, or the operator cannot

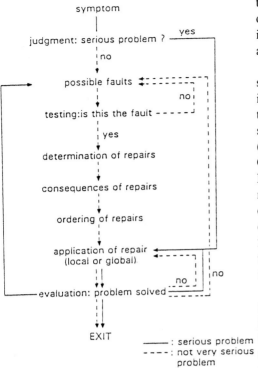

Fig. 1. Global strategies as applied by expert operators

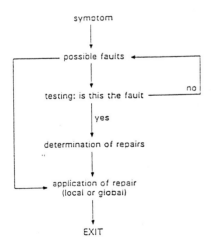

Fig. 2. Global strategies as applied by inexperienced operators

think of any other faults than the ones he already tested, he will be inclined to use a global repair to alleviate the problem.

The model describing the diagnostic strategy employed by relatively inexperienced operators differs from the expert model and is far more simple. Firstly, some of the categories (Judgment, Evaluation, and Consequences) are lacking altogether. Novices jump much more quickly to repairs, without realizing whether a certain repair actually is right and optimal for a certain situation. Figure 2 gives an overview of a model for the diagnostic strategy employed by inexperienced operators.

The model describing the diagnostic strategy employed by relatively inexperienced operators differs from the expert model and is far more simple. Firstly, some of the categories (Judgment, Evaluation, and Consequences) are lacking altogether. Novices jump much more quickly to repairs, without realizing whether a certain repair actually is right and optimal for a certain situation. Figure 2 gives an overview of a model for the diagnostic strategy employed by inexperienced operators.

In an electronics troubleshooting domain, Schaafstal and Schraagen (1993) found similar problems for novice maintenance technicians. One of the conclusions of that research is that novices need to develop robust, flexible troubleshooting strategies that are based on a functional understanding of the system.

Thus, in conclusion, the task structure for diagnosis in technical environments may be different for experts and novices in a certain domain. If one wants to use the task structure as in interpretation scheme for the development of tools for training, the task structure used by expert subjects may serve as the normative task structure (the goal to work towards), and can be used as such.

4 Diagnosis in Technical Environments: Local Strategies

Much of the work that may be interpreted as investigating local strategies in diagnosis has to do with local strategies that are used to determine the fault given the set of symptoms. In terms of the task structure, this fault finding process includes the process of testing, and an ordering of the faults according to likelihood. As described by Jansweijer et al. (1989), sometimes symptoms are strong indicators for certain faults and in these cases the symptom is related more or less directly to the remedy. Often these relations are indirect. This type of reasoning is known as *heuristic classification.* A slightly different association is the one where a symptom can be translated into disturbed functions. For example, a puddle of water underneath the washing machine probably leads to the conclusion that the water-contain function of the washing machine is disturbed. It is best to focus on that function and to exclude other functions such as the timer-control or motor-function. A third type of knowledge that is used to interpret symptoms is knowledge about the expected appearance of the 'inside' of the device. The physical appearance of parts and components is compared to an expected outlook. A loose wire has to be connec- ted again. Otherwise symptoms such as, for instance, a hot or burnt component, smoke, sparks or a strange sound give an immediate focus for diagnosis.

Rasmussen (1986) identified three search strategies employed by technicians: *functional search, topographic search,* and *symptomatic search.* In functional search, the faulty component is hypothesized from the normal functional relationship between a system and a specific part of the system. This search is a special type of the topographic search as discussed below. The information pattern is scanned and familiar features are judged individually in a stream of good/bad judgments. If a feature is judged faulty, attention is typically turned immediately toward the subsystem related to that function. In topographic search, reference to the location of the fault is obtained from the topographic location of a measuring point. In symptomatic search, a set of observations representing the abnormal state of the system - a set of symptoms - is used as a search template to find a matching set in a library of symptoms related to different abnormal system conditions. Symptomatic search consists of a form of pattern-matching, often developed on the basis of experience, between the symptoms and the result in terms of a label, which may be a cause, effect, location, or an appropriate control action. Symptomatic search may be considered a form of heuristic reasoning.

Some of the different search strategies that have been described in the literature may be considered more powerful strategies than others. Obviously, heuristics (or symptomatic search), connecting symptoms to underlying faults, belong to the most powerful strategies an operator may have, although they are only applicable in a narrow domain, and have no wider generality beyond this domain. Therefore, they are likely to fail in any new situation. Less powerful, but still leading to conclusions rather efficient, are search strategies such as topographic search, geared towards diagnosis in technical domains, but more widely applicable than heuristic search. At the next level of generality are search strategies such as split-half approaches, in which the goal is to minimize the number of tests to localize the source of the failure. At the lowest level of specificity are so-called weak problem solving methods, such as means-ends analysis and generate and test, as described by Newell and Simon (1972). These search mechanisms are asserted to be a central component of general problem-solving skill and are very general in scope, thus trading power for generality.

The search strategies used by technicians may be different in different situations, and may also depend on the level of expertise. Since heuristics are mostly developed through practical experience and are tied to specific situations, they may become increasingly available with increasing levels of expertise. As demonstrated by Rasmussen (1986), topographic search strategies, although not informationally economic, may be preferred by technicians in domains such as electronic troubleshooting.

Although most of the research on search strategies focusses on fault finding, some research has been done investigating the strategies people use to optimize the number of tests needed to localize the source of the failure. Morrison and Duncan (1988) for example found that in a task comparable to electronics troubleshooting it was more efficient in terms of number of tests if subjects spent more time on utilizing overview information on the system, instead of simply testing units sequentially from right to left. However, it should be noted that the former strategy puts a much higher demand on working memory resources, which are only limited available, and secondly, that the less efficient strategy did not necessarily lead to a lower diagnostic performance.

5 Diagnosis in Technical Environments: Domain Knowledge

Now that we have adressed what has been found about the task structure in diagnosis and the corresponding local strategies, the question remains what kind of domain knowledge plays a role in diagnosis in technical environments. Early work on expert systems seemed to imply that there was only one underlying model of domain knowledge. Work along this line gave rise to the *model-based approach*, which postulates that expert system building should start with an encoding of the first principles of a domain, for example, qualitative or quantitative models of the behavior of the device to be diagnosed (e.g., Davis, 1984). In most of the cases, this work concentrates on models about the structure and behavior of the device. However, as described in Steels (1990), it is possible to think of a variety of models, each focussing on different aspects of the problem domain. For diagnosis, for example, one could think of a structural model describing part-whole relationships between components and subsystems, a causal model representing the cause-effect relationships between properties of components, a functional or behavioral model representing how the function of the whole follows from the function of the parts, a fault model representing possible faults and components for each function that might be responsible for the fault, and an associational model relating observed properties with states of the system. Which of these models would be the one to use? Clearly, all these models are useful and have complementary utility in problem solving. Thus, the question is not what model to use exclusively, but what type of model or type of domain knowledge is appropriate in certain stages of the diagnostic reasoning process.

Most of the research on types of domain knowledge used concentrates on the process of fault finding. Jansweijer, Benjamins, and Bredeweg (1989) for example, found that the type of model that is of primary use to the service engineer of the UV-recorder is a model of the *function* of the device on different levels of abstraction. The service engineer knows the set of subfunctions that realizes a higher level function. The subfunctions can either be a set of independent subfunctions or a series of subfunctions that enable each other. Each subfunction can itself be described in the same way until, at the lowest level, a function is realized by a component that cannot be decomposed further, or of which the decomposition is of no interest since it is not repairable, but has to be replaced entirely.

In this way, a multi-fold representation on different levels of abstraction exists of the device. On the highest level functions are described with global parameters covering functions as expected by a naive user. At the lower level, the functions are described with parameters covering more detailed and inner functions of the device. A high level function of a washing machine for example is 'the cleaning of dirty wash', with a parameter of the 'cleanliness' of the linen. A lower level function of a washing machine for example would be heating the water.

It is clear that people know a lot more about the device than just the functioning and the structure of a device as shown by Kieras (1982, 1987). He suggests that most knowledge about devices is related to using the device, as opposed to how-it-works knowledge about the internal structure and operation of the device. The question is, though, whether the types of knowledge people use and report depends on their job-contents (an operator vs. a technician, or a technician vs. a manager), and there is suggestive evidence in the literature that this is in fact the case (Cuney, 1979).

If we take a closer look at the relationship between various types of underlying domain knowledge and stages in the diagnostic process as described in section 2, the following relationship is suggested by Schaafstal (1991), taken from an industrial domain (the paper and pulp industry):

Table 1. Relation between phases of the model and system knowledge used.
1 = Symptoms, 2 = Judgment, 3 = Possible faults, 4 = Ordering of faults, 5 = Testing, 6 = Determination of repairs, 7 = Consequences of application of repairs, 8 = Evaluation.

	1	2	3	4	5	6	7	8
Process flow		*	*		*		*	
Top. location					*			
Controls	*		*		*	*	*	
Function comp.	*	*	*			*	*	
Paper making	*	*	*	*		*	*	*
Normal values	*		*		*			*
Process dynamics	*		*		*			*
Functioning comp.			*		*			

The second domain of study, electronics troubleshooting in a radar system, also showed that people use a wide variety of system knowledge, in the same vein as the operators in the paper industry (Schraagen & Schaafstal, 1993). However, much more research in different domains is still needed to establish more firmly this kind of interaction between types of domain knowledge and stages in the diagnostic reasoning process.

This section may be concluded by the following remarks. Much of the earlier work on model-based reasoning focussed on models of the structure and behavior of the device. Although this work has lead to very interesting insights, in the long run this seems to be a too restrictive viewpoint, as pointed out by Steels (1990). Thus, a more flexible view towards the use of domain knowledge is needed, certainly if we take into account the flexiblity with which people use different types of knowledge, at different levels of abstraction and presumably also at different stages of the diagnostic reasoning process.

6   Implications for the Training of Troubleshooting Skill

One of the most striking findings in the literature, as summarized in Morris and Rouse (1985) is that instruction in theoretical principles is not an effective way to produce good troubleshooters. It is interesting to note that these results are quite consistent with reports from other domains such as process control (Morris & Rouse, 1985), in which explicit training in theories, fundamentals, or principles failed to enhance performance, and sometimes actually degraded performance. However, when theoretical instruction is combined with training people in how to use that knowledge, performance usually gets better (e.g., Miller, 1975).

It should be noted, though, that in the studies in which positive effects were found, the guidance involved was rather explicit: students were told to generate hypotheses, chunk information, and analyze symptoms in a prescribed way. This is a far more active approach than just providing an opportunity to use system knowledge, and should not be interpreted as evidence that the latter approach will produce better troubleshooters.

Thus, one of the elements that helps in training people to become better troubleshooters is an explicit guidance in the use of previously acquired theoretical knowledge. Another important factor in training of troubleshooting is the opportunity for practice which is also strongly advocated by many researchers in intelligent tutoring systems (e.g., Lesgold, 1992).

Not much is known about training in local strategies. A number of studies showed that supplying people with adequate procedures can have a positive effect on their troubleshooting performance (Potter & Thomas, 1976; Smillie & Porta, 1981). There is also limited evidence available that providing troubleshooters with good examples can have a beneficial effect on their performance (e.g., Johnson & Rouse, 1982). However, learning from examples may be confined to people with high ability, and appears to be dependent on explicit instruction to learn from the examples as well.

Training with respect to task structures is still a rather neglected area. This may partly be due to the misconception that training in domain, or system, knowledge will automatically result in good troubleshooting performance, since the two are closely linked. It may also stem from the idea that good troubleshooting skills will automatically evolve with experience on-the-job, and therefore explicit training will not help all that much: experience will do the work. In itself: this idea is valid: the expert troubles- hooters in our studies (Royal Dutch Navy and paper industry) became fine diagnosticians without explicit strategy training. However, the question is whether training in diagnosis as a whole can be speeded up and be made more efficient if strategy training is taken into account. A final reason for the absence of strategy training is the fact that good strategy training is difficult to accomplish and involves quite some analysis before good strategies have been identified and made sufficiently explicit for the incorporation in regular training courses.

7 Implications for the Development of Tools for Learning

The training of strategies requires a learning environment with sufficient possibilities for practice, and guidance in using a good strategy. This is not always easy to accomplish in real-life settings, since due to risks involved in those situations it is not always possible to freely experiment with installations or devices. A second problem involved is that in a real-life setting one has no control over problems that occur, and therefore it is hard to establish a training program solely on the basis of what happens in practice. Therefore, ideally one would need training tools and training environments that enable a trainee to systematically work through series of problems that have been controlled with respect to the current focus of training and in which appropriate, individualized, feedback can be given as well. In this way, it becomes possible to devise flexible learning tools, that enable individual trainees to follow their own learning trajectory. Only now, these environments become available, often as a result of the application of AI-oriented research. Third, the relationship between the training of domain knowledge and the training of strategies how to apply that knowledge is not very well understood. Recent efforts towards the development of coached practice environments for the training of troubleshooting, such as demonstrated by the Sherlock project (Lesgold, Lajoie, Bunzo, and Eggan, 1992), are rather promising in terms of their training results, and suggest that strategy training in relation to the acquisition of the relevant domain knowledge is possible and worth the effort.

Thus, to conclude with: strategy training, although important, is a neglected area in the training of troubleshooting skill, which certainly deserves more attention. This attention is now gradually growing, partly based on technological improvements. However, before strategy training, as part of the training of troubleshooting skill as a whole can be accomplished, there is a serious need for good methods for accomplishing cognitive task analyses, such that the strategies used and knowledge involved is made explicit. The method summarized in this chapter, but more fully discussed in Schaafstal and Schraagen (1992) is meant to be a contribution to this issue.

References

Anderson, J.R. (1983) The architecture of cognition. Cambridge, MA:Harvard University Press.

Anderson, J.R. (1987) Skill acquisition: Compilation of weak-method problem solutions. Psychological Review, 94, 192-210.

Bainbridge, L. (1984) Diagnostic skill in process operation. Revised version of invited review paper presented at the international conference on occupational ergonomics.

Cuney, X. (1979) Different levels of analysing process control tasks. Ergonomics, 22, 415-425.

Davis, R. (1984) Diagnostic reasoning based on structure and behavior. Artificial Intelligence, 24, 97-130.

Jansweijer, W.N.H., Benjamins, R., & Bredeweg, B. (1989) Diagnostic reasoning of the service engineer. Paper submitted to Conference on Second Generation Expert Systems, Avignon, 1989.

Johnson, W.B., & Rouse, W.B. (1982). Training maintenance technicians for trouble shooting: Two experiments with computer simulations. Human Factors, 24, 271-276.

Kieras, D.E. (1982) What people know about electronic devices: A descriptive study. Technical report No.12. UARZ/DP/TR-82/ONR-12. University of Arizona, Department of Psychology.

Kieras, D.E. (1987) What mental model should be taught: Choosing instructional content for complex engineered systems. University of Michigan, Technical Report No. 24.

Lesgold, A. (1992) Going from Intelligent Tutors to Tools for Learning. In C. Frasson, G. Gauthier, & G.I. McCalla (eds.), Intelligent Tutoring Systems. Second International Conference ITS'92. Lecture Notes in computer Science, Vol. 608. Berlin: Springer-Verlag.

Lesgold, A., Lajoie, S., Bunzo, M., & Eggan, G. (1992) SHERLOCK: A coached practice environment for an electronics troubleshooting job. In J.H. Larkin & R.W. Chabay (eds.), Computer-assisted instruction and intelligent tutoring systems. Shared goals and complementary approaches. Hillsdale, NJ: Lawrence Erlbaum.

Miller, E.E. (1975) Instructional strategies using low-cost simulation for electronic maintenance. Tech. Rep. HumRRO-FR-WD(TX)-75-20. Alexandria, VA: Human Resources Research Organization.

Morris, N.M., & Rouse, W.B. (1985). Review and evaluation of emprirical research in trouble shooting. Human Factors, 27, 503-530.

Morrison, D.L., & Duncan, K.D. (1988) Strategies and tactics in fault diagnosis. Ergonomics, 31, 761-784.

Newell, A., & Simon, H.A. (1972). Human problem solving. Englewood Cliffs, NJ: Prentice-Hall.

Potter, N.R., & Thomas, D.L. (1976) Evaluation of three types of technical data for troubleshooting. Tech Rep. 76-74 (3). Brooks, AFB, TX: Air Force Human Resources Laboratory.

Rasmussen, J. (1986) Information processing and human-machine interaction. An approach to cognitive engineering. Amsterdam: Elsevier Science Publishers.

Schaafstal, A.M. (1991) Diagnostic skill in process operation. A comparison between experts and novices. PhD thesis, Rijksuniversiteit Groningen.

Schaafstal, A.M. & Schraagen, J.M.C. (1992) A method for cognitive task analysis. IZF rapport 1992 B5.

Schaafstal, A.M. & Schraagen, J.M.C. (1993) Training of systematic diagnosis: A case study in electronic troubleshooting. In P. Brna, S. Ohlsson, H. Pain (eds.) Proceedings of AI-ED 93. Edinburgh, AACE.

Steels, L. (1990) Components of expertise. AI Magazine, summer 1990, 28-49.

Problems of Adaptive Action-Oriented User-Interfaces

Pertti Saariluoma and Michael Miettinen

Department of Psychology, University of Helsinki,
SF-00014 University of Helsinki, Finland

Abstract. Human actions are chunked: Low-level action components are organised into hierarchical systems. A user-interface which takes into account the hierarchical and chunked organisation of human actions, we call action-oriented. In an action-oriented interface, all action components are hidden behind general action labels and when working with an action-oriented interface, the actions are called the action labels. A way of realising action-oriented user-interface is to let the interface monitor human behaviour and adaptively modify itself. One experiment was conducted to study psychological problems in the use of adaptive interface which follows action-oriented principles.

Keywords. User-interface, adaption, chunking, attention

1 Introduction

People normally chunk their actions into wholes (Chase and Simon 1973, Ericsson and Kintsch 1991, Miller 1956). For example, when taking something we do not think about moving shoulders and elbow joints, wrists and fingers but instead, we just take the object. Taking is an action and all the required subprocesses are subordinated under this one action label in our minds. Information processing, which is build on chunked actions, could be termed action based.

Human thinking and communication is action-based. The main goal is important and the operative details are as far as possible hidden behind the high-level action concepts. The chunked character of human actions should be respected in designing user-interfaces and we call a user-interface which is close to this ideal, action-oriented. Instead of forcing users into mentally loading manual process control, an action-oriented user-interface requires nothing but information about the user's intended actions. The name of the action, however complex, should be enough to get a computer to carry it out with minimal, if any, human involvement.

Two amplifications are needed: Firstly, the concept of action oriented user-interface is polar. Interfaces are neither totally action-oriented nor standard, but more or less action-oriented. Secondly, an action-oriented interface is different from the notion of adaptive user-interface (Murray 1991, Wetzenstein, Ollenschläger and Wandke 1990). Action-oriented user interfaces need not be adaptive because they can be realized without any adaptation. Neither needs an adaptive user-interface to be action-oriented. Nevertheless, adaptive interfaces provide interesting technical opportunities for the designing of action-oriented user-interfaces.

The technical accomplishment of the chunking required in action-oriented interfaces is in principle easy, because it can be realized by writing macros. In this way it is possible to improve action-orienting in most standard interfaces. However, the range of users' needs, the variation of the programs and the programming environments make the practical designing of action-oriented interfaces difficult. An ideal action-oriented interface presupposes knowledge about users' and user-groups' abilities, mental models, and intentions, and this information is, for the most part inaccessible in the planning and manufacture of human-computer interfaces.

The design of action-oriented interfaces can also be enhanced by the users who can modify the interfaces to make them more suitable for their abilities and personal needs. This process can be fostered by providing suitable software to aid the modification. Machine learning and adaptive interfaces offer promising perspectives for interactive modification (Murray 1991, Wetzenstein-Ollenschläger and Wandke 1990). The interfaces themselves may learn to register users' needs and abilities by monitoring their behavior. They may either modify themselves or at least provide easy-to-use methods for the supervised modification.

In this paper our main interests are not technical but psychological. We are attempting to understand the psychological processes involved in working with action-oriented interfaces. A priori, we assume that one of the most difficult challenges for psychology in developing action-oriented interfaces is learning. Individuals' work-patterns develop in the course of time and training, and hence their expectations concerning the user-interface change. The users should also learn to use the facilities supplied by the interface and to know how to use their knowledge to make the interface to answer their needs.

2. Experiment

2.1 Introduction

Our main experimental task is menu navigation. This task was selected because it is known that novices prefer menus but, with increasing expertise may find them less convenient (Card 1984, Paap and Roske-Hofstrand 1988, Vandierendonck, van Hoe, de Soete 1988). Consequently, the problems of learning and interface adaptiviness seemed to be more relevant in menu navigation than in, e.g., programming. Of course, this does not mean that we think that menu navigation is the only task in which the idea of action-oriented interface is relevant. We consider the concept of action-oriented interface as a general and versatile concept which can be discussed in practically any interface context.

The user's knowledge is an essential factor of his behavior in a menu environment. This knowledge may be divided into task-knowledge and environmental knowledge. The former refers to the content-specific knowledge about goals and contents of a current computational task and the latter to knowledge about the behavior of the interface. Some of users are accidental and do not have much information about the task or the interface while others are experts in both. To observe the effects of these factors in our experiment, the familiarity of the task-environment was varied.

A second factor which could affect users, is the task complexity. If tasks are simple, it would seem natural to assume that current practice would be sufficient. The benefits of the action-oriented interfaces should become greater when the task demands increase. This is why the task complexity was varied. We also decided to use computer cuing in macro construction. It is well-documented in the cognitive literature that cues have beneficial effects in problem solving (Maier 1930, 1931). Also, Wetzenstein- Ollenschläger and Wandke (1990) have shown that subjects, in using an adaptive interface, may be encouraged to select more complex-action levels by computer cuing. This is why we thought that it would be easier for our subjects to use macros if the computer would suggest them.

2.2 Method

2.2.1 Subjects

Thirty two male students were used. They were computer-science students and cognitive science students at Helsinki University. All students had a good basic knowledge of computers and applications software. The age of the subjects ranged between 22-26 years and the subjects were divided in four equally sized groups.

2.2.2 Materials

The experiments were run with a standard 386SX PC with VGA monitor. A menu navigation program called ACONA (Action Oriented Navigation Program) with macro facility and computer cuing system was written with Pascal. ACONA is a basic menu environment. It presents a number of options for the user and the users' task in navigating is to select from various options one by pressing the correspondingly numbered key. Navigation takes place by moving from one menu to another until the target is reached. When the target has been found, the system backtracks to the beginning and presents the next task.

The task number and the number of tasks in the experiment are presented to the subjects in the middle of the first row of screen. The target is shown in the middle of the seventh row. The current menu node is presented underlined in the middle of the tenth row and the menu items indicating the next menus are located under it. The number of the alternatives in each menu was four. The maximum depth of the search tree was five and thus the total number of nodes was 161.

ACONA hand a facility which actively suggested macros. It monitors the paths subjects frequently use. If a path is used four times, the program interrupts, reminds subjects that they have used this route several times and asks if the subjects would like to make a macro.

The interface asks "Do you want to make a macro from the first element (e.g. Copenhagen) to the last element (e.g. Helsinki) (Y/N)?". If the answer is negative, no macro is made. If the answer is positive, the interface asks the subject name to the macro. The maximum number of characters in a name was 8. Self naming was selected because the literature of command names supports the use of mnemonic names and the literature of cue-validity has convincingly shown the superiority of self-naming (Barnard and Grudin 1988, Mäntylä 1986).

From this point on, the macro can be called up by pressing the esc-key. Then the program prints a macro index which lists the names of all the macros, numbered in alphabetical order. To call up a macro, the subject presses the correspondingly numbered key and the system moves cursor to the macro endpoint menu. In this way, macros allow the chunking of the menu navigation processes.

2.2.3 Procedure and design

The subjects were told that they should act as salesmen or saleswomen. The subjects' task was to move from Copenhagen to another city or town as quickly as possible. Copenhagen was the root node in all subtasks and in all conditions. The menu system presented city names as options or menu items. Thus moving from one city or town to another required normal menu navigation.

to establish the appropriate communication. Our model, therefore, does not suffer from the same computational complexity as the context-change approach. In fact the implementation is extremely simple and time-delay does not play any role in the generation of the speech acts.

However, we have to take into account that the types of cognitive states used in the model should be extended in the future . It is our experience from natural dialogue experiments that deep nestings of belief (> 2), such as 'A believes that B believes that A believes that p', are unnecessary to model, since they do not play an important role in dialogue modelling. An important extension, however, is the inclusion of so-called 'mutual belief' (see e.g. Clark & Marshall 1981). First, modelling mutual belief enables the dialogue partners to leave out superfluous information (Beun 1991) and, second, it enables dialogue participants to communicate information that can be used in reference to objects.

Furthermore, our model describes (or generates) elementary dialogue phenomena which are also observed in Conversational Analysis (see e.g. Levinson 1983). First of all, in the example presented we can observe the local management of *adjacency pairs*, i.e., the prototypical regularity in the sequences of speech acts, such as question/answer (moves 3–4[4] and moves 6–7) and the closing of the dialogue (moves 9–10).

Second, we observe *insertion sequences* in the example, such as move 3–4 and move 2–7. Clearly, in a theoretical model as the one presented, we can, depending on the problem to be solved and the initial belief state, generate an arbitrary number of levels of sequences and the answer to an original question may be many utterances apart. Empirical research should disclose how deep human participants are going in real conversation.

An important drawback of the natural language example is that the dialogue looks still superficial, especially without the extra control utterances. An extension, along the line of Levinson's *preference organization* model (Levinson 1983), in which linguistic markers are added in the dialogue if non-preferred speech act sequences are generated, seems therefore inevitable.

Also, the representation of domain knowledge should be extended drastically. However, extending the model with, for example, predicate logic has important consequences for the dialogue protocol, since formulas may be undecidable and, as a result, dialogue partners could speak until infinity.

An extension of the domain language may also influence the need for other types of cognitive states. For example, the inclusion of negation introduces the possibility of conflicting or inconsistent beliefs. Clearly, we cannot simply add a proposition p to a belief state of one of the participants if he or she already believes that ¬p. In those cases a solution could be to extend the model with belief about the partners belief, so that inconsistent beliefs can be separated. Depending on, for example, the sequel of the dialogue, the partners' expertise and the roles that the partner play in

---

[4] Strictly speaking, move 4 is not an answer, but a denial of the precondition to answer the question.

the interaction (such as teacher/student, student/student, expert/apprentice) the agent may drop his or her original belief and accept the other's belief.

This paper has been concerned with certain basic aspects of communication. To clarify fundamental principles in dialogue we have choosen a simple model based on the cognitive states of the participants, the speech acts they can perform to exchange information, and the underlying rules for the generation of the speech acts and the update of the cognitive states. Exploring the model with different cognitive states and different communicative strategies may give important insight in both human/human and human/machine communication. It should be stressed, however, that the rules for dialogue are rudimentary and that extensions along the lines indicated above will have far reaching consequences from a formal and a computational point of view.

Acknowledgements

This research was supported by the Cooperation Center Tilburg and Eindhoven Universities, The Netherlands.

References

Airenti, G., Bara, B.G. & Colombetti, M. (1993) Failures, exploitations and deceits in communication. Journal of Pragmatics, 20. 303-326.

Baker, M. (1994) Negotiation in Collaborative Problem-Solving Dialogues. In: R.J. Beun, M. Baker & M. Reiner (eds.) Dialogue and Instruction. Berlin: Springer-Verlag.

Beun, R.J. (1991) A Framework for Cooperative Dialogues. In: M.M. Taylor, F. Néel & D.G. Bouwhuis (eds.) Proceedings of the Second Venaco Workshop on the Structure of Multimodal Dialogue. Maratea, Italie.

Beun, R.J. (1994) Mental state recognition and communicative effects. Journal of Pragmatics, 20.

Bunt, H.C. (1989) Information Dialogues as Communicative Action in Relation to Partner Modeling and Information Processing. In: Taylor, M.M., Néel, F. & Bouwhuis, D.G. (eds.) The Structure of Multimodal Dialogue. Amsterdam: North-Holland.

Carlson, L. (1985) Dialogue Games: An Approach to Discourse Analysis. Dordrecht: Reidel Publishing Company.

Gazdar, G. (1981) Speech act assignment. In: A.K. Joshi, B.L. Webber & I.A. Sag (eds), Elements of Discourse Understanding. Cambridge: Cambridge University Press.

Grice, H.P. (1975) Logic and Conversation. In: P. Cole & J. Morgan (eds.) Speech Acts. Syntax and semantics, Vol. 11. New York: Academic Press.

Levinson, S.C. (1983) Pragmatics. Cambridge: Cambridge University Press.

Perrault, C.R. (1990) An application of default logic to speech act theory. In: P.R. Cohen, J. Morgan & M.E. Pollack (eds.), Intentions and Communication. Cambridge, Mass.: MIT Press.

Models of User Behaviour and Measures of Usability

Tom Bösser

ACit - Advance Concepts for interactive technology GmbH
Spiekerhof 6-8, D 48143 Münster, acit@eurokom.ie

Abstract. The use of models of human-computer interaction is discussed, including principles and applications which become feasible due to the availability of cognitive models with predictive power, noteably
- the use of a model of user interaction for the evaluation of the quality of usage of the dynamic model and of the presentation component of user interfaces
- the cognitive model as a knowledge model, describing the required contents of training material and documentation for specific, well defined skills.
It is argued that models of skilled behaviour are valid for the intended application, and provide a basis for efficient evaluation of the quality of usage of interactive systems.

Keywords. Cognitive models, human-computer interaction, rational behaviour, measures, usability

1 Models of User Behaviour as a Basis for Design, Analysis and Evaluation of Interactive Systems

The pragmatic objective of research into human-computer interaction is the development of methods and principles which aid the development of interactive, computer based devices with a high quality of usage, corresponding to the demands of the customers who buy, and the users who use these systems. Behavioural theory is a basis for research in human-machine interaction, but also develops new topics and perspectives in response to the problems recognized in application domains, some of which will be discussed here.

A specific feature of human-computer interaction is the fact that it occurs in a complex and meaningful domain, which can be described and captured with precision, including the interaction of the human user with a hardware/software system. This has been recognized and exploited by researchers, notably Card, Moran & Newell (1983) and Kieras & Polson (1985), who have developed models of human-computer interaction, and have also defined some measures based on the analysis of these models which indicate aspects of usability.

In the attempt to develop these approaches further into a practicable and efficient method for the evaluation of interactive systems, we have defined a conceptual and formal basis for the representation of user tasks, system functions and user procedures (called the SANe - Skill Acquisition Network - model) and we have developed efficient tools for the analysis of interactive systems, the description of user tasks and the simulation and evaluation of user procedures. Only a brief description can be given here, see Bösser & Melchior (1992) for more detail. The SANe toolkit is a commercially available set of software tools which includes syntax-directed graphical editors for the development of task models, of functional models of hardware/software devices, and for the simulation of user procedures.

Here we will describe the underlying principles of the cognitive modelling approach, and analytic measures which represent important aspects of the quality of interaction with devices.

2 Models of Behaviour - What Can They Represent?

Models in any domain can be constructed to represent selective aspects of the domain at appropriate levels of abstraction. An often used separation is the description of a system in terms of

structure / function / dynamics

The *structure* of a system describes the component modules. In behavioural science such components could be memory, sensors, effectors, cognition, motivation and others, i.e. functional modules.

On the *functional* level the functions operating within and between modules, and the state-changes effected by these functions are described.

The *dynamic* model describes the time course and dynamic parameters of the processes which govern the operation of the functions.

Although structural and functional models of behaviour serve an important purpose, predicting performance aspects of behaviour requires a valid dynamic model of behaviour for a defined domain. This has proven to be one of the most difficult tasks in behavioural science, where valid dynamic models with predictive power have been demonstrated in limited domains only (e.g. Fitt´s law). We argue that cognitive models of skills are well suited to the calculation of meaningful parameters of dynamic performance, and can also serve as a model of procedural knowledge.

3 The SANe Model of Skilled Behaviour

A SANe (Skill Acquisition Network) model represents skilled interaction with well-defined machines. This excludes problem solving - the situation where the user may have a goal, but does not know a procedure to attain it. It is also assumed that the HW/SW system with which the user interacts behaves in a predict-

The depth of the search was varied by presenting target cities with either the depth of two or four. The difficulty of the task was also varied by using in one situation, very familiar cities, e.g. Amsterdam, London, Berlin, etc., or by using, in another situation, towns less well known to our Finnish subjects e.g. Erwitte, Hulia, Piney, etc. The major variable was the macro option. Half of the subjects had the opportunity of defining and using macros but the other half had no macro option available.

The subjects were tested individually. They made 32 navigation tasks in all. The only within-subject variable was the depth. Familiarity with cities and the macro option were between- subject variables. The tasks were presented in eight groups of four tasks of the same depth, i.e. 2 or 4. To control the learning process, the presentation was ordered so that after a task group of depth 2 came a group of depth 4 and vice versa. The presentation was counterbalanced by presenting a half of the subjects with depth 2 first and half of the subjects with depth 4 first. This was done to avoid more than four sequences of the same depth tasks.

2.3 Results

The main results are presented in Figure 1.

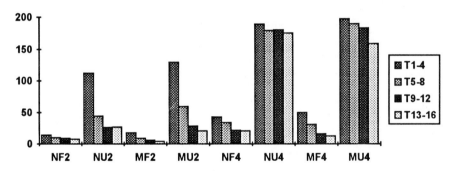

Fig. 1. The average processing times in seconds. N = No macro, M = Macro; F = Familiar, U = Unfamiliar; 2 = Depth two, 4 = Depth four; T = Task series number.

The following main effects and interactions were significant: task-time training, $F(3, 224)=175.87$, $p<.001$; depth $F(1,224)=2791.29$, $p<.001$; familiarity, $F(1,224)=5302.26$, $p<.001$; training x macro $F(3, 224)=8.64$, $p<.001$; training x depth $F(3, 224)=26.17$, $p<.001$; training x familiarity, $F(3, 224)=44.74$, $p<.001$; familiarity x depth, $F(1, 224)=1528.54$, $p<.001$, as well as the three-way interaction between training, depth and familiarity, $F(3, 224)=67.71$, $p<001$. However, the macro effect is not significant $F(1,224)=0.77$.

Table 1. The frequencies of constructed and used macros during the time of experiment by all subjects in the successive four series (S)

	FAMILIAR CITIES			UNFAMILIAR TOWNS	
Series	Macros defined	Macros used	Series	Macros defined	Macros used
S1	1	0	S1	0	0
S2	9	3	S2	2	1
S3	15	6	S3	4	3
S4	17	8	S4	5	4

Macro construction was common in tasks with unfamiliar towns, but the differences were small. The number of macros used was high and increased with learning series in both familiar and unfamiliar groups.

2.4 Discussion

Domain knowledge is used in navigation planning in a menu system. The increase in tree size causes increasingly more problems for the subjects. In an unfamiliar environment the menu-tree depth is an essential factor. Interestingly, the macro facility interacted with task-specific learning. This means that when the number of solved tasks increased, subjects benefited from use of the macro facility. Also, the more familiar people are with the task, the more macros they construct and use.

In the beginning of experiments the macro index is empty and thus no macro use is possible. To learn to use macros takes some time and so does the building of the basic macro library. Therefore, the actual macro effect can take place only when the number of trials increases. This clearly explains why no significant macro-effect was found. In using macros, subjects may lose time in the beginning but, when the number of tasks and the basic macro storage increases, the real benefits of an adaptive interface become apparent.

The psychology of action oriented user-interface relies on chunking. Human actions have hierarchical structures in which low-level basic actions are associated into wholes by chunking. Chunking is the way human information processing avoids the limits of working memory (Chase and Simon 1973, Ericsson and Kintsch 1991, Miller 1956). The mental load caused by acting in an environment depends essentially on human ability to chunk task-necessary environmental information. The more difficult the chunking, the more mental load the task causes and the more difficult performance will be (Gopher and Donchin 1986). Thus the idea is to remove all the obstacles of natural chunking from an interface and to use all the technical potential in computers to foster the chunking of actions.

A problem with many computer-interface systems is that they divide actions into rigid sets of elements and, in this way, impaire the chunking of action components. If each menu during the navigation process must be separately processed during the navigation process, the natural chunking process is disturbed. People learn the standard paths in a menu system, their information collection changes, and before long, they will find it burdensome to go through the piecemeal processes again (Card 1984, Vandierendonck, van Hoe, de Soete 1988).

When the users try to achieve some action-goals and when their apperception has abstracted one action plan, they are not very willing to pay attention to the modification of the interface (cf. Saariluoma 1992). It is one thing to navigate in a menu system and another to modify it. Computer cuing seems to provide an effective means to solve this problem. (cf. also Wenzenstein-Ollenschläger and Wandke 1990).

On the whole, the idea of action-oriented user-interface has been insufficiently researched. These first experiments suggest that action-oriented and adaptive user interfaces, though not being one and the same thing, have much in common. The combination outlined in this paper could be characterized action-oriented adaptive user-interface. This notion seems to have some flexibility. For example, it allows very effective personalization of the interface design. The macro systems created by one user can be stored in a personal file and thus the same interface may be modified in very different directions so that the interface may be built differently by each of its users depending on their personal needs. This we find is one of the most interesting future aspects of action-oriented adaptive interfaces.

References

Barnard, P.J. and Grudin, J. (1988) Command names. In: M. Helander (ed.) Handbook of human-computer interaction. Amsterdam: North-Holland (pp. 237-255).

Card, S. (1984). Visual search of computer menus. In: H. Bouma and D. Bouwhuis (eds.) Attention and performance, vol. 10. Hillsdale, N.J.: Erlbaum (pp. 97-118).

Chase, W.G. & Simon, H.A. (1973) The mind's eye in chess. In: W. Chase (ed.) Visual information processing. New York: Academic Press (pp. 215-281).

Ericsson, K.A. & Kintsch, W. (1991) Memory in comprehension and problem solving: A long-term working memory. Institute of Cognitive Science, University of Colorado , Boulder. Publication Number 91-13.

Gopher, D. and Donchin, E. (1986). Workload - an examination of the concept. In K.R. Boff, L. Kaufman & J.P. Thomas (eds.) Handbook of perception and human performance. Vol. II: Cognitive processes and performance. New York: Wiley (pp. 41/1-49).

Miller, G.E. (1956) The magical number seven plus or minus two: Some limits on our capacity for processing information. Psychological Review, 63, 81-97.

Murray, D. (1991) Modelling for adaptivity. M.J. Tauber and D. Ackermann (eds.) Mental models and human-computer interaction, vol. II. Amsterdam: Elsevier (pp. 81-95).

Maier, N.R. (1930) Reasoning in Humans I: On direction. Journal of Comparitive Psychology, 12, 181-194.

Maier, N.R. (1931) Reasoning in Humans II: The solution of a problem and its appearance in consciousness. Journal of Comparitive Psychology, 12, 181-194.

Mäntylä, T. (1986) Optimizing Cue Effectiveness: Recall of 500 and 600 identically learned words. Journal of Experimental Psychology, 12, 66-71.

Paap, K.R. and Roske-Hofstrand, R.J. (1988) Design of Menus. In: M. Helander (ed.) Handbook of human-computer interaction. Amsterdam: North-Holland.

Saariluoma, P. (1990) Apperception and restructuring in chess players' problem solving. In: K. Gilhooly, M. Keane, B. Logie & G. Erdos: Lines of thought: Reflections on the psychology of thinking. London: Wiley.

Vandierendonck, A., van Hoe, R, and de Soete, G. (1988) Menu search as a function of menu organization, categorization and experience. Acta Psychologica, 69, 249-278.

Wetzenstein-Ollenschläger, E. and Wandke, H. (1990). Toward adaptive human-computer interfaces, In D. Ackermann and M.J. Tauber (eds.) Mental models and human-computer interaction, vol I. Amsterdam: Elsevier (pp. 231-252).

Part 2

New Media: Enabling Technologies

New Media: Enabling Technologies

Introduction

The term 'medium' has a wide variety of meanings. However, for the purpose of this section a medium is regarded as a communication channel that supports human-computer communication. Obviously, within human-computer systems media are of major importance as a means of facilitating information flow from human to computer and from computer to human. The contributions in this section address new media to support human-computer communication and the enabling technologies upon which they depend.

In his paper, Jacob describes the area of human-computer interaction techniques and especially the new types of interaction techniques that are being developed at his laboratory: interaction techniques based upon eye movements and interaction techniques based upon the use of three-dimensional pointing. Gaver's paper argues the case for the more extensive use of sound effects, such as, auditory icons and background noises, in educational software. His paper describes how the use of sound can improve the quality of the interaction that users experience, i.e., help coordinate activities, promote guided exploration, and increase motivation. Barker introduces the concept of electronic books as a means of providing interactive learning environments. He discusses the basic nature of electronic books and offers a taxonomy of currently available products. Two case studies involving the use of 'telemedia books' are presented to illustrate the scope and potential of this new medium for interactive distance learning. Brok and Splunder discuss the design of screen-based control panels that involve 3-D view setting based upon the use of a 2-D mouse input device. The evaluation results that they have obtained indicate that their technique leads to the production of interfaces that are easier to learn, easier to use and involve no reduction in accuracy. In their paper, Tiritoglu and Juola discuss how the use of animated icons can promote the learning of the functions that are represented by those icons in a drawing application.

Natural language is increasingly being used as a medium to support human-computer interaction. Tufis et al. describe the techniques and the crucial role of natural language generation in a foreign language learning and tutoring system that is based on conversation in meaningful situations.

Overall, the papers in this section provide many useful examples of the ways in which new media and their enabling technologies are being used to develop and apply new techniques of human-computer interaction within many difficult and challenging application domains.

New Human-Computer Interaction Techniques

Robert J.K. Jacob

Human-Computer Interaction Lab, Naval Research Laboratory, Washington, D.C., U.S.A.

Abstract. This chapter describes the area of human-computer interaction technique research in general and then describes research in several new types of interaction techniques under way at the Human-Computer Interaction Laboratory of the U.S. Naval Research Laboratory: eye movement-based interaction techniques, three-dimensional pointing, and, finally, using dialogue properties in interaction techniques.

Keywords. human-computer interaction, interaction techniques, eye movements, gesture, pointing, dialogue

1   Introduction

Tufte [9] has described human-computer interaction as two powerful information processors (human and computer) attempting to communicate with each other via a narrow-bandwidth, highly constrained interface. A fundamental goal of research in human-computer interaction is, therefore, to increase the useful bandwidth across that interface. A significant bottleneck in the effectiveness of educational systems as well as other interactive systems is this communication path between the user and the computer. Since the user side of this path is difficult to modify, it is the computer side that provides fertile ground for research in human-computer interaction. This chapter describes interaction technique research in general and then describes research in several new types of interaction techniques under way at the Human-Computer Interaction Laboratory of the U.S. Naval Research Laboratory (NRL).

Interaction techniques provide a useful focus for human-computer interaction research because they are specific, yet not bound to a single application. An interaction technique is a way of using a physical input/output device to perform a generic task in a human-computer dialogue. It represents an abstraction of some common class of interactive task, for example, choosing one of several objects shown on a display screen. Research in this area studies the primitive elements of human-computer dialogues, which apply across a wide variety of individual applications. The basic approach is to study new modes of communication that could be used for human-computer communication and develop devices and techniques to use such modes. The goal is to add new, high-bandwidth methods to the available store of input/output devices, interaction techniques, and generic dialogue components. Ideally, research in interaction techniques starts with studies of the characteristics of human communication channels and skills and then works toward developing devices and techniques that communicate effectively to and from those channels. Often, though, the hardware developments come first, people simply attempt to build "whatever can be built," and then HCI researchers try to find uses for the resulting artifacts.

2 Eye Movement-Based Interaction Techniques

One of the principal thrusts in interaction technique research at NRL has been eye movements [3, 5]. We have been interested in developing interaction techniques based on eye movements as an input from user to computer. That is, the computer will identify the point on its display screen at which the user is looking and use that information as a part of its dialogue with the user. For example, if a display showed several icons, the user might request additional information about one of them. Instead of requiring the user to indicate which icon is desired by pointing at it with a mouse or by entering its name with a keyboard, the computer can determine which icon the user is looking at and give the information on it immediately.

Our approach to this interaction medium is to try to make use of natural eye movements. This work begins by studying the characteristics of natural eye movements and then attempts to recognize appropriate patterns in the raw data obtainable from an oculometer, turn them into tokens with higher-level meaning, and design interaction techniques for them around the known characteristics of eye movements. A user interface based on eye movement inputs has the potential for faster and more effortless interaction than current interfaces, because people can move their eyes extremely rapidly and with little conscious effort. A simple thought experiment suggests the speed advantage: Before you operate any mechanical pointing device, you usually look at the destination to which you wish to move. Thus the eye movement is available as an indication of your goal before you could actuate any other input device.

However, people are not accustomed to operating devices in the world simply by moving their eyes. Our experience is that, at first, it is empowering to be able simply to look at what you want and have it happen, rather than having to look at it and then point and click it with the mouse. Before long, though, it becomes like the Midas Touch. Everywhere you look, another command is activated; you cannot look anywhere without issuing a command. The challenge in building a useful eye movement interface is to avoid this Midas Touch problem. Carefully designed new interaction techniques are thus necessary to ensure that they are not only fast but that use eye input in a natural and unobtrusive way. Our approach is to try to think of eye position more as a piece of information available to a user-computer dialogue involving a variety of input devices than as the intentional actuation of the principal input device.

A further problem arises because people do not normally move their eyes in the same slow and deliberate way they operate conventional computer input devices. Eyes continually dart from point to point, in rapid and sudden "saccades". Even when the user thinks he or she is viewing a single object, the eyes do not remain still for long. It would therefore be inappropriate simply to plug in an eye tracker as a direct replacement for a mouse. Wherever possible, we therefore attempt to obtain information from the natural movements of the user's eye while viewing the display, rather than requiring the user to make specific trained eye movements to actuate the system.

We partition the problem of using eye movement data into two stages. First we process the raw data from the eye tracker in order to filter noise, recognize fixations, compensate for local calibration errors, and generally try to reconstruct the user's more conscious intentions from the available information. This processing stage uses a model of eye motions (fixations separated by saccades) to drive a fixation recognition algorithm that converts the continuous, somewhat noisy stream of raw eye position reports into discrete tokens that represent the user's intentional fixations. The tokens are passed to our user interface management system, along with tokens generated by other input devices being used simultaneously, such as the keyboard or mouse.

Next, we design generic interaction techniques based on these tokens as inputs. The first interaction technique we have developed is for object selection. The task is to select one object from among several displayed on the screen, for example, one of several file icons on a desktop. With a mouse, this is usually done by pointing at the object and then pressing a button. With the eye tracker, there is no natural counterpart of the button press. We reject using a blink for a signal because it detracts from the naturalness possible with an eye movement-based dialogue by requiring the user to think about when he or she blinks. We tested two alternatives. In one, the user looks at the desired object then presses a button on a keypad to indicate his or her choice. The second alternative uses dwell time—if the user continues to look at the object for a sufficiently long time, it is selected without further operations.

At first this seemed like a good combination. In practice, however, the dwell time approach proved much more convenient. While a long dwell time might be used to ensure that an inadvertent selection will not be made by simply "looking around" on the display, this mitigates the speed advantage of using eye movements for input and also reduces the responsiveness of the interface. To reduce dwell time, we make a further distinction. If the result of selecting the wrong object can be undone trivially (selection of a wrong object followed by a selection of the right object causes no adverse effect—the second selection instantaneously overrides the first), then a very short dwell time can be used. For example, if selecting an object causes a display of information about that object to appear and the information display can be changed instantaneously, then the effect of selecting wrong objects is immediately undone as long as the user eventually reaches the right one. This approach, using a 150-250 ms. dwell time gives excellent results. The lag between eye movement and system response (required to reach the dwell time) is hardly detectable to the user, yet long enough to accumulate sufficient data for our fixation recognition and processing. The subjective feeling is of a highly responsive system, almost as though the system is executing the user's intentions before he or she expresses them. For situations where selecting an object is more difficult to undo, button confirmation is used rather than a longer dwell time.

Other interaction techniques we have developed and are studying in our laboratory include: continuous display of attributes of eye-selected object (instead of explicit user commands to request display); moving object by eye selection, then press button down, "drag" object by moving eye, release button to stop dragging; moving object by eye selection, then drag with mouse; pull-down menu commands using dwell time to select or look away to cancel menu, plus optional accelerator button; forward and backward eye-controlled text scrolling.

Eye movement-based interaction techniques exemplify an emerging new style of interaction, called non-command-based [7]. Previous interaction styles all await, receive, and respond to explicit commands from the user to the computer. In the non-command style, the computer passively monitors the user and responds as appropriate, rather than waiting for the user to issue specific commands. Because the inputs in this style of interface are often non-intentional, they must be interpreted carefully to avoid annoying users with unwanted responses to inadvertent actions. Our research with eye movements provides an example of how these problems can be attacked.

3   Three-Dimensional Interaction

Another area of interaction technique research at NRL has been an investigation of three degree of freedom input [4]. In studying interaction techniques, each new piece of hardware that appears raises the question "What tasks is this device good for, and how should it be incorporated into interface designs?" Such questions are typically answered specifically for each new device, based on the intuition and judgment of designers and, perhaps, on empirical studies of that device. Our work in three degree-of-freedom input provides an example of how greater leverage can be achieved by answering such questions by reasoning from a more general predictive theoretical framework, rather than in an *ad hoc* way.

We begin by posing the question for the three-dimensional position tracker, such as the Polhemus 3SPACE or Ascension Bird trackers. While directly answering the question "What is a three-dimensional tracker good for?" we also try to shed light on the next level question, i.e., "How should you answer questions like *What is a three-dimensional tracker good for?*" Concepts such as the logical input device provide descriptive models for understanding input devices, but they tend to ignore the crucial pragmatic aspects of haptic input by treating devices that output the same information as equivalent, despite the different subjective qualities they present to the user. Taxonomies and other frameworks for understanding input devices have tended to hide these pragmatic qualities or else relegate them to a "miscellaneous" category, without further structure.

Instead, we draw on the theory of processing of perceptual structure in multidimensional space [1]. The attributes of objects in multidimensional spaces can have different dominant perceptual structures. The nature of that structure, that is, the way in which the dimensions of the space combine perceptually, affects how an observer perceives an object. We posit that this distinction between perceptual structures provides a key to understanding performance of multidimensional input devices on multidimensional tasks. Hence two three-dimensional tasks may seem equivalent, but if they involve different types of perceptual spaces, they should be assigned to correspondingly different input devices.

The three-dimensional position tracker can be viewed as a three-dimensional absolute-position mouse or data tablet; it provides continuous reports of its position in three-space relative to a user-defined origin. The device thus allows the user to input three coordinates or data values simultaneously and to input changes that cut across all three coordinate axes in a single operation. (A mouse or trackball allows this in only two dimensions.) Such a device is obviously useful for pointing in three-space, but it is also applicable in many other situations that involve changing three values simultaneously. We considered two tasks that both involve three degrees of freedom, i.e., that require adjusting three variables. For comparison with the three-dimensional tracker, we used a conventional mouse (for two of the three variables in the tasks) and then provided a mode change button to turn the mouse temporarily into a one-dimensional slider for the third variable.

A naive view of these two alternatives suggests that the three-dimensional tracker is a superset of the two-dimensional mouse, since it provides the same two outputs plus a third. Thus the three-dimensional tracker should always be used in place of a mouse (assuming ideal devices with equal cost and equal accuracy), since it is always at least as good and sometimes better. Our intuition tells us that this is unlikely—but why? The goal of this research is to develop a firmer foundation from which to draw such judgments. To do this, we extend Garner's theory of processing of perceptual structure, [1] first developed with fixed images, to interactive graphical manipulation tasks and thereby use it to shed light on the selection of multidimensional input devices. Garner observed that relationships between the attributes of an object can be perceived in two ways that differ in how well the component attributes remain identifiable. Some attributes are *integrally* related to one another—the values of these attributes combine to form a single composite perception in the observer's mind, and each object is seen as a unitary whole; while other attributes are *separably* related—the attributes remain distinct, and the observer does not integrate them, but sees an object as a collection of attributes.

Our hypothesis is that the structure of the perceptual space of an interaction task should mirror that of the control space of its input device. To examine it, we considered two interactive tasks, one set within an integral space and one in a separable one, and two input devices, one with integral dimensions and one, separable. This yields a two by two experiment, with four conditions. We expect performance on each task to be superior in the condition where the device matches that task in integrality/separability. That is, the interaction effect between choice of task and choice of device should far exceed the main effects of task or device alone.

For the integral three-attribute task in the experiment, the user manipulates the x-y location and the size of an object to match a target, since location and size tend to be perceived as integral attributes; for the separable task, the user manipulates the x-y location and color (lightness or darkness of greyscale) of an object to match a target, since location and color are perceived separably. The difference in perceptual structure between these two tasks is in the relationship of the third dimension (size or greyscale) to the first two (x and y location); in all cases, the x and y attributes are integral.

For the integral device condition, we use a Polhemus tracker, which permits input of three integral values. For the separable condition, we use a conventional mouse, which permits two integral values, to which we added a mode change to enable input of a third—separable—value. Our hypothesis predicts that the three degree of freedom input device will be superior to the two degree of freedom (plus mode change) device only when the task involves three integral values, rather than in all cases, as with the naive hypothesis mentioned above.

Our experimental results strongly supported this hypothesis. We found that neither device is uniformly superior to the other in performance. Instead, we find significantly better performance in the experimental conditions where the task and device are both integral or both separable and inferior performance in the other two conditions. These results support our extension of the theory of perceptual space to interaction techniques, which predicts that the integral task (size) will be performed better with the integral device (Polhemus) and that the separable task (greyscale) will be performed better with the separable device (mouse).

4   Dialogue Interaction Techniques

Another direction in our research is the notion of dialogue interaction techniques [8, 6]. In a direct manipulation or graphical interface, each command or brief transaction exists as a nearly independent utterance, unconnected to previous and future ones from the same user. Real human communication rarely consists of such individual, unconnected utterances, but rather each utterance can draw on previous ones for its meaning. It may do so implicitly, embodied in a conversational focus, state, or mode, or explicitly. Most research on the processes needed to conduct such dialogues has concentrated on natural language, but some of them can be applied to any human-computer dialogue conducted in any language. A direct manipulation dialogue is conducted in a rich graphical language using powerful and natural input and output modalities. The user's side of the dialogue may consist almost entirely of pointing, gesturing, and pressing buttons, and the computer's, of animated pictorial analogues of real-world objects. A dialogue in such a language could nevertheless exhibit useful dialogue properties, such as following focus. For example, a precise meaning can often be gleaned by combining imprecise actions in several modes, each of which would be ambiguous in isolation. We thus attempt to broaden the notion of interaction techniques in these two dimensions (multiple transactions and multiple modes).

A useful property of dialogue that can be applied to a graphical interface is focus [2]. The graphical user interface could keep a history of the user's current focus, tracking brief digressions, meta-conversations, major topic shifts, and other changes in focus. Unlike a linguistic interface, the graphical interface would use inputs from a combination of graphical or manipulative modes to determine focus. Pointing and dragging of displayed objects, user gestures and gazes as well as the objects of explicit queries or commands all provide input to determine and track focus.

Human dialogue often combines inputs from several modes. Deixis often involves a pointing gesture that does not precisely specify its object; the listener deduces the correct object from the context of the dialogue and, possibly, from integrating information from the hand gesture, the direction of the user's head, tone of his or her voice, and the like. The user could, similarly, give a command and point in a general direction to indicate its object. The interface would disambiguate the pointing gesture based on the recent history of its dialogue with the user and, possibly, by combining other information about the user from physical sensors. An imprecise pointing gesture in the general direction of a displayed region of a map could be combined with the knowledge that the user's recent commands within that region referred principally to one of three specific locations (say, river R, island I, and hill H) within the region and the knowledge that the user had previously been looking primarily at islands displayed all over the map. By combining these three imprecise inputs, the interface could narrow the choice down so that (in this example) island I is the most likely object of the user's new command.

We call these higher-level interaction elements dialogue interaction techniques, and we have begun designing and testing them in our laboratory. We are also developing a software architecture for handling these properties that span more than one transaction. It treats them as orthogonal to the usual lexical, syntactic, and semantic partitioning of user interface software. Our first system demonstrates the use of a focus stack in an interactive graphics editor. In the future, we will expand to a richer representation of dialogue than a stack, to support a wider range of dialogue interaction techniques.

5   Conclusions

This chapter has provided an overview of a variety of new human-computer interaction techniques we are studying and building at NRL. Interaction techniques like these, when applied to the design of specific interfaces, increase the useful bandwidth between user and computer. This seems to be the key bottleneck in improving the usefulness of all types of interactive computer systems, and particularly educational systems, which depend heavily on dialogues with their users.

Acknowledgments

I want to thank my colleagues at the Naval Research Laboratory, Dan McFarlane, Preston Mullen, Manuel Perez, Linda Sibert, and Jim Templeman, who have worked on much of the research I have described in this chapter. This work was sponsored by the Office of Naval Research.

References

1. Garner, W.R.: The Processing of Information and Structure, Lawrence Erlbaum, Potomac, Md. 1974
2. Grosz, B.J.: Discourse. In: D.E. Walker (ed.) Understanding Spoken Language. pp. 229-284. New York: Elsevier (North-Holland) 1978
3. Jacob, R.J.K.: The Use of Eye Movements in Human-Computer Interaction Techniques: What You Look At is What You Get. ACM Transaction on Information Systems. pp. 152-169. April 1993
4. Jacob, R.J.K., Sibert, L.E.: The Perceptual Structure of Multidimensional Input Device Selection: Proc. ACM CHI'92 Human Factors in Computer Systems Conference. pp. 211-218. Addison-Wesley/ACM Press 1992
5. Jacob, R.J.K.: Eye Movement-Based Human-Computer Interaction Techniques: Towards Non-Command Interfaces. In: H.R. Hartson, D. Hix (eds.) Advances in Human-Computer Interaction, Vol. 4, pp. 151-190. Norwood, N.J: Ablex Publishing Co. 1993
6. Jacob, R.J.K.: Natural Dialogue in Modes Other Than Natural Language. In: R.J. Beun (ed.) Natural Dialogue and Interactive Student Modelling. NATO ASI Series F. Berlin: Springer-Verlag 1994
7. Nielsen, J.: Noncommand User Interfaces. Comm. ACM 36(4), pp. 83-99 (April 1993)
8. Perez, M.A., Sibert J.L.: Focus in Graphical User Interfaces. Proc. ACM International Workshop on Intelligent User Interfaces. Orlando, Fla.: Addison-Wesley/ACM Press 1993
9. Tufte, E.R.: Visual Design of the User Interface. Armonk, N.Y.: IBM Corporation 1989

"Class, You're Not Making Enough Noise!" The Case for Sound-Effects in Educational Software

William W. Gaver

Rank Xerox Cambridge EuroPARC
61 Regent Street, Cambridge CB2 1AB, UK

Abstract. Nonspeech audio cues used in educational software can substantially increase functionality. Sounds can increase the tangibility of interfaces, help coordinate activities, and promote guided exploration. In addition, sounds are fun, and thus increase motivation. These functions for sound are illustrated by a number of interfaces which use auditory icons, everyday sounds designed to convey information by analogy with everyday sound-producing events.

Keywords. Human-computer interfaces, educational software, collaboration, multimedia, auditory interfaces, sound, ecological psychology

1 Introduction

In this paper, it is argued that educational software could benefit in a number of ways by the incorporation of sound-effects much like those used in movies, radio dramas, and video games. Classes should be filled with the sounds of roaring machines, running water, even breaking glass – not made by the real thing, of course, but by educational software.

If this seems crazy, consider KidPix™, an award-winning drawing program for children produced by Bröderbund Software (see Fig. 1). KidPix is fun: It incorporates a large number of innovative graphical tools with which kids can explore and play. This figure shows what a few of them do. Pick one paintbrush and drops of ink follow the cursor. Pick another and trees grow wherever you press the mouse button. Yet another turns smooth mouse motions into rough scribbles. Use one of the "rubber stamps" to put little drawings wherever you click. And if you do not like the result, you can erase it in a number of highly satisfying ways – my favourite is the bomb.

KidPix is an interesting program in part because it uses the power of the computer to go beyond the usual literal metaphors used in painting programs. But it is the *sound* that makes it more than just a novel drawing program: all the tools are accompanied by clever, useful, and appropriate sound-effects. Use the dripping paintbrush, for instance, and you hear the drops of paint seep down the screen. Use the scribbling paintbrush, and you hear a pencil scribbling on paper. Stamp an owl on the tree branch, and you hear the stamp slap against the page. And when you

Fig. 1. KidPix™ uses a variety of sound-effects to accompany drawing.

blow up the screen, you hear the explosion – the effect would not be nearly so powerful otherwise.

Are these sounds just gimmicks? Perhaps. But here it will be argued that the sounds used in KidPix add significantly to its success in a number of ways, and that these advantages are applicable to many other programs.

1.1 What Sounds Add to Interaction

First, sounds increase the *tangibility* of the interface, and help to explain what is happening. Remember that the users of KidPix are unlikely to trouble with manuals or help systems – if they can read at all. The sounds help to make the program self-explanatory. Consider how confusing the scribbling paintbrush would be if it were not accompanied by the appropriate noise. Or how prosaic the bomb-eraser would be if it "blew up" your screen without making a sound. Sounds like these reinforce the visual expressions of a metaphor. By adding redundant information about what is happening, they make the tools seem more real (and thus the interface more transparent). Because they also add new information – for instance, about the putative tool and surface, in the case of the scribbling paintbrush – they can convey new information about what is going on in the interface.

Second, sounds can help *coordination* with others, by allowing other kids (and teachers) to hear what they cannot see. You do not need to be looking at the screen to know what tools a kid is using – you can hear the scribbling, dripping, and explosions. This may not be so important for programs like KidPix, but it is potentially quite useful for educational software, particularly collaborative systems in which several people may be working in the same program at the same time.

Finally, sounds promote *guided exploration*, by selectively indicating attributes of interest. Real sounds inevitably accompany actions, determined by the laws of physics. Sound-effects have to be created; programs do not naturally make sounds. This means that the designers of sound-effects have the opportunity to design sounds that highlight some aspects of an event and not others (in fact, they cannot avoid it). So the scribbling paintbrush stresses the gestures of pencil on paper, while the dripping brush leaves out the surface, and emphasises the viscosity of the "ink." Again, this may not be so important for entertainment software like KidPix, but it can be valuable for educational software.

2   Auditory Icons

The sounds used in KidPix™ were designed to be fun, not useful. It is doubtful that the designers sat down and asked themselves, "how can the sounds we use increase tangibility, promote coordination, and help with guided exploration?" They were, after all, primarily concerned with making their program entertaining and useful enough to sell. Thus while most of the sounds in this program are remarkably apt, few are actually that useful.

Over the last several years, on the other hand, there has been research concerned with just these issues. The result is a strategy for creating *auditory icons*, everyday sounds designed to convey information about computer events by analogy with everyday events (Gaver, 1986). The sounds used are similar to those used in KidPix. But because the purpose of auditory icons is to provide information, rather than entertainment, a richer, more principled set of design principles have evolved.

The basic idea behind auditory icons is to map computer events to analogous sound-producing events (see Fig. 2). For instance, when a user selects a file, the act of clicking the mouse while the cursor is positioned over the icon suggests that a tapping noise might be an appropriate mapping. The result is a simple sound-effect, much like those used in KidPix.

But auditory icons go beyond the sounds used in KidPix because they are *parameterized*; that is, meaningful parameters of the computer and sound-producing events are mapped to one another. For instance, the size of the file might be indicated by the size of the virtual object you hear tapped. The type of file can be conveyed by the material of the tapped object. And the overall disk space might be mapped to the overall reverberation applied to the sound, so that an empty disk sounds like a large, echoing hall, and a full disk sounds liked a small, cramped room. Parameterizing auditory icons has two effects. First, it allows families of auditory icons to be created, which convey rich information in lawful ways. Second, it increases the variability of the sounds heard from the interface, and thus helps prevent any given sound from becoming annoying through repetition.

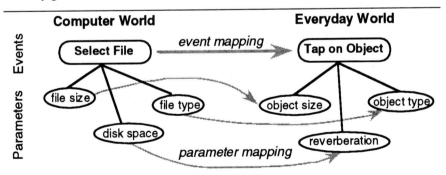

Fig. 2. Auditory icons are created by mapping events in the computer world to sound-producing events in the everyday world. They may be parameterized by mapping attributes of the computer and sound-producing events to one another.

Auditory icons rely on a new approach to the psychology of sound and hearing that stresses our tendency to hear sounds in terms of the events that cause them (Gaver, 1993a, 1993b). For instance, if you are walking down a street and hear a sound, you are less likely to ponder its pitch, loudness, and timbre (all attributes of sound studied by traditional psychophysics) and more likely to hear it as a large automobile heading your way – and jump! This experience of *everyday listening* implies that we can start to describe sounds and their perceptual correlates in terms of events. Instead of describing a sound in terms of its pitch and the acoustic correlate of frequency, for example, we might describe it in terms of the size of its source and the associated acoustic correlates. This perspective leads to a new approach to the psychology of sound and hearing, as suggested above. More important, for the purpose of this paper, it leads to a new set of conceptual tools for building auditory interfaces in which computer events are mapped directly to sound-producing events. This is the strategy behind auditory icons.

The rest of this paper describes auditory icons and their potential uses in educational software. The discussion centers around the three functions of increasing tangibility, supporting coordination, and guiding exploration. Each of these functions is illustrated by a system that uses auditory icons. The first is the SonicFinder, an auditory extension to the desktop metaphor which makes the world of the computer more tangible and more self-explanatory. The second is SoundShark, and a related application ARKola, which adds sound to a prototype system of collaborative software meant to support distance education. The last is the Environmental Audio Reminder (EAR) system, which uses sound to convey selected information about events going on in our office environment.

3 Increasing Tangibility: The SonicFinder

Educational software must achieve a number of goals. The primary one, of course, is to teach students about the subject matter at hand. But to do this, the students must learn to use the software itself. Thus a second goal is that the software should be readily learned and ideally self-explanatory. In addition, software should motivate students both to explore the particular contents it offers and the relevant domain more generally. This is a third challenge facing designers of educational software.

Auditory icons may help in creating interfaces that are easy to learn and which motivate users by increasing the tangibility of the interface. A good example of this is the SonicFinder (Gaver, 1989). This is an extension to the Finder, the application used to organize, manipulate, create and delete files on the Macintosh. Creating the SonicFinder required extending the Finder code at appropriate points to play sampled sounds modified according to attributes of the relevant events. Thus a variety of actions make sound in the SonicFinder: selecting, dragging, and copying files; opening and closing folders; selecting, scrolling, and resizing windows; and dropping files into and emptying the wastebasket. Most of these sounds are parameterized, although the ability to modify sounds was limited by the sampling software used. So, for instance, sounds which involve objects such as files or folders not only indicate basic events such as selection or copying, but also the object's types and sizes via the material and size of the virtual sound-producing objects. In addition, the SonicFinder incorporates an early example of an *auditory*

A) Selection	B) Dragging	C) Deleting

Fig. 3: In the SonicFinder, many user-initiated events are accompanied by meaningful auditory icons, increasing tangibility and ease of learning.

process monitor in the form of a pouring sound that accompanied copying and that indicates, via changes of pitch, the percentage of copying that had been completed (see also Cohen, 1993).

Fig. 3 shows an example of an interaction with the SonicFinder. When a user selects a file icon (Fig. 3A), a tapping sound is played which provides feedback about the event and also provides information about the file size and type. As the user drags the icon towards the wastebasket, a scraping sound is played (3b), which not only indicates that the object is being moved, but also reflects the size of the file and what it is being dragged over (i.e., its home window, another window, or the desktop). This sound stops either when the user releases the object, or when it hits a possible container such as a folder. Finally, when the user throws the icon into the wastebasket (3C), marking it for deletion, the sound of crashing glass is heard. This provides useful feedback about the nature of the interaction, and also reflects the number of other objects in the wastebasket.

Sounds like these serve to provide redundant information about events in the system, and thus increase its tangibility. Once users become accustomed to the SonicFinder, they feel somehow removed from the interface if the sound is turned off. The sounds seem to make interactions more immediate to users.

Sounds also convey information that is not conveyed graphically. For instance, the size and type of files is not indicated in most modes of the graphical display, yet can be readily judged (at least qualitatively) from the selection sounds. Sometimes sounds seem to convey information more effectively than graphic feedback. For example, hearing when a dragged object is over a container seems more effective than highlighting for helping people avoid playing chase-the-wastebasket, and in moving files to new windows without losing them in unnoticed folders. Finally, there is some anecdotal evidence that the SonicFinder helped some new users understand the underlying metaphor of the Finder; by emphasising the tangibility of icons, they support the interpretation of simple line-drawings as "objects" that can be moved, opened, etc.

In sum, the SonicFinder demonstrates the potential for auditory icons to provide rich information in intuitive ways. This can be helpful in making systems obvious, and thus in allowing users – whether students or not – to focus on the content offered by the software rather than the task of figuring out how to use it. In addition, auditory icons can increase the feeling of *direct engagement* (Hutchins, Hollan and Norman, 1986) with interfaces. They reinforce the feeling that the model world presented by graphical interfaces is a real one that can be interacted with in meaningful ways. Finally, interfaces that use auditory interfaces are more fun: Just as erasing the screen in KidPix would be boring if the bomb were silent, so selecting a file in the Finder is somehow less satisfying when it does not make a noise.

4 Supporting Coordination: SoundShark and ARKola

One of the potential problems with using educational software is that it may separate students from each other and from their teachers, turning classrooms into collections of individual users, each staring intently into his or her own screen. Thus another challenge for the designers of educational software is to develop products that support communication and coordination amongst students and their teachers. Auditory icons can help with this both within the physical classroom, and within collaborative virtual worlds used as "classrooms" for distance education.

4.1 SoundShark

An example of this latter role for sound is provided by SoundShark, an auditory version of SharedARK (Smith, 1989). SharedARK is a collaborative version of ARK, the Alternate Reality Kit. Developed by Smith (1987), ARK is designed as a virtual physics laboratory for distance education. The "world" appears on the screen as a flat surface on which a number of 2.5D objects may be found. These objects may be picked up, carried, and even thrown using a mouse-controlled "hand." They may be linked to one another, and messages may be passed to them using "buttons." Using this system, a number of simple physical experiments may be performed. In addition, SharedARK allows the same world to be seen by a number of different people on their own computer screens (and is usually used in conjunction with audio and video links that allow them to see and talk to one another). They may see each other's hands, manipulate objects together, and thus collaborate within this virtual world.

SharedARK is a multiprocessing system, with the potential for several "machines" or self-sustaining processes to run simultaneously. In addition, it provides a very large world to users, in that the space for interaction is many times larger than the screen (depending on available memory, it may cover literally acres of virtual space). This means that simultaneous users of the system may not be able to see each other (or more accurately, the hands that represent them), despite their being in the same "world" and potentially changing it in ways that might affect each other.

To help collaboration in this large, complex world, we extended the SharedARK interface with auditory icons that indicate user interactions, provide background information about ongoing processes and modes, and support navigation. The result is called SoundShark (Gaver and Smith, 1990). Many user actions are accompanied by auditory icons which are parameterized to indicate attributes such as the size of relevant objects. In addition, ongoing processes make sounds that indicate their nature and continuing activity even if they are not visible on the screen. Modes of the system, such as the activation of "motion," which allows objects to move if they have a velocity, are indicated by low-volume, smooth background sounds.

These auditory icons are helpful for individual users. More interesting, the sounds support collaboration among remote users. Because each sound can be heard throughout the "world," collaborators can hear each other even if they cannot see each other. In addition, the distance between a user's hand and the source of a sound is indicated by the sound's amplitude and by low-pass filtering. This not only seems to aid navigation (prompting us to develop "auditory landmarks", objects whose soul function was to play a repetitive sound that could aid orientation) but allows collaborators to hear the distance and even direction of their partners.

4.1 The ARKola Simulation

Our experiences with SoundShark suggested that auditory icons could help collaboration amongst distributed colleagues interacting in a virtual environment. To test this, we developed a special application within SoundShark that we used for observing people's use of the system. Our aim was to assess the usefulness of auditory icons for collaborators within the system as well as for individual users.

The application we came up with is a model of a softdrink plant called the ARKóla bottling factory (Fig. 4; Gaver et al, 1991). It consists of an assembly line of 9 machines which cook, bottle, and cap cola, provide supplies, and keep track of financing. The plant was designed to be fairly difficult to run, with the rates of the machines requiring fine tuning and with machines occasionally "breaking down," necessitating the use of a "repair" button. In addition, we designed the plant to be too large to fit on the computer screen, so participants could only see about half the machines at any given time.

Each of the machines makes sounds to indicate its function. For instance, the "nut dispenser" makes wooden impact sounds each time a nut is delivered to the cooker, the "heater" makes a whooshing flame-like sound, the "bottler" clangs and the "capper" clanks. In addition, the rate of each machine is indicated by the rate of repetition of the sounds it makes, and problems with the machines are indicated by a variety of alerting sounds such as breaking glass, overflowing liquid, and so forth.

As with SoundShark, the sounds were designed not only to be useful for individual users, but also to be helpful in coordinating partners running the plant. We

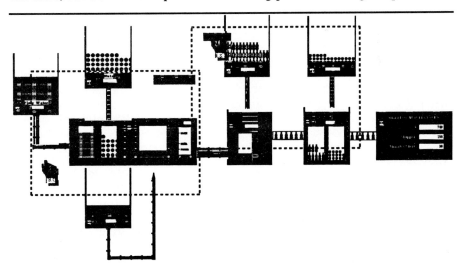

Fig. 4. The ARKola bottling plant simulation (about one fourth actual size). Rectangles show the extent of the plant each user sees at a given time.

tested this in a simple observational study. Six pairs of participants were asked to run the plant with the aim of making as much "money" as they could during an hour-long session. Each pair ran the plant for two hours, one with and one without auditory feedback (with the order, of course, being counterbalanced). We observed their performance from a "control room" via video links as they ran the plant, and videotaped their activities for later analysis.

Our observations indicated that sounds were effective in helping individual users keep track of the many ongoing processes. The sounds allowed people to track the activity, rate, and functioning of normally running machines. Without sound, people often overlooked machines that were broken or that were not receiving enough supplies; with sound these problems were indicated either by the machine's sound ceasing (which was often ineffective) or by the various alert sounds. Perhaps most interesting, the auditory icons allowed people to hear the plant as an integrated complex process. The sounds merged together to produce an auditory texture, much as the many sounds that make up the sound of an automobile do. Participants seemed to be sensitive to the overall texture of the factory sound, referring to "the factory" more often than they did without sound.

These observations support the idea, introduced in Section 3, that well-designed sounds can help new users learn how a system works. These observations also support the thesis of Section 4, that sounds are particularly useful in guiding exploration of systems by providing information about a relevant subset of events. Finally, sound seemed to add to the tangibility of the plant and increased participants' engagement with the task. This became most evident with a pair of participants who had completed an hour with sound and were working an hour without. From the video, their increasing boredom with the silent plant is obvious (as are several mistakes that they attribute to the lack of sound). Finally, one of the pair remarks "we could always make the noises ourselves..."

Our major findings, however, related to the role of sound in collaboration. In both the sound and no-sound conditions, participants tended to divide responsibility for the plant so that each could keep one area on the screen at all times. Without sound, this meant that participants had to rely on their partner's reports to tell what was happening in the invisible part. With sound, each could hear directly the status of the remote half of the plant. This led to greater collaboration between partners, with each pointing out problems to the other, suggesting solutions, and so forth. The ability to provide foreground information visually and background information using sound seemed to allow people to concentrate on their own tasks, while coordinating with their partners about theirs. It was an effective way of linking participants in this model world without forcing them to be together all the time. This is likely to be a very useful feature for helping with the balance between self-guided work and coordination in educational systems of the future.

5 Guiding Exploration: EAR

Still another challenge facing designers of educational software is in balancing between tightly-constrained teaching systems and systems that allow free exploration on the part of students. Traditional "drill and test" systems seem boring, have dubious efficacy, and make limited use of the potential power that computing offers. Newer "exploratory learning" systems, on the other hand, may be confusing and, moreover, make it difficult to coordinate the material that students actually learn as they wander through complex virtual environments.

A middle ground between these extremes may be found in systems which support *guided exploration* of complex environments. The idea is to constrain students' explorations of rich informational spaces to a set of trajectories that cover a subset of relevant information. For instance, fictional characters have been used to guide access to a historical database using the conventions of narrative flow (Laurel et al., 1990). Systems such as these offer a good deal of flexibility to teachers: Students may be assigned one particular trajectory, permitted to chose amongst a number of alternatives, or allowed simply to wander freely through the information space.

Auditory icons can help create systems that offer guided exploration by allowing a subset of information to be presented at a given time. From this point of view, sounds can be designed not to convey all possible information, but to present that which is necessary to highlight a particular task. For instance in SoundShark different sounds might be used for lessons involving gravity (for which mass, distance and the like are important) than for those involving the coordination of complex processes (such as ARKola, in which the relative rates of the machines was most important). Using sounds, different aspects of the "world" can be emphasised for different purposes.

5.1 Environmental Audio Reminders

The key to using sounds that guide exploration is in designing them to clearly represent only the relevant information for a given task, as opposed to all the information available. As an example of this, consider the Environmental Audio Reminders (EAR) system we use at EuroPARC (Gaver, 1991). This system plays a variety of nonspeech audio cues to offices and common areas inside EuroPARC to keep us informed about events around the building. EAR works in conjunction with the RAVE audio-video network (Gaver et al., 1992; Buxton and Moran, 1990), which connects all the offices at EuroPARC with audio and video technologies using a computer-controlled switch, and *Khronika* (Lövstrand, 1991), an event server which uses a database of events in conjunction with software daemons to inform us of a wide range of planned and spontaneous, electronic and professional events. EAR, then, consists of sounds triggered by Khronika when relevant events occur, which are routed using the RAVE system from a central server to any office in the building.

This system is set up to play sounds that remind us about a range of events. For instance, when new email arrives, the sound of a stack of papers falling on the floor is heard. When somebody connects to my video camera, the sound of an opening door is heard just before the connection is made, and the sound of a closing door just after the connection is broken. Ten minutes before a meeting, the sound of murmuring voices slowly increasing in number and volume is played to my office, then the sound of a gavel. And when we decide to call it a day, one of us may play the "pub call" to interested colleagues, who then hear laughing, chatting voices in the background with the sound of a pint glass being filled with real ale in the foreground.

Many of the sounds we use in EAR may seem frivolous because they are cartoon-like stereotypes of naturally-occurring sounds. But it is precisely *because* they are stereotyped sounds that they are effective. More "serious" sounds – such as electronic beeps or sequences of tones – would be likely to be less easily remembered than these. In addition, we have taken some care in shaping the sounds to be unobtrusive. For instance, many of the sounds are very short; those that are longer have a relatively slow attack so that they enter the auditory ambience of the office subtly. Most of the sounds have relatively little high-frequency energy, and we try to avoid extremely noisy or abrupt sounds. So though the sounds we use are stereotypes, they are designed to fit into the existing office ambience rather than intruding upon it.

EAR serves as a useful example of many of the themes of this paper: They are effective because they are stereotyped sounds that are easily learned and remembered. They promote coordination by making information available to the distributed members of our labs. The overall effect is to allow us to hear events as if they were just outside our offices, despite the fact that these events are either too distant to hear naturally or have not even occurred yet.

The point here, however, is that while EAR creates an intuitively accessible auditory environment that complements and supplements our everyday one, it is not a slavish imitation of *all* the sounds we might potentially hear around our building. We do not play the sounds of people entering and leaving the building, for instance, or those of people typing, moving things in their offices, etc., though in principle we could. These events do not appear relevant to the tasks that we are supporting, and thus would merely be distracting. Instead we choose the sounds we play to indicate an important subset of the ongoing activities in the building. Moreover, individual users may tailor the system, registering interest in some events (for instance, meetings), but not others (for instance, pub time). In this way, the system supports a guided trajectory through the information that might be available. It offers the ability to maintain awareness of remote events without distracting or confusing us with too much data.

6   Conclusions

None of the systems described in this paper – KidPix, the SonicFinder, SoundShark and ARKola, or EAR – were explicitly designed for educational purposes. But all have something to say about how to make such systems easier to use, more motivating, more supportive of group work, and better able to guide students in their learning about complex, rich environments. Sounds can make systems easier to learn and more enjoyable to use. They are useful in supporting coordination without enforcing togetherness, because they can allow background information to be conveyed using the auditory channel while foreground, task-specific information can be provided visually. Finally, by providing only a subset of information, it is possible to use auditory icons to guide exploration along trajectories that are useful and desirable. So if the idea of designing noisy educational software may have seemed counter-intuitive at the start of this paper, it should now be possible for readers to imagine a day when teachers will be pleading with their students to make *more* noise.

References

Buxton, W., and Moran, T. (1990). EuroPARC's integrated interactive intermedia facility (iiif): Early experiences. In Proceedings of the IFIP WG8.4 Conference on Multi-User Interfaces and Applications, Heraklion, Crete, September 1990.

Cohen, J. (1993). Kirk here: Using genre sounds to monitor background activity. Adjunct Proceedings of INTERCHI'93, Amsterdam, May 1993,. ACM, New York.

Gaver, W. W. (1986). Auditory icons: Using sound in computer interfaces. Human-Computer Interaction 2, 167 - 177.

Gaver, W. W. (1989). The SonicFinder: An interface that uses auditory icons. Human-Computer Interaction 4 (1).

Gaver, W. W. (1991). Sound support for collaboration. Proceedings of the Second European Conference on Computer-Supported Collaborative Work (Amsterdam, September 1991) Dordrecht: Kluwer.

Gaver, W. W. (1993a). How do we hear in the world? Explorations of ecological acoustics. Ecological Psychology (5) 4.

Gaver, W. W. (1993b). What in the world do we hear? An ecological approach to auditory source perception. Ecological Psychology (5) 1.

Gaver, W. W., & Smith, R. B. (1990). Auditory icons in large-scale collaborative environments. Proceedings of Human-Computer Interaction – Interact'90, Cambridge, U.K., August 1990 Amsterdam: North-Holland.

Gaver, W. W., Moran, T., MacLean, A., Lövstrand, L., Dourish, P., Carter, K., & Buxton, W. (1992). Realizing a video environment: EuroPARC's RAVE system. Proceedings of CHI'92 , Monterey, CA, May 1992, ACM, New York.

Gaver, W. W., Smith, R. B., & O'Shea, T. (1991). Effective sounds in complex systems: The ARKola simulation. Proceedings of CHI 1991, New Orleans, April 28 - May 2, 1991, ACM, New York.

Hutchins, E. , Hollan, J. , & Norman, D. (1986). Direct manipulation interfaces. In D. A. Norman & S. W. Draper (Eds.), User centered system design: New perspectives on human-computer interaction. Hillsdale, NJ: Lawrence Erlbaum.

Laurel, B., Oren, T., and Don, A. (1990). Issues in multimedia interface design: Media integration and interface agents. Proceedings of CHI'90, Seattle, April 1990, ACM: New York.

Lövstrand, L. (1991). Being selectively aware with the Khronika system. In Proceedings of ECSCW'91, Amsterdam, September 1991.

Smith, R. (1987). The Alternate Reality Kit: an example of the tension between literalism and magic. Proceedings of CHI + GI 1987, Toronto, April 1987, ACM, New York.

Smith, R. (1989). A prototype futuristic technology for distance education. In: E. Scanloon, T. O'Shea (Eds.) New Directions in Educational Technology. NATO ASI Series F, Vol. 96 Berlin: Springer-Verlag, 1992, pp. 131-138.

Electronic Books and their Potential for Interactive Learning

Philip Barker

Interactive Systems Research Group, Human Computer Interaction Laboratory, School of Computing and Mathematics, University of Teesside, Cleveland, UK

Abstract. The growing popularity and importance of electronic books opens up many possibilities for the dissemination of instructional material. Electronic books are made possible because of the availability of low-cost, high-capacity storage facilities based upon the effective use of digital optical storage media - particularly, compact disc read-only-memory (CD-ROM). Because of their portability, robustness and pedagogic potential such books offer a powerful mechanism by which to implement distance learning programmes. This paper describes and discusses the basic nature of electronic books and those special features that make them particularly suitable for the support of both open and distance learning. Two ongoing projects in which we are currently involved are then briefly described.

Keywords. Electronic books, interactive learning, interface design

1 Introduction

Over the centuries, since the introduction of the printing press, books have obviously played a fundamental role in a wide range of information dissemination and knowledge transfer activities. Some years ago we analysed the role of conventional books in technical knowledge dissemination processes [1]. We identified a number of important limitations of such books (see table 1) and suggested that some new form of book was needed in order to overcome the limitations of those that are printed on paper.

In our original publication [1], we used the term 'electronic book' to describe a new form of book whose pages were composed, not of static printer's ink, but from dynamic electronic information. Generally, we now use this new term to describe information delivery systems that are capable of providing their users with access to pages of reactive electronic information with which they can interact. As can be seen from fig.1, the pages of information which make up an electronic book are organised conceptually just like the pages of a conventional book.

Generally, an electronic book may be thought of as being a collection of reactive and dynamic pages of multimedia information (that can embed text, pictures and sound) [2]. The information contained within these pages is of three basic types:

aesthetic (which is used both to help reinforce the underlying book metaphor and also to provide an ergonomically 'pleasing' appearance); informative (which is intended to instruct or inform those who use a particular book); and either implicit or explicit control functions. The control options that are available are important because they enable users to specify the nature of the information that they wish to retrieve from a given book and how this retrieved material is to be displayed within the confines of the host delivery platform. Some examples of simple primitive control options for electronic books are illustrated in fig. 1. The most commonly used functions are: next page; previous page; goto page N; exit book; and so on.

Table 1 Basic Limitations of Conventional Books

- difficult to reproduce
- expensive to disseminate
- difficult to update
- single copies cannot easily be shared
- easily damaged and vandalised
- bulky to transport
- embedded material is unreactive and static
- cannot utilise sound
- cannot utilise animation or moving pictures
- unable to monitor reader's activity
- cannot assess reader's understanding
- unable to adapt material dynamically

Unlike conventional books, those that are published on electronic media require some form of 'delivery platform' to facilitate access to them. The basic architecture and composition of a typical electronic book delivery platform is illustrated schematically in fig. 2.

The most commonly used multimedia information storage medium for publishing electronic books is compact disc read-only-memory (CD-ROM). Typically, this makes available about 650 Mbytes of storage. The storage space available with a CD-ROM disc can be used in a variety of different ways for the storage of multimedia information such as text, sound, static pictures, animation, computer programs and a very limited amount of motion video. Typical figures that are often quoted to reflect the storage capacity of a CD-ROM disc are: 200,000 pages of A4 text; or 20,000 low-quality (PCX) image files; or 2,000 TV quality still images; or 30 seconds of video; or 18 hours of low-quality sound. The way in which the available storage is used within a given electronic book production will depend critically on the 'media mix' needed by the particular publication concerned.

Obviously, the actual amount of material that can be stored on a CD-ROM disc will depend upon whether or not any form of data compression technique is applied to the information before it is committed to storage. Normally, in order to store full-motion video pictures on a CD-ROM various types of compression (and decompression) technique must be applied.

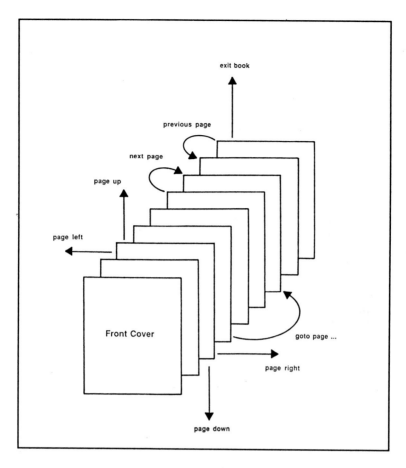

Fig. 1. Conceptual model for an electronic book

2 Types of Electronic Book

Depending upon the type of information that they embed and the kinds of facility that they make available, electronic books can be classified into the following basic categories: text books; static picture books; moving picture books; talking books; multimedia books; polymedia books; hypermedia books; intelligent electronic books; telemedia electronic books; and cyberspace books. Each of these categories of electronic book is briefly discussed below.

As their name suggests, text books are composed of pages of textual material that have been organised into suitably sized 'chunks' of information. The chunk size that is employed will depend upon the screen size that is used for information display and the number of chunks/page that it is required to present simultaneously. Static picture books consist of a collection of pictures that are organised into some particular theme; the pictures may be of various 'qualities' with respect to their resolution and the range

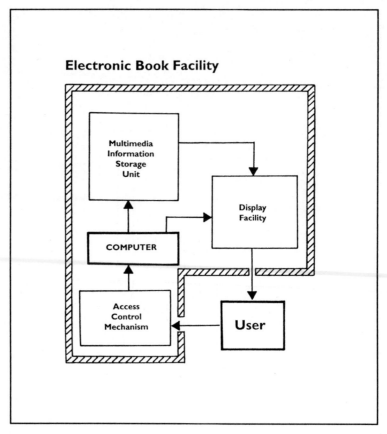

Fig. 2. Basic structure of an electronic book delivery station

of colours that they embed. Moving picture books are constructed from either animation clips or motion video segments - or combinations of each of these; the 'mix' used will depend upon a variety of factors such as the purpose of the electronic book and the 'message' that it is to 'convey'. Talking books depend for their success upon recorded sound (both high- and low-quality) that is used in conjunction with a variety of 'interactive audio' techniques to facilitate end-user control of information and knowledge transfer.

Multimedia books use various combinations of two or more communication channels (either in sequence or simultaneously) in order to encode a particular message. Such books use text, sound, pictures and moving images that are basically organised in a 'linear' fashion. The materials are delivered by means of a single delivery medium (such as magnetic disc or CD-ROM). Polymedia books, in contrast to multimedia books, use a combination of several different media (CD-ROM, magnetic disc, paper, and so on) in order to deliver their information to end-users.

Hypermedia electronic books have much in common with multimedia books in that they depend upon the use of multiple communication channels. However, unlike multimedia books, hypermedia books employ 'non-linear' organisations of information based upon the use of web-like structures. Because of the embedded intelligence that they contain, intelligent books are capable of dynamic adaptation as a consequence of interaction with end-users. Undoubtedly, two of the most exciting types of book that we are currently developing are telemedia books and cyberspace books. The first of these uses telecommunication facilities to augment the capabilities of a CD-ROM publication in order to support highly interactive distributed distance learning activities [3]. Cyberspace books are used as a means of providing their readers with access to various types of virtual reality facility; such books employ different kinds of interactive simulation environment in order to provide end-users with participative, 'real-life' encounters that they would not normally be able to experience.

Because of their importance in the context of distance and independent learning activities, telemedia books will be discussed in more detail in the following section of the paper.

3 Telemedia Books and Distance Learning

As we have suggested above, electronic books can be used to support a wide range of learning and training applications. They are particulary important in the context of supporting distance learning, individualised self-supported learning and co-operative group learning at a distance [3]. The way in which we envisage this happening is illustrated conceptually in fig. 3.

Embedded within this figure is the idea of students learning by electronic means through the use of electronic classrooms. Such classrooms may exist in two basic forms. First, they may exist physically in a particular geographical location - being composed of a relatively small number of interactive workstations contained within a given room or building. Second, they may exist in the form of a 'virtual classroom' that is composed of an almost limitless number of learning stations that are physically distributed anywhere in the world - for example, in home environments, in people's places of work, in public places such as libraries, and so on.

We envisage that a very large proportion of the delivery platforms for interactive learning will be of a highly portable nature - based upon the use of various types of portable computer system (such as lap-tops, hand-held computers, notebook computers and various sorts of consumer products based upon technologies such as CD-I and CDTV). We refer to such environments as 'portable interactive learning environments'. The use of such technology is attractive because it means that many aspects of learning and training can transcend institutional boundaries. Of course, it is anticipated that all the workstations used to support this type of learning will incorporate the type of architecture that was previously illustrated in fig. 2. They will therefore be capable of making large amounts of multimedia and/or hypermedia

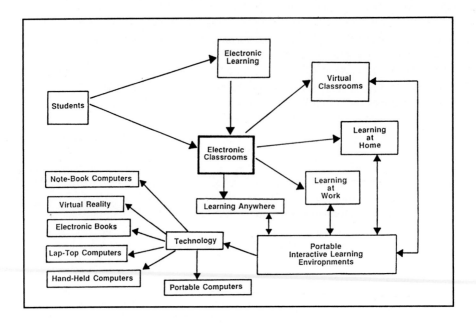

Fig. 3. The role of electronic books in distance education

information available through the medium of electronic books that are published on optical media such as CD-ROM.

Obviously, the use of stand-alone workstations similar to those described above (and illustrated schematically in fig. 2) would only go part of the way to realising the overall needs of learners and trainees in a virtual classroom situation. It is therefore important to consider what other functions a portable learning environment needs to provide. Naturally, an important aspect of conventional classrooms that must be provided within virtual classrooms is 'class contact' with other students and tutors. In order to meet this requirement it is necessary to provide various forms of 'person to person' communication facilities (for example, by means of electronic mail, bulletin boards, telephone, video-phone and/or conferencing facilities). Such facilities not only allow fellow students to communicate with each other but also support, if necessary, communication with tutors and subject matter experts who make themselves available for use as 'human learning resources'. The type of computer-based learning environments needed to support this approach to learning and training is illustrated schematically in fig. 4.

Fundamental to this type of workstation is the presence of an appropriate connection to a host telecommunication facility. This may take a variety of different forms. It might be a simple modem and 'dial up' connection (made through a telephone network) to some other compatible modem attached to a remote host computer. Alternatively, the workstation may be connected directly (via a suitable network card) to a local area network and then, through a series of wide area networks to some remote site that might be located almost anywhere in the world. Obviously,

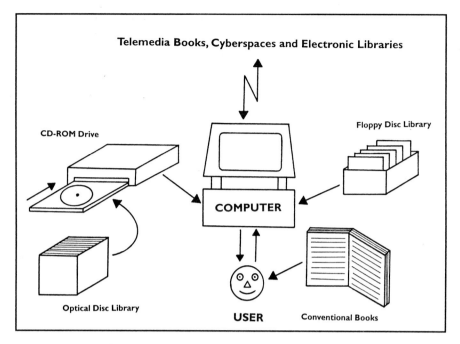

Fig. 4. Polyfunctional workstation for electronic book delivery

as well as supporting distant person-to-person communication such workstations are also able to support access to a wide range of other remote resources such as electronic libraries and either down-loadable or shared cyberspaces.

As we have suggested earlier, electronic books that are designed in such a way that they are able to take advantage of a telecommunications infra-structure similar to that described above are referred to as telemedia books. We envisage a variety of different uses for such books within the context of distributed distance learning both within academic and non-academic organisations. Two examples of systems that we are currently developing will be briefly described in order to illustrate how such books may be used.

The simplest type of telemedia book for use in a delivery platform similar to that shown in fig. 4 is one which uses CD-ROM for the bulk publication of large amounts of interactive course material for use by students. However, also embedded in the electronic book (in the form of a reader service) is an electronic mail facility that is referenced through an icon. This facility can be used in a variety of ways to support communicative exchanges between students and for the transfer and/or sharing of materials. The work that we are currently undertaking in our 'interactive language learning project' illustrates this approach to the use of telemedia books for learning French. The essential course material is embedded upon a CD-ROM (as an electronic book) that allows individual students to listen to and practice speaking French. They can also test their writing ability by sending electronic mail communications to each other and to fellow students and tutors located both within the UK and in France.

The second telemedia book project that we are currently working on involves the design of support material in the form of 'interactive manuals' for use within an electronic performance support system (EPSS) that is to be used within the context of office automation. The EPSS system is intended to provide just-in-time (JIT) training at a particular point of need. The system that we have been designing and prototyping is intended to offer this type of support within a geographically distributed multi-centre organisation. The interactive manuals that embed the technical and procedural information necessary for the organisation are published on CD-ROM. The communications infra-structure running above this basic publication level is accessed as a standard facility within a telemedia 'company services' handbook that enables employees to gain access to each other and to sources of expert help and advice. This enables employees to share skills and when necessary develop new ones through tele-tutoring techniques and JIT methods.

4 Conclusion

Books are an important mechanism for the storage and communication of information. Conventional books are published on paper as a collection of pages of static information. Therefore, in many ways, the concept of a book is intimately bound to this medium. This has both advantages and disadvantages - some of which have been discussed in this paper. Of course, there is no inherent reason why the concept of a book has to be media dependent. Other media could equally well be used to publish books or embed the book concept. For example, conventional books could be 'televised' on television but because of the low interactivity of this medium users would loose the ability to 'turn pages'. However, by using a more interactive medium (such as a computer) to publish a book, many of the properties of conventional books can be emulated. It is therefore important to realise that the properties of a book will depend very much upon the nature of the medium (or 'media mix') used for its publication. In this paper we advocate the use of telemedia electronic books as a useful resource for promoting and supporting distance education and cooperative group learning at a distance. Two examples of the use of electronic books for distance learning have been briefly described. Obviously, many more exciting possibilities of this approach yet remain to be explored.

References

1. Barker, P.G. and Manji, K.A., New Books for Old, Programmed Learning and Educational Technology, 25(4), 310-313, (1988).
2. Barker, P.G., Electronic Books, Special Edition of Educational and Training Technology International, 28(4), 269-368, (1991).
3. Barker, P.G. and Giller, S., Electronic Books for Distance Learning, 759-761 in Volume 2 of the Proceedings of the Ninth International Conference on Technology and Education, Paris, France, 16-20 March, (1992).

A Change of View: The Parameter Projection Problem in Three-Dimensional View Setting

Eric Brok[1] and Peter van Splunder[2]

[1] Open university, Faculty of Engineering, Box 2960, 6401 DL Heerlen, the Netherlands.
[2] PTT Research, Insitute for Applied Social Science Research, Box 421, 2260 AK Leidschendam, the Netherlands.

Abstract. An experimental on screen control panel for 3D view setting is described. The design requires only a regular 2D mouse input device. The user sets the desired viewpoint by direct manipulation of metaphoric icons, which is more facile and natural than by setting several slide control bars.

This specific control panel is also adressed as an illustration of a general interface design issue: the internal technical parameters of the computer program must be projected onto the user interface with great care to avoid confusion in the user.

Keywords. Interface design, 3D graphics, interaction techniques, virtual controllers, rotation control, view setting, parameter projection problem

1 Introduction

Usually the functioning of a computer program is determined by a set of internal parameters. Many of these parameters are to be controlled by the end user. Seen from the view of a computer programmer, it would be most obvious to expose these parameters directly to the user. But in many cases the technical parameters by itself are not organized in a way that the user can grasp easily. The user probably relates to the situation at hand by very different conceptual entities. In short there is a gap between technically significant parameters and psychologically significant parameters. To facilitate human-machine communication these two sets have to be projected carefully onto each other. We will call this issue the *parameter projection problem* (PPP). We will discuss this issue further by an example interface.

The example concerns view setting in three-dimensional graphics. Before turning to the PPP-issue, we want to make clear that in 3D graphics there is also an optical projection problem. First three-dimensional objects have to be projected onto the flat screen. Mathematics deals with that quite well. Second and more problematic is the two-dimensional on-screen manipulation of three-dimensional objects. Simply pointing at an object can be already ambiguous (Bier, 1990). It is now widely acknowledged that creating and manipulating 3D objects is a complicated task (e.g. Veniola, 1993).

One way to deal with this issue is to develop advanced mechanical interaction devices. Datagloves, 3D glasses, 3D mouse devices (e.g. Venolia, 1993) and the like seem to bring truly three-dimensional interaction literally within reach. Existing CAD/CAM applications often use hardware dials to rotate three-dimensional objects. This is another way of diverting interaction away from the flat screen. We acknowledge those approaches, but this paper will discuss an interface that only requires on-screen interaction with a 2D mouse. (The design of this interface however could easily be adapted to true 3D input.)

Chen, Mountford and Chellen (1988) describe several virtual controls for rotating 3D objects. Most promising seems what they call the 'virtual sphere' (see also Evans, Tanner & Wein (1987)). This control is a virtual trackball that can be manipulated by mouse cursor. Rolling it up or down makes the selected object pitch (see also table 1). Dragging sideways makes the object yaw. And (unlike physical trackballs) dragging along the circumference makes the object roll. However promising, this control concerns only rotation. The current paper explicitly focusses on the *combined* task of translation and rotation of the 'camera' through space.

2 The example program

The control panels we will discuss are part of a prototype application program. We will first take a quick glance of this program called PLEXI[1] itself. PLEXI enables the user to furnish a three-dimensional room (see fig. 1). Because arranging furniture mainly concerns movements along the floor, this interaction takes place in a 2D ground plan window.

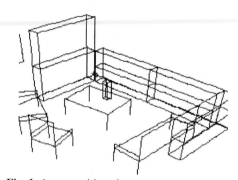

Fig. 1. A room with a view.

The room is also continually depicted in a seperate '3D window'; of course the window itself is 2D, but a 3D structure is projected onto it. The user must communicate the desired viewpoint to the computer. For this, PLEXI supplies two very different control panels, on which this paper will focus.

To appreciate the PPP-issue in this example some technical details should be noted. The program is written in Pascal. It uses a library module which calculates projections of 3D wire frame structures onto the screen. The module needs several parameter values to determine the view on the scene (see table 1 and fig. 2).

---

[1] Readers might wonder why the program is called PLEXI. In reality solid objects can obscure parts of each other. Simulating this in computer graphics requires considerable computing effort. Therefore the program pictures wireframe furniture only. But in a funny mood we claimed that the program was still perfectly realistic; it is specifically made for those fancy interior decoraters who furnish entire rooms by *plexiglass* furniture only.

Table 1. The parameters that determine a view.

Parameter	Effect	Reference
Yaw	Rotate camera around...	y axis
Pitch	Rotate camera around...	x axis
Roll	Rotate camera around...	z axis
Scale	Closeness of camera to...	center of space
MoveX	Move rotation center along...	x axis
MoveY	Move rotation center along...	y axis
MoveZ	Move rotation center along...	z axis

Y

X

Z (out of page)

Yaw

Pitch

Roll

Fig. 2. The axes and rotations as defined by the library module.

3 Two different views

3.1 The slide bars control panel

Seen from the viewpoint of a programmer it would be most obvious to expose these technical parameters directly to the end user. This approach results in the control panel in fig. 3. There is a seperate slider for each parameter. The yaw, pitch and roll vary from -180 to +180 degrees. The move parameters vary from -100 length units to +100 length units.

Using this control panel we experienced some problems. First of all, the names of the parameters poorly explain their effects, especially for non-English native speakers. But most confusing of all, the different parameters interact mutually. For example the effect of rotation around y axis depends on the displacement of the centre of the space. This is of course stereometrically coherent but can be psychologically hard to interprete and predict. The control panel does not support a consistent mental model about the relative effects of each of the parameters when combined. Related studies too suggest that users often find cummulative rotation around all three axes hard to monitor and control (Chen, Mountford and Sellen, 1988).

3.2 The icon based control panel

We decided to change our view from the programmers' to the users'. For the moment we forgot all we knew about the 3D Pascal module. Another control panel was designed from scratch that would make more sense to the user. The new design was based on two general interface design concepts: *methapors* and *direct manipulation*. Metaphoric interfaces explicitly use everyday objects and events from outside the com-

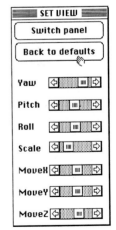

Fig. 3. The slide bars panel.

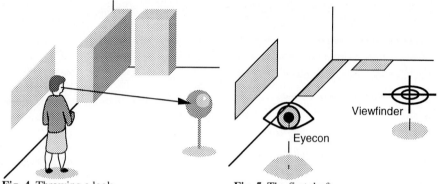

Fig. 4. Throwing a look.   **Fig. 5.** The first draft.

puter realm to support computer-based tasks. Metaphor guides the construction of a mental model about the functioning of the computer program. Metaphor is a powerful resource for design because it exploits prior knowledge; by analogical reasoning even novice users will know what to expect from the system and how to respond to specific situations (Gardiner and Christie, 1987). A second and strongly related design concept is direct manipulation. It requires visual representation of the domain of discourse (e.g. by metaphoric icons). Then the user can perform operations by pointing, dragging and editing objects. The benefits of direct manipulation as opposed to command lines or menus, include rapid learning, fewer errors, high user satisfaction and encouragement of explorative user behavior (Schneidermann, 1991).

The new PLEXI control panel involves direct manipulation of methaporic icons. It introduces a third-party perspective in which the user sees herself, watching a part of the scene (see fig. 4). The user can then simply displace the icon representing herself to the desired viewpoint and displace the focus spot to direct her look towards a certain spot. Actually this is not quite that simple because both viewer and focus spot should be manipulated in all three dimensions. Fig. 5 shows our first draft and fig. 6 the implemented version. Viewer and spot are represented by methaporic icons, which we will call Eyecon and Viewfinder respectively. This new control panel looks like the actual room. On the floor are the continually updated contours of the furniture arrangement. These can not be manipulated in this panel. The position of Eyecon relates to the 'camera' viewpoint in space. The position of Viewfinder specifies the focus spot at which the 'camera' is

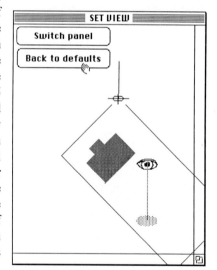

Fig. 6. The implemented 'eyecon' control panel.

aimed. The user can modify the horizontal position of an icon by dragging its shadow along the floor in any direction. The icon itself moves automatically along, keeping straight above its shadow. Directly, the icon can be dragged only vertically[2] which determines the height. In this way the user can specify a viewpoint by one to four meaningful movements instead of one to seven technical parameter changes.

Once the eyeconic control panel was devised, its parameters had to be projected to the seven technical parameters which the Pascal module required. This is the actual PPP issue (see fig. 7).

Table 2 shows in a glance how the visual appearance of the two control panels relate to the changing 3D view. The first three views show merely how seperate parameters effect the view. View number 4 however serves to demonstrate the clear advantage of the eyecon panel in combined translation and rotation. Would you be able to guess the slide bar settings right to get this peep through the window?

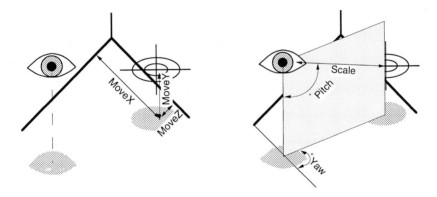

Fig. 7. Actual projection of internal parameters onto interface semantics.
The position of the shadow of Viewfinder along the floor determines the *x-z displacements* and the distance from Viewfinder to its shadow determines the *y-displacement*. Thus Viewfinder represents the centre of space. The direction in degrees from Eyecon to Viewfinder along the floor determines the amount of *yaw*. The difference in heigth (icon-to-shadow distance) between Eyecon and Viewfinder determines the *pitch*. The *roll* parameter is not implemented but could be assigned to local rotation of Eyecon around its own centre (by dragging at its edges). *Scale* was calculated as the 3D-Euclidian distance between Eyecon and Viewfinder, multiplied by a heuristic factor.

---

[2] If users would be allowed to drag the icon in an oblique direction, it would be impossible to decide which combination of x, y and z-movement they intended.

Table 2. Four views and their control settings. From left to right: four views, the respective arrangements of the eyecon panel and the respective settings of the slide bars.

Viewno.	View	Eyecon panel	Slide bars panel
1			Yaw Pitch Roll Scale MoveX MoveY MoveZ
2	Basic manipulations		Yaw Pitch Roll Scale MoveX MoveY MoveZ
3			Yaw Pitch Roll Scale MoveX MoveY MoveZ
4	A look through the window		Yaw Pitch Roll Scale MoveX MoveY MoveZ

4 Experiment

In order to learn more about the usability and learnability of the eyecon panel, a small scale experiment was carried out. This experiment was designed to compare the eyecon panel directly to the slide bars panel regarding learnability by novices.

4.1 Method

Subjects. Five male and five female right-handed adult subjects were tested. Five of the subjects had an academic degree, three of which in mathematics. All subjects were familiar with using a mouse device. They had no prior experience with PLEXI or any other 3D graphics system.

Apparatus. The experiment was run on an Apple Macintosh LCII computer with color display and a one-button mouse. The software (PLEXI itself and the experiment control) was written in Pascal. Accuracy was recorded on line. Task completion time was recorded by a hand held stopwatch. The roll parameter was hidden in the slide bar panel because it was not implemented in the eyecon panel either.

Tasks. Subjects were asked to perform a series of matching tasks. On the screen they were presented a plain room seen from a certain position. Then they were shown a picture on paper of a certain desired view and they were asked to match the screen picture in angle and size to the paper copy. Both target and screen picture were wireframe rendered. Subjects decided themselves when the match was sufficient.

Each series consisted of four matching tasks:

task 1	from view 1 to view 2 (see table 2)
task 2	from view 1 to view 3
task 3	from view 1 to view 4
task 4	from view 4 to view 1

Both task completion time and accuracy of match were measured. Accuracy was calculated as the sum of the squared differences between the two views on the parameters yaw, pitch, scale, moveX, moveY and moveZ. Subjects were not allowed to switch to default view settings during the tasks.

Design. According to a within subject design, each subject performed the same task series with both control panels. Order of control panel was counterbalanced: half of the subjects used the icon based panel first, the others used the slide bars panel first. This condition was equally divided over sex because gender might relate to ease or style of spatial reasoning. Verifying such effects however would require a much broader study.

Procedure. All instructions were provided by the test leader. In addition to a general introduction to the procedure, screen layout and upcoming tasks, each session consisted of *twice* the following sections, once for each control panel:

- Introduction to the control panel
- Self-discovery with this panel for five minutes
- Supplementary explanation by experimenter if neccessary
- Task 1 to 4 using this panel

To make sure that subjects really tried to understand each control panel during the discovery period, they were asked to explain verbally how each icon or slide bar related to the 3D picture. In two cases for each panel this revealed serious misconceptions and some supplementary explanation was provided by the test leader. At the end of the session the subject was asked a 1 to 10 rating for the usability of each control panel.

4.2   Results

Performance in style and completion time differed even more between subjects than we already expected. Fig. 8 shows the quantitative results. Fig. 8a shows that (averaged over subjects) all tasks were completed fastest with the eyecon panel. The difference is particular large regarding task 3. Fig. 8b shows accuracy of task result. For the simpler tasks (1 and 2) the slide bars gave least error. For the more complex tasks the eyecon panel gave least error. Fig. 8c shows that the average rating was higher for the eyecon panel than for the slide bars panel.

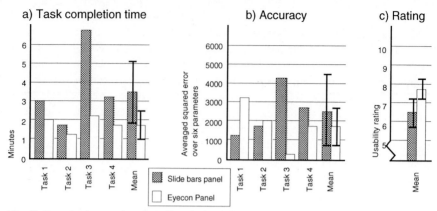

Fig. 8. Quantitative results of small scale (n = 10) user test.

4.3 Discussion

Different strategies. Completion time very much depended on choice of strategy. The 3D window always depicts the centre of space (which is centre of focus and rotation as well). But because this centre point is projected onto the 2D screen, it does not reveal its actual 3D position compared to the room. Often the centre point only *appears* to coincide with a particular part of the room, and drifts away when rotating the room around. Using the slide bars panel a cumbersome strategy (which was discoverd by only one subject) should be adopted to overcome this problem. When using the eyecon panel there is no need for such a strategy because the 3D position of the centre point is explicitly represented by the Viewfinder.

Also the two control panels proved to call for very different strategies according to the use of feedback information. Using the slide bars panel it proved very hard to predict the effect of each slide shift; the subjects continually watched the 3D window to receive indispensable feedback. But using the eyecon panel it proved unneccesary to watch the intermediate results.

Task difficulty and completion time interaction. We expected an interaction effect between control panel type and task difficulty. Tasks 1 and 2 did not require moving the focus spot at all. So in the eyecon panel the Viewfinder should not be displaced and in the slide bars panel the moveX, moveY and moveZ slides should not be scrolled. Therefore both panels were expected to be quick and easy for these tasks. The advantage of the eyecon panel was expected to emerge only in tasks 3 and 4. Results for accuracy actually revealed such interaction. The results for task completion time did not, because task 1 and 2 did not turn out to be as simple as was expected, which depended strongly on first action choice. Although tasks 1 and 2 did not *require* changing the focus spot, subjects still often did and found themselve lost in space, which was most severe using the slide bars panel.

We are primarily interested in the usability of the eyecon panel, so user difficulties with the bars panel will not be discussed in detail any further. The major drawbacks for the eyeconic panel proved to relate to three seperate issues which we will now adress briefly.

Dragging technique. In this version of the eyecon panel, an icon can only be dragged along the floor by dragging its shadow. The unnaturalness of this technique proved persistent; some subjects repeatedly tried to drag an icon itself horizontally even when they already knew they should drag its shadow. Moreover, if an icon lies exactly on the floor, it obscures its shadow. Fortunately this technique is not intrinsic to the eyecon panel. In response to these observations an alternative version of the panel was implemented. In this version the icon can be dragged along the floor directly. To move the icon further or closer above its shadow a modifier key must be depressed during the dragging. This scheme brings along extra movements (it involves the keyboard or a second mouse button) but will probably prove more natural.

Relating different views. The second issue is inherent in the use of the metaphor, of a person walking around an object (as opposed to turning an object around in your hands). Remember that the control panel shows a static third party perspective in which both viewer and object are represented. So if the room is watched from behind, left in the control panel becomes right in the 3D window. (This also happens when using the slide bars panel.) This extreme example demonstrates that the user must be able to relate the static directions in the panel to the changing directions in the 3D window. Fortunately most subjects succeeded in this quite well.

Cluttering windows. The eyecon control panel inroduces yet another view-like window to the screen. Because too many viewing windows can be cumbersome it would be wise to integrate some of the windows. The control panel intrinsically can not coincide with the 3D view because a viewer can not see herself standing in her own view on the scene. But the control panel could coincide with the ground plan window rather easily.

5 Conclusions

The eyeconic control panel clearly shows considerable improvement in learnability and ease of use (without loss in accuracy) compared with the slide bars panel. Subjects generally rated the eyecon panel higher in ease of use. Observations gave rise to several ideas for further improvement of the eyecon panel such as change of dragging technique and integration with the ground plan window.

Whenever one writes a computer program based on existing library modules it can be very tempting to duplicate the internal organization of parameters directly to the user interface. In general and certainly in our example this can lead to communicational problems. Technical parameters can differ from psychological entities and they can interact in ways that are difficult to predict. A deliberate *change of view* can be necessary to design a more user-oriented organization of parameters.

References

Bier, E. (1990) Snap-dragging in three dimensions. In: Proceedings Workshop on Interactive 3D Graphics. ACM/SIGGRAPH, 183-196.

Chen, M., Mountford, S. J., & Sellen, A. (1988). A study in interactive 3D rotation using 2D control devices. Computer graphics 22, 4, 121-129.

Evans, K. B., Tanner, P.P. & Wein, M. (1981). Tablet based valuators that provide one, two or three degrees of freedom. Computer Graphics, 15, 3, 91-97.

Gardiner, M.M. & Christie, B. (eds.). (1987). Applying cognitive psychology to user-interface design. Chichester: Wiley.

Schneidermann, B. (1991). A taxonomy and rule base for the selection of interaction styles. In: B. Schackel, S. Richardson (eds.) Human factors for informatics Usability, 325-342. Cambridge, UK: Cambridge University Press.

Animated Icons Promote Learning of Their Functions

Alp Tiritoglu[1] and James F. Juola[2]

[1] Department of Design, University of Kansas, Lawrence KS 66045, USA
[2] Department of Psychology, University of Kansas, Lawrence KS 66045, USA

Abstract. In the present research the benefits of animated icons were examined. A subset of static icons was taken from a CAD program and converted into animated icons. Subjects were tested about their understanding of the functions of the icons before and after the animation took place. In addition, a questionnaire was given to assess the subjective opinion of users about their experience. It was found that animated icons have a positive effect on comprehension of icons and the tasks they represent. Finally, some major issues relevant for effective use of animated icons in user interface design are discussed.

Keywords. Icons, animation, graphical user interfaces, CAD user interfaces, animated icons, learning, designing animated icons

1 Introduction

The number and complexity of computer programs are increasing daily. Society has reached a point where its members can find an application for almost every need. However, having the application does not help the users if they cannot understand the program. Most programs require some time to learn to do even a simple task.

Computer Aided Design (CAD) is one area in which many applications have been developed. Since the concept of drawing by hand or using conventional methods is different from using a computer, users have to learn new concepts in drafting with computers. Many users struggle with these programs at the beginning of their learning process. Icons are widely used to make the user interfaces more friendly and self-explanatory. However, there are many cases in which icons do not carry the meaning intended. Animation is one of the solutions to the communication problem that give another dimension to icons.

In the present research the potential benefit of *animated icons* is investigated, as an alternative solution to static icons. An existing CAD application, MicroStation[1] v3.5, is taken as a platform. MicroStation is a 2D and 3D CAD application package, and its user interface is based on Graphical User Interface (GUI) techniques. In MicroStation's user interface, almost every function is attached to an icon. Although some icons in MicroStation are obvious in function, others are abstract on different levels. Since interactive and dynamic programs require constant manipulation, there

[1] MicroStation is a trademark of Integraph, Inc.

is a potential for using animated icons in applications for all types of users to increase learning and comprehension of a system. The present research investigates whether animated icons actually aid people in understanding their functions and accomplishing the task. It also emphasizes principles and possible pitfalls in designing animated icons for user interface design.

2 Method

2.1 Task Analysis and Simulation of Animated Icons

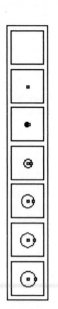

Fig. 1a.
Sequences of
frames that show
'Place Circle
Center' function.

The purpose of our task analysis was to understand how users interact with icons on the MicroStation platform. At this stage the goal was to create the most useful animated icons for the users. Users' actions in activating icons and how they use the related functions were examined iteratively. Sequences of actions; e.g., drawing a circle, were recorded and used in generating animations. People who were experienced in MicroStation were interviewed for possible modifications in order to fine-tune the animations. At different levels of the design process, people from various disciplines were questioned to find out whether the animations made sense to them.

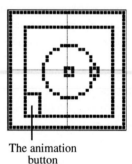

The animation
button

Fig. 1b. A 32 by 32
grid in which the icon
is defined

In the development of animated icons, animations were integrated into the existing static icons. The way users select the icons and how they interact with them was kept the same. However, for animation, a new button was added to the lower-left corner of the icons. (see Fig. 1b) When the animation button was selected, the animation took place in the area in which the icon was defined (32 by 32 pixels). Once the animation was completed, the icon reverted to its original shape. Animations could be viewed as many times as the user needed. This gave the user a chance to watch the animations more than once.

The MicroStation user interface was designed on the basis of direct manipulation techniques, and almost every graphical function is attached to an icon. MicroStation's user interface was simulated by using the HyperCard[2] background feature with active buttons in the foreground. Twenty-four icons were simulated and converted to animated icons. Except for the selected and implemented, all other icons were dimmed to preserve the same global look and feel of MicroStation, and to make the available icons more distinctive.

---

[2] HyperCard is a trademark of Apple Computer, Inc.

2.2 Experiment and Questionnaire

Sixty subjects were divided equally and randomly into control and experimental groups. Each group participated in a two-part experiment. In the first part of the experiment, subjects were asked to look at the 24 static icons on the screen and write down their possible meanings. At this point the subjects of both groups were allowed to look at the screen and individual icons, but they were not allowed to activate any of the icons or related functions. In the second part of the experiment, the control and the experimental groups were allowed to activate static icons and their functions, but only the experimental group were permitted watch the animated icons. Control and experimental groups were given equal opportunities to try the functions on the MicroStation platform. The first part of the experiment was limited to 40 minutes and the second part to 75 minutes.

Subjects were asked to complete a three-part questionnaire: prior, during, and following the experiment. Questions asked prior to the experiment primarily related to the subjects' level of knowledge pertaining to the use of computers and icons. During the first and second part of the experiment, control and experimental groups were asked to describe in writing the meaning of the 24 icons and how they appeared to function during the application. In addition, their verbal comments were noted. Each response of subjects for functions of icons was graded between '0' and '4' with '0' the lowest and '4' the highest grade. Evaluation of answers for the icons took place in five categories: 0: No relation or no explanation at all, 1: There are some implications, but no explanation or wrong explanation, and no methods, 2: The function is understood, but the method is not explained or the method is wrong, 3: The function is understood, but the method is not totally correct, 4: The function is completely understood including the steps needed to be taken to operate it.

Following the experiment both control and experimental groups were asked to complete the third part of the questionnaire, a semantic differential analysis (image profiling) test. The experimental group was also asked to complete an additional questionnaire to evaluate animated icons based on their experience during the experiment.

3 Results

On the basis of the initial questionnaire subjects within each group were divided into non-experienced, beginner, intermediate, and advanced computer users with

Table 1. Beginners, intermediate and advanced groups who are compared using t-test.

	t-Test: Two-Sample							
	Beginners		Intermediate		Advanced		All Groups	
	Control	Experimental	Control	Experimental	Control	Experimental	Control	Experimental
Mean	17.08	44.91	18.03	36.46	33.78	18.96	21.39	36.08
Variance	133.65	207.10	138.94	247.28	783.72	256.81	309.63	295.26
Observations	10	9	13	16	7	5	30	30
df	17		27		9.70		58	
t	-4.67		-3.50		1.06		-3.27	
p	p<0.000		p<0.00		p>0.05		p<0.01	

tosh or other icon-based system experience. For later analysis, the non-experienced and beginner subgroups were combined.

The main performance measures were the written descriptions given for each of the 24 icons by subjects before and after working with the system. The final results and the compairison of groups using t-test are shown in Table 1. Significant differences were found between the improvement scores for the control and experimental groups. Specifically, the experimental group showed a greater gain in accuracy of describing functions. There was no significant difference in the improvement scores for the advanced experimental and control groups. This result was probably due to a subject selection error in advanced control and experimental groups. Therefore the ceiling effects limited the amount of gain made by the advanced subjects in Part 2. Overall,

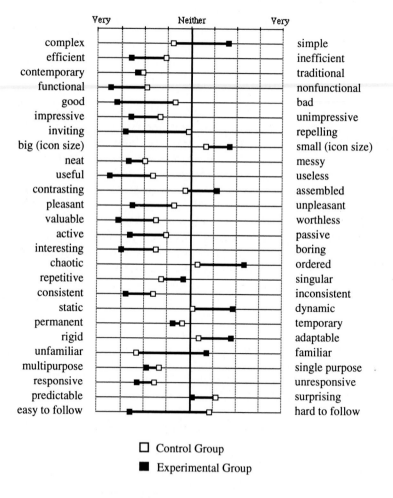

Fig. 2. Semantic Differential Analysis of Control and Experimental Groups

however, the 36% gain shown by the experimental group is highly significantly greater than the 21% gain shown by the control group.

Fig. 2 shows the semantic differential mean scores for the two groups of subjects, which clearly indicate a higher overall impression of the system for the experimental group. These results are supported by the indication of the experimental group expressed in the final questionnaire that they would generally like to have animated icons available in other applications and as help to indicate icons' functions.

4 Discussion

The results showed that the experimental group, which had experience with animated icons, improved 15% more in acquisition of knowledge about icons' functions than did the control group, who had experience with static icons, during a short session in which they used the icons in a CAD environment. It is important to note that all of the animations developed in this research were based on existing static icons. In other words, the starting point in designing animated icons was not a set of novel animated icons, but an existing, established set of static icons. Presumably, if the same icons had been designed as animated icons from the beginning, the increase in understanding would be even more substantial than that shown here.

Association between the symbol in the icons and the objects they refer to is sometimes indirect. For example, in the second part of the experiment some subjects were confused by the shape given to "move" or "copy" icons. These icons have rectangular shapes, however their functions are capable of moving or copying any entities on the screen. Therefore, novice users thought that specific icons could work only with rectangularly shaped objects. This is a good example of poor mapping, and it should be anticipated at the outset, namely at the design stage of the system. We can see the same problem with "Fence" functions in which the iconic representations of the functions make sense only after those functions have been learned. The intention of the icons should be the other way around. The user should be able to understand what the icons stand for prior to using their functions.

Some icons require prior operations or objects (e.g. move, copy, or fence operations). In other words, the user is supposed to use the functions to change the state of an existing object. Such icons usually do not carry this information at all. Animation can be a solution to this problem by indicating that prior operations or objects are required for specific icons. Another way to deal with this problem is to turn off the functions that cannot be used (e.g., dimmed icons, or faded icons).

In terms of subjective opinion, from the post experiment questionnaire for the experimental group showed that nearly all subjects indicated that animated icons were better for explaining system functions than static icons. Most subjects also agreed that even though an icon, in this case an animated icon, presents a functions clearly, sometimes the user is still not entirely satisfied unless he/she tries the function.

Help features, such as animated icons, do not necessarily improve understanding of the system for advanced users. However, animated icons could be used as reminders if the applications involve remembering many functions as in MicroStation.

The semantic differential analysis gives us a concise view of subjects' personal opinions. From the profile (see Fig. 2) we can see that subjects think animated icons feel simpler to use than static icons. In this example, animated icons clearly have a more positive effect on users than static icons.

4.1 Cognitive Aspects

Animated icons should tend to facilitate visualizing complexity and conceiving tasks and problems in visual terms. Visualization is an important concept in user interface design. Visualizing what is happening facilitates learning and helps in constructing a mental model of the system.

Wertheimer (1959) pointed out that the same problem can be solved more easily by restructuring a figure, sometimes by including motion. Motion does not bring a third dimension, however it helps to visualize how things are related to each other and how they interact with each other successively in space and with time. Many problems can be solved by manipulating images. Some recent studies indicate that the ability to manipulate spatial information can make human-computer interaction tasks easier to perform (Eberts, 1989). Eberts found that showing how tasks are performed with computer graphics was beneficial when the subjects were later asked to solve problems when the graphics were not available.

Memory is an important factor in the design process, because it is a critical limiting factor in human information-processing. In a CAD application such as MicroStation, the number of functions and how they are performed are almost impossible to remember unless the user has years of experience. Animation is a quick way to remember and refresh the memory through visualization. In general, recall is better if the context of remembering fits the learning context of memorization.

Consistency is another important factor in learning. We know that it is easier to recognize patterns in consistent environments. Regardless of where the animations are used, in animated icons or in animated help screens, they should be consistent in terms of presenting common clues. Users could then determine some likely features when they see new animations. It appears that learning is generally under the control of the subject. However, the way information is organized is a key factor in learning. Information organization is usually based on order, classification, or semantic relations among entities. Animated icons facilitate the learning process by giving semantically organized information about the functions and the syntax of their use. In addition, animations aid in seeing the whole picture of the concept presented with less cognitive load than many other forms of communication media.

Abstract icons require more time to learn than pragmatic icons, such as rotating an entity vs. drawing a rectangle. Abstract icons and related functions seem to be equally difficult for both experienced and novice users. During the first part of the experiment, it was observed that regardless of their experience level, all subjects had the same difficulties in understanding certain abstract icons; e.g., fence manipulations. After viewing the animation, there was a significant increase in comprehension of abstract icons. However, animation does not change the fact that abstract functions require more trial-and-error in order to be understood and learned completely as opposed to empirical functions.

Animated icons appear to be helpful in constructing a mental model of the system for the users. However, animated icons can also be misleading due to the fact that they are usually simplified to be more understandable. Therefore, in designing animated icons, the designer should consider the fact that the scenario chosen for the animation has a direct impact on users' mental models of the system.

4.2 The Design of Static and Animated Icons

There are some major issues that the designer should keep in mind to create successful and meaningful icons. Some of these issues are also valid for animated icons.

Static icons should be designed as clearly as possible so that the user does not have to learn the meaning of the icon from other sources such as on-line help or manuals. Although establishing a direct map between the real world and an icon is difficult, it plays an important role in the success of icons. Symbols are also used in icon design, but they require an initial learning procedure. Sutcliffe (1989) stated that an absolute boundary between symbols and icons is illusory because as soon as a symbol's meaning has been learned it will become a meaningful image.

The size of icons is another important issue in designing effective icons. According to Sutcliffe (1989) simple icons can be effective in dimensions of 0.5 cm. square and complex icons can be successful in 1.0 cm. square. Sutcliffe (1989) noted that giving a clear outline is also important to help visual discrimination.

In any system icons should have consistent graphical characteristics such as line thickness, patterns, and colors. In addition, graphical elements distinguishing one icon from other icons must be clear to the user (Brown, 1988).

Animated icons introduce new issues to icon design such as scenario development, visualization and more important, motion. Baecker and Small (1990) define animation as follows: "Animation is not the art of DRAWINGS-that-move but the art of MOVEMENTS-that-are-drawn. What happens between each frame is more important than what exists on each frame. Animation is therefore the art of manipulating the invisible interstices that lie between frames. The interstices are the bones, flesh, and blood of the movie, what is on each frame, not merely the clothing." (Baecker and Small, 1990, p. 251). Developing a scenario for icons is directly related to icon mapping in time. First, icons have to be designed as part of the animation, not as a separate icon that follows an animation. Second, besides making functions clear, animation is capable of increasing the information represented and showing the necessary steps to be taken to activate their related functions. Therefore, task analysis is necessary to extract the points and steps for each function. Animation should be kept in simple form. There are two main reasons for this: first, complex animation requires significant computer power, and second, simple forms of animation can be more effective in terms of learning. The following steps are key factors in developing a scenario in animated icons:
- analysis of task domain
- identification of the functions
- analysis of basic characteristic of the functions
- analysis of steps to be taken to execute the functions
- analysis of integration of the functions with respect to the system

5 Conclusion and Future Research

The present research examined animated icons in the context of an educational tool, a tutorial, a help utility, or a reminder for complex functions. The results indicate that there is a significant potential in using animated icons in user interface design, not only for operating system level user interfaces or CAD applications but also for any product that may use animated icons (e.g., audio systems, VCRs, copy machines, and cameras).

It should be noted that all the animated icons were presented in a CAD environment. Therefore the results obtained from this research generalize primarily on how users interact with animated icons in an environment in which domain specific knowledge is required. We may assume that if animated icons help users who are not literate about the domain, they would definitely help those who have domain-specific knowledge. This assumption suggests that animated icons could be used as a tutoring tool to teach the syntax of an application for advanced users.

In general, icons are two-dimensional pictures. In recent user interface systems, a pseudo third dimension has been used in many icons (i.e., usually a shading around the icon, e.g., buttons, switches). The pseudo third-dimension mostly helps to make representational icons more realistic. However, a real three-dimensional icon has not yet been created. We have no idea what kind of results we may expect if we create an environment that uses real three-dimensional icons for user-computer interaction. It seems that virtual reality is one field in which three-dimensional icons can be used experimentally. Tools and functions would become more realistic than their two-dimensional representations. In this case, the users would perhaps hold the icons, change their parameters (object-oriented icons; e.g., an eraser icon would erase part of a raster image but also the same eraser icon would delete an entity if it is used in vector-based image).

If we include a third dimension and motion into icons, then we should question the term "icon." In this case, we may leave icons in their two-dimensional environment and call our new tools "*idols*".

References

Baecker, Ronald., Small, Ian. (1990) Animation at the Interface. In: Brenda Laurel (ed.) The Art of Human-Computer Interface Design. 251-267.: Addison-Wesley

Brown, C. Marlin "Lin". (1988) Human-Computer Interface Design Guidelines.: Ablex Publishing

Eberts, Ray E., Eberts Cindelyn G. (1989) Four Approaches to Human-Computer Interaction. In: Hancock, P.A., Chignell (eds.) Intelligent Interfaces. 69-127.:Elsevier

Sutcliffe, Alistair. (1989) User Psychology. Human-Computer Interface Design. 7-48.: Springer

Wertheimer, Max. (1959) Productive Thinking. New York: Harper

Generating Natural Language in an Immersive Language Learning System

Dan Tufis[1], Henry Hamburger[2], Raza Hashim[2] and Jiqian Pan[2]

[1] Center for Research on Machine Learning and Language Processing, Romanian
   Academy, Calea Victoriei 125, Ro71102, Bucharest 1, Romania
[2] Dept. of Computer Science, George Mason University, Fairfax, VA 22030 USA

Abstract. Our computer-based conversational partner is designed to provide practice for beginning foreign language students. The conversations take place in realistic situations that are expressed both visually and verbally, so that the student can see what he/she is talking about. Besides clarifying meaning, this situational immersion also insures contextual appropriateness. Natural language generation plays a crucial role in such a system, especially for interacting with a beginner, since clearly the learner must first be exposed to the words and constructions of the new language before being expected to produce them. In this paper we therefore stress generation, especially its so-called strategic aspects, in relation to the situations in which the student is immersed. Although developed for foreign language practice, the approach applies to other learning environments, with language generation serving an interface role.

Keywords. ICALL, language immersion, knowledge representation, interlingua,natural language generation

1 Overview: Language Tutoring and Language Generation

This paper describes the techniques and crucial role of natural language generation - in particular its high-level aspects - in a foreign language learning and tutoring system that is based on conversation in meaningful situations. Such a learning environment is motivated by important trends in foreign language pedagogy; see Richards and Rodgers (1986). The system engages the student in tightly integrated linguistic and graphical two-medium communication. (On these two media, see Cohen, 1991). For this reason and because the conversation is grounded in realistic situations represented in coherent, realistically structured domains (microworlds), we say that the system is immersive: the student is immersed in a situation.

The objectives, along with the rationale, significance and organization of the system, are presented at greater length by Hamburger and Hashim (1992). Maney (1993) presents a more detailed justification and describes FLUENT-1, a working system in which situations are presented via realistic interactive graphics and are discussed in the target language using a pattern-matching approach to natural language processing. FLUENT-2, major portions of which have been built, uses tools of artificial intelligence to achieve greater flexibility in several aspects of the system, including the generative approach to dialog management described in this paper. The new system will thereby dramatically enhance the linguistic range of the tutor, in comparison to the completed FLUENT-1 prototype. Both systems attempt to resolve the tension between educational and conversational continuity delineated in Hamburger and Maney (1991). Briefly put, the two continuities mean that the system must say things that make sense in the situational context yet do not violate the precept that new linguistic material should be introduced gradually, according to a pedagogically sound syllabus.

FLUENT-2, implemented in MCL2 (Macintosh Common Lisp with objects), is designed to communicate both graphically and linguistically, and in both directions between the tutor and the student. However, here we will address only the system's generation of language. Language generation plays an especially crucial role for interacting with a beginner, since clearly the learner must first be exposed to the words and constructions of the new language before being expected to produce them. Natural language generation is widely viewed as a multi-level process. Here we distinguish two levels: deciding on the message to be conveyed to the listener and actually producing it. These two levels are sometimes called the strategic and tactical levels of generation. More often than not, the two levels use different representations, placing more emphasis on domain and language aspects respectively.

Strategic generation is accomplished principally by the view processor. This module operates on domain knowledge representations - including plans, actions, objects, their properties, classes and their inheritance hierarchies - to produce a language-independent representation of the output sentence. The view processor operates on views, which are abstractions of relevant things to say, from various viewpoints. In the implementation, views must include process information about how to extract situational information from the current action and microworld state. The tutorial strategy component of the system must choose a view, reflecting an aspect of the current situation, to guide what it says. The view-processor creates a frame-style structure that is the knowledge representation (KR) of the forthcoming sentence from the viewpoint of the tutor. The KR reflects both the situation and the chosen view. The view may prescribe that the action itself be mentioned, or its role in a plan or the resulting state. These and some other broad categories of views have several members each. We have identified over 40 candidate views and implemented several of them by extracting and manipulating structural information from such places as the various slots of an instantiated action rule or its arguments, which are objects in the current microworld. Some views are at the level of an object, others at the level of an event, and some put events into a still broader perspective with respect to other events or time. It is up to the tutorial strategy module - or tutor - to select a view that both makes sense in the situation and will yield linguistic output that is comprehensible to the student. The tutorial strategy module is discussed in Hamburger (1993).

Tactical generation is handled by the generation side of the natural language software of the Athena Language Learning Project or ALLP (Felshin, 1993). The ALLP generator operates on a linguistically oriented semantic representation called interlingua (IL) to produce a sentence, phrase or paragraph in any of several natural languages. There is actually another phase, between the two just described, that converts the language-independent KR structure produced by the view processor to the corresponding quasi-language-independent IL structure. This KR-to-IL conversion is the job of the KRIL module.

The ALLP system maintains some focus information and, if provided with appropriate information, takes care of several discourse phenomena. IL structures (ILSs) are not, however, as abstract and language independent as representations in lexical cognitive structures (Jackendoff, 1990). For instance, although "I like Mary" and "Me gusta Maria" are realizations of the same lexical cognitive structures, they have different ILSs. An ILS also differs considerably from the relatively concise domain-oriented KR, since the ILS contains structure relating to language in general and also to the particular language currently in use. In summary, the path from action to language takes place in three steps: formulation proper linguistic realization.

2 From Action to Language

Essential to our approach to carrying on a conversation about a dynamic situation of a language-independent microworld-oriented KR; conversion to IL; and the is the ability to reformulate a given microworld entity into something to say. Actions are an especially useful basis for linguistic outputs, so we focus on them. In some cases, the tutor's linguistic move is to comment on the action just carried out in the microworld by either the student or by the tutor, leading to a description of the action itself or how it changes something. Alternatively, having chosen a potential action, the tutor may tell the student to do it, or ask the student something about it. Yet another class of linguistic moves is that in which the tutor produces a follow-up reaction to a student response. If, for example, the student's graphical move is unresponsive to the preceding command, the tutor may formulate a statement involving two actions - contrasting the actual to the expected one. Where two actions are involved, as in the preceding example of an action-based command and the graphical response, it must be possible to compare the meanings of the two. Even though one of the actions shows up outwardly in language while the other has arisen from a graphical move, the comparison must take place within a single representation system, specifically that of the microworld. To be sure to have the needed structures available, we maintain a history list of all the actions for both tutor and student, not only those that occur but also the potential ones that are used for producing linguistic output. Comparing the two actions is not merely a matter of an equality test, since the action commanded may be less specific than a suitable response. Moreover, if the tutor has told the student to execute a plan rather than an action, the job of evaluating the responsiveness of the student's next action becomes significantly more difficult, since many kinds of actions may advance the plan, given that it is not, in general, merely an inflexible linear sequence of actions.

The microworld-oriented representation - the KR - that the view processor builds has two parts, WHAT-TO-SAY and HOW-TO-SAY, corresponding to the distinction between the basic meaning of an instruction, question or comment and the specific way of linguistically realizing it. More specifically, WHAT-TO-SAY includes the objects, events, states, and relationships that are to be linguistically realized, whereas HOW-TO-SAY includes tense, aspect, mood, voice, reference definiteness, and so on.

After the view processor has determined what to say and how to say it, the KRIL module (which is not yet fully implemented) must translate from these domain KR structures into IL structures. It is important that this translation produce IL structures that will yield smooth natural language output. For instance, the IL should specify the appropriate use of pronouns for repeated reference to the same object in the same sentence or for anaphoric reference to a previous clause, sentence or even graphic move; e.g., "You can't do *that*."

The mapping from KR to IL relies heavily on information provided by the dictionary of the language in use. In many cases, a KR entity is mapped to its corresponding lexical entry in the current dictionary. This is the case for object classes, property values, action types and relations. Note, however, that an individual object is first mapped into the class it belongs to and then differentiated, as necessary, by properties that distinguish it from other members of the class. From the lexical entry, the KRIL module extracts the information it needs to build IL fragments which are further integrated into the final IL structure. This lexical information, which is especially important in the case of verbs, includes such things as thematic structures, selectional restrictions and prepositional attachment requirements. Since the process of building an ILS is driven by this kind of language-specific lexical data, the resulting ILS is partially language-specific. Nevertheless, it is important to note that the process itself is language-independent at the level of code.

3 Generation Criteria at the Dialog Level

Merely specifying the action on which it is based does not determine the tutor's linguistic output. We have already noted the variety afforded by views, and this section will show how the choice is further enriched by interaction types and syntactic variants.

Interaction Types. The interaction type specifies (i) an assignment of roles in the dialog for the tutor and the student, as themselves or possibly as microworld characters, (ii) which one of them initiates the interaction; (iii) whether each particular turn consists of action or language, and (iv) for each linguistic turn, whether it is a command, question, answer, comment, suggestion or description. Eight simple two-move interaction types arise just from the fact that either the tutor or student can initiate the move sequence with an action, command, question or statement (followed by an appropriate response). Particularly relevant to language generation are the interaction types we call Movecaster, in which the student carries out any action and the tutor comments on it; Commander in which the student acts in response to a command; and Quizmaster, in which the tutor poses a question.

The choice of interaction type is one of the crucial decisions by the tutorial strategy module, since it has powerful effects on the level of difficulty for the student. Perhaps most crucial in this regard is whether the interaction type requires the student to engage in the production of language; just comprehend it to give an appropriate action, or, least difficult, simply acknowledge exposure to a presentation. The various interaction types also provide important variations in sentence structure by requiring declaratives, imperatives and questions, thereby enhancing language experience and also affecting difficulty. The interaction type also influences the values chosen for some surface generation parameters, including tense, mood, aspect, voice and person. Moreover, the choice of interaction type affects which information-level views are appropriate, thereby indirectly giving the interaction type further impact. Additional dialog factors that are not controlled by the interaction type include whether a request is direct or indirect, formal or informal, specific or generic, intensional or extensional.

Closely related to the interaction types are extensions of them that deal with follow-up language suitable for the learning and tutoring situation. This additional kind of dialog factor consists of what we call "evaluative continuation types," which let the tutor approve ("Right!"), reject or correct a student's graphic move ("No! I told you to pick up the red book not the blue one"), or assist a student's linguistic move. An example of such assistance that is implemented in FLUENT-1 can occur when the tutor asks a Wh-question that requires a linguistic response. If the student is unable to respond, the tutor can convert the question to multiple choice format. More such continuations and other interaction types are under development, as well as work allowing for the possibility of breaks for conversational repair.

Finally, note that by their nature interaction types play a key role in dialog management by making successive turns coherent. For example, using a Commander interaction type means that after a command is given the system goes on to process the right general kind of response to commands, namely a student action. It does this by accepting and interpreting mouse movements and mouse button events. At the next higher level of dialog organization, the interactions themselves should also form a coherent succession. To achieve this, we have a method of defining tutorial schemas built out of interaction types and plans. For example it is possible to define a tutorial schema that calls for executing a plan with accompanying comments from the tutor and then, in effect, giving the student step by step instructions to execute that plan again with different objects.

Language Structure. Language structure variations are important to FLUENT both for coverage of the language and to make the dialog as colloquial as possible. Choices of this kind influence where the microworld operator (a predicate or relation) and its arguments turn up in the phrase structure of the resulting sentence. Many of these devices are valid only for specific languages and/or require particular verb case-frames. In simple sentences, the operator typically corresponds to the main verb, possibly affected by a preposition; note, for example, the microworld equivalence of "The cup contains juice" and "There is juice in the cup." Depending on the language, the operator may in some cases be realized as a verb, a verb plus a particle, or verbal locution; e.g.,"take advantage," "avoir beau." Which possibilities are allowed depends on the structures available in a particular language and the particular lexical items, especially verbs, that are permitted in those structures. The structural variations controlled at this level include some of the so-called movement phenomena such as topicalization and the choice between active and passive voice, as well as the use of semantically related verbs like "buy" and "sell" that denote the same action but with arguments permuted.

Of particular utility to the tutor for adjusting the level of difficulty are language maneuvers that permit the inclusion or omission of some of the arguments, for example, ergative constructions ("the cup broke" vs. "you broke the cup"), truncated passives ("the water was turned on" vs "the water was turned on by the girl") causatives ("someone fed the baby" vs. "the baby ate") and the inclusion or omission of various kinds of optional phrases. Depending on the interaction type and on evaluative continuation, a decision might be made on producing contrastive and/or elliptic phrases ("The cup not the pot!").

Given that a particular object is to be referred to, various aspects of language can work to identify it uniquely. If it is the only instance of its type, its class name suffices, e.g., "the cup." This is also the case if it is uniquely prominent in some way, by virtue of mention or action. If the set of objects in the class exceeds one, it may be possible to find one or more properties to use for modification to get a set with only one element or only one prominent element, e.g., "the gray cup" meaning the only one at all or the only one on a tray being offered. Properties can be immutable, as in the case of color, but need not be, and this can have language consequence; e.g., the "ser"/"estar" distinction in Spanish. A temporary property may be current or historical, e.g., "the cup on the table" vs "the cup that you used to water the plant."

A property may pertain only to the object itself or can relate it to another object, by such relationships as location, possession, possessor and function: "the cup on the table", "the person with the coffee pot", "the woman's chair", "the key to the safe." Abstract relationships are also possible, including order, comparison and exclusion: "the second cup (from the left)," "the bigger cup," and "the other cup" or "the cup not on the table." Ordinals and superlatives necessarily reduce set size to one, on their usual interpretations, which affects their position within the noun phrase (see Crain and Hamburger, 1992).

The various ways of restricting the extension of a noun's class by applying modifiers need not yield just a single entity, but may instead yield a set of cardinality two or more. Consider the various determiners and quantifiers that are possible in this case in English. One can use "a" to refer to an arbitrary member of the set, "some" (or "some of the") with the noun pluralized to refer to any proper subset of cardinality greater than one (so that the original set must have had at least three elements), or "the" (or "all the" or "all of the") with plural to refer to the entire set. "Each" or "every" can be used with the singular for roughly the same effect. In addition, "none of the" with plural or "no" with singular or plural can deny an attribute for each of three or more elements, and similarly for "neither (of the)" with two elements. Additional phenomena brought into play for collectivities as opposed to individuals are complementary subsets ("the other," "the rest of the"), cardinal numbers, and graduated quantification for both numerosity and quantity ("few," "many," "most," etc.). Complementarity can be used with each of the others. One can have, for example, "many other," "three other" or "all the other" preceding a noun and its modifiers. It seems then, that "other" acts semantically like a restrictor, despite its syntactic peculiarities. Finally, note that nouns denoting substances like "water" (which are mass nouns in some languages) fit with some of these constructions, including "some," "other" and "all."

4 Generation Criteria at the Microworld Level

At the microworld or domain level, there are several decisions to be made that together we refer to as view selection. Views are abstractions of what the tutor can say. They have to do with an action itself and other things in the microworld that are related to it, including objects, plans and possibly time, as well as certain aspects of the dialog.

The educational purpose of views is to introduce a wide range of language aspects. In addition, to the extent that views (like microworlds and interaction types) differ in difficulty, they provide another tool to let the tutor achieve a language output that is of educational benefit for the current student. Not only are some views more difficult than others, but also the varying of views is challenging. It is important to note, though, that while adding views leads to greater conversational flexibility, this very flexibility may also cause ambiguity about what is being said. To avoid letting this undermine the FLUENT immersion strategy, there must be careful control of the use of views and/or parallel development of visual communication of the corresponding ideas, so that the student has some basis for knowing what view is in use.

Since there are many views, it will help to organize them into categories. To do so, note that in response to some particular action, the tutor can comment on the action itself, the resulting state, or on a subplan, say the one that has just been completed or the one that can now commence. Thus there are action views, state views and plan views.

The two principal inputs to the view component are the current view, selected by the tutorial strategy module, and the current event, in the form of a fully instantiated action rule. In the case of plan views, it must also be possible to make reference to the current plan. It may seem obvious that state views need access to the objects and their properties, but state views also need to know what the current action is, so that the system can talk not about arbitrary objects but about those that have been actively involved in what is going on.

The most directly relevant slots of the action rule for view processing are its header and the slot that holds its knowledge updates. The header tells the nature of the action and the objects involved. The knowledge updates are needed, like the action itself, for relevance: not only should the tutor talk about the objects that are changing, but also it should be talking about what the changes are.

The output of the view component is a pair of frames, in a simple knowledge representation language, that contain essentially all the information necessary to determine the tutor's language output. This output is passed to the KRIL component for translation to the interlingua structure upon which the NLG system operates to give the actual sentence or phrase in the current language.

The most straightforward of the action views is one that simply presents an action without reference to context, moreover choosing the most prominent action. In Movecaster, this is the action that the student has just carried out. In

Commander, the action is one chosen by the tutor. Although the choice of action may be based on a plan, the plan is not mentioned in this view. The interaction type determines the tense, mood and aspect. Commander, of course, takes the imperative, while Movecaster uses a (recent) past (e.g., "Elle vient de ramasser la tasse").

Events of the kind described above are associated with action rules in the microworld. We distinguish these conceptual level actions from the more primitive actions that are carried out using the mouse. These latter actions, though ordinarily too fine-grained to warrant attention in the conversation, are distinguishable at the level of the interface and might be discussed if the student were to give evidence of misunderstanding the interface. In this case the student should be addressed as a user of the computer, not as a character in the microworld. Examples here might be "Move the hand to the cup." or "Press down the mouse button."

One may also wish to speak about the non-occurrence of a possible action. The action might be one that was anticipated, perhaps because of being next in a plan, in which case it can (but need not) be part of a more complex plan view. Other non-occurring events can be constructed in relation to the action that did occur by using the same operator with another argument (see the discussion of "other" under objects, above). These views seem most appropriate when used in combination with others. An example of combining with the action that did occur is, in Movecaster, "He did not pick up the spoon. He picked up the cup." or more flowingly, "He picked up the cup, not the spoon." A Commander example that contrasts actions rather than objects is "Do not put down the cup. Use it to get some water." On the usefulness of such commands, see Di Eugenio (1993).

Commenting on an action at various relative times or in relation to the time of surrounding events gives rise to temporal views as well. Among state views, a view can involve referring only to the object acted upon or can result in commenting on a collectivity of objects sharing its type, and so on. It is even possible to have "rejection views" for dealing with failed and impermissible actions in Movecaster. Discussing disallowed and discouraged actions should be helpful for correcting misperceptions when tutoring non-linguistic subject matter (Hamburger et al., 1993).

5 Concluding Remarks

We are creating a two-medium conversational system for foreign language learning, drawing upon techniques of language pedagogy to motivate aspects of the design, and upon techniques of artificial intelligence for flexibility in the implementation. We have found useful the constructs described herein, including action rules, views, interaction types, and tutorial schemas. The approach may lead to interfaces for learning environments with subject matter other than language.

Acknowledgement This work is supported by grant IRI-9020711 from the U.S. National Science Foundation.

References

Cohen, P. R. (1991) The role of natural language in a multimodal interface. Menlo Park, CA: SRI International Technical Note 514.

Crain, S. and Hamburger, H. (1992) Semantics, knowledge and NP modification. In Levine, R. (Ed.) Formal Grammar: Theory and Implementation. Oxford: Oxford University Press.

Di Eugenio, D. (1993) Speakers' intentions and beliefs in negative imperatives. In Rambow, O. (Ed.) Proceedings of the Association for Computational Linguistics Workshop on Intentionality and Structure in Discourse Relations. Columbus, Ohio, June 20.

Felshin, S. (1993) A Guide to the Athena Language Learning Project Natural Language Processing System. Cambridge, MA: Massachusetts Institute of Technology.

Hamburger, H. (1993) Structuring Two-Medium Dialog for Language Learning. Army Research Institute: Workshop on Advanced Technologies for Language Learning. Washington, April 20-22. To appear in Holland, M., Kaplan, J. and Sams, M. (Eds.) Intelligent Language Tutors: Balancing Theory and Technology. Hillsdale, NJ: Lawrence Erlbaum Associates.

Hamburger, H., Tufis, D. and Hashim, R. (1993) Structuring two-medium dialog for learning language and other things. In Rambow, O. (Ed.) Proceedings of the Association for Computational Linguistics Workshop on Intentionality and Structure in Discourse Relations. Columbus, Ohio, June 20.

Hamburger, H. and Hashim, R. (1992) Foreign language tutoring and learning environment. In Swartz, M. L. and Yazdani, M. (Eds.) Intelligent Tutoring Systems for Foreign Language Learning. NATO ASI Series F, Vol. 80, pp.201-218. Berlin: Springer-Verlag.

Hamburger, H. and Maney, T. (1991) Twofold continuity in language learning. Computer-Assisted Language Learning, 4, 2, 81-92.

Jackendoff, R. S. (1990) Semantic Structures. Cambridge: MIT Press.

Maney, T. (1993) The FLUENT-1 Foreign Language Tutoring System. Doctor of Arts project, George Mason University, Fairfax, VA.

Richards, T.C. and Rodgers, T.S. (1986) Approaches and Methods in Language Teaching. Cambridge: Cambridge University Press.

Part 3

Artificial Intelligence, Software and Design Techniques

Artificial Intelligence, Software and Design Techniques

Introduction

The papers presented in this section follow three themes: The role of social interaction between agents; the role of dialogue in learning and problem solving; the use of visual display in programming and knowledge elicitation.

The papers by Brainov and Connah both discuss the importance of the social interaction of agents and both consider how the interaction between agents can be achieved. Brainov's solution is in the tradition of distributed AI and his system is implemented using a blackboard architecture and contract net protocols. Connah, on the other hand, treats cooperation and other social issues in the framework of situated agents. It is interesting that when conflicts arise because of the conflicting desires of students in Brainov's model, the solution which he proposes includes strictly social remedies such as the formation of cooperative or competitive groups of students. This is in sharp contrast to the rather mechanical solutions that are usually proposed for arbitration in this kind of situation. Focus of attention is also seen as being a central issue by both Brainov and Connah.

Both Ragnemalm and Mikulecký use dialogue to provide intelligent assistance for the user in his or her interaction with a complex system. In Ragnemalm's case the dialogue is with a learning companion which helps the user to use a simulator of an industrial process. The dialogue described by Mikulecký is with the front end of an expert system. In both cases the ability to provide explanations is important and Mikulecký places particular stress upon the active role of the computer in the dialogue. Chmyr and Pilipenko propose formal models to describe instructional dialogues.

Singer and Soubie discuss the problem of acquiring non-verbal expertise, i.e., in their case the expertise required to understand pictures or sequences of pictures in the context of a game (rugby football). They also describe a language to elicit visual knowledge to develop a knowledge-based system that can analyze symbolic translations of video sequences of the game so that tactical improvements can be suggested.

Kasiński points out the difficulty of programming robots, using conventional robot programming languages, to perform complex micro-manipulation or to operate in an unusual environment. The solution he proposes is a simulation method in which the robot is programmed by the user who can see its simulated operation and the action with the environment. One of the difficulties of the approach is to generate a sufficiently realistic model of the robot's world. In this work Kasiński takes a rather broad view of what constitutes a robot and so any results from the work should have a correspondingly wide application.

Cooperative Problem Solving as a Basis for Computer Assisted Learning

Sviatoslav Brainov

Institute of Mathematics, Acad. G. Bonchev str. bl.8, Sofia 1113, Bulgaria

Abstract. In this paper we present a new approach for computer assisted learning. This approach incorporates features of intelligent tutoring systems and distributed problem solving. It has been designed to permit multiperson-multimachine interaction and to stimulate a social dimension in the learning activity of the students. A framework called DEE (Distributed Educational Environment) that supports multiagent learning activity on the basis of cooperative problem solving is described. The DEE is organized as a network of autonomous problem solvers.

Keywords. Computer assisted learning, distributed problem solving, cooperation, task allocation, conflict resolution, blackboard-based systems

1 Introduction

The proliferation of computer networks and the recognition that much human activity involves groups of people have provoked interest in distributed problem solving. One of the main approaches in distributed problem solving is person-machine coordination. This approach provides a useful means for managing a collection of people and machines working together in a coordinated and cooperative way. Within this approach research in distributed problem solving has a great impact in the area of computer assisted learning. The currently accepted paradigm in the computer assisted learning of one (student)-to-one (computer) interaction may be improved by absorbing some ideas from multiagent interaction theory.

In this paper we present a framework called DEE (Distributed Educational Environment) that supports multiagent learning activity on the basis of cooperative problem solving. The DEE is organized as a network of autonomous problem solvers. Students may participate in the network by one of the existing nodes. The DEE may be considered as a departure from the conventional one-to-one teaching model to one that engages many learners and teachers. In our opinion the process of learning as a coordinated multiagent activity more directly reflects the nature of human learning.

The main intention behind the DEE is to support the social dimension in the learning activity of the students. Interaction between the students participating in the network may stimulate their motivation. Since cooperation is an integral part of social interaction [1], a group of students may achieve more by working together than by working alone. The DEE allows the students to communicate between each other, to form groups of interests, to pursue a goal by common efforts and so on. In such a way different student's viewpoints may be analyzed and a common cognitive space may be constructed. The ability of the DEE to coordinate different users resembles participant systems [2] to a great extent. In contrast to conventional participant systems, the DEE has its own problem solving abilities and domain expertise.

One of the major requirements on educational systems is on their ability to adapt. In computer assisted learning systems the only way to obtain the adaptation abilities is by using and developing the user model. In the DEE, adaptation abilities reside in the multiagent organization which may be changed dynamically in the course of teaching. Repeatedly changing needs of the students may be met in the DEE by dynamically rearranging the problem solving structure, the structure of roles and priorities.

One of the major difficulties which arises when using a conventional educational system is connected with resource limitations. Individual computational agents have bounded rationality, bounded resources for problem solving and bounded domain and didactic expertise. The primary contribution of the DEE is that it makes it possible to combine the resources of different intelligent nodes.

Another significant problem that often arises in computer assisted learning is the incompatibility between the computer knowledge representation and the students' mental models. Discrepancies in conceptual models often make it difficult for the students to follow the computer guidance. The DEE permits different knowledge representation schemes and knowledge perspectives. This makes it possible for the system to capture non-trivial solution paths and exhibit more extensive diagnostic policies. The architecture of the DEE fits the open-systems model [6]. Open systems have no fixed boundaries and are easily extendible with new knowledge bases or intelligent agents.

The remainder of this paper commences with a description of the architecture of the DEE. We then discuss the organization of communications. Finally, we summarize our approach and propose some open problems.

2 Distributed Educational Environment

The DEE is organized as a network of autonomous intelligent nodes. The distribution can arise because of spatial distance, deductive difference or semantical distance. Each student may participate in the network by means of particular nodes supplemented with teaching abilities and didactic expertise. These nodes are called 'tutors'. Out of the network context, the tutor node may be considered as a single intelligent tutoring system [10]. Besides the tutor nodes the network may include other types of nodes: problem experts, teaching experts and so on.

The interface between the network and the student is realized through the tutor node. Because of bounded resources and bounded rationality this node is not able to deal effectively with all the problems to be solved. It is more reasonable to use the knowledge and problem solving skills of multiple nodes, each of which handles some part of the total problem. In the case of functional and knowledge specialization among the nodes this approach guarantees the better use of network resources. In the DEE the initial task allocation is done by the tutor node. After that each node manages its activity on its own, allocating subproblems of the original problem to other nodes.

Each node in the network has an extended blackboard-based architecture [4,5]. The node blackboard is intended to contain only the dynamically local context of computations. The global context of the current situation is maintained by global blackboards associated with each student. The student blackboard is divided into two areas. The first one, called the student area, represents student's belief model. Belief changes occur as implications of some student or node action. The second area, called the network area, contains network goals, partial solutions, current hypotheses, plans and so on. All the nodes are able to obtain and modify information from the network area.

Belief revision in the student area is managed by the tutor node associated with the student. The student may exchange messages with other students by communicating with their tutor nodes. After such communication the tutor nodes are responsible for the subsequent belief revision in the student areas.

Besides monitoring the student area the tutor node is also responsible for the monitoring of the network area in the student blackboard. All the read and write data-access requests from the other nodes are handled by the tutor node. Since the different nodes are not guaranteed to modify the blackboard uninterruptedly, the tutor node has to ensure the syntactic and the semantic integrity of the blackboard information. This integrity is achieved by supplementary labels for each blackboard element denoting the nodes the element is associated with. As an example, the plans in the network area are labelled with the addresses of the nodes executing them, the hypotheses are labelled with the addresses of the nodes proposing them and so on. If some modification in the blackboard is made all the nodes it involves are informed by the tutor node. In such a way redundant work is avoided and the node processing power is concentrated in more promising solution paths. Another advantage of such a labelling mechanism is that it provides the network with a global view of the current situation. Given such a global view, many conflicts between the nodes may be avoided and better distribution of the processing load may be achieved.

Plan synchronization is carried out by the tutor node. Since the plans of different nodes are connected by temporal and spatial resources and causal relations, interaction between the plans must be controlled. When incompatibility between the plans occurs the tutor node may postpone some plan execution or reallocate the task of replanning to another node. After the modification of the blackboard plans the nodes executing these plans must rearrange their activity according to the modifications. In such a way the tutor node may not only keep a watch over the activity in the network but control this activity. The central role the tutor node plays is relative to its student blackboard. There may be other tutor nodes and other students in the network. In this case all the tutor nodes have the same authority and conflicts between them must be resolved by negotiations [9].

3 Communication Protocol and Internode Interaction

A convenient method for internode communication is the contract net protocol [3,11]. It provides a powerful mechanism for task allocation, since it permits a more informed choice from among the alternative nodes to which tasks may be allocated. The key element in the task allocation is the negotiation procedure. The negotiations involve two nodes which are called manager and contractor. The manager generates a task to be done and the contractor agrees to perform the task. The manager announces the existence of the task to all potential contractors. Each contractor evaluates its own level of interest with respect to the type of the task and the available resources. If the task is found to be of sufficient interest, the contractor informs the manager about its readiness to perform the task. The manager may choose from among the several potential contractors. It selects those contractors which better match the task requirements. A contract is thus an explicit agreement between a node that generates the task and a node that executes the task. The nodes are not constrained to be only managers or only contractors. It is possible for a node to be simultaneously both manager and contractor for different contracts. As an example, in the process of executing the task the contractor may deliver parts of the task to another contractors. In this case this node is a contractor in respect to the whole task and a manager in respect to the parts of the task.

In the DEE the initial tasks are generated by the tutor node. The announcement of these tasks is carried out by placing them on the student blackboard. After negotiations the tasks are allocated to contractors and the contractors' names are placed on the blackboard. In this way all the nodes are acquainted with the network activity. Furthermore, by virtue of this publicity, several contractors in a given contract may share partial results and communicate between each other. In the conventional contract net protocol such communication is not possible because the task allocation information is inaccessible.

The mechanism of task allocation by a global blackboard helps work duplications to be avoided. As an example, a node may check the student blackboard whenever it receives a new task. If such a task has already been performed by another node, the first node may simply copy the results.

The global blackboard approach is also well suited to the management of communication. By examining the student blackboard the nodes may reason about each others' present activities. It allows the nodes better to predict the effects a message will have on the other nodes. Predictions lead to reduced communications because only necessary data need to be communicated. In fact, the student blackboard plays the role of the activity map in which all the points of task and result sharing are marked. The nodes use the activities allocation information to recognize and establish communication links, to discover how activities may be reordered to avoid harmful interactions and to promote helpful interactions.

More interesting communication problems arise when there are many students and many tutor nodes in the network. While the tutor nodes have higher priority in respect to other kinds of nodes, the priorities of all tutor nodes are equal. This requires more complex decisions about the interaction between the students and the tutor nodes. In the DEE three heuristics are proposed for conflict resolution between the network and the students:

1. Group formation. When conflict arises between the students the current individual student goals may be changed to equivalent ones which promote cooperation.
2. Group destruction. When conflict arises between a student group and the network the students are given competitive goals.
3. Changing the focus of attention. When internal conflict arises between the tutor nodes the students are given other problem situations. In such a way plans and preferences of the tutor nodes are changed.

4 Conclusions

In this paper we have presented a new approach for computer assisted learning. This approach incorporates features of intelligent tutoring systems and distributed problem solvers. It has been devised to permit multiperson - multimachine interaction and to stimulate the social dimension in the learning activity of the students. Several perspectives for further research remain. A mechanism for internode cooperation must be developed. On the basis of this the tutor nodes may control the student groups and influence the behaviour of each student. For these purposes economic and game-theoretic models may be useful [7,8].

References

1. Axelrod, R.: The Evolution of Cooperation. Basic Books 1984
2. Chang, E.: Participant Systems for Cooperative Work. In: M. Huhns (ed.) Distributed Artificial Intelligence, 311-339. London: Pitman 1987

3. Davis, R., Smith, R. G.: Negotiation as a Metaphor for Distributed Problem Solving. Artificial Intelligence 20 (1), 63-109 (1983)

4. Durfee, E. H.: Coordination of Distributed Problem Solvers. Boston: Kluwer Academic Publishers 1988

5. Hayes-Roth, B.: A Blackboard Architecture for Control. Artificial Intelligence 26, 251-321 (1985)

6. Hewitt, C.: Open information systems semantics for distributed artificial intelligence. Artificial Intelligence 47, 79-106 (1991)

7. Malone, T. W.: Toward an interdisciplinary theory of coordination. Tech. Report CCS 120 MIT Sloan School of Management, Cambridge   MA 1991

8. Rosenschein, J. S., Genesereth, M.R.: Deals Among Rational Agents. In Proceedings of the 1985 International Joint Conference on Artificial Intelligence, 91-99 (1985)

9. Rosenschein, J. S., Zlotkin, G.: Negotiation and Task Sharing Among Autonomous Agents in Cooperative Domains. In Proceedings of the 1989 International Joint Conference on Artificial Intelligence, 912-917. Morgan Kaufmann Publishers 1989

10. Sleeman, D., Brown, J. S.: Intelligent Tutoring Systems. New York: Academic Press 1982

11. Smith, R. G.: The Contract Net Protocol: High - Level Communication and Control in a Distributed Problem Solver. IEEE Transactions on Copmuters C-29, 12, 1104-1113 (1980)

The Design of Interacting Agents for Use in Interfaces

David Connah

Institute for Perception Research
P.O. Box 513, 5600 MB Eindhoven, The Netherlands

Abstract. In this paper situated agents are contrasted with agents which rely on a planning-based model of action. It is suggested that situated agents are particularly appropriate for skill-based tasks and that skill forms the basis of many important applications. The impact of situated agents on representation and the importance of social interaction and emergent behaviour are also discussed.

Keywords. Situated agents, skill, social behaviour, emergent behaviour

1 Introduction

First let me indicate what kind of agent I have in mind. I will not attempt a rigorous definition but will rely rather on the common-sense, everyday meaning that people give to the word. Broadly speaking agents 'do' things; they are (apparently) capable of acting autonomously or, in Laurel's phrase (Laurel 1991), they are capable of *initiating action*. I would like however to repeat the distinction made by Laurel between two varieties of agent. Agents can be seen as acting on behalf of someone else; for example, an estate agent who sells your house for you or an insurance agent. They can also be seen simply as acting in their own interests and most 'biological' agents (people, animals) are in fact acting in this way most of the time. Much of the literature has dealt with the first kind of agent - Apple Guides come to mind immediately - but the second kind is in fact more general and subsumes the first kind. In what follows I am thinking of this more general kind of agent.

The use of the word agent is not new in Artificial Intelligence (AI). What is more recent is the notion of *situated* agents. If there is a date at which people in AI began talking about situated agents that date is probably about 1984. Many of the ideas which contributed to this notion are however much older than that and have often been drawn from completely different disciplines such as sociology, anthropology and philosophy. 1984 (if that is the right date) was when people in AI began to realise that some of the problems that were causing such trouble in AI might be eased (or even go away completely) if a different approach was tried. Let me introduce the idea of situated agents by talking about models of action.

2 Models of Action

Until a few years ago, it was almost universally the case that the actions of agents were described and implemented in terms of a planning model. Roughly speaking this means that agents were thought to have goals. In order to achieve these goals they constructed internal models of (part of) the world and then, by reasoning about these models, they constructed a plan of action. In its simplest form such a plan is a sequential list of actions to be taken by the agent. Once the plan had been constructed it would then be executed by the agent, usually resulting in some externally observable behaviour or actions. In this model goals, plans, internal representations of the world and reasoning go hand-in-hand to cause the behaviour of the agent. This is perhaps not the whole story; the agent, on this theory, has in some sense to *intend* to act before action becomes possible. This gives rise to a belief-desire psychological model to explain intention. All of these things to a large extent hang or fall together.

Nowadays, however, this is not the only model. There is another theory called situated action theory (Suchman 1987). In this model an agent acts in a way which is 'appropriate' to its situation. Here 'appropriate' refers to a behaviour which evolution, learning, or design has engendered in the agent to ensure its survival and the satisfaction of its interests. The 'situation' is a potentially complex combination of external and internal events and states. In this model there is no suggestion of planning, desires, beliefs etc. but there are other ideas that are implied by the model. The most important of these is that agents have to be closely coupled to their environment. This is so because it is only through their direct perception of the world that they can be aware of their situation and only by this awareness that they can act appropriately. Thus perception is essential for this model but the model also has implications for such things as representation, emergent behaviour, social behaviour and skill.

Many of the things that we want to do with agents can be done by skilled (as opposed to 'intelligent') agents and situated action theory is very well suited to the description and implementation of such agents.

I will start to describe some of the implications which the theory has for the design of agents by discussing, in the next section, the particular kind of representation that is a common feature of situated agents.

3 Representation

There are problems associated with creating an internal representation of the world. First there are the overheads associated with the construction of the model. Then there is the difficulty of ensuring that the model is always up-to-date. This is particularly difficult if there are other agents in the world causing it to change in unpredictable ways. Is there an alternative kind of representation that doesn't come up against these problems? The answer provided in the situated agent paradigm is to say that the world is the best representation of itself (Brooks 1991). In this case there are no overheads for model construction and maintenance, and the model is always accurate as well as being as rich as only the real world can be. But there is more to it than this. When an internal model has to be constructed there is no way in which the agent can know at the time of construction which parts of the model are going to be of importance and which not. Indeed, as this is likely to change with time, any information that could conceivably be required must be embodied in the model. In the 'no-internal-representation' case the agent need only, at any given moment, perceive that part of the world that is currently of interest. In other words there is a *focus of attention*.

Let me try to clarify some of these ideas with the help of an illustration[1].

The task at hand is a task in the blocks world. The agent is presented with a table on which there are piles ('columns') of blocks. Each block has a letter on its front face. The task of the agent is to use the blocks on the table to create a copy of the rightmost column on the table. The world in which the agent has to perform its task is shown in Figure 1.

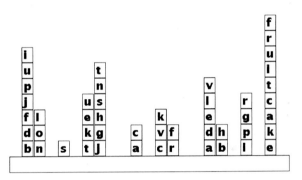

Fig. 1

Faced with such a task an AI programmer would typically try to deal with it in terms of planning (Rich 1983, p.259, Nilsson 1980, p.275). This would involve creating a representation of the world in the form of symbolic descriptions and a set of operators to act on those symbolic descriptions. There would also be an explicit symbolic description of the goal of the program or agent and some reasoning process by which the agent would discover how to change the current state of the

---

1. Chapman in (Chapman 1991) said "I believe that implementations in AI most often serve as *illustrations* of approaches" and "Approaches are learned in part from the practice of reimplementing illustrative programs". The work described here is taken from my re-implementation and extension of Chapman's Blockhead program (Chapman 1989).

world into the goal state. The planning paradigm also requires some method of detecting when a solution has been found and, in some cases, a method of recognising when a solution is nearly correct (Rich 1983). A simple plan is a list of operators taking the original state into the goal state step by step.

The situated action approach to the same task differs in every respect from that of planning. There is no symbolic description of the world; there is only the world itself. There is no reasoning process[2] but only actions which are appropriate to the situation of the agent. In the current implementation at least, there is no explicit goal; the *designer* has an explicit goal but the goal-like behaviour of the agent is emergent from its atomic situated actions.

Perception in this example is simulated by intermediate level vision. This simulation is accomplished by means of markers (Chapman 1989, Chapman 1991, Ullman 1984). A marker is a device within the visual system of the agent which can be used to (detect and) mark specific features in its visual field. For example the bottom or the top of a column of blocks. It can also be used to track some ongoing activity such as marking the place where the next block is to be placed. This kind of marker merely marks a position in the visual field of the agent. It is the responsibility of the agent to get the marker to the right location in the first place. Markers are the only visual interaction that the agent has with the world. In other words if there is no marker at any given time on a particular spot the agent can have no knowledge (at that time) of what is there or even of the existence of the location[3].

The actions of the agent can be divided into two parts: internal and external. Internally the agent manipulates a small set of markers enabling it to find blocks, decide which ones should be moved and subsequently keep track of them. Externally it manipulates the blocks in ways determined by the internal states of the markers. It is not a difficult matter to extend the program so that if the construction of the copy is interrupted either maliciously or by some 'natural' event like the pile collapsing, the agent can still recover from the situation using exactly the kinds of actions it used in constructing the pile in the first place. This kind of recovery is difficult or impossible when using an internal representation but then it is never seen as necessary since nothing can interfere in the only world the program knows: the internal representation itself. This is why the blocks world, as usually described, is so unrealistic.

This is by no means the full story on representations; in particular, I am not suggesting that agents never use internal representations. I am simply saying that for many of their activities internal representations are not only not necessary but may be counter-productive.

---

2. In a sense there *is* a reasoning process but it is 'built-in' to the actions which are determined by the situation. This kind of implicit reasoning is a common feature of skilled activity.

3. Note that markers can also be used to mark 'virtual' objects such as the gap between two objects or the space into which something has to be placed.

4 The Social Nature of Agents

It was remarked earlier that much of AI has been concerned with the operation of a single agent in a passive world. The apparent assumption has been that once one agent had been successfully designed it would simply be a question of adding other rather similar ones.

Although one can think of applications where an agent acts in isolation, the majority of cases involve interaction between agents.

An example of a specifically social activity is provided by cooperation (Hickman and Shiels 1990). Here there is an implicit communication between agents which is effected by the actions of the agents in the world. Of course in one sense *all* communication travels via the world (sound, light etc.) but I am referring to something different in this case. Suppose two bricklayers are building a wall. As one of them lays a brick in place the shape of the wall is changed and the other bricklayer is guided in his placement of the brick by the new shape of the wall. All that is required is the ability of the bricklayers to perceive the current state of the wall and to have actions which are appropriate to that state. The *significance* of each action is dependent on the state of the wall.

I will illustrate this process with an example suggested by a demonstration program (Wavish 1991). This program is in the nature of a game or entertainment based on the idea of a sheep dog rounding up sheep and driving them into a pen. The demonstration is a simulation of a system containing seven agents: a sheep dog, five sheep and a shepherd. The idea is that the dog should round up the sheep and drive them towards the shepherd. For this to happen both the sheep and the dog must, in some simple way, be able to perceive each other. As far as the dog is concerned, its surroundings are notionally divided into eight sectors centred on the dog itself. It has a rudimentary 'vision' system which informs it of which octants contain sheep. (This is all; it doesn't know how many sheep or how far away they are). The sheep on the other hand are 'aware' of the presence of the dog when it gets too close for comfort. Given this rather basic perceptual ability, what behaviour should we write down that will cause the dog to round up the sheep and herd them towards the pen? The following four behaviours are sufficient:

• if the dog is running along with the sheep on its right hand side and there are no sheep in the dog's front-right octant, it should turn right until sheep appear in that octant (similarly if it is running with the sheep on its left).

• if, at any time, the shepherd appears in one of the dog's three front octants, it must reverse its direction of travel.

• if the dog approaches a sheep too closely the sheep must move (run) away from the dog.

• the sheep must avoid colliding with each other.

The result of these four behaviours is that the sheep are compressed into a flock

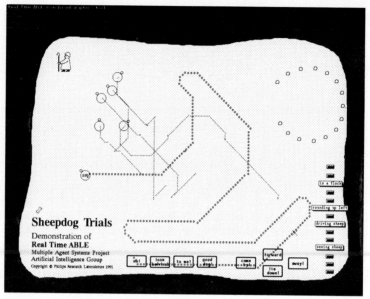

Fig. 2

and that the dog weaves to-and-fro behind the flock, driving it towards the shepherd. This behaviour can be seen in Figure 2.

Ignoring the details of the diagram, one can clearly see the tracks of the sheep and of the dog as it weaves to-and-fro.

Two points are illustrated by this fragment of the demonstration.

1) The behaviour of the agents is *situated*. In this simple example it is easy to write down, for example, what conditions must hold for the sheep to run away from the dog.

2) The flocking and herding of the sheep is not achieved solely by the dog's behaviour as one might assume but requires the complementary behaviour of the sheep. It is, in this sense, a kind of social behaviour in which all the agents are co-involved.

5 Emergent Behaviour

When watching the demonstration of the sheep and sheepdog, observers find it is natural to describe it in terms of words or phrases such as 'flock', 'rounding up', 'herding the flock' and so on. None of these concepts is explicitly represented in the program but they are ascribed by the observer to the behaviours of agents in the system. This behaviour is emergent from the interaction of other behaviours such as running towards the sheep or running away from the dog.

The stability of the emergent behaviour in this case is important. The overall behaviour of the group of agents is not predictable in detail by the observer (although it is deterministic) and different starting positions of the agents lead to sequences which, in detail, are completely different. However the behaviour at the level of the flock (and this indeed is what leads us to *ascribe* the term 'flock') is extremely stable and robust; it can be deliberately disrupted (e.g. the player can pick up and move the dog or any or all of the sheep) and will fairly rapidly return to the stable flocking and driving behaviour.

6 Skill

The idea of skilled agents has already figured in this lecture. In fact one of the changes in viewpoint that I would like to argue for is that agents should primarily be seen as skilled rather than intelligent. There are at least three reasons for this. The first is that skill is in many ways a more straightforward concept than intelligence. The second is that for many, perhaps most, of the things we want agents to do in real applications, skill is what is required and the final reason for concentrating on skill is that one can speculate that reasoning is based on skilled activities in the real world and is not something that is pursued by people in a completely abstract way (Chapman and Agre 1986).

Wavish has written a program which demonstrates precisely these kinds of skills in an agent. His agent plays the game of Tetris. In this game (if you are not familiar with it) blocks of various shapes appear to fall under gravity and land either on the 'ground' or on top of blocks which have previously fallen down. The aim of the player is to manipulate these blocks as they are falling either by rotating them or by moving them sideways (translating them) in such a way as to fit them into holes in the already existing heap of blocks. If the player does this successfully (by completely filling rows of blocks) then he or she scores points. It is an important part of the strategy to keep the height of the heap down since otherwise it reaches a level at which the game is terminated. The game is shown in progress in Figure 3.

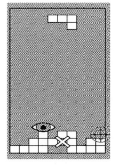

Fig. 3

The agent plays the game in a situated manner. It scans the heap (hence the 'eye' icon[4]) looking for certain patterns in its top surface and it then applies rotations and translations to the block depending on which block is falling and which patterns it finds.

The impression that one gets on watching the agent play is of some (fairly small) degree of intelligence but in fact nothing that we would normally think of as intelligence is involved. Most of the time, although the agent is by no means optimised, it seems to choose a reasonable location and orientation for the block. At all events the scores it achieves are roughly speaking an order of magnitude better than my best score. I would not like to think that this was a true reflection of our relative intelligences although I can bear to think that it is more skilful than I am.

7 The Future of Situated Agents

Research on situated agents has not been going on for very long. The theory is still patchy and there are few, if any, commercial applications extant. Nevertheless, it is an area which is developing fast and which seems to have great potential. An attempt has been made in this lecture to introduce the topic by discussing some of the important issues but how will the theory develop and what kinds of application can we expect in the future?

Probably the hottest topic at present is that of learning in situated agents. The Tetris agent described in the previous section was hand-crafted; the various combinations of block shape and heap patterns were chosen and refined by the programmer. Whilst this is feasible for small programs it would constitute a bottle-neck in the writing of larger ones. For this reason it has been suggested by several people that it will be necessary for agents of this kind to be learning agents. Work in this direction has been done by Maes (Maes 1991, Maes 1993) and Chapman (Chapman 1991). This work is still in its early stages and Chapman, in particular, has reported that his attempts to harness back propagation methods has been disappointing. He concluded that in future it would be necessary (because of the situatedness of the agents) to look at learning methods which are much more directly linked to the ways in which the perceptions and actions of the agent are effected.

The discussion of representation in the lecture was confined to those situations in which the world of the agent could be used as the only representation required by the agent. This was an important insight made in some of the early work on situated agents (Brooks 1986, Agre & Chapman 1987). However it is unlikely to be the whole story; the issue of representation goes beyond this. There is, for example, the particularly interesting situation in which dynamic external representations (e.g. speech, drawings, writing) are used by an agent as part of its current situation. As

---

4. The other icons visible in the diagram represent the various markers that the agent uses in playing the game. See the section on representation.

Clancey says (Clancey 1991): *"We don't know what we want to say until we say it."* There is much work to be done on this question of representation; the most that can be said of work to date is that it has challenged the accepted view about internal representations and opened up the whole field to a radical re-appraisal.

In the section on the social behaviour of agents I emphasised the complementary nature of the behaviour of agents. This is really just a hint of a much more radical position which I think will eventually have to be embraced in this paradigm although it is not clear at present how this can be done. I am referring to the idea that cognition and intelligence, if you will, are not things that are contained within the head of the agent but are products of the social interaction of agents (Coulter 1979, Costall 1991). If this line of argument holds up it is fruitless to continue to try to make agents more intelligent simply by putting more and more 'clever' things into them. They will only behave in ways which we would remotely call intelligent if they have a rich interaction with each other and with the world. It is because of this requirement for a rich and close interaction that I feel that situated agents are perhaps our best bet at the moment.

Finally applications. I am not aware of any genuinely commercial applications of situated agents that have been made so far. There have, on the other hand, been quite a lot of projects which have demonstrated their potential. It seems likely that the man-machine interface will be one area where applications will appear before long. In the slightly longer term multi-media, virtual reality and interactive drama (Bates 1990) are all areas where skilled agents could be expected to play important roles. Agents are being introduced into educational systems: work is proceeding in this area at IPO (van Hoe and Masthoff 1993). They can also be expected to appear in training scenarios and command and control training exercises. In short there is no lack of potential applications and the technology is maturing rapidly. We can expect the results of the fusion of the two in the fairly near future.

References

Agre, P.E. and Chapman, D. (1987) "Pengi: An Implementation of a Theory of Activity", Proceedings of the AAAI Conference, Seattle, Washington

Bates, Joseph (1990) "Computational Drama in Oz", Working notes of the AAAI Workshop on Interactive Fiction and Synthetic Realities, Boston, July 1990

Brooks, R.A. (1986) "A Robust Layered Control System For a mobile Robot", IEEE Journal of Robotics and Automation, vol. RA-2, No. 1, March 1986, 14-23

Brooks, R.A. (1991) "Intelligence without representation", Artificial Intelligence 47 (1991), 139-159

Chapman, D. (1989) "Penguins Can Make Cake", AI Magazine, Winter 1989, pp.45-50

Chapman, David (1991) "Vision, Instruction, and Action", MIT Press, Cambridge MA

Chapman, D and Agre, P.E. (1986) "Abstract Reasoning as Emergent from Concrete Activity" in "Workshop on Reasoning about Actions and Plans", eds. Georgeff and Lansky, Timberline, Oregon, Morgan Kaufmann

Clancey, W.J. (1991) "Israel Rosenfield, The Invention of Memory: A New View of the Brain", Artificial Intelligence, 50 (1991), 241-284

Costall, A. (1991) "Graceful Degradation", in "Against Cognitivism: Alternative Foundations for Cognitive Psychology", Arthur Still and Alan Costall (eds.), London, Harvester Wheatsheaf (1991)

Coulter, J. (1979) "The Social Construction of Mind: Studies in Ethnomethodology & Linguistic Philosophy", Macmillan Press

Hickman, S.J. and Shiels, M.A. (1990) "Situated Action as a Basis for Cooperation", in "Proceedings of the 2nd. European Workshop on Modelling an Autonomous Agent in a Multi-Agent World", Paris, 1990, Elsevier Science Publishers (North-Holland)

van Hoe, R.R.G. and Masthoff, J.F.M. (1993) "A multi-agent approach to interactive learning environments" in "Collaborative problem solving: theoretical frameworks and innovative systems" AI-ED 93 Workshop, Edinburgh, Scotland

Laurel, B. (1991) "Computers as Theatre", Addison-Wesley, 1991

Maes, P. (1991) "Learning Behaviour networks from Experience", Proceedings of the First European Conference on Artificial Life, MIT Press, 1991

Maes, P. (1993) "A Learning Interface Agent for Scheduling Meetings", Proceedings ACM - SIGCHI, Florida, 1993

Nilsson, N.J. (1980) "Principles of Artificial Intelligence", Tioga Publishing Co.

Rich, Elaine (1983), "Artificial Intelligence", McGraw-Hill

Suchman, L. (1987) "Plans and Situated Actions: the problem of human-machine communication", Cambridge University Press

Ullman, S. (1984) "Visual Routines", Cognition, 18, pp. 97-159

Wavish, P.R. (1991) "Exploiting Emergent Behaviour in Multi-Agent Systems", in "Proceedings of the 3rd. European Workshop on Modelling an Autonomous Agent in a Multi-Agent World, Kaiserslautern, 5-7 August 1991, eds. Y. Demazeau and E. Werner, Elsevier Science Publishers (North-Holland), 1991

Simulator-Based Training
Using a Learning Companion

Eva L. Ragnemalm

Department of Computer Science, University of Linköping, S-581 83 Linköping, Sweden,
E-mail: elu@ida.liu.se

Abstract. This article describes how a Learning Companion can be used in simu-lator-based training. The main advantage of this approach is that it retains the exploratory quality of the simulator while still closely following the student's rea-soning in a dialogue.

Keywords. Simulator-based t raining, learning companion

1 Introduction

This article discusses an ongoing project aimed at improving simulator-based training systems. The ultimate intention is to provide intelligent assistance for training process-control operators to perform diagnosis of dynamic systems. In or research domain, paper and pulp manufacture, the training goal is to increase the operator's understanding of the process, focusing specifically on teaching him[1] to apply his factual knowledge to a diagnostic problem. The training is intended to supplement classroom instruction and on-the-job training.

One difference between skilled process operators and novice operators is the ability to diagnose errors efficiently. Skilled operators follow a diagnostic proce-dure that appears to be independent of the part of the plant in which it was learned (Schaafstal 1991). Teaching this diagnostic procedure to novice operators might involve presenting a suitable fault situation on a simulator and following the oper-ator through the steps of the procedure. The problem is that many of the steps are not normally verbalized or otherwise made explicit.

This problem could possibly be solved by engaging the user in a dialogue using a Learning Companion, LC, (Chan and Baskin 1990). The benefit of the learning companion would be the possibility of analysing the student's reasoning using a dialogue, while still preserving the exploratory nature of learning with a simulator.

In the following sections I will first describe the educational situation today and how it might be changed. Then I will briefly describe the entire system I envisage, followed by a more detailed discussion of how a LC could appear to the student.

---

[1] In this text I will use the pronoun "he", since the operators in the domain are often male.

2 Education of Process Control Operators

Education of process operators today includes both classroom instruction (teaching the facts about the system, from chemistry to process control theory) and on-the-job training, in the form of apprenticeship. One problem with using apprenticeship to teach diagnosis is that errors don't occur on cue, that is when the student is ready to learn that specific error.

This problem can be remedied by using a real-time, dynamic simulator as a tool for the training. Using the simulator, errors can be introduced on demand, when needed to illustrate the symptoms and reactions in the plant. The simulator should also be interactive, so that the student can perform the kinds of actions he would on the plant. (Hollan et. al. 1984, Baines et.al 1992)

To further enable learning at the most convenient time for the student (thus ensuring good motivation), it is useful to have a computer tutor capable of controlling the education to some extent, and thus permitting the student to practice and develop his skills under computer supervision. Such a tutor should be able both to gauge the student's knowledge in order to present suitable problems, and should be able to answer questions pertaining to the exercises. This includes abstract questions on plant functionality as well as reasons for certain occurrences. (Lajoie and Lesgold 1989, Machietto and Kassianides 1991, Goodyear 1991, Cheikes and Ragnemalm 1993)

In order to teach the diagnostic procedure, and more precisely, to check if the student is using it, it is helpful to engage the student in a dialogue during the process of problem solving. While it would be possible to have the training system take the role of, for instance, a Socratic tutor (a tutor who guides the student's reasoning by asking questions.) (e.g. Burton and Brown 1982), it can also take the role of a co-learner (Dillenbourg and Self 1992) or a Learning Companion, LC, (Chan and Baskin 1990). An attractive side-effect is that the use of peer-to-peer dialogue also makes the learning situation more similar to reality, where diagnosis takes place as a cooperative effort among the operators in the control room. The LC concept also permits us to use pedagogical methods like coaching (Sokolnicki 1990), where the Tutor does not interact as closely with the student as when using a Socratic method.

This does not mean that the LC should replace the Tutor, however. Inherent in the Learning Companion concept, is the idea that the LC has no more knowledge than the human student. This means that we can not dispense with the Tutor component, since we still need to guide the learning process and supply new knowledge to the student.

3 The System

The training system I propose would contain a number of interacting components. The first three would be interacting directly with the student:

1 A Simulator, modelling the system (for instance the bleaching plant or an evaporator system) that is to be used for training. The simulator is used both for presenting problems and testing solutions. Although it needs to have good representational fidelity to the real system, but a full scale simulator replicating the control room layout is not necessary, since the goal is not the training of manual dexterity skills.

2 A Tutor, responsible for the planning of the education. Depending on the pedagogical strategy chosen, it needs more or less extensive pedagogical knowledge, and needs to have access to a model of the student's knowledge (the Student Model, see below). In order to provide explanations and answer questions from the student, it also needs access to the knowledge of an expert process control operator.

3 A Learning Companion, whose main purpose is to provide information for the Student Model (see below) and specifically to determine whether the student is following the desired diagnostic procedure. To be able to cooperate with the human student, it must also be capable of reasoning about the process and carrying on a discussion on the subject. It should, to be credible in the long run, be capable of learning at the same rate as the human student, and must thus have a dynamic knowledge base separate from that of the Tutor.

4 A Student Model is needed by the Tutor in order to adapt its plans to the student. The SM contains the system's beliefs about the student's knowledge. It does not interact with the student, it represents him. It is updated both by the LC (regarding current activities) and the Tutor (when something has been learned, or a need to learn has been identified).

4 Example

The diagnostic procedure that we wish to teach the student has nine steps (Schaafstal 1991):

1 Identification of symptoms.
2 Judgement: How serious is the problem (the consequences of it).
3 Determination of possible faults.
4 Ordering of faults according to likelihood.
5 Testing (finding evidence for/against a certain fault).
6 Determination of repairs.
7 Consequences of application of repairs.

8 Ordering of repairs (according to consequences).

9 Evaluation of repair action taken.

The only steps that entail interaction with the simulator are step 5 and the implicit implementation of the repair itself between steps 8 and 9. This means that to a system with a coaching tutor, the other steps are invisible. But a system capable of observing and analyzing a dialogue between the student and a LC can trace the other steps as well. This can be done either just following the student through the task, noting whether the procedure is followed or not, or correcting the student when the LC detects deviations. Correction can be either implicit or explicit. An example where implicit corrections are used follows.

An evaporator system (see Fig. 4.1.) is a common component in many chemical systems. Its purpose is to concentrate liquid solutions by means of evaporating the water content. It consists of an evaporator tank where the solution is heated by high-pressurized steam, a separator tank where the liquid solution is separated from some of the steam evaporated, and a cooling system where this steam is condensed and led away from the solution. There is also a feedback loop that allows part of the solution to circulate through the system again, mixed with new feed, while the rest is drawn off.

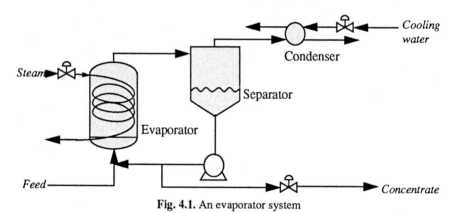

Fig. 4.1. An evaporator system

Situation: the level of solution in the separator has started to increase slowly, and the temperature is also rising, the concentration going down:

Speaker	Statement	Comment
Student	The Separator level is rising! If it gets too high, the separator will overflow!	Identifies a symptom (1) and makes a judgement.(2)
LC	The concentration is decreasing.	Returns to Id. of symptom (1) with no further comment
Student	... and the temperature has increased.	Also returns to Ident. of symptoms (1)

Cont. on next page.

Speaker	Statement	Comment
LC	At this rate we still have 5 minutes before the concentration is too low and 10 minutes before separator overflow.	No more symptoms, proceeds to refine earlier Judgement (2)
Student	Ok, so what's causing it? Clogged outlet from the separator? If so, we must stop the feed!	Possible fault (3) Determ. of repair (6)
LC	It could also be a plug in the incoming steam pipe.	Returns to Possible faults (3)
Student	No, in that case the pressure and the temperature would be going down, and that is not the case. But it could also be a partial plug in the cooling water pipe. That would explain the slight increase in temperature.	Test (5) Possible fault (3) Test (5)
LC	Plugging in the outlet is quite common. What other symptoms would that give?	No more possible faults, proceeds to Ordering (4), initiates Test (5)
Student	Well, definitely not an increase in temperature.	Test (5)
LC	Ok, that means it's probably a plug in the cooling water. How do we fix that?	Prompts student to go to (6)

...

To be capable of carrying on a dialogue like this, the LC needs to be able to reason about the diagnosis in each of the steps, and attribute each of the student's comments to one step. In order to detect when things are missing in the discussion it must generate all the things that should be mentioned, and tick them off as covered. It should also update the student model so that exercises where the missed steps are crucial can be chosen for illustration and practice.

5 Implementation

The issue of whether the student's reasoning can be traced with the aid of a Learning Companion could be tested by implementing a small experimental LC like the one illustrated above. It could be constructed as a module consisting of an expert system capable of doing diagnosis in a small domain, and a communication module which, using (severely) restricted natural language, is capable of conveying phrases like the ones above.

How well the LC succeeds in tracing the student's adherence to the steps can be evaluated by devising exercises and sequences of student input with gaps, and checking if the LC detects those gaps.

The impact of this technique on the learning of the diagnostic procedure can be measured by the number of corrections the LC makes during an exercise, and possibly comparing that with students who have practised on the same exercises without the LC.

6 Summary

This poster presents the idea that a Learning Companion could be used as a technique to trace the performance of steps that are not ordinarily verbalised during problem solving, as an alternative to having a Socratic tutor question the student.

References

Burton, R.R. and Brown, J.S. (1982) An investigation of computer coaching for informal learning activities. In Sleeman D. and Brown, J.S., editors, *Intelligent Tutoring Systems*, Chapter 4, pages 97-98. Academic Press.

Chan, T.-W. and Baskin, A.B. (1990) Learning companion systems. In C. Frasson and G. Gauthier, editors, *Intelligent Tutoring Systems: At the Crossroads of Artificial Intelligence and Education*, pages 6-33. Ablex, New Jersey.

Cheikes, B.A. and Ragnemalm, E.L. (in press) Simulator-based training-support tools for process-control operators. In *Proceedings of the NATO Workshop on Natural Dialogue and Interactive Student Modeling, 1992*.

Baines, G.H., Gunseor, F.D., Haynes, J.B. and Scheldorf, J.J. (1992) Benefits of using a high fidelity process stimulation for operator training and control check-out. *Tappi Journal*, pages 133-136, January. Presented at the TAPPI 1991 Engineering Conference.

Dillenbourg, P. and Self, J.A. (1992) PEOPLE POWER: A human-computer collaborative learning system. In Frasson, C., Gauthier, G. and McCalla, G.L., editors, *Proc. of ITS '92*, pages 651-660. Lecture Notes in Computer Science, Vol. 608: Springer Verlag.

Goodyear, P. (1991) A knowledge-based approach to supporting the use of simulation programs. *Computers in Education*, 16(1):99-103.

Hollan, J.D., Hutchins, E.L. and Weitzman, L.M. (1987) STEAMER: an interactive, inspectable, simulation-based training system. In Kearsley, G.P., editor, *Artificial Intelligence and Instruction; Applications and Methods*, chapter 6, pages 113-134. Addison-Wesley.

Lajoie, S.P. and Lesgold, A. (1989) Apprenticeship training in the workplace: Computer-coached practice environments as a new form of apprenticeship. *Machine Mediated Learning*, 3(1):7-28.

Machietto, S. and Kassianides, S. (1991) Computer based training of process plant operators. Prepared for presentation at "CIM in the Process industry".

Munro, A., Fehling, M.R., and Towne, D.M. (1985) Instruction intrusiveness in dynamic simulation training. *J. of Computer-Based Instruction*, 12(2):50-53.

Schaafstal, A.M. (1991) *Diagnostic Skill in Process Operation: A Comparison Between Experts and Novices.* PhD thesis, University of Groningen, Institute for Perception TNO, P.O. Box 23, 3769 Soesterberg, The Netherlands.

Knowledge–Based Interfaces for Existing Systems

Peter Mikulecký

Department of Computer Science, Institute of Management and Information Technology, 501 91 Hradec Králové, Czech Republic

Abstract. The complexity of computer exploitation has increased rapidly as computers became components in complex systems. This is true even if we consider existing software systems and/or packages. To use them meaningfully requires days, or more frequently weeks, of practicing with the necessity of studying thick manuals. This seems to be especially critical in the case of expert systems or large database systems, where the user typically expects to begin useful work almost immediately. The moral of this is that computer users, regardless whether they program or not, are expecting *more and more assistance from the systems* they use.

We do believe that it is the idea of *active (or co-operative) assistance* to the computer users, which seems to be both essential and achievable in designing *intelligent interfaces to existing complex software systems*. In our paper we present some remarks about *active assistance*, including some problems from the area of *advice giving*. Some recent *projects of active advice-giving systems* will be mentioned briefly and an example of a simple active advice-giving system will be described.

Keywords. Knowledge-based user interfaces, advice-giving, active assistance

1 Introductory Remarks

The computer is becoming an ever more important part of our society. Nowadays, personal computers and various complex software products, e.g. data- base-like products, expert and other knowledge-based systems, desk top publishing systems and others, are being heavily utilized by users who previously belonged to the category of casual or occasional software users. Therefore, there is increasing awareness of the value of tools providing expert assistance in the use of just mentioned software products. This expert assistance should require the use of appropriate user interfaces. In other words, the quality of interaction between man and machine can be considered to be essential in all areas where computer support is used.

"The user interface to a software system can spell the difference between success and failure. Sometimes, function does not seem to count. If the program does a good enough job, if the users see an easy to use, easy to learn, helpful, pleasant interface, they love it. The interface might be the most significant sales aspect of a software

product ...", writes Wexelblat in [20]. Everyone, who came in touch with a sophisticated user interface, is likely to agree.

For over a decade, there has been extensive research in the area of intelligent man-machine communication. However, the results in this area and their dissemination into practice have not been entirely satisfactory. The recent impressive results in user modeling (see, e.g. [7] or [8]) are awaiting their incorporation into really used existing (software) systems. Much progress can be realized in this area by moving away from toy problems to practical, industrial situations, and by developing general tools to build both active systems and user models. A relatively successful attempt in the direction relevant to the one discussed here seems to be the FOCUS Project (Esprit 2 Project: 2620) [5]. However, tools for active systems are largely non-existent at present.

The majority of really used existing (software) systems are imperfect systems. Imperfect systems can show an imperfect behaviour because their users are unskilled. This is very frequently the case in many practical applications where the users have not been using the computer systems before. The system should then try to compensate for this lack of skills by active advisory and helping behaviour. As soon as a system becomes sufficiently complex, its user can rarely master it fully. For instance, in the case of an information system containing large amounts of diverse data, a user can seldom ask the right question. Often she/he never knows which question to ask. Even if the system answers a question correctly, the answer may not be what the user really wanted, for perhaps she/he should have asked another, related question whose answer would have been more helpful to achieve intended goals (see a couple of papers by Siklóssy, e.g., [14] or [15]).

As we have stressed earlier (see [11], [12]), one approach to making existing systems more perfect could lie in the incorporation (using computer simulation) of the appropriate guidance given by an experienced helper – an expert in programming, or in the effective usage of given program package or database system. Such a helper or advisor can play the role of an *active assistant* in solving complex problems, in giving qualified advice if the programmer/user lacks the relevant knowledge, or in guiding the novice while constructing his/her first program or using a complex database system for the first time.

In order to fulfil the role of a helpful assistant to computer users, an intelligent system must learn about its user, and must try to guess intelligently at the user's goals. Such systems were first called *impertinent* [15], because they impertinently said what they had not been asked. Now they are called *active systems*. Active systems were first described, together with methods for their design by Siklóssy [14], [15]. Recent application to an active, optimal advisor for train passengers in the Netherlands is described in [17], [18] or [19]. Another recent application will be described later in this paper.

We do believe that the idea of *active (or co-operative) assistance* to the computer users is essential in designing *intelligent interfaces* (or *intelligent front-ends* to existing complex software systems. In what follows we intend to present some thoughts about the *active assistance*, discussing some problems of the *advice giving* first. Some recent *projects concerning active advice-giving systems* will be mentioned briefly and an example of a simple active advice-giving system QEAPS [2] will be described in a more detail.

2 Remarks About Advice-Giving in User Interfaces

We share the conviction of Carroll and McKendree [1] that advice giving could become the first successful domain for intelligent interfaces. They sketched the situation in the field of *human-computer interaction* as follows:

In general, people want to use computers, because they want to get something accomplished. This is good in that it gives users a focus for their activity with a system and increases their likelihood of receiving concrete reinforcement from their work. On the other hand, this same pragmatism can make an individual unwilling to spend any time learning about a system. To consult even on-line tutorials or programmed self-instruction manuals is, for the majority of people, a distraction from effective work. It means, that there is a *conflict between learning and working* that inclines new users to try to skip training, or to skip some parts of it, sometimes with disastrous consequences. From the same reason experienced users are likely to use the procedures they already know, regardless of their efficacy.

As Wexelblat [20] pointed out, the situation is especially critical in the case of expert systems, where the user of an expert system expects to begin useful work almost immediately. We can confirm from our own experience this same attitude like users of database systems.

The negative influence of the learning versus working conflict could be reduced through the use of various kinds of knowledge-based advice giving systems, e.g. by *intelligent system monitors* [1], *active collaborative systems* [15], or *supervising expert systems* [10]. These could integrate the time and effort spent on learning with actual use of a system. This *advice-giving approach* contrasts with the more typical drill and practice style of contemporary on-line tutorials and the confusing verbosity of typical context-insensitive help commands (see, e.g. [6]).

The main idea behind *supervising expert systems* (cf. also [11] and [12]) lies in designing an expert system in front of a user system (e.g., a database system) in order to improve the user friendliness and the applicability of the user system in such way that the expert system would be able:

- to analyze and recognize a given problem from the defined problem area (e.g., scheme-conversion in a database),
- to use expertise based on the knowledge-base in giving advice on the most suitable, available method for solving the problem,
- to give advice on how to use the underlying system effectively and efficiently,
- to advise in correcting possible errors.

More about the further development of the idea of supervising expert systems can be found in [13].

Advice-giving systems will need to have knowledge if their advice is to be useful. These systems are distinguished chiefly in that they store information about the underlying existing user system, about its commands, conditions, procedures, etc., and can access this information and provide it to users as on-line training and help. Further, if the advice-giving system is to behave properly across a range of users, the system should at least implicitly contain a model of its users. A recent discussion of user models can be found in [8]. The field of user modelling is essential for increasing the quality of advice-giving in active systems.

3 Remarks About Active Systems

Active systems (or following Siklóssy, *active collaborative systems*) not only answer questions from the user, but they will also give additional information not directly requested by the user, and might suggest other questions that may be more pertinent to the user's goals. In addition, active systems include a component which broadcasts information that may interest the user, even when the user did not request any information or ask any questions. Active systems differ in their behaviour from passive systems which wait for questions from the user and consider their task to be finished after providing the answers.

Following [16], we can list some of the inadequacies of passive systems, which simply answer a question. There are four such inadequacies, namely:

- the system may fail to inform the user that a modified question, closely related to his initial question, has a "significantly better" answer, which would help the user better to achieve his goals.
- the system may fail to inform the user that his question includes presuppositions which are not actually valid, so that the answer given may be misleading or meaningless.
- the system may fail to provide the user with additional information which the user would normally expect, and which he must now request explicitly.
- the system may fail to inform the user of the additional, related topics that the system is ready to pursue at the user's request.

All of these inadequacies should be avoided when using an active system, which, in the case of existing user systems, is an active knowledge-based interfacing system in front of the user system. A pretty example of an active advice-giving system is the TRAINS system, described in [17], [18] or [19]. However, the TRAINS system is not an interface in front of some existing user system. It is an active assistant in looking for an optimal train route in the time-table of the Dutch Railways. In what follows, we intend to describe briefly an active knowledge-based interface QEAPS [2]. It aims to be an intelligent and active collaborating device helping the user in mastering the Q-editor, a recent popular sharware text editor. The system QEAPS has been developed recently in the scope of a master thesis at the Department of Artificial Intelligence, Comenius University, Bratislava, under the supervision of the author of this paper.

The system QEAPS has been developed with the aim of helping novice users better and more quickly to master their usage of the Q-editor. It can be also used by more experienced users as a supervising and practicing device, preventing the users from mistakes typical of moderately experienced people, or leading the users to work with the editor more efficiently.

The QEAPS system starts with some initial evaluation of the user's abilities or experience in using the Q-editor. This evaluation should be given by the user and it includes four basic types of users: professional, experienced user of computers but lacking experience in using the Q-editor, moderately experienced computer user with no experience in Q-editor usage, novice. The initial evaluation is the basis for a dynamic user evaluation during the session with the Q-editor. The evaluation is decreased or increased in the accordance with the number of user's failures and successes. As a result of this evaluation, the form, frequency and contents of the advice is adjusted. For instance, an experienced user needs less advice which should be brief and on a more technical level, while a novice needs the advice frequently and perhaps in a more readable and understandable form. The evaluation just described creates a basis for user modelling to the extent necessary for successful advice-giving in using the Q-editor.

Active advice-giving in the QEAPS system is based on monitoring of the user's activities. All the user's keyboard activities are filtered first through the QEAPS monitoring module and compared to some templates of activities, representing legal as well as optimal sequences of keys which should be pressed by the user in the particular situation. If a difference is found, the system evaluates it in order to decide whether it is a mistake or only a less effective key sequence. The QEAPS system will then actively produce advice which (depending on the evaluation of the user) either prevents the user from making mistakes or helps him to perform a desired step more efficiently.

The active advice-giving system QEAPS has been implemented in Turbo Pascal 6.0 under the MS DOS 5.0. It runs even on PC 286 machines and is rather modest in memory requirements and relatively fast in response. The system has been created experimentally, for scientific purposes. However, some first positive reactions from academical users show that this approach of creating small applications for particular existing and largely used systems could be very promising. A more informative paper about the QEAPS system will be published.

4　Concluding Remarks About Possible Future

Further development of our knowledge-based advice-giving user interface could be as follows:

- the implementation of the theoretical results into a linguistic interface capable of use in a knowledge-based advice-giving user interface.
- the implementation of a working advice-giving system in front of a widely used commercial database system (e.g., the ORACLE or INGRES) and/or a popular text processing system.

We are convinced that the area of knowledge-based advice-giving user interfaces as well as the possible further application areas are promising areas giving scientifically and economically very interesting results. The future in the area should bring a number of interesting user friendly applications to such existing software systems as complex databases, desk top publishing systems, large scientific program libraries, graphical packages, and, last but not least, knowledge-based systems themselves. We do not expect the full natural language capability to be necessary, we believe in the power of small restricted language processing modules. Our experience in this direction seems to be promising. But one never knows.

Acknowledgements

All the work just described has been done while the author was with the Department of Artificial Intelligence, Comenius University, Bratislava, Slovakia. The author is indebted for the support from the grant A-08/1991 during the period 1991-1993. The author also wishes to express his gratitude to all the colleagues from Bratislava thanks to whom the years in Bratislava have been fruitful and pleasant.

The author wishes to express his deepest thanks to Maddy D. Brouwer - Janse for giving him an opportunity to spend a very pleasant and interesting ten days at the NATO ASI, and to David Connah as well as Tom Bösser for their help in preparing the final version of this paper.

References

1. Carroll, J. M., McKendree, J. : Interface design issues for advice giving expert systems. Comm. ACM 30, 14-31 (1987)
2. Bódi, V.: Active advice-giving systems. Diploma Thesis, Dept. Artificial Intelligence, Comenius University, Bratislava 1993 (in Slovak)
3. Furnas, G. W., Landauer, T. K., Gomez, L. M., Dumais, S. T.: The vocabulary problem in human-system communication. Comm. ACM 30, 964-971 (1987)
4. Furtado, A. L., Moura, C. M. O.: Expert helpers to data-based information systems. In: L. Kerschberg (ed.) Expert Database Systems, 581-596, Benjamin and Cummings 1986
5. Hague, S., Reid, I.: Esprit 2 Project 2620 - FOCUS. Fourth Annual Report - Summary of Progress. FOCUS/NAG/16/23.2-P Document, NAG Ltd., Oxford 1993
6. Houghton, R. C., Jr.: Online help systems: A conspectus. Comm. ACM 27, 126-133 (1984)
7. Kobsa, A., Wahlster, W. (eds.): User Models in Dialog Systems. Berlin: Springer-Verlag 1989
8. Kok, A.: A review and synthesis of user modelling in intelligent systems. Knowledge Eng. Review 6, 21-47 (1991)
9. Mikulecká, J., Mikulecký, P.: Yet another knowledge-based front-end-to-database project. In: F. Belli, F. J. Rademacher (eds.) Industrial and Engineering Applications of Artificial Intelligence and Expert Systems, Proceedings, Paderborn 1992. Lect. Notes Comput. Sci. 604, 622-625, Berlin: Springer 1992
10. Mikulecký, P., Kelemen, J.: Supervising expert systems: An attempt to organize certain mathematical software intelligently. In: Proc.Int.Conf. "Berliner Informatik-Tage '82", 313-325, Berlin 1982

11. Mikulecký, P.: On knowledge-based software tools. Computer Physics Communications **41**, 397-401 (1986)
12. Mikulecký, P., Kalaš, I., Kelemen, J.: Representation of meta-knowledge in expert systems. Computers and AI **5**, 223-234 (1986)
13. Mikulecký, P.: An Overview of Intelligent Front-ends and Advice-giving, Computer Science Preprint No. CS5-91, Department of AI, Faculty of Math. and Physics, Comenius University, Bratislava 1991
14. Siklóssy, L.: Question-asking question-answering systems. In: J.-C.Simon, L. Siklóssy (eds.) Proc. Int. Seminar on Intelligent Question-Answering and Data-Base Systems, 151-163, I.R.I.A., Rocquencourt 1977
15. Siklóssy, L.: Impertinent question-answering systems: Justification and theory. In: Proc. 1978 ACM Nat. Conf., 39-44, Washington D.C. 1978
16. Siklóssy, L.: Active Collaborative Systems. Unpublished manuscript. 1985
17. Tulp, E., Siklóssy, L.: TRAINS: An active time-table searcher. In: ECAI'88 Proceedings, 170-175, Munich 1988
18. Tulp, E., Siklóssy, L.: TRAINS: A case study of active behaviour. In: Proceedings of Int. Workshop on Ind. Appl. Machine Int. and Vision, Tokyo 1989, 259-263, New York: IEEE 1989
19. Tulp, E., Siklóssy, L.: Searching time-table networks. AI EDAM **5**, 189-198 (1991)
20. Wexelblat, R. L.: On interface requirements for expert systems. AI Magazine, 66-78, Fall 1989

Dialogue of Partners as a Method of Non-Formal Problem Solving

Igor Chmyr

Institute of Low Temperature Engineering and Energetics. 1/3 Petra Velikogo St., Odessa
270100, Ukraine

Abstract. Human-machine dialogue can be used not only for organizing the interface, but also as a "solver" for non-formal problems. Methods used by experts in a teaching process are non-formal. We can build a dialogue scenario that simulates an expert's work. The system described in this paper, contains such a scenario, an access method to a set of stimuli.

Keywords. Computer and human dialogue, dialogue scenario, dialogue simulation

1 Simulation of an Expert's Work in the Dialogue Process

Software and hardware resources of modern computers, and particulary those resources that involve human-computer interaction make computers ideal assistants in self-education and teaching.

In last year's reviews, and particulary in the manuscripts that appeared in connection with the NATO Special Program on Advanced Educational Technology (running from 1988 to 1993), many effective approaches for innovative computer program design are described. Let us enumerate some of the methods that were proposed: explanation-based learning [1]; immersion-style environment [2]; hypothesis-driven learning [3]; exploratory learning [4], and so on.

Is it possible to find a certain "common denominator," a universal approach, among the methods that were described, to be used as a basis for design computers teaching programs?

Inside the frames of computerized educational methods it looks very much like the "common denominator" has not been found.

Our opinion is that a universal approach, as mentioned above, has to be described as a computer system that is able to store and realize methods for non-formal problem solving in general. Of course, this system must emulate all applied teaching methods of experts.

Our approach is based upon the supposition that computer-human dialogue, which is perceived not only as a process, but as a knowledge-base, can store both communicative information and "expert logic".

A dialogue between a computer and a human (where the computer remains the active partner), appears like a human-expert work during non-formal problem solving. The analogous properties of both processes are enumerated in Table 1.1.

Table 1.1. The properties in common between non-formal problem solving, by human experts and computer-human dialogue.

The main properties of non-formal problem solving by human experts	The main properties of computer and human dialogue (where the computer remains the active partner)
Multi-step process. At every step an elementary action is executed and a certain intermediate result is obtained.	Multi-step proccess. At each step a computer passes a portion of information to a human and receives a related answer.
An expert knows which elementary action is next, after a concrete result has been obtained. "Expert logic" is knowledge about the connection between the previous result and following action.	The computer program determines the next portion of information which is to pass to a human after the previous answer has been analyzed.
Often, (particulary during teaching) the action and the result obtained are in relationship: "the whole and the part."	Often the information which is passed to a human has a question status, and the answer which the human returns to the computer is a part of the subject of the question .

Thereby, we will describe a computer system for storing and implementing methods of non-formal problem solving, as a system wich would serve to simulate an expert's work by means the computer-human dialogue.

Explanation of terms:

Stimulus. A logical portion of information that is passed from computer to human in a single step. The stimulus may have any duration and be passed through video- and/or audio-channels.

Reaction. Information that is relevant to the stimulus and is passed from human to computer.

Dialogue step. A stimulus with a set of expected and non-expected reactions.

Dialogue scenario. A knowledge base that stores all dialogue step descriptions that are united by "expert logic."

2 A Scenario as an Access Method to the Storage of Stimuli

A computer as an active partner generates a goal oriented sequence of stimuli. This goal is to obtain a solution to a problem. The scenario generates the subsequent stimulus after the reaction from the passive partner has been received.

The idea is that a scenario does not "calculate" the ordinary stimulus, but finds the stimulus in the memory – *StimulStore*.

The scenario, in essence, is an access method to the *StimulStore* registers, and it supports two functions:

- to store "expert logic" for problem solving;
- to generate a current stimulus index for *StimulStore*.

We will use the abbreviation *DiAM* for "dialogue access method" in the following text. A number of applied scenario analyses allow us to conclude that *DiAM* has a network organization. Every node of this network corresponds to dialogue step in the process, and every step corresponds to the elementary dialogue contact act.

In relation to a navigating algorithm (an algorithm that defines the next node index) all *DiAM* nodes are divided into two types:

- nodes with unconditional transition (*Node1* type);
- nodes with conditional transition (*Node2* type).

With *Node1* nodes every recognizing reaction corresponds to only one next node index.

With *Node2* type nodes every recognizing reaction corresponds to a set of node indices. The next node index is choosen contingent upon the reaction meaning accepted at the previous step.

Every *DiAM* node will be simulated by a set of interpretative data which defines one dialogue step. A *DiCycle* will be used as an abbreviation of this interpretator.

Node1 structure is shown in Fig. 2.1.

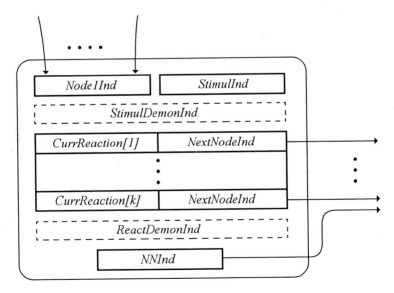

Fig. 2.1. The unconditional transition node organization

The following abbreviations are used in Fig. 2.1:

Node1Ind - the index of *Node1* node;

StimulInd - the index of *StimulStore* register;

StimulDemonInd - the index of "demon," which serves the stimulus;

CurrReaction[1]...CurrReaction[k] − current recognized reaction indices;

{NextNodeInd} − a set of next node indices for recognizing reactions;

ReactDemonInd − the index of "demon," which serves the reaction;

NNInd − the next node index, which is used when a reaction was not recognized.

"Demon" is an optional, non-resident process that is used in those cases when we need an action that the *DiCycle* cannot execute.

A data set that describes *Node1* is interpreted in the following order:

Stimulus phase. The description of the stimulus which is stored in a *StimulInd* register is interpreted. If the description contains *StimulDemonInd*, then this process is loaded and executed.

Reaction phase. The current reaction is accepted and the relevant index is formed. If the description contains a *ReactDemonInd*, then this process is loaded and executed.

Navigation phase. The next node index is defined. For *Node1* nodes we may write the navigational rule:

> if <*CurrReaction[i] is formed*> then <*transit to NextNodeInd[i]*>
>> else
>>> if <*CurrReaction is unrecognized*> then <*transit to NNInd*>

The Node2 organization assumes that all passive partner reactions from the first to the final step are stored in a specific memory, which we will call *PathMem*.

Node2 structure is shown in Fig. 2.2.

In Fig. 2.2 we used the following additional abbreviations:

PathMemInd   − the index of *PathMem* reqister;

PastReaction[1] ... PastReaction[k] − the indices of recognizing reactions in the previous step.

A *Node2* data set interpretation differs from a *Node1* data set interpretation only in the navigation phase. The navigation rule for *Node2* is as follows:

> if (<*CurrReaction[i] is formed*>) and
> (<*PastReaction[j] in the PathMemInd step is also formed*>)
> then <*transit to NextNodeInd[i,j]*>
>> else
>>> if <*CurrReaction is unrecognized*> then <*transit to NNInd*>

A *DiAM* network may be described by various mathematical methods (Petri nets, for example), but it is more constructive to describe *DiAM* as an abstract relational database. This description has two important advantages:

- it does not prevent a complex node elements classification;
- it converts the *DiAM* into data which is easy to edit.

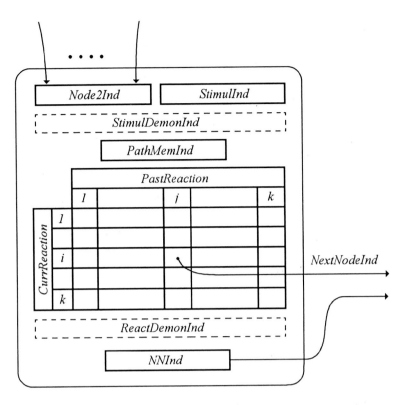

Fig. 2.2. The conditional transition node organization

In the following example of *DiAM* data base description we use the notation from [5]. In this example *DiAM* consist of three relations:

$$DiAM = \{Step, Node1, Node2\}$$

where

    Step = *{NodeInd, NodeType, StimulInd, StimulDemonInd,*
        ReactDemonInd, NNInd}

    dom(NodeInd) = {1, ..., NodeQ};

        NodeQ   - the total quantity of *DiAM* nodes;

    dom (NodeType) = {1,2};

    dom (StimulInd) = {1, ..., StimulQ};

        StimulQ - the total quantity of *StimulStore* registers;

                NodeQ≥ StimulQ

    dom (StimulDemonInd) = {<StimulDemon names table>};

    dom (ReactDemonInd) = {<ReactDemon names table>};

    dom (NNInd) = {1, ..., NodeQ}.

A single *DiAM* node is described as one *Step* relation cortege.

$Node1 = \{\underline{Node1Ind, CurrReactionInd}, NextNodeInd\}$

$dom\,(Node1Ind) = \{1, ..., Node1Q\}$

$Node1Q$ - the total quantity of unconditional transition nodes;

$dom\,(CurrReactionInd) = \{1, ..., k\}$

k - the quantity of recognizing reactions available for each node;

$dom\,(NextNodeInd) = \{1, ..., NodeQ\}.$

The correspondence between a single $Node1$ node and surrounding nodes is described as being less then or equal to k corteges of the $Node1$ relation. (See Fig. 2.1).

$Node2 = \{\underline{Node2Ind, CurrReactionInd, PathMemInd, PastReactionInd},\\ NextNodeInd\}$

$dom\,(Node2Ind) = \{1, ..., Node2Q\}$

$Node2Q$ - the total quantity of conditional transition nodes;

$$Node1Q + Node2Q = NodeQ$$

$dom\,(CurrReactionInd) = dom\,(PastReactionInd) = \{1, ..., k\}$

$dom\,(PathMemInd) = \{1, ..., N)$

N - the total quantity of $PathMem$ registers;

The correspondence between a single $Node2$ node and surrounding nodes is described as being less than or equal to k^2 corteges of the $Node2$ relation. (See Fig. 2.2.)

We may call this $DiAM$ organizational approach, datalogical. Scenario creation is a permanent editing process. The datalogical approach allows us to design a full-screen scenario editor that simplifies and accelerates the editing process and gives experts the possibility to create scenarios by themselves.

3 The Architecture of "Dialogue Solver"

The computer environment needed for the simulation of expert work by means of computer-human dialogue consists of the following units.

1. Temporary storage for dialogue process, $PathMem$, stores a sequence of passive-partner reactions from the first step to the step when a solution to the task has been obtained.

2. Stimulus permanent storage, $StimulStore$, is a direct access storage that stores an indexed set of stimuli descriptions.

3. Dialogue access method, $DiAM$, is a database which stores a problem-solving method. For every input reaction $DiAM$ provides access to a single indexed element of $StimulStore$.

4. Dialogue processor, $DiCycle$, is a resident process that provides step-by-step interpretation of scenario.

5. Demons-procedure library, $DemonLib$, is a set of external procedures which fulfill functions not covered by $DiCycle$.

Demon-procedures have no limits. They can work with any program-accessed storages of a computer.

The main aim of *StimulDemon* is to execute video or audio effects that cannot be executed by *DiCycle*.

In general, *ReactDemon* can be used in those cases when *DiAM* serves as a dialogue shell for a computational-algorithm kernal of an applied program.

Reactions obtained can be used in several ways:

- to define a next node index;
- to be stored for future use by demon procedure;
- to explain the logic of a task-solving process when we use a chain of stimuli and reactions to form a deductive conclusion.

The *PathMem* must store the "history" of a dialogue process. Let every *PathMem* register consist of the following set of fields.

PathMemInd - the index of dialogue process step.

NodeInd - the index of *DiAM* node.

PastReactionInd - the index of the reaction that was chosen. (In the case when a stimulus contains a list of reactions and one reaction has been chosen).

PastReactionSense - a verbal description of the reaction.

PastReactionValue - the value of the reaction that was engaged. (In the case when a stimulus has predetermined the reactions of external input).

The architecture of non-formal problem "dialogue solver" is shown in Fig. 3.1. In this figure numbers are used to show the sequence of acts during the interpretation of dialogue step.

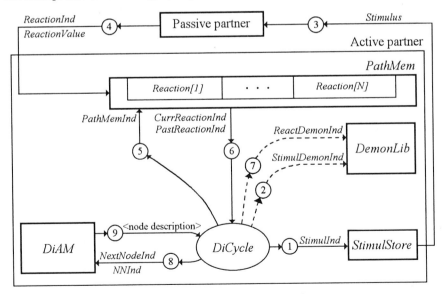

Fig.3.1 The architecture of a system which can solve problems using a "dialogue method."

4 Conclusion

An approach to the building of a system that is oriented to non-formal problem solving by means the simulation of expert work has been described.

The simulation of expert work may be realized when a computer plays an active role in human and computer dialogue.

The probable sphere of application of this approach is the transmission of knowledge, education and design.

We have used the approach described for the design of software tools and have applied this software (named "Dialogue Processor") to simulate expert work in the teaching of foreign language and design engineering. This work was executed in the "Dialogue Systems Laboratory" in the Odessa Institute of Low Temperature Engineering and Energetics (Ukraine).

Acknowledgements

In addition to the natural acknowledgement to my colleagues in our "Dialogue Systems Laboratory", the author would like to thank Dr.ir. Maddy D. Brouwer-Janse for her assistance and supporting.

References

1. Carlo Tasso, Danilo Fum and Paolo Giangrandi: The use of explanation-based learning for modeling student behavior in foreign language tutoring. In M.L. Swartz and M. Yazdani (eds.) Intelligent tutoring systems for foreign language learning. NATO ASI Series, Vol. F80, 151-170. Berlin: Springer 1992
2. Henry Hamburger and Raza Hashim: Foreign language tutoring and learning environment. In M.L. Swartz and M. Yazdani (eds.) Intelligent tutoring systems for foreign language learning. NATO ASI Series, Vol F80, 201-219. Berlin: Springer 1992
3. Peter Reimann: Modeling active, hypothesis-driven learning from worked-out examples. In E. De Corte, M.C. Linn, H. Mandl and L. Verschaffel (eds.) Computer-based learning environments and problem solving. NATO ASI Series, Vol F84, 129-148. Berlin: Springer 1992
4. Richard Ennals: Computers and exploratory learning in the real world. In P.A.M. Kommers, D.H. Jonassen and J.T. Mayes (eds.) Cognitive tools for learning. NATO ASI Series, Vol F81, 139-146. Berlin: Springer 1992
5. Maier D.: The theory of relational databases. Computer Science Press 1983

Modeling a Partner in a Dialogue

Oleg P. Pilipenko

Odessa State University
2 Petra Velikogo St., Odessa 270100, Ukraine

Abstract. We propose a formal model, based on automata, for dialogue systems. This model is used as a methodological base for Dialogue Processor — a CASE-tool for the development of dialogue systems which can conduct dialogue according to a stored scenario.

Keywords. Formal model, automaton, dialogue system, partners' dialogue

1 Partners' Dialogue

Functions of a dialogue system are problem-independent and are determined only by specifics of human–computer interaction. This fact allows us to separate user interface from application programs and to build a formal model for dialogue systems [1]. Such a model can be used as a methodological base for CASE-tools to develop dialogue systems. This model of dialogue should be constructive: simple enough to be implemented and complex enough to cover a wide range of dialogue processes.

Some authors consider the human-computer dialogue as a sequence of question-answer pairs. Participants' roles are strictly determined - one of them is asking (active) partner, another is answering (passive) partner. However, our experience shows that this kind of dialogue is not widespread in everyday communication. It is found almost exclusively in formal teacher/student settings.

More frequently initiative in dialogue is passed from one participant to another. We call this kind of dialogue *partners' dialogue*. The answering partner can intercept initiative when he does not understand a question or does not have enough information to answer a question. In this case the initiative is intercepted for a short time. The answering partner may also intercept initiative when the asking partner fails to formulate a question correctly and the answering partner needs to ask series of questions to define the asking partner's demands more precisely and to give an acceptable answer finally. In the last case the initiative is intercepted for more time.

It is particularly important to be able to model the partners' dialogue in order to develop modern dialogue systems. Partners' dialogue is more productive because it imitates our natural usage of dialogue.

2 The Automaton Model

Some authors use automaton models to describe dialogue sytems. Proposed paper extends traditional models to describe partners' dialogue.

Let us define an automaton, P, as the quadruple $< S, D, E, h >$, where S is a set of automaton states, where the initial state, s_0, and the final state, s_n, are distinguished; D is a set of inputs; E is a set of outputs and $h : S \times D \rightarrow S \times E$ is a function that calculates the automaton output, e, and next state, $\bar{s}$, according to the current state, s, and automaton input, d, (user's action). Along with (or instead of) step function, h, we may consider output function $f : S \times D \rightarrow S$ and transition function $g : S \times D \rightarrow E$ such that $h(s,d) = \big(g(s,d), f(s,d) \big)$.

We shall introduce some sets: Q is a set of user's questions, A is a set of user's answers, Q' is a set of automaton questions and A' is a set of automaton answers. There is null answer, a_0, in A'. For each s_k we shall define special sets: Q_k a set of discernible user's questions, and A_k a set of discernible user's answers. Let there exist an input, d_0, which cannot be recognized as a discernible user's question or answer at any step:

$$d_0 \notin \bigcup_{k=1}^{n} Q_k \,, d_0 \notin \bigcup_{k=1}^{n} A_k \,,$$ and $d_0 \in D$. The set of inputs to automaton consists of possible user's questions and answers ($D = Q \cup A$), and its set of outputs contains its own answers and questions which it asks while intercepting initiative in dialogue ($E = Q' \cup A'$).

Let us consider classes of automaton states. Automaton can:
—answer a user's question and wait for the next question;
—ask a question and wait for a user's action;
—answer a question, intercept the initiative, ask the user a question, and wait for the user's action.

We denote them accordingly, S^1, S^2 and S^3. The final state s_n remains not embedded in any set. We can note that $S = S^1 \cup S^2 \cup S^3 \cup s_n$.

There is some natural order of states from different categories. We shall describe this order in the terms of constraints for functions g and f.

Let us examine the transition function, g. Assume that the automaton is in the s_k state. If $s_k \in S^1$ and the user's action, d, is not recognized as a discernible question or answer, the $g(s_k, d)$ state belongs to S^2. If $s_k \in S^2 \cup S^3$ and the user's action is not recognized or recognized as a discernible answer then the $g(s_k, d)$ state belongs to S^2. If there is no such state, s, that $g(s, d) = s_n$ for some d, then our dialogue system will never stop. Such kind of dialogue system is permissible, nevertheless we believe that for some (at least one) nodes $s_k \in S^2 \cup S^3$ under some answer of user, d, dialogue terminates (transits to the final state s_n). The logic of the dialogue process assumes that a dialogue has its goal, so dialogue stops after the goal is attained. If $\exists k \; \exists d \; (d \in Q_k \; \& \; g(s_k, d) = s_n)$, in other words, if dialogue system can terminate directly after it accepts a question, we may consider its behavior incorrect, «impolite»: instead of answering the user's question, the dialogue system terminates.

Let us examine the output function, f. Assume that automaton is in the s_k state. If user's action, d, is recognized as question ($d \in Q_k$) then the automaton can proceed by answering the question ($f(s_k, d) \in A'$), or intercepting the initiative and asking the user a question of its own ($f(s_k, d) \in Q'$). If a user's action is recognized as an answer ($d \in A_k$) then automaton will ask the user a new question or will answer the most recent unanswered question.

Consider the automaton cycle. If the current automaton state is $s_k \in S^2$, the automaton will ask a question. If $s_k \in S^1 \cup S^3$, automaton will begin step with visualization of the answer which was obtained on the previous step. If $s_k \in S^3$, after the answer is visualized automaton will intercept the initiative and ask the question $q \in Q'$ connected with the current state. Following any of the given situations, the automaton will wait for the user's action. In any state the automaton must recognize some of the user's actions as questions. The accepted user's action is either recognized as a question from Q_k or an answer from A_k, or it remains unrecognized. According to accepted action automaton produces an output $e = f(s_k, d)$. If the action remained unrecognized then $f(s_k, d) = f(s_k, d_0)$. Then automaton transits to the new state $g(s_k, d)$.

Automaton starts from the state s_0. Automaton can start dialogue as an active partner, asking the user a question, or as passive partner, waiting for the user's question. In the first case $s_0 \in S^2$. In the second case we consider that $s_0 \in S^1$ and that automaton will start this step with visualization of the null answer, a_0. When automaton transits to the s_n state, it stops.

3 The Net Model

The correspondence of automata and graphical presentations is discussed in [2].

The state-transition diagram of the automaton mentioned above can be mapped to a network $G = \langle S, \Gamma \rangle$ with the node set S and the relation Γ that sets up a correspondence between node s_i and the set of nodes $\Gamma(s_i)$ which are the ends of the edges starting from this node. All edges starting from each node are numbered (probably, with gaps). In this way all elements of every $\Gamma(s_i)$ are numbered (see Fig. 3.1). Let us slightly change the transition function g so that $g : S \times D \to N$, where N is the set of the natural numbers. Transition will occur from the current node, s_k, to the node ending the edge with number $g(s_k, d)$. We shall not represent the final node s_n. The dialogue system will finish its work when there is no edge which starts from the current node and has number $g(s_k, d)$.

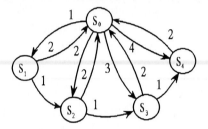

Fig. 3.1. Sample dialogue scenario network

We call the couple of the step function h and the network G augmented with edge numbers the *dialogue scenario.*

4 Implementation of the Net Model

This net model is useful as a formal base for the universal dialogue interpreter which can conduct dialogue according to a stored dialogue scenario.

4.1 General Issues

The step function, h, can be implemented by the internal facilities of the dialogue interpreter or by the use of *external processes*. Some answers to the user's questions and/or transition codes can be calculated by a separate executable modules invoked by system. In the case of the usage of external processes we need to be able to move data between the dialogue system and the external process.

Database or knowledge base can be connected to such a dialogue system. It can contain some facts, data or rules about how to analyze the user's questions or how to synthesize answers. Then some steps of dialogue can be connected with modifications of the database or knowledge base.

In order to implement a generator of dialogue scenarios based on the abovementioned net model, we need to choose an interpretation of sets S, Q and A. We may consider any keystroke, mouse button click or mouse movement as a user's action. However, such interpretation would lead to an unnecessarily detailed dialogue scenario consisting of an unmanageably large number of nodes. To reduce complexity of the dialogue scenario networks we can use their recursiveness. We can replace some subgraphs with nodes and thus increase the «granularity» of nodes and of possible user questions and answers. We can substitute nodes for subgraphs satisfying the following condition: All edges entering a subgraph enter the same node. We call such subgraphs substituted by nodes *scenario units*.

Objects that are commonly used in interfaces, such as entry fields, menus, dialogue boxes with pushbuttons, radio buttons and check boxes, may be considered as standard scenario units.

Conception of the scenario units allows us to develop dialogue scenarios by means of incremental refinement. We can provide the reusability of scenario units: the same units can be used instead of the different nodes or even in different dialogue scenarios.

To facilitate the generation of dialogue scenarios we should maintain library of the scenario units. Such a library may also contain individual dialogue steps, objects that form dialogue steps, and even elemens of objects (bitmaps, texts, fonts and so on).

It can be useful to store more extensive information on history of the current dialogue session. For example, if user can access such information then he can quickly determine where he is and optimally navigate through the dialogue scenario network. Presence of the history of the current dialogue session allows to make help subsystem of the dialogue system more context sensitive. It even will be possible to predict the user's intentions and prompt for ways to complete them.

There arises a practical question: how can we divide scenario into scenario units? If we consider a dialogue system as multifunctional software tool, we may incapsulate separate functions of a system into scenario units. We also may divide scenario so that long term initiative transitions are connected with separate scenario units. These approaches are complimentary because, on one hand, any dialogue system may be considered as a means to achieve goals. On the other hand, to achieve a goal dialogue system conducts dialogue and during this dialogue partners' roles may be changed.

4.2 Generating Dialogue Scenario

In order to create a dialogue scenario we need a dialogue scenario generator which can do some standard operations on the net G. At least it should be capable of selecting the current node and the current edge; inserting a new node or a new edge; deleting a node or an edge; modifying the current node or the current edge.

Since all nodes are numbered, we may select current node by specifying its number. Also it is convenient to select a node «next» to the current — a node at the end of the current edge. When a new node is selected as current, the first edge (or the edge with the least number) becomes current.

Insertion of the new node should be accompanied by creation of new edges, at least one entering the new node. In order to prevent isolated nodes it can be useful to create an edge between the current node and the new node automatically on the insertion of the new node.

Deletion of the current node should be accompanied by deletion of all edges entering the node. It can be done automatically by complete look over of all net edges.

On deletion of the current edge the dialogue scenario generator should detect appearances of the isolated nodes. If such a situation occurs, it is necessary to forbid deletion of the current edge or to warn user that deletion of the last edge entering a node automatically causes deletion of that node.

Modification of the current node, s_k, can be accomplished by a change of the node class, or by a change of the means of visualization of the answer and/or question, or by modification of the step function, $h(s_k, d)$. If we change the node class, the dialogue scenario generator should check whether the above-mentioned constraints (see Chap. 2) of function h are conformed. We may modify the step function, $h(s_k, d)$, by changing the output function, $f(s_k, d)$, or by changing the transition function, $g(s_k, d)$. We also may modify the current node substituting a scenario unit for it.

Modification of the edge number changes conditions on which the dialogue transits from the node at the start of the edge to the node at the end of the edge or changes the order of states on some paths of the dialogue process.

4.3 Recommendations on the Development of the Dialogue Scenarios

We recommend generating dialogue scenarios by means of incremental refinement. We can start the generation of any scenario with the network $G_0 = <\{ s_0 \}, \{ < s_0, s_0 > \} >$ which consists of one node and one edge starting from and ending at that node (see Fig. 4.1). Further we can extend the net explicitly, adding new nodes and edges, or implicitly, substituting scenario units for some nodes.

Fig. 4.1. Network G_0

We recommend providing all or, at least, some nodes with *common dialogue actions*. Those actions are called common because they have common meaning in any dialogue scenario. They are: entrance (one step advance); exit (a return of one step); scenario unit exit; scenario exit.

One step advance makes sense if there is some natural step order. For example, during editing sessions (as editing text with word processor) it is natural to advance to the process of editing of object after object is selected. At this step the return to the selection of the new object or cancellation of the editing session we may consider as actions under some uncommon conditions.

A return of one step is necessary if selection of the next dialogue step can be made incidentally. Providing one step return is especially recommended for the steps, which interpretation can take long time or leads to essential changes in the database (knowlege base) connected with the dialogue scenario.

A scenario unit may have some nodes from which there is an exit (transition to the final state, s_n). Along with the normal exit and exits on the errors we recommend providing an exit on cancellation. Users often choose system functions by mistake and will need a clearly marked «emergency exit» to leave the unwanted state without having to go through an extended dialogue. The only way to distinguish how the recent scenario unit terminated is the transition code (value of the function g) on the last step of this unit. We believe that engineer of the dialogue scenario should have an opportunity to generate scenario in such a way that different exits out of scenario unit are distinguished. On the other hand, it is convenient not to distinguish different exits of one kind (for example, cancellation on the first step of the scenario unit or after some steps of the dialogue). To satisfy these requirements we permitted numbering edges with gaps (see Chap. 3).

We can consider scenario exit as the dialogue system termination or as switching to another dialogue system with the option of restarting dialogue from the step at which that switching occurred.

A dialogue restart is very important for multitasking environments and for dialogue systems, which need a long time to complete the dialogue. We can treat educating systems and knowledge transfer systems as systems of the second class. To restart dialogue, we need to have an opportunity to start dialogue not only from step s_0, but from any step belonging to some set $\left\{ s_{i_1}, s_{i_2}, ..., s_{i_m} \right\}$. Along with that we need to provide possibility of storing a restart step number and probably last answer of the dialogue system.

4.4 The Dialogue Processor

The model of a dialogue partner was implemented in the Dialogue Processor project. The Dialogue Processor consists of the Dialogue Generator to generate dialogue scenarios, and the Dialogue Interpreter to interpret these scenarios. The Dialogue Generator stores a generated scenario as a metafile — a stream of objects. The scenario determines dialogue steps (net nodes) and permissible transitions (net edges). Each dialogue step can include passive audio- and video-objects, active video-objects and description of external process that the step invokes. Passive objects are used to express a question or an answer for a user's question. Active video-objects are used to give the user an opportunity to answer a question or to ask his own question.

Passive video-objects are panels with static text or bitmaps. Animated passive video-objects and audio-objects add an expressive force to generated dialogues. Active video-objects are standard dialogue panels - menus, choice lists, or dialogue boxes with entry fields and choice fields of different kinds.

5 Prospects

The Dialogue Processor uses object-oriented technology and stores dialogue scenarios as streams of objects. Further development of the object-oriented databases will allow storage in one database dialogue objects and application objects as well which promotes the creation of more complex dialogue systems.

The proposed model can be extended to describe training of the dialogue partner. If we assume that the step function, sets of net nodes and edges, or sets of discerning questions and answers depend on time, we obtain a model of a non-stationary dialogue system. If we add system actions that modify the above-mentioned elements of a dialogue system, we obtain a model of the instructable partner of the dialogue process.

References

1. Hisashi Nakatsuyama, Makoto Murata, Koji Kusumoto. A new framework for separating user interfaces from application programs. SIGCHI Bulletin Vol. 23 No. 1 (1991)
2. Indranil Chakravarty, Michael F. Kleyn. Visualisms for describing Interactive Systems. In: G. Clocton (Ed.) Engineering for Human-Computer Interaction. Elsevier Science Publishers B.V. (North-Holland) 1990

A Visual Knowledge Elicitation Language and Methodology for Acquiring Non-Verbal Expertise

Benjamin Singer[1] and Jean-Luc Soubie[2]

[1] Aramiihs Laboratory 31, rue des Cosmonautes 31077 Toulouse Cedex, France
[2] Irit Laboratory 118, route de Narbonne 31062 Toulouse Cedex, France

Abstract. In this paper we propose a Visual Knowledge Elicitation language and methodology for picture understanding, in order to take into account visual expertise for interpreting static pictures or dynamic image sequences. The domain of expertise considered here is that of team games, with an application to rugby.

Keywords. Knowledge Acquisition, Visual Knowledge, Picture Understanding

1 Introduction

In this contribution we propose a specific Visual Knowledge Elicitation (VKE) language for images or image sequences understanding. This domain independent language is included in a knowledge acquisition software tool implemented on a Color Sparc station.

The first part of the paper details the scientific problem in distinguishing and comparing verbal and visual approaches to Knowledge Acquisition (KA). Non-verbal approaches are illustrated by means of more striking associated methodologies, which in general include both KA methods and software tools. The knowledge partition in deep and surface levels, according to Steels [5], is then described to justify our restriction to the acquisition of surface knowledge. The second part of the paper examplifies our contribution by a specific acquisition technique, based on a VKE language, applied to the interpretation of symbolic image sequences of team games, using rugby as an example. The third part deals with the representation and structuring stages, for the verbal and visual knowledge, following the MACAO methodology and using the MACAO software tool.

In conclusion we point out the originality of our KA approach, and the generality of the results achieved for a growing number of similar tasks, which currently includes a major picture understanding activity.

2 Research Framework : Non-Verbal KA Methodologies

The KA methodologies, which are recognized and used today and which follow data-driven or model-driven approaches, are in fact only verbal i.e. are based either on transcribing the expert's verbalizations (from directed or non-centered interviews) or on existing written documents which capitalize the expertise.

There are however many new requirements nowadays, particularly these related to the growing number of technical tasks involving an interpretation activity of image or image sequence. So designers are led to propose new non-verbal KA methods and to realize the associated software tools. Thus we can use the term of Visual Knowledge Acquisition (VKA).

The specific methodology proposed here has been applied to the study of team games, and particularly to the understanding of rugby image sequences taken from real matches. A new recording technique is used to associate a colour video image sequence with any game sequence. The new technique was a single fixed camera with a fixed lens which is attached to a crane and records a continuous trend of all the actors in the game (ball, single players, subsets of players).

For our domain, the study is restricted to the acquisition of the surface knowledge from Pierre Villepreux's model [6], because the deep knowledge has been already correctly formalized by Deleplace's logical model, called "real-time Tactical Choice Systematics". At any time t of a game sequence, this model gives all the possible options at $(t + \Delta t)$ in an n-ary decision set formalism.

3 Our Non-Verbal Approach based on a Visual Knowledge Elicitation Language

The context of our study is that of image sequence understanding in the domain of team games, using rugby as an example [2]. The aim of our research project is to realize a KBS for analyzing game sequences from video image sequences of a given team, in order to propose tactical improvements during the training stages for future matches [3]. Such a system is to be seen as a software tool to assist tactical decision-making. Its definition has been preceded by a domain formalization step, and a reasoning model based on a typical game sequence partition, and on different inference levels [1]. The interpretation is carried out by the expert on symbolic image sequences - and no longer video. Such sequences are reconstructed from the data from an image processing module, which takes digitalized color video images as input. Such a module is located upstream of the VKE software tool [4].

3.1 Visual Diagramming Languages for Knowledge Acquisition

Casner has proposed an interesting contribution to Problem Solving Methods for visual knowledge processing, by formally defining, then using in separate domains, diagramming languages. Such languages, which can be seen as particular languages for VKA, differ from iconic languages because they are defined as strict mathematical transformations between a set of perceptual codes (such as patterns, colors, or spatial combinations of isolated objects) and a set of interpretations, whose goal is to associate a semantic level with the use of these perceptual codes. The diagramming language uses iconic representations, spatial distributions and graphical symbols to represent the entities at an individual level (players), a collective level (teams, attack, defense) and a meta-collective level (global movements, strategies). Such diagrams refer to the associated concepts.

3.2 Visual Knowledge Elicitation

3.2.1 Choosing the Experts

Our approach, which is focused on knowledge acquisition and representation, embodies Pierre Villepreux's expertise. Pierre Villepreux was a high-level competition player and is nowadays a famous coach and technical director : he is considered by other coaches to be a high-level theorist of the game [6]. Our choice is explained by the theoretical formalization level reached by the expert and by the existence of a more general model, consistent with this expertise and which is necessary to understand it. Proposed by René Deleplace, such an including formal framework is the so-called "real-time Tactical Choice Systematics" or "deleplacian logical model", which is both theoretical and practical.

3.2.2 Integrating the VKE Language into a KA Software Tool

Our VKE language has been integrated with a specific visual KA software tool. Its specifications follow an object-oriented design and programming methodology, and the supporting language is C++ under SunView and X Windows environments unified by OpenWindows. It runs on a Color Sparc IPC Workstation. The VKE language is based on selecting isolated and global objects (discrete or not), in order to represent pertinent subsets of the symbolic picture which is being considered. Besides designating objects, the expert can give the trajectory of the manipulated subsets in terms of parallel or sequential movements. Thus owing to an explicit selection mechanism, here implemented by a mouse, he draws the (object, concept) pairs he manipulates during his reasoning.

Thus we can associate visual information - which can be approximated by quite simple geometrical models - to reasoning sequences, and movement expression characteristics, that current tools for acquisition and structuring do not allow one to take into account or to capture in order to design more and more efficient KBs. This elicitation language is above all domain independent.

3.3 Complete Definition of the VKE Language

The actual language design process using the extended BNF formalism has these complementary parts : initial static definition, then dynamic description for use by the expert. Thus to turn specification into action, we have to follow two steps.

3.3.1 Static Definition of the VKE Language

The BNF formalism is seen as a Knowledge Representation formal language. By combining them, we give the BNF productions of our static VKE language. The associated formal grammar is composed of a finite set of productions (its cardinality is 16), and starts from the <VK ELICITATION> axiom. The rules are numbered for convenience of reference. No ordering is in fact implied. Headings are inserted to facilitate locating sections of the grammar. The resulting sections are to be used as a rough guide only.
Terminal symbols : any string in lower case,

Non-terminal symbols : any variable between inferior and superior meta-symbols,
Start symbol : VK ELICITATION,
Meta-symbols : BNF constructors and operators,
Rules :
Start symbol
  1. <VK ELICITATION> ::= (<Space-Time> . <Movement>)$^+$
Space and time
  2. <Space-Time> ::= [<Object> trajectory]
Movement definition
  3. <Movement> ::= <Space-Time> <Relative speed> <Sequentiality>
Object definitions
  4. <Object> ::= <Isolated object>| <Global object> . <Shape name>
  5. <Isolated object> ::= visual representation of an elementary entity {e.g., ball}
  6. <Global object> ::= <Discrete global object>| <Non-discrete global object>
  7. <Discrete global object> ::= visually countable set of isolated objects
  8. <Non-discrete global object> ::= visually non-countable set of isolated objects
Shape selection and description
  9. <Shape name> ::= name given by the expert to the global object shapes
Speeds
10. <Relative speed> ::= <Less fast speed>| <Equal speed>| <Faster speed>
11. <Less fast speed> ::= first option of "ad-hoc" visual conventions
12. <Equal speed> ::= second option of "ad-hoc" visual conventions
13. <Faster speed> ::= third option of "ad-hoc" visual conventions
Displacements
14. <Sequentiality> ::= <Sequential movement>| <Parallel movement>
15. <Sequential movement> ::= sequential related to the last manipulated object
16. <Parallel movement> ::= parallel in relation to the last considered object

3.3.2 Dynamic Definition of the VKE Language

During their use by the expert, there is a running order for the commands. Such an order is defined by the following formal grammar given in the BNF formalism. It is composed of a set of p production rules (p = 15). The rules are numbered for convenience of reference, but no ordering is implied. Headings are inserted to facilitate locating sections.
Terminal symbols : any string in lower case,
Non-terminal symbols : any variable between inferior and superior meta-symbols,
Start symbol : FUNCTIONS,
Meta-symbols : BNF constructors and operators,
Rules :
Start symbol
  1. <FUNCTIONS> ::= (<Initializing> . <Processing> . <Finishing up>)$^+$
Initialisation step
  2. <Initializing> ::= <Filename> . <Acquisition start>
  3. <Filename> ::= the coordinates filename corresponding to the current image
  4. <Acquisition start> ::= reads the coordinates file, shows the initial spatial
     distributions

Ending step
  5. <Finishing up> ::= <Session writing> . <End of acquisition>
  6. <Session writing> ::= file writing of the expert's work session
  7. <End acquisition> ::= quit the KA software tool
Working sessions
  8. <Processing> ::= (<VK ELICITATION>│ <Chrono>│ <Match>│
                  <Parallel Simulation>│
                  <Sequential Simulation>│ <Domain Modelling>)*
  9. <VK ELICITATION> ::= see the previous section
  10. <Chrono> ::= temporal context of the image {in minutes and seconds}
  11. <Match> ::= spatial context of the game {team names, competition, stadium}
Parallel and sequential animations
  12. <Parallel Simulation> ::= parallel movement of all the objects whose
                      trajectory has been explicitly given by the expert
  13. <Sequential Simulation> ::= sequential movement of all the objects whose
                      trajectory has been explicitly given by the expert
Deep knowledge modelling
  14. <Domain Modelling> ::= [<Inflexion>]│ (<Inflexion> . <Inflexion>)$^{+}$
  15. <Inflexion> ::= visual representation, according to Deleplace's theory of the speed vector and inflexion limits; eventually visualization of these basic concepts in hidden mode, because there are not always useful during the expert's work.

3.4 Acquisition Sessions with the Expert

3.4.1 User's Interface

Discrete and non-discrete objects, relative speeds, sequential or parallel displacements, and other functions have been implemented : the "Start-Acquisition" and "End-of-Acquisition" options, which respectively initialize the expert's work by reading the input data file (2D (x, y) players coordinates) and quit the software tool. The semantic difference between the VKE language and the complementary functionalities is integrated into the interface itself and is composed of three parts :
- an *horizontal command area*, located horizontally on the screen, and including the functions (the processing options and the filename associated to the picture),
- a *vertical commands area*, located on the right side of the screen, and dedicated to the options of the VKE language,
- the *central command area* contains an aerial symbolic representation composed of a bird's eye view of the static background, including all the (2p+1) individual actors i.e. the p attackers, the p defenders and the ball.

3.4.2 Geometrical Models for Pattern Approximation

The expert can draw discrete or non discrete global objects, which represent convex or concave patterns given by their closure. Any closure is defined by its polygonal approximation, seen as a set of segments. Our aim is to find in this case the most suitable pattern model of this drawn on the screen by the expert. There is no restriction about the patterns that could be designed : the expert can propose the pattern he wants when solving a problem. Such an approach is of a double interest: on the one hand for the expert, in order to help him to describe and formalize the patterns he uses in his resolution models by simple geometrical figures, and on the other hand for the knowledge engineer, in order to capture non ambiguous objects for the knowledge representation and structuring phase.

We want to provide the expert with a generic geometrical palette. There are a large number of analytic models. Nevertheless for our domain the following hierarchy of classes is sufficient : conics, parallelograms, and polygons.

3.4.3 Domain Dependent Functions

The three domain dependent functions are the following :
- spatial context (match and competition framework),
- temporal context (time in minutes and seconds) associated to the current image sequence owing to the "Chrono" button,
- for any isolated object considered and taking into account its specific individual role (attacker or defender), the Deleplace button is dedicated to visualizing the concepts coming from the deep knowledge i.e. the deleplacian modelling of general movement phases : module and direction of the speed vector, the inflexion angle generating the inflexion cone.

3.4.4 Handling Sessions

The following screen copy is an image of a current visual knowledge acquisition session. We can see that a geometrical pattern model palette is proposed to the expert on the right side : it is composed of the first four figures mentioned in the last previous section : ellipse, circle, rectangle and square. After drawing any pattern, the expert wants to approximate it by one of these options in choosing the associated button : the software tool automatically adjusts the model to the pattern which has been drawn.

3.4.5 Interactive Simulation of the Reasoning Steps

The "Sequential Simulation" and "Parallel Simulation" buttons allow the user respectively to visualize at any time and in real-time a behavioral simulation of the players motions only for these whose trajectory has been explicitly given by the expert. There are two options. If the action is sequential, the software makes a complete displacement of the players being considered one after another. In the case of simultaneous trajectories, players are all animated in parallel step by step.

The expert proceeds to such simulations either after each reasoning substage, or at the end of the working session. The visual trail of each simulation is printed on a paper sheet, by interactive screen hardcopies.

3.4.6 Disk Writing of Visual Information

Keeping in mind the knowledge representation phase for the KB structuring, we want to have a trail of the acquisition work with the expert. So a Session Backup option is proposed and enables the writing to disk of all the information associated with isolated or global objects. Concerning the special "Ball" object, if a player is keeping it at t, the data are simply duplicated. For discrete or non discrete global objects, the same procedure is executed. Indeed, even if the visual counting of isolated objects is not possible, these objects are in fact present within the symbolic representation.

4 Non-Verbal Knowledge Representation and Modelling

4.1 Why a Modelling Stage is Essential

For understanding pictures, defining and implementing a VKE language is not sufficient. Indeed we have to consider a knowledge representation and structuring phase in order to design the KB. This is done by using the MACAO methodology and running the associated software tool. More precisely for any problem solved by the expert, by using the semantic nets formalism for domain modelling, and the schemas formalism for reasoning modelling.

4.2 The MACAO Knowledge Modelling Methodology and Tool

MACAO is a knowledge elicitation and modelling methodology which has two generality levels i.e. is both domain and expert independent. A well-known decomposition of expertise transfer for KBs design distinguishes for the data, their elicitation, abstraction, analysis, structuring then validation. The aim of this KA methodology is to assist the whole expertise transfer process, to design the complete Abstract Conceptual Model of the KB. So this typical data-driven acquisition methodology enables us to construct an Abstract Conceptual Model by knowledge elicitation by solving all the major classes of problems.

4.3 How Verbal Knowledge is Processed with MACAO : Static and Dynamic Knowledge Modelling

The dynamic knowledge associated with the reasoning is expressed with MACAO by using schemes graphs. Such a modelling stage is induced from the knowledge acquisition and linked to the schemas representation language.

For instance, to solve the problem "Attaque-Jeu-Déployé", two graphs are necessary : one to model the static knowledge (domain) and the other the dynamic knowledge (reasoning), by using resp. the semantic nets and schemas formalisms.

4.4 Extending MACAO to Take Into Account Visual Information

4.4.1 Quick Description of the Extension

Concerning the representation phase, we have to extend the scheme structure in order to take into consideration the visual knowledge manipulated during the expert's inferences. Such an extension is done by inserting a link on the graphic visualization (characteristic pattern on a symbolic image) corresponding to all the specific concepts manipulated in the scheme. This insertion implies an updatery of the existing structure by including a logical link in the CONTEXT and GOAL fields, by adding a new "DISPLAY IMAGE" button, to show respectively the input defensive and the output offensive spatial distributions, which can be perceived following the corresponding patterns.

The consequence of such an extension consists in the design of two symbolic picture directories, structured by typical defense and attack distribution patterns.

4.4.2 Generalizing our Approach to Related Visual Expertise

It seems obvious that we could easily transpose our approach to the growing number of tasks which nowadays include a picture understanding activity, using either fixed images or image sequences. There are plenty of applicative domains, such as static or dynamic imageries in sportive or technical areas.

Indeed our technique for elicitating non-verbal expertise is generic and could be first applied to other ball games, because the status of the manipulated objects remain exactly the same for isolated players, sets of players and trajectories. No significant changes arise in the visual acquisition technique, and the same methodology could be run with a football high-level expert for instance.

5 Conclusion

The originality of our approach consists of the proposed VKE language. Indeed our visual KA methodology, for non-verbal expertise, is based on this generic VKE language, which has been defined precisely, and whose use has been shown in the domain of team games. Its basic interest is that it is rather suitable to the specific needs in picture understanding than the usual verbal methods. Let us now compare it with Casner's diagramming language, and with Gaines'interactive visual language. All are seen as formal languages, and so have been formally defined syntactically and semantically. All are fully interactive and congenial to the user. In the three languages, interpretations through concept names are associated with the visual entities. The difference is that the Gaines inter-translatability between the visual and textual languages is not respected here.

References.
1. B. Singer, P. Villepreux. Towards formalizing the semantic analysis of team games, with the example of rugby. International Review MISH, 114, 19-33, Paris, France (1991)
2. B. Singer, J.L. Soubie. Taking into account Non Verbal Expertises : a Visual Knowledge Elicitation Language and Methodology for Picture Understanding. Proceedings of the Seventh European Knowledge Acquisition Workshop (EKAW'93), 2, 207-225, Toulouse and Caylus, France (1993)
3. B. Singer, P. Villepreux, J.L. Soubie. Designing a tactical decision-making Knowledge Base for team games, with the example of rugby. Proceedings of the 5th ACAPS Fall International Conference (ACAPS'93), Caen, France (1993)
4. B. Singer, J.L. Soubie, P. Villepreux. Contribution of Artificial Intelligence to knowledge acquisition and modelling in the field of team games. Design of an Expert System for tactical decision-making in rugby. Review Science & Motricity, 21, Paris, France (1993) [French]
5. L. Steels. Components of Expertise. AI Magazine, 11 : 2, 28-49 (1990)
6. P. Villepreux. Rugby de mouvement et disponibilité du joueur. INSEP Diploma Report, Paris, France, 1987 [French]

Visual Programming of Robots in Virtual Environments

Andrzej Kasiński

Department of Control, Robotics and Computer Science
Politechnika Poznańska, 60-965 Poznań, Poland

Abstract. The advantages of graphical simulators over conventional, task-level robot programming languages are discussed. In particular, the way of preparing application programs for robots operating in abnormal operating conditions is described. The role of interactive and visual feedback for early program and action failure detection is pointed out.

Keywords. robot programming, computer graphics, automated geometrical reasoning

1 Introduction

In our paper we take a broader perspective on what is usually considered to be a robot. In the following text we look at the robot as a device that is able to merge and fuse sensorial data into some internal representation of the world (action environment) and given the goal of its operation it is able to produce a certain behavior. So to program a robot for action means to establish the relationship between the goal, sensorial input and feedback information and the resulting behaviors.

Our research is motivated by the practical observation that programing even a routine task for industrial robot applications is done more efficiently by using available graphical simulators than by using classical robot programing language with its domain-specific semantics. The efficiency can be measured by the time required to produce a reliable robot program as well as by the ease of detecting a priori possible program bugs and programmed action failures [1]. The key issue here is the augmentation of the interactivity of the program development process and the possible integration of the programer's implicit knowledge (skill) into that process. The problem becomes particularly important when relatively complex manipulation tasks like fine motion among cluttered obstacles or grasping an unknown item with a multi-fingered robot hand are taken into account. Micro-manipulation and some rather special applications of robots, such as in-orbit operation, make the problem of the reliable a priori or in-line programing of these tasks even more important issue [2]. In these cases the expressive power of the language seems to be inadequate and the lack of interactive "conceptual feedback" from the model of the problem is more apparent.

If we change the geometrical scale of the robot operation or enter a specific environment (such as in space, in underwater or nuclear environment) we have to give up many common sense based principles. Furthermore, some new factors may appear and some more usual ones no longer apply. At the same time some of the model laws of physics (gravity, friction, external force fields) may have to be suspended or modified. We call a model of the environment with such properties a virtual environment. In virtual environments the nature and scale of the phenomena are distorted and this could seriously affect that part of the programing language which is concerned with robot-centered semantics. Our proposal is to avoid those problems by supporting conceptual modeling of the robot scene by visualization, animation and selective rendering of some relevant aspects of the robot world [3].

2 Visual Programming of Robots as a Method

Visual programming is an idea and programming style which, by taking the advantage of available computer vision technology and computer graphics, supports the application programmer in his job of task synthesis [4]. This should not be mixed with pictorial programming using icon-based languages. Modern techniques of computer animation and rendering as well as pattern recognition methods, symbolic reasoning and learning algorithms are of particular relevance to the visual programing. Real world, i.e. the robot and its environment, are represented for programing purposes by the internal computer models which are special data structures or more recently are objects. The most important task (and the key to the success of visual programming) is to maintain consistency between realistic properties and model properties. The important issues of model building, validation and maintenance are not discussed here although this could be an important source of potential failures (both at the programing stage and during action). Physical properties of elements participating in the action which are substantial to the goal of operation are modeled as model attributes or in more involved cases as a number of laws that can be modified and manipulated by the programed. This option opens the way for creating virtual environments.

In graphical simulators for robot task programming the internal models are visualized and animated in a more or less realistic way. The level of scene rendering differs depending upon the computational power of the platform and the cost of the system [5]. The on-line interaction of the programmer with models is possible in most cases. The results of those interventions are communicated in visual form on the spot. This interactive property of visual programing creates a conceptual link between the programmer internal model of the environment and the computer model embedded within the simulation system. Moreover there is a visual feedback in the classical sense between the model and the agent.

In most cases some additional tools for analysis are available such as attention focusing mechanisms (in standard case these are view-point selectors, projections and cross-sections, zooming, time-diagrams or in more advanced systems: selective rendering and visualization together with the exchange of the geometrical representations). Domain specific libraries of functions and transforms as well as the knowledge base with rules and methods are included. Thus the mental load upon programmer can be shifted from maintaining and manipulating a model of the scene to the analysis and interpretation stages of the programing process.

Visual programing and the user controlled animation engine are particularly useful for assessing the dynamic properties of the system and for verifying the behavioral aspects of the program. The right way to understand the dynamic relationships is to display the behavior of the model at different time scales and then to observe restricted parts of the display (or some aspects of the model). This is an important educational aspect of the method. The visual programing approach creates ways to introduce the skill-based knowledge, experience and observation of the programmer into the robot programing process without significant risk by using the simulator. What has to be pointed out is the fact that in contrast to the normal case most of the experience gained with respect to the virtual reality cannot be reduced to common sense principles.

The most promising areas of application for visual programming are:

— educational and skill capturing systems,
— tele-operation and virtual presence systems,
— action programing systems and debuggers,
— failure detection and monitoring systems.

3   How to Control the Programmed Behavior?

Robot task programing systems are among the most complex dynamic modelers of the realistic phenomena. They have to integrate geometrical reasoning with simple physical models of the elements of the scene. Moreover they have to be oriented towards action. Finally, it has to be pointed out that computational resources available are usually limited. The last remark imply a certain need for economy of problem representation.

Simulation and the analysis of robot behavior are obviously helpful in assembling a reliable working application program. However the complexity of the scene and the hidden properties of the active elements are the main reason for failures in the real world performance of the program. Running a simulator to evaluate the target program is sometimes not enough to avoid future failures. Therefore it is necessary to provide the simulator with some checking mechanisms. The standard approach is to include in the system some automatic safety measures such as collision detection and location procedures. This is a good solution for the robot trajectory programing issues. The interaction of the robot with the environment requires some additional measures to be taken. The simple physics of bodies in contact is added to the system in order to work out in semi-automatic way the conditions for the static equilibrium. A good example of using phenomenological models in simulation systems is friction, which is extremely important in such common tasks as proper grasping. Nested models of friction are introduced by defining embedded objects with growing complexity and fidelity of friction modeling [1].

The appropriate "layer" of the nested model is called for depending on situation. The required accuracy in calculating grasp stability being determined by the goal of operation. If the program fails during the real run there is always the possibility of reconsidering the plan taking into account more complex models of reality (here friction model).

Another possibility to support robot task programing using simulator is to render visible those aspects of the phenomenon which are not normally visible. This refers in particular to the system of active and reactive forces acting during grasping which are in some systems made visible as vectors [6]. Moreover these forces are made individually available for direct tuning while the force balance maintenance system responds with a new display of the equilibrium situation. That kind of the interactive working provides the user with the opportunity of making sensitivity analysis of the solution obtained by simple tuning. Friction models can also be made visible by introducing so called friction cones. This gives the user some means of evaluating safety margins for a particular grasp.

To study dynamic aspects of the robot behavior the underlying dynamics models must be added to the modeler and the analysis is made after the run. Time plots and state space trajectories are examined in order to understand the requirements for robot control which are associated to the execution of the particular trajectory. A very useful option is the interactive tuning of the action time-scale to study some critical sections of the trajectory in detail. Animation of geometrical models is only used to show timing of the task and to reassure the programmer that the coordination and collision avoidance issues have been solved correctly.

The most evident and popular method of supporting the control of the robot behavior is by providing the programmer with selective attention focusing mechanism. Standard solutions which are frequently encountered in most robot simulators are: changing a viewpoint and perspective, projection, cross-section or hidden lines removal and zoom in order to study some fragments of the scene in more detail.

4   Representation Issues

Usually we are restricted to the use of economic means of expression to visualize robot scene. This because of the computational load involved by the on-line synthetic picture animation algorithms, computational activity in the background and the rendering cost. However these limitations become recently not so critical due to the available resources and computational power of modern workstations. The platforms that are used for robot visual programming vary from Silicon Graphics powerful workstations to IBM PC compatible microcomputers. Our proper experience in implementing robot simulators is with the bottom line equipment. Our first graphical robot simulation and programming systems were based on wired-frame models without hidden lines removal. Thus polyhedral representation schemes were used and there was no possibility of modeling in an adequate way many practical situations, in particular those related to grasp planning. The reason was a discontinuity in the model surface curvature. Today we are able to run models with up to 15 degrees of freedom and animate them in real-time with hidden line removal and collision detection using 486 PC models.

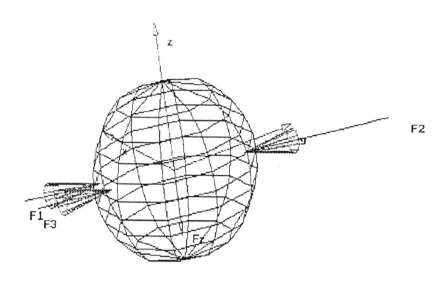

Fig. 1. Graphical screen of the automatic grasp planning sysyem. Grasping a sphere with three-fingered robot hand

5   Conclusions

Issues in visual programming of robots were characterized briefly and some problems relating to the implementation of graphical simulators were discussed in more detail. The experience of the author results from the supervision of several implemented student projects and M.S. theses on robot simulation where all the mentioned above issues and presentation techniques were tested and verified. Currently we are studying the problems of using generalized cylinders and NURBS as internal models for robot geometry. The preliminary results are promising. Another challenging problem under study is to capture the geometrical model of the robot directly from the scene by using computer stereo-vision system and pattern matching methods. On Fig. 1 we give an example of the graphical output of the system for contact detection and automatic grasp synthesis. Here active (external) force and grasping forces at contact points (suggested automatically) are visible. Grasp synthesis in that case was performed for the spherical item and the robot hand had three fingers.

Acknowledgements

Author would like to thank J. Kurasz for his contribution to the development of the system.

References

1. Kasiński, A.: Man-Machine Aspects of Computer-aided Interactive Grasp Planning. In: Analysis, Design and Evaluation of Man-Machine Systems. IFAC Publication. Ed. H. Stassen. Pergamon Press 1993 Oxford. pp.71-76.
2. Minsky, M. et al.: Feeling and Seeing: Issues in Force Display. ACM Computer Graphics., no.5, 1990, pp.235-243.
3. Kasiński, A.: Development of the Intelligent Graphical Front-End for Robot Grasp Planning. To appear in NATO ASI Series F, Berlin: Springer 1994.
4. Flynn, P.J., Jain, A.K.: CAD-Based Computer Vision: From CAD Models to Relational Graphs. IEEE Trans. on PAMI, vol.13, no.2 Feb. 1991, pp.114-132.
5. Trostmann, E. et al.: ROPSIM, A Robot Off-Line Programming and Real-Time Simulation System Including Dynamics. Prepr. IFAC 3rd Int. Symp. on Robot Control SYROCO'91, Vienna, September 1991, pp.423-428.
6. Gatrell, L.B.: CAD-Based Grasp Synthesis Utilizing Polygons, Edges and Vertexes. Proc. IEEE Int. Conf. on Robotics and Autom. Scottsdale AR, IEEE Press 1989.

Part 4

Advanced Applications

Advanced Applications

Introduction

The papers presented in this section address issues that pertain to the deployment of advanced interaction techniques, methods and dialogue representation in educational systems.

A comparison between computer-aided instruction and computer-assisted language learning with respect to the role of natural language in the instructional discourse is presented by Offereins. Addressing individual differences is a complex issue that is often neglected by designers of educational software. Hibino presents an interactive multimedia system for foreign language learning that is designed to address individual learning styles and needs of students. Komissarova gives a pragmatic survey of psychological characteristics, such as interpersonal relations, role functions of student and system, pertaining to instructional systems. Accessing data in a timely and natural manner is a difficult problem for many databases and especially for multimedia databases. Espinosa and Baggett propose a method for accessing, navigating and browsing through complex multimedia databases based on the concept of cohesive elements.

Several applications were presented that illustrate the possibilities of new technologies for the design of educational systems in different subject domains. An interactive instruction tool for the teaching of handwriting of languages that utilize non-Roman alphabets is discussed by Heller et al. The paper by Patterson presents a methodology for the design, implementation and evaluation of a multimedia system for the training of pilots and engineers on an aircraft braking system. Spaai et al. use an intonation meter with visual feedback of the speech contour to teach intonation to prelingually, profoundly deaf children. Their results indicate that this type of system has promising possibilities for use with the disabled. Pais et al. discuss an interactive software system that offers easy and efficient analysis of the transient state of the chemical recovery cycle of a pulp mill. Santos presents a general model for information systems that work over the telephone. A language for dialogue definition and a modular architecture with speech recognition and generation, and natural language understanding components is described. Velázquez-Iturbide discusses the limitations of functional programming environments for educational purposes. He proposes a minimum set of requirements that are needed to use these environments for teaching complex programming concepts. Alexandrov and Milanova describe an advice-giving module for the use of a computer numerical control machine in a computer-aided manufacturing system.

Interactive Learning and Natural Language Systems

Margriet Offereins

Department of Computer Science, University of Twente, P.O. Box 217, 7500 AE, Enschede, The Netherlands. e-mail: grietje@cs.utwente.nl

Abstract. The biggest problem with applying the processing of natural language in computer-assisted instruction (CAI) is the lack of a direct link between the architecture of the natural language interface and the architecture of a CAI system. This paper is a proposal for solving this problem. A first approach focuses on the use of natural language user interfaces in CAI. It is shown that the design of interfaces for CAI is based on instructional discourse planning that hardly involves processing of natural language. A second approach focuses on computer-assisted language learning (CALL). This approach is promising, as it supports the integration of language in interaction and in learning.

Keywords. Natural language processing, user interfaces, interactive learning, computer-assisted instruction, computer-assisted language learning

1 Introduction

People learn by communicating with each other in natural languages. In interactive learning, computers are applied to facilitate learning in particular knowledge domains. It is our intention to determine the ways natural language is used in interactive learning.

Most systems for CAI have been developed by structuring the knowledge domain. The interface environment presents pieces of knowledge constrained by the way they are structured and are accessible in the system. These system-oriented paradigms for CAI systems do not support the analysis and generation of natural language. The planning of the discourse of the instruction does not involve natural language processing. The use of natural language is restricted to providing prepared explanations, hints, help and feedback to the learner. As such, it is integrated in the knowledge that is taught by the system. Much overhead is generated when the capacity for processing natural language is incorporated into CAI.

In computer-assisted language learning (CALL) the same problems occur, but the difference is that the knowledge domain itself is about natural language.

Dialogues of natural language in these systems are supported by knowledge of vocabulary, syntax and grammar of the language. An integration of both applications is valuable. It provides spin-offs for natural language interaction in general and for interactive learning in one's own natural language.

Four sections follow. The first deals with interactive learning and instruction and shows what is meant by a system for CAI. The second section discusses natural language interfaces for CAI. The third section explores natural language as the knowledge domain for interactive learning in CALL. The final section gives the conclusions.

2 Interactive Learning and Instruction

Systems for computer-assisted instruction (CAI) are useful and have been successfully applied in many domains now. In systems for CAI the learning domain is bounded. Therefore a CAI system is an appropriate application for communication by natural language.

An analysis of natural language dialogues for instruction is required to find out if there is a need to develop natural language interfaces for CAI. First we present a general architecture of a system for CAI from the knowledge perspective. Then we show that instructional discourse planning is important for the design of systems for CAI, but does not lead to the use of sophisticated natural language interfaces.

2.1 General Architecture of CAI

A general architecture of a CAI system is depicted in the figure below (Fig. 1). It consists of knowledge components that are interrelated in various ways.

The instruction that is performed by the system applies knowledge about the learner's performance for the restructuring of the pieces of knowledge that are taught and the control of the interaction with the learner. The system only produces predefined utterances of natural language that are derived directly from the knowledge domain.

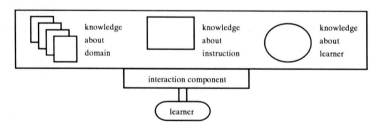

Fig. 1. The general knowledge components of a CAI system

As an example, a system for CAI is considered in a problem solving domain such as algebra or geometry. Table 1 gives examples of the knowledge components that are involved. The interaction component deals with incoming and outgoing knowledge sources of respectively the user and the system, and is equipped with tools to enhance the instructional environment with, for example, an execution or simulation environment.

Knowledge components in a problem solving domain	
Knowledge about domain :	exercises, solutions, feedback, bug catalogue
Knowledge about learner :	user model
Knowledge about instruction :	exercise selection, diagnosing learner's solution, selecting appropriate feedback, evaluating learner's performance
Interaction component	
Knowledge sources :	learner's solution, feedback, questions, menu selection, mouse clicks, keyboard strokes
Tools :	code window, text editor, programming language environment

Table 1. Knowledge components of a CAI system in a problem solving domain

2.2 Planning of Discourse and Instruction

Discourse planning is strongly related to the planning of the instruction and the design of an instructional language. The instructional dialogues in CAI are hardly combined with techniques for processing natural language. The planning and design of instructional dialogues is done merely to support the design of the knowledge structure for the material that is taught by CAI systems (Woolf 1988).

In cooperative problem solving and coaching, there is a need to develop CAI interfaces from a user-oriented approach. The dialogues are based on analysis of human discourse in performing learning tasks. For example, analysis has been done of dialogues in cooperative problem solving by (Erkens and Andriessen 1993). The results of the analysis are used for the development of a dialogue monitor for an intelligent cooperative educational system. For the factual interaction with the system a menu-based natural language interface has been constructed.

Another example is the research on didactic discourse in intelligent help systems in (Winkels, Breuker and Sandberg 1988). This research resulted in the development of a discourse planner for a generic coach. The discourse in an intelligent help system is meant for support of the use of a computer application environment. The learning principles are specified in the form of relations between concepts in the domain of the application.

3 Natural Language Interfaces to CAI

Natural language interfaces are either word, sentence or dialogue based. They stress a particular style of instruction. A style of instruction is viewed here as a possible combination of methods and techniques that are used for guiding the user in learning. For example, the degree of feedback that is provided, or the freedom the user is allowed in elaborating an exercise without having the system interrupt or control the sequence of steps that are taken.

An interface stresses the style of instruction. There are criteria for the design of an interface for instruction. There are different natural language interfaces that are applicable, but they hardly meet the criteria for a well-designed interface for instruction.

3.1 Criteria for Interfaces

A well-designed interface for CAI stresses a particular style of instruction and enhances the quality of instruction. The following three aspects characterize the style of instruction of a CAI system:

- *modes of communication*: The interface supports one or more communication modes, such as a language for dialogues in natural language, a window for comments of the system, menus, screen graphics, or a workspace for doing exercises.
- *control*: The interface puts an amount of control on the user. It shows the user what he is allowed to do. It narrows down the user's possible actions. This is of help for monitoring and identifying what the user's actions are. These actions are evaluated in the instruction process.
- *support*: The interface provides support to the user. Restricted modes of communication, windows with different functionality and menus support the user in following a specific path in learning. A special window with on-line help messages or hints keeps the user activated.

Dialogues in natural language for instruction require the design of a specific set of tools for the analysis and generation of language in the knowledge domain that is taught. The following linguistic criteria apply to the design of tools for processing instructional natural languages (Burton and Brown pp. 56 in: Wenger 1987):

- *efficiency*: The learner should not have to wait for the parser to complete its task.
- *habitability*: Within its domain, the system should accommodate the ranges of ways in which learners are likely to express the ideas.
- *robustness against ambiguities*: The system should not expect each sentence to be complete and unambiguous.

- *self-tutoring*: The interface should make suggestions and handle unacceptable inputs in such a way as to clarify the scope of possible interactions.

The notion of *semantic grammar* is used in the attempt to build practical natural language interfaces to educational systems (Burton and Brown pp. 55-65 in: Wenger 1987) and databases. The aim of semantic grammar is to characterize a subset of natural language well enough to support casual user interaction. In a semantic grammar the choice of word and phrase categories is based on the semantics of the intended application domain as well as on the regularities of the language. An interface that is based on semantic grammar has knowledge about the application domain built in at very low levels of processing. This means that the interface has to be entirely rewritten for a new application domain.

3.2 Instructional Interfaces

In the following, natural language interfaces for CAI are discussed. They support different styles of instruction and learning. Plain dialogues do not benefit a well-designed CAI system. They require extra overhead for communication, at the expense of the quality of instruction in the knowledge domain.

Menu-Based Natural Language Systems. A menu-based system of natural language supports the user in showing the system's boundaries. The way the menu-system is set up can narrow the scope of ambiguity and misinterpretation of language for both the user and the system. The expressive power of natural language is combined with the ease of use of menus (Miller 1988). For example, in "Bridge", a CAI system for teaching programming, a problem solving task starts out with menu-entries of informal language phrases to support the learner in correctly defining the plans for solving the problem (Bonar 1991). The selection of entries in the menu also triggers internal knowledge bases and processes that are attached to the menu's entries and that are relevant for supporting the next phases of the task.

Hypertext-Based System. A system based on hypertext provides additional information on items that are highlighted in the text. It is up to the user to select an item to learn what it is. Each item that can be selected is the top of a stack of one or more hypertexts.

Question Answering System. A question answering system gives the user complete control in learning. The system has to deal with the user's typing and spelling errors. The domain is restricted to the context of a fixed database of knowledge. The result of parsing a question is mapped to a database query. The answers that are given are based on facts that are explicitly present in the database.

Dialogue System. A dialogue system imposes no control on the user. The quality of the instructional dialogues in plain natural language is poor. The user can type any answer or question and leave it up to the system to proceed with the dialogue in a way that makes sense. The limits of both the linguistic and the conceptual coverage of the system are difficult for users to infer. The system has to deal with the user's typing and spelling errors. There is a huge overhead of knowledge for language processing. Techniques of analysis for the processing of dialogues in natural language are therefore often word spotting algorithms that are based on the recognition of certain keywords. For example, the "Albert" system (Oberem 1991), a CAI system in elementary physics, conducts a dialogue in English to help the learner in analysing a problem in elementary physics. The communication is based on the recognition of keywords in the responses of the learner to the system's inquiries.

4 Computer-Assisted Language Learning

In systems for computer-assisted language learning (CALL) the knowledge that is taught is about natural language. There are several CALL systems for teaching different language skills. In the following, examples are given of CALL systems for teaching spelling and grammar in native and in foreign languages. These examples all combine language technology with the teaching of language.

4.1 Teaching a Native Language.

One CALL system that teaches German (Schwind 1987) consists of a grammar knowledge base, a module that generates exercises, a natural language and a graphic interface and an error explication module. The grammar knowledge base allows different access modes for variously analysing sentences, producing sentences, analysing and explaining errors and answering student's queries. The interaction is done in either French or German. Exercises are given in dialogue form in which the student may ask questions in the context of the exercise, that are about the system's explanations, the exercise or the properties of the German language in general.

Another CALL system that teaches Dutch (Pijls, Daelemans and Kempen 1987) consists of an expert system of linguistic knowledge, a didactic module including a subcomponent for diagnosing the learner's knowledge, a bug catalogue, an instruction module, an exercise generator and a user interface with a powerful graphical tree editor. This tree editor supports graphical manipulation and animation of tree structures that correspond to the syntactical structures of sentences. This tree editor is used for different exercises about the composition or decomposition of sentences.

4.2 Teaching a Foreign Language

One CAI system for teaching non-native speakers English is the system VP^2 (Schuster and Finin 1986). The exercises are about the translation of Spanish sentences in English. This system is of interest as a grammar of the native language is used as a model of the user in teaching a foreign language. The theory behind this is that learning a new language is done by comparing and contrasting constructs of the language in the new language with those in the native language.

The use of products of natural language for learning foreign languages may lead to a language-independent CALL system, according to (Yazdani 1989). Grammar rules of French, parsing techniques and error-reporting modules are kept separate and distinct from one another to support an "open-ended" approach to development in the CALL environment.

Another system for CALL in Spanish is "CALEB" (Cunningham, Iberall and Woolf 1986). This system uses an architecture based on production rules for teaching Spanish. The emphasis is put on the communication between the CAI system and the learner. Therefore the system is comprised of a rich interactive environment. Word-oriented responses are typed at the keyboard and action-oriented responses are performed with the mouse and pictured objects. However, the system has only a limited set of topics and pieces of language, like a phoneme, syllable, word or phrase and is based on predefined exercises and answers.

Another CALL system for Spanish, the "Computer-Assisted Language Learning Environment" (CALLE) (Rypa 1992) is based on linguistic knowledge of syntax and grammar. The dialogue-based system operates in a window environment in which a target text to be translated can be queried to yield linguistic information to the learner. A major goal is to promote inquiry into the patterns of the target language. Natural language processing provides data to diagnose the learner's input.

5 Conclusions

Employing natural language in the design of interfaces for CAI does not enhance the instructional value of a CAI system and can cause a great deal of overhead for language use and understanding, unless the instruction is related to teaching language. In that case, linguistic knowledge and tools for processing natural language are useful for a variety of tasks and support natural language dialogues in learning languages.

References

Bonar, J.G. (1991) Interface Architectures for Intelligent Tutoring Systems. In H. Burns, J.W. Parlett, C. Luckhardt Redfield (eds.): Intelligent Tutoring Systems: Evolutions in Design. Chapter 3, pp. 35 - 67. Hillsdale, NJ: Lawrence Erlbaum

Cunningham, P., Iberall, T., Woolf, B. (1986) CALEB: An Intelligent Second Language Tutor. In IEEE Conference on Systems, Man & Cybernetics, pp. 1210 - 1215

Erkens, G., Andriessen, J. (1993) Cooperation in Problem Solving and Educational Computer Programs. To be published in Tennyson, R. (ed.): Computers in Human Behavior. New York: Pergamon Press

Miller, J.R. (1988) The Role of Human-Computer Interaction in Intelligent Tutoring Systems. In M.C. Polson, J.J. Richardson (eds.): Foundations of Intelligent Tutoring Systems. Chapter 6, pp. 143-191. Hillsdale, New Jersey: Lawrence Erlbaum

Oberem, G.E. (1991) The Development and Use of Artificial Intelligence Techniques for the Delivery of Computer-Assisted Instruction on Advanced Computers. Research Report. Rhodes University, Grahamstown.

Pijls, F., Daelemans, W., Kempen, G. (1987) Artificial Intelligence Tools for Grammar and Spelling Instruction. Instructional Science no. 16, pp. 319 - 336

Rypa, M. (1992) CALLE: A Computer-Assisted Language Learning Environment. In F.L. Engel, D.G. Bouwhuis, T. Bösser, G. d'Ydewalle (eds.): Cognitive Modelling and Interactive Environments in Language Learning. Proceedings of the NATO Advanced Research Workshop in Advanced Educational Technology. Series F: Computer and Systems Sciences, Vol. 87, pp. 175 - 182. Berlin: Springer-Verlag

Schuster, E., Finin, T. (1986) VP^2: The Role of User Modelling in Correcting Errors in Second Language Learning. In A.G. Cohn, J.R. Thomas (eds.), Artificial Intelligence and its Applications, pp. 197 - 209. Chichester: John Wiley & Sons

Schwind, C.B. (1987) An Overview of an Intelligent Language Tutoring System. In Advances in Artificial Intelligence, Proceedings of ICAI 1986, pp. 189 - 205. London: Hermes

Wenger, E. (1987) Artificial Intelligence and Tutoring Systems. Los Altos, CA: Morgan Kaufmann

Winkels, R., Breuker, J. Sandberg, J. (1988) Didactic Discourse in Intelligent Help Systems. In Proceedings ITS '88 Montreal, pp. 279 - 285

Woolf, B. (1988) Intelligent Tutoring Systems: A Survey. In H. Schrobe and AAAI (eds.) Exploring Aritificial Intelligence, Chapter 1, pp.1-43. Los Altos, CA: Morgan Kaufmann

Yazdani, M. (1989) An Artificial Intelligence Approach to Second Language Teaching. In Maurer (ed.): Computer-Assisted Learning. Second International Conference Computer-Assisted Learning (ICCAL '89), pp. 618 - 624. Lecture Notes in Computer Science. Berlin: Springer-Verlag

The Learner's Partner: Foreign Language Learning and Real World Encounters

Stacie L. Hibino and Edna A. Coffin

Project FLAME, University of Michigan, 188 Frieze Building,
Ann Arbor, MI 48109-1285, USA

Abstract. The Learner's Partner (LP) is a pedagogical model using interactive multimedia for foreign language learning. This model is designed for individual student use (or for use by pairs of students) and focuses on several aspects of language acquisition, including: viewing and listening, reading, writing, speaking, comprehension, and cultural understanding. A variety of activities are provided at increasing levels of interactivity and difficulty, thus providing some scaffolding to the student while addressing individual learning styles and needs. This paper provides a detailed description of the LP model and presents some research questions related to evaluation of its use in the classroom.

Keywords. Foreign language, multimedia, computer-aided instruction, interactive learning environments

1 Introduction

A number of computer systems have been developed for foreign language learning. Some focus on simulations, some on cultural aspects, and others on drill and practice. Many of these systems, however, either tend to focus on only some aspects of language learning (e.g., some simulations focus on listening and responding skills, but not speaking skills), or they focus on language learning *out of context* (e.g., drill and practice).

Our approach to the use of computers in foreign language learning is to design and develop multimedia pedagogical models which address several aspects of language learning within a cultural context. These models integrate pedagogy with functionality and form, allowing the same model to be used to develop applications for several different languages.

We use video and audio to set the stage for the student, so that learning takes place within a realistic and cultural context. In the case of the Learner's Partner (LP) model, we use various activities to address several aspects of language learning, including: viewing and listening, reading, writing, speaking, comprehension, and cultural understanding.

This paper describes the LP model, using several examples from one of the Spanish LP applications. Some research questions related to evaluating the LP in the classroom are also presented, followed by a short summary.

2 Description

The LP model uses video to provide cultural context, modeling, and real world encounters. Two types of video segments are used — real-life scenarios (e.g., buying a bus ticket) and short cultural reports. Activities for the scenarios focus primarily on comprehension and speaking skills, leading up to role playing. Activities for the cultural reports focus on comprehension and writing, leading up to student research reports.

2.1 Introductory and Table of Contents Screens

When the program starts, the student is presented with a title screen, a video introduction, and a table of contents. Each of these is described below.

Title Screen. The title screen provides the following information to the student: the type of application (e.g., Learner's Partner), the language of the application (e.g., Spanish), and the title or main topic of the application (e.g., México Distrito Federal (a unit about Mexico City)).

Video Introduction. Following the title screen, the student is prompted to confirm that the correct videodisc (and side of videodisc) is in the player and is presented with a short video introduction.

Table of Contents. The table of contents lists video chapters related to the main topic. These video chapters are split into two subgroups, corresponding to their type; video scenarios are listed before short cultural reports. The student can select a chapter by clicking it.

2.2 Real-life Scenarios

The activities menu for the real-life scenarios (i.e., "Conversaciones" in the Spanish applications) includes seven activities, presented to the student in four organizing groups:
1. Getting Started
    View and Listen
    Listen and Read
2. Words and Meanings
    Vocabulary in Context
    Comprehension
3. Let's Practice
    Listen and Repeat
    Listen and Write
4. Your Turn
    Role Playing

The level of student interactivity increases with respect to the order listed above. The activities in these video scenario chapters are designed to help the students focus and improve their speaking and conversational skills. Each of these activities is described in more detail below.

View and Listen. View and Listen introduces the video chapter to the student, thus providing a context for the other activities. The objective is to obtain a basic overall understanding of the scenario by focusing on visual and oral cues, rather than trying to translate the conversation word for word. The video can be played segment by segment, or all at once. In addition, the student has the option to view a text transcription of the video as it is being played.

Listen and Read. In Listen and Read, the student focuses on matching spoken phrases with their written counterparts. The student is presented with the transcription of the video in a scrolling text field. When the Play All button is used, the whole video scenario is played, and lines are highlighted as they are being spoken. Individual lines (i.e., phrases) can be played by double-clicking directly on the line the student wishes to hear. A test mode is available within this activity, in which a phrase or sentence is played and the student must select the line with the corresponding text. The test is open-ended and the students can try to match as many lines as they wish.

Vocabulary in Context. The main objective of this activity is to listen to vocabulary words within the context in which they are spoken, and then to match the words to corresponding pictures. The student is presented with a list of vocabulary, a small video window, and a grid of pictures with which to match the words. The student clicks a line from the list of words or phrases, views and listens to the words in context, and then clicks on the corresponding picture. If a correct picture is selected, the vocabulary text is placed underneath the picture as a caption. If an incorrect picture is selected, the student is asked to listen more carefully and the video context is automatically replayed.

Comprehension. Comprehension focuses more on details of the video, allowing the students to work on improving their viewing (and listening) skills. In this activity, the student views a short video segment (which may or may not include audio), watching for clues to answer the question presented. The student answers the question by selecting from a list of potential answers. Some of the answers may be similar, but only one is correct. Thus, the student must watch and listen to the video carefully, in order to gather the relevant information for answering the question. When the student selects an answer, detailed feedback is given to confirm a correct answer or to highlight any problems with an incorrect answer.

Listen and Repeat. In this activity, students record themselves repeating the native speakers in the dialogue of the video scenario. A segment is played, and the student selects a line to record. The individual line is played and the student uses a recording panel to practice repeating the selected line. Students can play and record themselves as many times as they wish, they can play the original speaker as many times as they wish, and they can compare themselves to the native speaker (using a Compare button which plays the native speaker followed by the student's recording) as many times as they wish. In this way, the students work on both their speaking and listening (aural) skills.

Listen and Write. This activity is essentially a dictation activity in which the students listen to a line of the video scenario, and type the transcription of it. Buttons are provided to insert special characters (e.g., é) directly into the text, thus allowing students to focus on the actual transcription without having to worry about memorizing special key combinations.

Role Playing. This activity provides a structure in which the student can take on the role of one of the persons in the scenario. The students construct their dialogue within the context of the original video. They select words and phrases from a set of lists to build sentences. These sentences (which may now be different from the original dialogue) are then recorded. When all the sentences are complete, the students can use a Play All button to hear the new dialogue, which includes themselves, and one of the original speakers.

2.3 Short Cultural Reports

The activities menu for the short cultural reports (i.e., "Reportajes" in the Spanish applications) is organized in the same four groups as the video scenarios.   There are eight activities for each of these video chapters, however, and the focus is on writing and composition rather than speaking and conversation.

1. Getting Started
   View and Listen
   Listen and Read
2. Words and Meanings
   Comprehension
   In Other Words
3. Let's Practice
   Listen and Repeat
   Listen and Write
4. Your Turn
   Let's Write
   Moving On

The basic activities (i.e., View and Listen, Listen and Read, Comprehension, Listen and Repeat, and Listen and Write) are the same in both the scenario and cultural video chapters. The few activities in the short cultural reports that are different are described in more detail below.

In Other Words. This activity focuses on the students' listening skills. The students play a video segment, listening for key phrases and identifying the main focus. The students then play three audio segments (without video or text support), listening for the one which best summarizes the video segment that was played. The students select their audio segment of choice, and receive feedback on their selection.

Let's Write. While Listen and Write form a kind of recall activity (i.e., students can generate text by recalling what was said), Let's Write focuses on the composition of short paragraphs. The student selects a topic related to the current video chapter, and is presented with three questions related to that topic. Each question has corresponding video that the students can play to gather information in order to compose an answer. This activity was designed to be an intermediary step between dictation and free form composition.

Moving On. This activity varies from video chapter to video chapter, but focuses on composition within the following contexts: 1) allowing the students to explore some cultural aspects in more depth, and 2) helping the students to compare the cultural aspects presented in the video with characteristics of their own culture.

2.4 Additional Aids for the Student

A number of aids are available to the student while using the LP. These include a simple online dictionary, a small online student notebook, and a progress chart. The dictionary contains all of the words in all of the applications within the same foreign language. This dictionary can be accessed from any of the LP activities.

The student notebook has three primary uses: 1) allows students to take notes while using the LP, 2) provides a place for the students to store (and later expand) short compositions completed in the LP (e.g., paragraphs from Let's Write or stories from Moving On), and 3) provides an avenue for the teachers to tailor the use of the LP to their classroom needs (e.g., a teacher can ask students to do View and Listen for a video chapter and use their notebook to take notes on the main points, so that they can later write a summary of the video chapter in their own words).

The Progress Chart keeps track of how much time students have spent on each activity of each video chapter. The students, teachers, and developers all have access to this information (though students only have access to their own progress chart).

3 Research Questions

In evaluating the design and use of the LP, we will look at research issues related to evaluating educational software in general, as well as specific issues related directly to the LP. General issues focus on the interface and on transformation: are there places in the application where the interface interferes with the students' activity or goals? How does the technology *transform* the way we do things in the classroom? how do teacher-student interactions and roles change? what do students learn through the software? how does the use of the technology change the way students learn?

Regarding a specific issue directly related to the LP, we are interested in examining any correlation between the use of the LP and individual learning styles. Is the time spent on different LP activities correlated to individual student's learning styles? E.g., do textually-oriented students focus on "Listen and Read" and "Listen and Write" while graphically-oriented students focus on "View and Listen" and "Vocabulary in Context?"

4 Summary

The LP model for foreign language learning uses multimedia to integrate culture and context with practice and exploration. The two types of video used (scenarios and short cultural reports) provide natural threads of focus on speaking and writing, while also providing context for general activities in viewing, vocabulary, and comprehension. Although some initial interface testing has been conducted, classroom studies are just beginning.

Acknowledgements

Learner's Partner applications are being designed and developed by several members of Project FLAME (Foreign Language Applications in a Multimedia Environment) at the University of Michigan. Besides the authors of this paper, the design and development team include: Gonzalo Silverio (Spanish), Joanna Porvin (French), and Pamela Colquitt (Chinese).

Psychological Peculiarities of Man-Machine Communication in Instructional Systems

Helena Kommisarova

Psychological Institute of the Ukraine, 2 Pankovskaya, Kiev, Ukraine 252033

Abstract. A survey is given of psychological features and problems that are typical in man-machine communication in instructional systems. Role functions, and the relations between the student and the system are discussed. Psycholinguistic parameters of textual information are suggested.

Keywords. instructional systems, psychological problems, eductional psychology, student-computer collaboration, psycholinguistics, readibility

1 Introduction

The main objective is a pragmatic survey of psychological features characteristic of man-machine communication (MMC) in instruction systems, and of psychological problems that can occur that have not been covered elsewhere in this volume. These are problems involving the psychology of education, of interpersonal relations and issues of comfortable communication, for example, the readability of textural information. These issues are being studied by the author and by other ex-soviet psychologists (see acknowledgements).

2 MMC Versus Live Communication with a Teacher

In the following, inter-personal problems of collaboration are considered. How does MMC, when one collaborator is non-human, differ from human-to-human communication? What is required to make the interface more supportive in its "attitude" and in its interactions?

First of all, the communication between student and instructional system (IS) can be compared to that between student and human teacher. The following two peculiarities can be noted, *reverse asymmetry* and *redefinition*.

In traditional instruction, human communication is assymetric in favor of the teacher, who controls the situation and the learning process. He/she usually initiates interaction with the student, makes decisions about the interaction's course and about its interruptions, manages time and evaluates the student's activity and performance. However, in computer-assisted instruction the situation is quite different. The IS maintains implicit control of the learning process with respect to instructional objectives and goals and ways of reaching them. But the system should explicitly emphasize the student's position of dominance and initiative in starting or interrupting communication and in choosing the path through the curriculum.

The second peculiarity manifests itself in attempts by the student to *redefine* the learning task to be a different one. One of the possible reasons for this is the student's emotional reaction to a judgmental attitude of the instruction system. The student may accept estimates of his/her progress given by a human teacher, but may not admit that evaluation of performance by a machine is legitimate. So the student often tries to prove the computer's stupidity by substituting for the real task a similar but different one. The mechanisms of this phenomenon can be clarified if two kinds of factor that contribute to the communicative behavior of each communicant are taken into account. For humans a set of factors was proposed by T.N. Ushakova.

Table 1

"Self" Factors	Factors Referring to the Partner
1. Motive	1. Logical Position of the Partner
2. Intellectual Capacity	2. Estimation of Emotional Status
3. Emotional Status	3. Social and Personality Status
	4. Situational (Temporal, Spatial, etc.)

Given this, the gap between "Social and personality status" ("Partner" #3 above) of the IS as a teacher (according to its role) and habitual stereotypes that regard the machine as a dumb tool can be appreciated. This cognitive dissonance makes the student feel emotionally uncomfortable and can cause negative reactions which can worsen the student's "emotional status" (Self" #3), decrease his motivation ("Self" #1), and evoke beliefs about the existence of a negative emotional attitude on the partner's (IS) side ("Partner" #2).

3 Instructional Systems Versus General-Purpose Systems

The educational setting has aspects that are unique. The main goal of instructional systems is not to necessarily solve problems related to particular subjects as many man-machine systems do, but rather to create desirable changes in the student *per se*.

A. In the case of instruction, MMC is a means of controlling the student's learning activities. Therefore, this interaction can be considered efficient if it allows the instructional objectives and goals to be reached.

B. In efficient instructional systems the subject of the dialogue is not restricted to the content of the learning task. In this situation the communication between computer and student should influence the latter's cognitive activity immediately; should facilitate its formation; should promote self-consciousness and the rise of reflection, etc.

C. In addition to minding external dialogue, instructional systems are (or should be) sensitive to the students' internal dialogue: This point is crucial. It should be noted that from the psychological point of view the dialogue is regarded not as an exchange of remarks--it emerges because of the existence of two positions, two views on the same problem. Promotion of the student's internal dialogue, which can be provided by the external man-machine dialogue is indicative of effectiveness of the dialogue in an instruction system.

Notice that the internal dialogue can be provoked by the IS's attempt to make the student understand the partner's logical position, as differing from his own. Thus making the student aware of the existence and of the essence of several different viewpoints about this problem, the system both forms the first "Partner"-factor and stimulates internal dialogue in the student. All of these features ensue from one another and are characteristic of MMC in the instructional context.

4 Psycholinguistic Features of Textual Information

The *naturalness* of communication is important. This problem was studied by A. Voiskunsky. The suggestion is that there are two kinds of naturalness involved in MMC depending on the direction in whichthe message passes. If communication goes from the user to the system, then psychological naturalness of communication is important: i.e. the way of sending the message should minimize the user's efforts while keeping the meaning of the message safe. Menu-based input meets these requirements. On the other hand, receiving a message from the system should be linguistically natural for the user, so that he can process the information obtained without extra effort. With regard to implementation, reduced output of natural language is the appropriate solution in this case. Maintaining a good approximation to human speech is important.

4.1 At the Level of Lexicology

At the level of lexicology, both quantitative and qualitative aspects can be considered. Quantitatively, certain specific ratios between types of words that are represented in the text should be kept. Experimental data show that proportions usual for oral speech or free written style are as follows: 17-22% nouns, 15-17% verbs, 8-9% adjectives, 14-16% pronouns, 9-12% adverbs, 1% numbers, 22-24% prepositions and conjunctions. Proportions can shift according to the domain of dialogue: in natural science more nouns are used, in mathematics more numerals can be used instead of adverbs, pronouns etc. In the official newspapers nouns occupy up to 40% while verbs account for only 4-5%.

From the qualitative point of view, careful usage of new words and terms is very important., New words need to be defined, and terms should be at least understandable in the context. New and special words should be introduced step-by-step, 2-4 new words per 100 words. Text can also become vague if flooded with old or rare words; so a normative vocabulary is preferable.

With respect to speed of communication, about 120 words per minute in written dialogue, depending on age of the student, on the subject matter and on the nature of the material. Improper speed of communication can cause negative reactions such as irritation or rejection.

The text should be emotionally *tinted* in a positively personal way (calling people by name, employing a supportive even "cheering" tone, administering approval whenever possible and using positive words even in negative replies). This increases the comfort and the friendliness of communication for students and thus enhances their willingness to communicate and to acquire new knowledge.

4.2 At the Level of Syntax

At the level of syntax, desirable characteristics were found by comparing the structure of clear text to that of complicated and effort-consuming text. Readability of the text was assessed by criticists, experts and by normal readers. The "derivation tree" was chosen for syntactical analysis. This technique has been developed by linguists in Russia and Ukraine such as Paducheva and Sevbo.

The technique allows the following of formal connections between words in terms of domination and control. This study gave strong evidence that values of specific parameters of syntactical structure are connected with the clarity of the text. To elaborate, the core idea of the technique is that each sentence has an hierarchical tree-like structure, each word (node) is controlled by a word at a higher level, and the predicate is the root of the whole tree. To evaluate the structure of the derivation tree, several parameters are estimated:

-Length of the sentence;
-Number of levels in the tree;
-Length of the arc, which is estimated by the maximum number of nodes situated under the arc connecting two nodes immediately (not mediated by any other node);
-Number of simple sentences (if a complex sentence is evaluated);
-Number of homogeneous groups
-Density of branching, the number of nodes controlled by the same node at an upper level
-Zigzag number, the number of nodes in which the preceding route changes its direction;
-Trend, defined by the ratio between left-side and right-side nodes in each case of branching.

The derivation tree is illustrated by example in Fig. 1. In the upper case there is a rather unbalanced structure. Poor readability of this sentence can be explained by the excessive values of *length, levels, arc,* and *zigzag.*

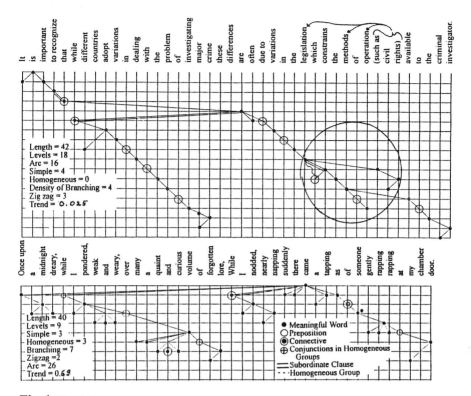

Fig. 1. Two derivations trees, the tope showing a sentence that is difficult to understand, the bottom showing a sentence of similar length that is easy to grasp.

Extreme right-side *asymmetry* combined with extreme *length-of-sentence* also overloads active memory. In addition, there is a distorted fragment (shown by the outlined region) with an improper sequence of words. At this level of comprehension the semantic analysis is usually made automatically, according to the syntactical structure of the sentence. In this case the reader will attach the group, "such as civil rights," first to "operation," then to "methods," and only afterwards to "legislation," to which it belongs. Therefore, two erroneous steps are inevitable before getting to the correct solution, and purposeful semantic analysis is necessary for this. Thus, immediate understanding is hampered. On the graph this situation can be seen as an "awkward" group of nodes, projections of which cross the lower arc.

The lower example of a derivation tree in Fig. 1 shows a much better structure, and the phrase is easily understandable, although it also has extreme values of *length* and *arc*. These latter characteristics could be a cause of cognitive overload for the reader, except that the text is *rhythmically* organized, in conjunction with *rhyme*. The illustrates one advantage of prosody.

With respect to the study of the correspondence between syntactical parameters and intelligibility of the text, the following results were obtained. First, certain parameters, such as *length, arc, zigzag,* and *levels* are extremely important for having a comprehensible text.

As a rule, the maximum length of the sentence should not exceed 20 words. The mean value for this parameter is 6-10 for clear texts and 2 or 3 times more in complicated texts.

The graph of the phrase structure should be rather symmetrical about its root, i.e. predicate. If the sentence is rather long (15-20 words), then left-side asymmetry with many subordinate groups before the predicate is undesirable. As a rule, long sentences are slightly symmetrical to the right.

The number of simple sentences, of similar/homogeneous groups, and the density of branching (which can't be determined strictly) should not be excessive. These indices are connected with the length of the sentence.

The number of levels in a graph should not exceed 7-9. This corresponds to the concept of "depth" (after Ingwe) and to the volume of active memory.

Existence of more than two zigzags in one and the same route is undesirable (except for cases when the direction is changed in the nodes corresponding to prepositions, to adverbs which show the degree of a certain quality or property and are connected with subordinate clauses; and when the direction is changed towards the negative article).

In addition to the zigzag number, possible intersections should be taken into consideration. It was found that, as a rule, projection of any senior master word that controls another word should not cross the lower segment of the same route. That means that between two words, one of which is subordinate to the other, there should be no extra word that controls the first master word. Additionally, *are length* should not be more than 7-9 nodes. Larger values are undesirable, but allowed if nodes under the arc include homogeneous groups. Beyond this level are the *hyper-syntactical level* and the *semantic level,* however, these are beyond the present scope.

5 Conclusions

Man-machine communication in the instructional context has its own psychological peculiarities of role functions and of pedagogical strategy in comparison with traditional instruction. The pool of psychological requirements, which involve perception, learning styles, and friendliness to the user, must be considered carefully to create efficient instructional systems. Also, the on-going study of psycholinguistic aspects of textual information has shown a dependence between certain formal parameters of the text and the property of readability, that also require the serious attention of those who design interfaces in education.

Acknowledgements

The majority of the research that has been noted here appears only in russian, most is reported in sources that are difficult to obtain. Those desiring access to this information may contact the author who here wishes to acknowledge the following: E.I. Mashbitz, V.V. Andriyevska, E.V. Paducheva, I.P. Sevbo, M.L. Smulson, O.K. Tikhomirov, S.I. Treskova, T.N. Ushakova, S.I. Treskova, and A.E. Voiskunsky.

A Design for Accessing Multimedia Information Using Cohesion

Roger Espinosa and Patricia Baggett
School of Education, University of Michigan, Ann Arbor, MI 48109-1259, USA

Abstract. A design for access of multimedia information based on cohesion is presented and initial testing is discussed. Elements in a database are cohesive if they refer to the same concept. The designer selects cohesive elements and sequentially links those referring to the same concept, forming a "subway line" for each concept. Cohesive elements can be in different modalities, e.g., graphics, text, photos. Users are given access via the "subway lines." At a given "stop" the user can either follow the subway line he or she is currently on (by default), or change to another subway line which crosses that stop but which links elements referring to a different concept. At each stop, a list of concepts, and thus subway lines crossing at the stop, can be made available for the user, acting as an index of currently active concepts. This method of accessing data was designed as an alternative to menus and keyword approaches. We have implemented the method in several domains, including a repair task, literature analysis, a history of mathematics, and lesson plans for elementary mathematics.

Keywords. Accessing information, hypermedia, multimedia, cohesion

1 Overview

1.1 The Problem

Often when one is presented with a large amount of computerized information, one is faced with developing a way for it to be browsed. This article describes a design for accessing computerized information. The information to be browsed can be lengthy and can consist of material from different modalities, such as text and pictures.

A unique feature of the approach given here is that after the material is divided into units by the designer, access links between units are based on cohesive elements in the material. Two elements are cohesive if they refer to the same concept, even if they occur in different modalities. Users can follow "subway lines" through the material; each line sequentially links elements referring to the same concept. At a given "stop" the user can either follow the subway line he or she is currently on (by default), or change to another subway line which crosses that stop but which links elements referring to a different concept.

1.2 Why this Approach?

• It is different from a hierarchical or menu structure and is advantageous for loosely connected heterogeneous material. It is also convenient for hierarchical material in which the hierarchy is not known to the designer.

• The design is motivated by a theoretical framework in cognition.

• At a given "stop" on a subway line the user is not forced to make a choice about where to go next; there is always a "default," namely, continue on the current subway line to the next stop. Only if the user wishes to follow a concept other than the one he or she is currently following must a decision be made.

2 Description of the Basic Design

2.1 The Data Structure and Visual Cohesion

Suppose that there is a large amount of material that is to be computerized and made accessible for browsing. The material is first divided into units (sometimes called frames or pages or screens). Each unit can be viewed as a node in a graph. The nodes are connected together by links, and a person using the system can traverse the material by traveling along the links. So a link represents the possibility of going from one node to another.

A determination of which nodes are linked together is made as follows. In each node, there is a set of designated elements. A link l between node i and node j is a relation between a unique element x in node i and a unique element y in node j. The link means that x and y are cohesive elements. For example, node i might contain a picture of a motor, and node j the word "motor." The picture and the matching verbal label refer to the same concept, and so can be designated as cohesive elements.

To give a brief background, the concepts of text cohesion and coherence have been used in similar ways by many authors (Halliday 1985; Halliday & Hasan 1976; Grimes 1975; Harris 1952; Kintsch & vanDijk 1978). Cohesion is a semantic relation between two items in a text. For Halliday & Hasan (1976) cohesion occurs through word repetition, a noun and its pronoun referent, use of synonyms, etc. According to these authors, the semantic continuity provided by cohesion is a primary factor in a text's intelligibility.

Baggett & Ehrenfeucht (1982) extended notions of text cohesion to visual, and to text-and-visual, or between-media, cohesion. They described a "cohesion graph" for 23 frames (still photos) taken from an animated movie of James Thurber's *The Unicorn in the Garden*. Nine of the photos and the cohesion graph created from all 23 arranged in the order in which they occurred in the movie, are shown in Figs. 1 and 2. The cohesion graph was formed as follows. Nineteen concepts whose referents occurred in the photos, such as characters (e.g., husband, unicorn, wife) and specific locations (garden, bedroom, etc.), were selected. If a referent to any of the 19 concepts (i.e., a cohesive element) occurred in a photo, a mark was made in the cohesion graph, as shown in Fig. 2. For example, it was determined that a picture of the husband occurred in 14 of the 23 photos. In the cohesion graph, the number of times cohesive elements occurred in two adjacent photos (when the photos were put in the order in which they occurred in the movie) was indicated. For the picture of the husband, this number was 11. The sum of these adjacencies was defined as the cohesion value for the photos. The cohesion value for the 23 photos in their correct order was 46. One experimental result from the study was that people who had not seen the movie, when asked to put the 23 frames in an order so that they "make a good story," gave orders which

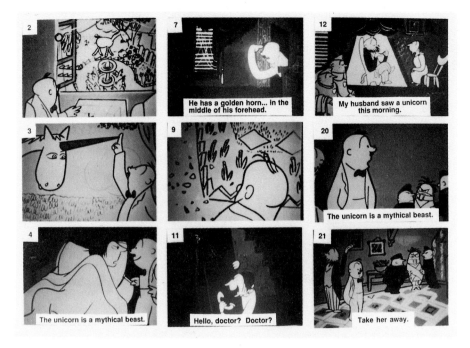

Fig. 1. Nine of the 23 photos used in *The Unicorn and the Garden* ordering task. Numbers in the upper left corners indicate the position in the actual story. Pictures drawn by Pam Hoge.

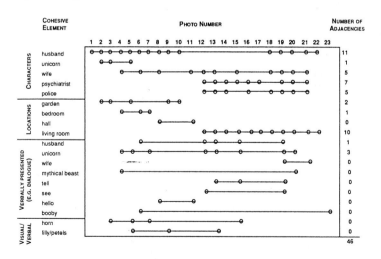

Fig. 2. Cohesion graph of movie photos in the order they occur in the actual story. Markers indicate that a cohesive element occurs in a given photo. The number of times a given element occurs in two adjacent photos is given under "Number of Adjacencies."

on average had a cohesion value of 55.1, or nearly 20% greater than in the actual story. One interpretation for this result was that associations in memory may be made by an awareness of the existence of similar elements (e.g., as postulated by the 1978 theory of Kintsch et al.).

Baggett, Ehrenfeucht, & Guzdial (1989) developed a prototype of an interactive graphics-based instructional system for assembly and repair, in which access was via visually (or graphically) cohesive elements. The graphics implementation, together with prototypes in literature analysis, a history of mathematics, and elementary mathematics lesson plans, will be briefly described in section 3 below.

2.2 An Example of a Graph and its Traversal

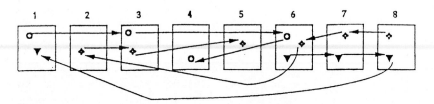

Fig. 3. A graph of eight units of information and three types of cohesive elements. The physical order is indicated by *1, 2, 3, etc.* and there are three cohesive elements: ○, ✦, and ▼.

Fig. 3 shows an hypothetical small example of a graph created from eight units of information. (In actuality, of course, graphs are considerably larger.) There are 3 types of cohesive elements in the figure, ▼, ○, and ✦. Note that the path linking together cohesive elements of a given type does not branch, but forms a single line. In a given frame, the user can select, for a specific cohesive element, the "next" or the "previous" frame that contains that element, or the "home" (or first) frame that contains the element. For example, in frame 3, where there is a second occurrence of ○, selecting "next" for ○ takes one to frame 6; selecting "previous" takes one to frame 1, and selecting "home" takes one to frame 1. Similarly, in frame 3, selecting "next" for ✦ gives frame 5; "previous" gives frame 2, and "home" gives frame 8.

2.3 Options Available to the User

The following options can be made available to the user in every frame: For any cohesive element in the frame, the user may be able to ask about (1) the name of the cohesive element; (2) the number of occurrences of the element in the entire material; and (3) the number of the occurrence in the frame the user is currently visiting. So for the cohesive element "page number," the user could find out how many pages (or units) of information there are in the whole presentation, and which one is currently being visited.

In Fig. 3 the user might be in frame 6 and ask about cohesive element ○. Suppose the presentation is about an object to be repaired. The user might be informed that the name of the cohesive element is motor. He or she can also find out that there are four occurrences of motor as a cohesive element, and that the current occurrence is number three. The actual instances of "motor" might be a moving video showing what happens when the motor is turned on, a cut-away diagram showing the interior of the motor, a text telling how to troubleshoot the object when the motor is dead, a list of parts in the motor, together with their photographs, etc.

The point is that all the instances refer to the same concept. A user following a cohesive element will receive information on the same concept, but possibly in different modalities. As noted above, a path linking together cohesive elements of a given type does not branch. The order of access is determined by the designer. Also, not every reference to the concept (e.g., motor) has to be designated a cohesive element. For example, if the reference is of minor importance in a frame, the designer may decide to omit it as a cohesive element in the frame.

To help the user keep from getting lost, a stack facility can be provided, so he or she can always go back to previously visited material.

Other options available to users can be quite elaborate. For example, a user may be able to request, "Take me to the ninth stop on this line," or "Take me to the stop on this line that intersects with such-and-such other line."

2.4 Responsibilities of the Designer

To design a presentation, a person must do five things:
1. Select a set of materials to be browsed.
2. Divide the material into units, which will be nodes in the graph.
3. Designate one or more parts of each unit as cohesive elements of a given type.
4. Give each cohesive element type (each subway line) a unique short name which will be available to a user.
5. Specify, for each element in each unit, what its predecessor and its successor will be, in terms of access.

2.5 Applying Results from Graph Theory to the Approach

It is desirable that any two nodes be connected by a short path. (It may be that the user needs to change subway lines in order to find the short path.) There is a theorem (Bollobas, 1985) which states that if a graph is created randomly, then the expected distance between two nodes (i.e., the length of a shortest path between them) is almost as small as is theoretically possible. (The theoretical minimum depends mainly on the valency of the graph, namely, the number of nodes that can be linked directly to one node). This result indicates that the designer does not have to worry about short connections between nodes. This property is expected to occur by itself.

3 Descriptions of implementations

In this section we briefly describe some implementations of the design. All were done on the Macintosh and are mouse-driven.

3.1 Graphics-based Procedural Instructions for Repair of a "String Crawler"

In a graphics-based instructional system for assembly and repair, access was via visually (or graphically) cohesive elements (Baggett et al., 1989). The object in question was a "string crawler," a battery-powered "vehicle" which traveled along a string when its switch was turned on. A user of the system could follow any of 21 different concepts (e.g. *motor, batteries, wire, switch box*) through the 41-frame presentation when given a task (to repair a broken string crawler). Cohesive elements were indicated by stars; clicking on a star or its related object moved the user to the "next" frame in the presentation that contained the object. There were 98 clickable stars in the presentation and thus an average of 2.4 per frame.

3.2 Emily Dickinson Poems

A frame from another implementation of the design, by the first author, are shown in Fig. 4. The implementation involved 183 Emily Dickinson poems and critiques of them offered by four authors. The cohesive elements in this case are 16 abstract themes, together with the poems themselves. In Fig. 4, a poem subway line, *[P 303] The Soul selects her own Society*, is shown. (The subway line is indicated below the banded line on the lower left-hand side of the screen.) The user is on stop 2 of 5 for this poem. Stop 1 was the poem itself, while stop 2 is the poem together with a critique of it by Charles R. Anderson. There are three other cohesive elements (subway lines) active in this frame; two are thematic: *Love Imagery* and *Sexuality Imagery*; the third is the poem *[P 249] Wild Nights - Wild Nights*, which Anderson also discusses in this frame. The user can get the menu of concepts, with those that are active in this frame blackened, by clicking on a compass icon. By clicking on any of the three active elements in the menu, the user can switch subway lines.

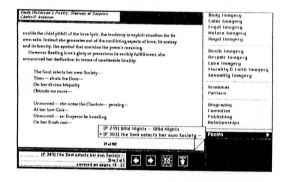

Fig. 4. Frame from an implementation involving the poetry of Emily Dickinson.

3.3 Where in History is Mathematics?

This implementation, done by students in two graduate software-design classes taught by the second author, involves the six different civilizations which according to current knowledge developed mathematics at least in part independently: Africa, Sumer-Babylon, India, China, Maya, and Inca. Concepts whose referents make up the list of cohesive elements include zero, counting schemes, tools, games, and famous individuals.

The implementation was originally laid out as a two-dimensional array. Names of the six civilizations labeled the columns, and each row was labeled by a concept. In theory, if all civilizations had references to each concept, the user could travel through the matrix horizontally or vertically. In reality, however, it was not the case that a reference to each concept was included for each civilization. For example, a reference to the concept of *zero* was included only in the civilizations of Maya, India, and China.

3.4 Lesson Plans for Elementary Mathematics

Another prototypical implementation of the subway model involves a database of 101 lesson units from a new curriculum for elementary mathematics. It was done by Barry Webster under the supervision of the second author, using materials written by Baggett & Ehrenfeucht (1993). The materials are meant for teachers. Concepts which can be followed through the materials in the prototype are identified (examples are *area, fractions,* and *money*), and teachers or curriculum planners can follow them through the material. The plan is for this prototype to be extended to a larger database (currently about 250 lesson units have been written); concepts yielding subway lines will be chosen from typical "scope and sequence" charts found in elementary textbooks. Teachers will have the materials available electronically, and if they want to browse all units which contain a certain concept (e.g. *fractions*), they can do so. Many lesson units contain illustrations, so that this implementation will have a multimedia database as it expands.

4 Advantages of this Approach

4.1 Importance of Cohesive Elements in Active Learning

Our work (Baggett & Ehrenfeucht, 1988; Baggett, Ehrenfeucht, & Guzdial, 1989) has shown that when material is presented passively to a learner (e.g., as in a videotape), the hierarchical structure of the material plays an important role in learning. But when the information is presented interactively, so that a user can traverse the material freely, cohesive elements are more important than hierarchical structure. This design gives principled access to information based on one's being able to follow a line of interest.

4.2 Independent Exploration

Since individuals are allowed to follow their own "tours" through lengthy material, rather than having to take "guided tours," they may take more active roles in exploring the material and get directly to the information that they want, quickly, without confusion, and without wading through irrelevant and distracting material.

4.3 Presence of a Running Index of Active Elements

On every frame the information that is available to the user about cohesive elements can be implemented to act as a constant index. This on-line index helps him or her follow a line of inquiry, quickly spot old and new important topics in a unit, and be kept aware of where in the information he or she currently is. This type of information is not available in a book. It should give users a good "feel" for the material, and help them locate what they want efficiently.

4.4 A Multimedia Alternative to Menus and Hierarchies

The system allows the designer to bypass having to find the hierarchical structure of material to be presented. It is based on retrieval of information by concepts designated as important by the designer, and independent of the medium in which they are presented. Users explore and learn by browsing and following their own choices of concepts through the data.

There have been attempts at developing on-line browsing systems in recent years, and electronic access to large bodies of material is the wave of the future. The novelty of our approach lies in arranging access so the users/learners can follow single cohesive lines through the material. The ideas are simple, and theoretical results in random graph theory indicate that the method can result in high efficiency for users in exploring. locating, and studying information.

References

Baggett, P. & Ehrenfeucht, A. (1982). Information in content equivalent movie and text stories. Discourse Processes, vol. 5, 73-99.

Baggett, P. & Ehrenfeucht, A. (1988). Conceptualizing in assembly tasks. Human Factors, 30 (3), 269-284.

Baggett, P. & Ehrenfeucht, A. (1993). A new elementary mathematics curriculum that incorporates calculators. Unpublished materials.

Baggett, P., Ehrenfeucht, A., & Guzdial, M. (1989). Sequencing and access in interactive graphics-based procedural instructions. University of Michigan School of Education Technical Report for Office of Naval Research, vol. 2 (1), August.

Bollobas, B. (1985) . Random Graphs. New York: Academic Press.

Grimes, J. (1975). The Thread of Discourse. Mouton Press, The Hague, 1075,

Halliday, M. (1985). An Introduction to Functional Grammar. Baltimore, MD: Edward Arnold.

Halliday, M. & Hasan, R. (1976). Cohesion in English. London: Longman Press.

Harris, Z. (1950). Discourse Analysis. Language, 28, 1-30.

Kintsch, W. & vanDijk, T. (1978). Toward a model of text comprehension and production. Psychological Review 85, 363-94.

WISH: Writing Instruction Script in Hebrew

Jon McKeeby[1], Yael M. Moses[2], Rachelle S. Heller[1]

[1]Department of Electrical Engineering and Computer Science
[2] Classics Department, George Washington University, Washington, D.C. 20052, U.S.A.

Abstract. This paper will describe an interactive instructional tool being developed at George Washington University for the teaching of handwriting of languages that utilize non-Roman alphabets. This tool, utilizing a microcomputer, videodisc player, stylus and graphics tablet, enables the student to receive instruction in letter formation, review the mechanics of the writing process, and test their handwriting accomplishments.

Keywords. multimedia, computer aided instruction, foreign languages, pen-based interfaces

1 Background

1.1 Early Handwriting Systems

In the early seventies two computer aided instruction (CAI) handwriting systems for non-Roman alphabets were developed. Abboud's system (1972), designed to instruct students in the writing of Arabic, consisted of a computer and a grease pencil. Students were instructed to write letters on the computer screen by using the grease pencil. After the student completed this task, the correct letter formation was presented on the screen, requiring the student to compare it to his or her own handwritten letter.

Following an empirical study, Abboud reported that at the completion four to eight hours of CAI instruction and four hours of classroom instruction students performed significantly better than students who were taught through either a programmed instruction course or an audio-lingual method. However, it should be noted that the audio-lingual method bases its instruction on listening and speaking with little or no writing. In addition to the increased proficiency in handwriting mechanics, Abboud reports that students who used the CAI system had a better attitude about class work and were more interested in continuing their Arabic language education.

Two problems of this system include the unconventional handwriting positioning and the inability to provide feedback relating to the student's inputted letter. First, the normal handwriting position consists of the student resting his/her arm on a desktop surface, as opposed to writing a letter on a computer screen with his/her hand positioned in the air. The second problem results from the student self-evaluation of a letter. Even though the student is able to gain some visual feedback from comparing a written letter against examples of the computerized letter, his/her evaluations may be interpreted incorrectly. In addition, a comparison of a written letter and a target letter does not provide the student with information about the correct mechanics of letter formation. Thus, the student's evaluation of his/her performance is, at best, incomplete.

The system by Chuang and Chen (1973) was designed to teach writing techniques, assist in the handwriting process stroke by stroke, evaluate student's writing, and provide informational feedback to aid the student in correcting mistakes in letter formation and letter appearance. The system allowed students to input letters by using a pen-stylus and graphics tablet. Students were then provided visual feedback by displaying their inputted letter and the computerized letter as well as instructional feedback describing mechanics used by the student to form the letter. Even though a completed system was described, no usability and empirical results were provided and the educational effects are not known.

1.2 Difficulties in Creating Successful Handwriting Instruction Systems

The major reasons for the limited success of the development of CAI handwriting systems include the extensive time necessary to create effective systems, input and output technologies (i.e., graphics tablets, computer displays, video output), the complex problem of recognizing letters and the inability to present a clear and computer instructional system. In order to present students with complete feedback pertaining to the process and results of a newly learned non-Roman alphabet, it is necessary to provide natural input techniques and visual feedback.

An instructional writing system is not true letter recognition if the target letter that is being compared to the inputted letter is known. In this case it is not necessary to sort through a complete set of letters. However, the comparison of an inputted letter and a target letter is complex because of the variability of writing style (i.e., proportional size and shape appearance) from one individual to another (Stallings, 1975).

Even though a picture and a description of the writing process may provide an adequate presentation of the letter, animation of the letter development and a live demonstration conducted by the instructor allows the student to visualize the complete handwriting process for each letter of the alphabet. Thus, a demonstration of the handwriting process is essential (Smith, 1987) in order to effectively instruct students.

2 The WISH System

Initially conceived and presented to the language faculty of The George Washington University by the professor of Hebrew, the objective for the WISH (Writing Instruction Script in Hebrew) system was to create a pilot project for the instruction of non-Roman languages such as Arabic, Greek, Hebrew and Cyrillic. The simplicity of cursive Hebrew (i.e., characters are not connected as in English nor are they contextual as in Arabic) provided an ideal character set for the initial pilot system.

WISH teaches the correct letter formation for each of the 27 cursive letters of the Hebrew alphabet. The WISH system allows students to observe the writing process, guide the student in writing each letter, examine the characters being drawn and completed, and provide immediate instructional feedback to aid the student in correcting errors in both character formation and appearance.

WISH handwriting development consists of two phases: a presentation stage and an interactive stage. The presentation stages uses video sequences and animation to guide students in the formation of cursive letters. These segments allow students to observe the actual positioning of the instructor's pen on lined paper as each letter is being formed. The video segments reinforce correct the handwriting process and are accessible for the student as a reference at anytime. Animation sequences are used to focus on the sequential formation of each character, stressing the character formulation and appearance attributes for each letter. Descriptions of the important attributes of the letters are provided on the screen. Students can trace the cursive letter using the stylus and tablet.

The presentation stage guides the student in the correct formation of the Hebrew cursive alphabet. However, to teach the handwriting process and formation of each letter, it is necessary to evaluate a student's handwriting process and product and provide feedback for improvement. After the presentation stage for a given letter, the student enters the letter writing section of the interactive writing stage. Students use a stylus on a tablet to write several examples of the cursive letter corresponding to the version that is displayed on the screen (Fig. 1). During this interactive stage, students' letters are examined and evaluated both by the student through self-inspection and by computer generated evaluations.

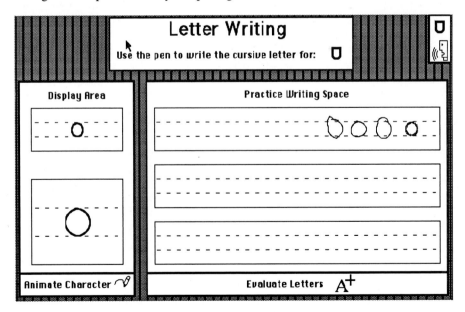

Fig. 1. The Letter Writing Screen

2.1 The Writing Module

As the student writes a letter, the written letter's (x,y) points and its boundary are calculated. From the boundary box, the letter is resized with respect to the target letter and then overlaid on top of the target letter through a transformation of the (x,y) points. The visual evaluation provided by overlaying the written letter on the target letter provides immediate constructive feedback to the student. In addition, the accuracy of the written letter is determined and feedback given to the user. To determine the acceptability of the written letter, it is necessary to perform a detailed evaluation by examining a variety of attributes (Fig. 2)

Shape:	Letter form/appearance
Proportional Size:	The size in relation to other written letters
Position:	The horizontal and vertical position
Stroke Direction:	Direction of pen stroke
Stroke Order:	The sequence in which strokes are formed. For letters that are formed with one stroke, stroke order is also used to refer to connectivity
Proportional Spacing:	The spacing between letters

Fig. 2. Letter Attributes

By clicking on the desired letter in the writing section, the user is able to review the attribute evaluation of for any letter (Fig. 3). After reviewing the letter evaluation, the student is able to return to the writing section. A student can continue to the next letter after writing a practice letter at least five times.

2.2 The Attribute Evaluation Module

Since the target letter is known, a true letter recognition algorithm is not needed, but rather a technique to match the written letter to the target letter. For example, if the computer system instructs the student to write the letter "A" and the student writes a letter "B", the algorithm will determine that the written letter was a bad letter "A" and then describe why it was a bad "A", never identifying it as a "B".

In addition to providing constructive feedback to the student, the evaluation algorithm must be able to identify the reasons the written letter was a 'good' or 'bad' match. To do so, it is necessary to perform a detailed evaluation of the written letter by examining each attribute. As the algorithm evaluates each attribute, a list of feedback responses is generated. This list describes the strengths and weaknesses of the written letter with respect to each attribute of the target letter. In addition, a guide is provided for the student to assist with future letter formation.

In order to identify the attributes of the Hebrew cursive alphabet, it was necessary to determine a set of general characteristics. A detailed attribute listing for each letter, identifying the optimal and acceptable letter, was created.

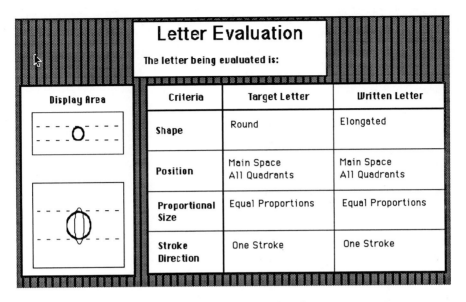

Fig. 3. The Letter Evaluation Screen

The shape of the written letter is the actual points of the letter entered through the use of the stylus and tablet as seen by the user. The other attributes of the written cursive letter are determined through the written letter's characteristics: bounding area, center, starting point, ending point, order of strokes and the character points. From these alone the stroke direction and stroke order of the written letter are determined and evaluated.

In order to determine a letter's proportional spacing and position attributes, the written letter's characteristics are used with a clock-face, a quadrant system and a spacing (Fig. 4). The clock face is used to identify the start and end of the letter and writing direction. The space component divides a writing space into three vertical spacing areas, the lower space, the main space and the upper space (all spaces are equal in size). The quadrant system is used to identify the center and horizontal positioning of a letter. The positioning of the quadrant and the distance of the vertical spacing are used to determine a letter's proportional attribute while the center of the quadrant system and three spaces are used to determine a letter's position.

The most difficult of all letter attributes to evaluate is the letter's shape. For the WISH system, the visualization of the character as well as a simple template matching algorithm are used to evaluate the correctness of the letter. Given that many of the the letters are comprised of arcs and straight lines, it was possible to develop mathematical equations to represent many of the Hebrew letters. From the size and proportion values of the written letter and the equation of the target letter, a template is created. For those letters that do not lend themselves to an equation, the digitized form of the letter is used as the template. The written letter is compared with the template. By using the size and proportional values of the written letter, the created template is equivalent in size to the written letter.   The creation of the comparison template in real time reduces complications of the template matching that are inherent to matching written characters.

The comparison process consists of counting the number of black and white points in the sample that match the defined points in the template. If the written letter and the template are greater than 85% equivalent, the shape is considered correct.

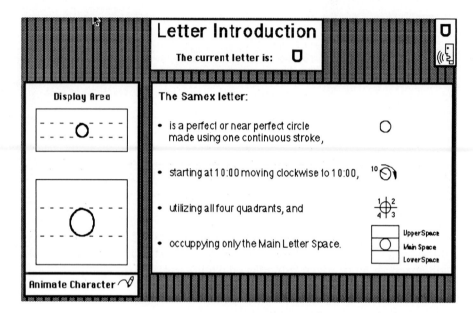

Fig. 4. The Space and Quadrant System

During the WISH introduction, the student is provided with a letter sample screen and is instructed to write samples of the *Samex* . From these the student's proportional size value is calculated. The size of the character is determined by forming a bounding box around the letter and determining its dimensions. The size is used to evaluate the proportional size attribute by comparing the entered character size to the student's written letter size.

In addition to proportional size value, the written letter samples are used to develop a template bounding box. This box involves the quadrant and component space system used to describe Hebrew letters. The template bounding box can be centered on top of the written letter and use to determine the written letter's positioning correctness.

Stroke direction is evaluated throughout the letter writing process with reference to stroke direction and position of the target letter attribute. For each target letter, a list of direction changes is maintained. As the stroke direction of the written letter changes during the writing process, its stroke direction list is updated. The stroke direction is determined through use of the previous and current (x,y) coordinates. Upon completion of the letter, the stroke direction list of the written letter is compared to the target with all differences noted in order to provide student feedback.

The stroke order of the written letter is determined by ordering the strokes as they are written by the student and comparing them to the order of strokes in the target letter. Since most letters use only one stroke, stroke order is also used to refer to connectivity. For letter that are only one stroke, the character is considered to be disconnected if the student lifts the stylus beyond the height of the proximity of the stylus and tablet while writing.

Proportional spacing, the spacing between letters and line, is only calculated when the student writes sequences of letters or words during the practice session. The distances are calculated by calculating the left, right, upper and lower spacing between characters. These calculations are performed by subtracting components of the bounding boxes.

3 Conclusions

An innovative, interactive learning environment for students to learn the writing mechanics needed to produce characters of a non-Roman language has been described. Currently, the primary objective is to create the CAI system to effectively teach Hebrew handwriting. Formative and summative evaluations are planned. Usability testing and educational impact studies will be conducted during the 1993-94 academic year. Modifications to WISH will be made to enable it to effectively teach other non-Roman languages including Ancient Greek, Russian, Chinese, Japanese, Korean and Arabic.

References

Abboud, V.C. (1972, March) The computer as an instructional device for the Arabic writing system. Computers and the Humanities, vol 6(4), pages 195-207.

Chuang, H.Y. and Chen, S. (1973, August). Computer aided instruction in Chinese characters. Proceedings of the First International Symposium on Computers and Chinese input/output Systems. pages 599-616.

Smith, W (1989). Modern technology in foreign language education: Applications and projects. National Textbook Company, Lincolnwood, Illinois.

Stallings, W.W. (1975) Approaches to Chinese character recognition. Pattern Recognition. Vol 8, pages 87-98

A Method of Evaluating the Usability of a Prototype User Interface for CBT Courseware

Garry Patterson

Dept. of Information Systems, The University of Ulster, Jordanstown, Co. Antrim. BT37 0QB, Northern Ireland

Abstract. This paper describes the evaluation process for assessing the usability of a prototype user interface for Computer-Based training (CBT) courseware. The MIDAS (Multimedia Interactive Design Aided System) model presents a methodology for the design, implementation and evaluation of multimedia CBT courseware. Results of the usability of the prototype application are presented which are based upon the evaluation criteria within the model. The evaluation results are analysed to test the performance of the prototype and their implications discussed. The implementation of the model presented is centered on the following application - *the training of pilots and engineers on the braking system of the British Aerospace Jetstream Aircraft.*

Keywords. Human-computer interface, computer based training, courseware, multimedia, evaluating usability, authoring

Introduction

The research project was conducted under the general perspective of the definition of methods and tools for the evaluation of an interface based on human factors criteria. The goal was to design an interface for use by CBT courseware users in an effective learning environment. This study presents one such method; the validation of human factors criteria proposed within the MIDAS framework ([Patterson'93]).

There are numerous different human factors methods currently available for the evaluation of interfaces. They each have advantages and drawbacks, the major problem however is that none of them allows a complete evaluation of an interface. Several classifications of such methods have been described ([Christie'90], [Karat'88], [Maguire'89] and [Senach'90]). Three main categories of methods can be distinguished depending on their orientation; theoretical models, expert judgement or the users. The latter approach is the one that will be stressed and used in this paper.

1 Evaluation Methods Based on Users

In this category, evaluation methods are based on various user related data. The data may consist of users' performance data collected during user interaction with existing or prototyped interfaces (behavioural data) or from cognitive indications (understanding and memory). The data may also consist of subjective information extracted from users' attitudes and opinions about the interface. Extracting and monitoring user data is performed with several tools that are more or less intrusive. Such techniques include on site observation, audio-video recording, physiological recording or concurrent verbalisations. These can influence users' behaviour. Conversely, questionnaires, subsequent verbalizations, individual or group interviews have less of an influence on users' performance. The use of an *Evaluation Booklet*, presented the user with a practical method in the form of a checklist. The method adopted is discussed in Sections 2 and 3.

2 The Evaluation Within the Methodology of MIDAS

2.1 Overview of the Method

The method is a practical tool, in the form of a checklist. It is based on a set of software ergonomics criteria, which a well-designed user interface should aim to meet. The checklist consists of sets of specific questions aimed at assessing usability. These provide a standardized and systematic means of enabling those evaluating a CBT system interface.

2.2 Sources of the Checklist Questions

The checklists have been developed with reference to a number of sources. A number of questions from the 'Usability: Screening Questionnaire' in ([Clegg'88]), and the format for these sections have been adapted from this source. In addition, early versions of Clegg provided the stimulus for a number of questions within Sections 1 and 10. Other sources for the checklist include ([Ravden'89], [Smith'86], [Gardner'87] and [Shneiderman'87]).

2.3 How Should the Checklist be Used?

A key feature of the method, and a prerequisite for using the checklist, is that the evaluator uses the system tasks which the CBT courseware has been designed to perform, as part of the evaluation. This takes place before completing the checklist, and represents the first step in the evaluation. Tasks used in the evaluation should be representative of the work which is to be carried out using the system, and should test as much of the system, and as many of its functions, as possible. Such tasks require careful construction and are extremely important to the validity of the user interface evaluation. There are a number of reasons for use of representative tasks:

[i] Tasks which are realistic and representative of the work for which the system has been designed provide the most effective way of demonstrating the system's functionality.

[ii] This approach enables those evaluating the interface to see it not simply as a series of screens and actions, but as part of the application system as a whole.

[iii] By carrying out tasks, evaluator's can be exposed to as many aspects of the user interface as possible, which is necessary if they are to comment usefully, and in

detail, on specific features, problems, strengths and deficiencies of the CBT courseware interface.

[iv] Many significant problems and difficulties of the courseware are only revealed when carrying out tasks.

[v] In some cases, there may be important aspects of usability which can only be captured by using the system (e.g. inflexibility of a menu structure when the task requires rapid movement between different parts of the system.)

In addition to the above points, important information can be gathered *by observing* an evaluator's performance when carrying out tasks in an evaluation. Observations and recording of task performance is extremely valuable in identifying those difficulties which evaluators experience when interacting with the system.

The method enables a variety of different people, with different background and expertise, to evaluate the same user interface. A particular benefit of this is that it enables end-users, such as the CBT students and trainers and designers who will use the system to access its usability before it is implemented into a full courseware package.

2.4 When Can the Method be Used?

The method can be used to evaluate usability both during and after design and development of the user interface. Where *prototyping tools* are available, it can enable early evaluation of an interface, or if alternative interfaces, so providing feedback at early stages in the design process. In this way, different configurations can be tested, and necessary improvements made, before reaching a fully operational state ready for implementation. At the later stages of development, it is more difficult to make major modifications to the interface.

2.5 Potential Financial Benefits of Using the Method

CBT user interface evaluation using this method may incur some immediate financial costs; for example, where the development process is lengthened, or through the involvement of end-users and others in the evaluation.

However, the importance of user interface design and of usability should not be underestimated, and its evaluation should be expected to take the time and effort worthy of its importance. In the longer term, the benefits which are likely to result from the evaluation will outweigh the costs for CBT courseware developers and companies which use their skills. Benefits may include:

- reduced training time for end-users;
- reduced support costs, due to fewer, and less significant difficulties;
- reduced need for amendments, modifications and revisions after implementation;
- where relevant, increased sales, as a more usable, well-designed and acceptable training environment is provided;
- a greater willingness among end-users to accept the training system and to use it effectively;
- a greater awareness among those developing CBT training courseware application systems of the requirements for 'user-centred' design.

In Section 3 the evaluation method is used to assess the usability of the prototype application user interface. In the light of experimentation, recommendations for changes to the prototype are made.

3 The Evaluation

3.1 Goal of the Evaluation

The goal is to assess the usability of a user interface for CBT courseware. The method, and in particular the checklist, enables an interface to be evaluated by a variety of people with differing expertise and backgrounds; including, for example, interface designers, other technical experts and, most importantly, representative end-users, who may or will actually use the system in practice. The method does not aim to solve problems, or to enable a quantitative assessment of usability. It provides a means of identifying problem areas, and the extracting of information concerning problems, difficulties, weaknesses and areas for improvement.

3.2 Method

3.2.1 Subjects

One hundred and twenty subjects participated in the study. There were 15 pilots whose experience in flying ranged from two to twenty-four years (M = 7.5; $S.D.$ = 6.5), and the remaining participants were the student and staff population registered with The University of Ulster. Male and female subjects participated. The ages of the subjects ranged from 18 to 40 years (M = 23.7, S.D. = 4.7).

3.2.2 Procedure

Each subject participated in one individual evaluation session. The evaluation consisted of a learning phase and identification tasks in interactive mode. The subjects then completed the Evaluation Booklet. In the learning phase subjects were invited to study the prototype application relating to The Braking *System of the British Aerospace Jetstream 32 Aircraft.* They were encouraged to work through the introduction, statement of objectives, operation of the brake system and component location modules. However, the subjects could at any stage return to the main menu screen, and execute the courseware in any order. This would also assess the systems' usability. The identification tasks followed the completion of the learning phase. During these tasks, subjects were presented with problems relating to answering questions on the location and operation of the braking system. No time limit was imposed on either phase. Times ranged from 25 - 40 mins. (M = 32.5, $S.D.$ = 6.5) for the pilots; 29 - 72 mins. (M = 50.5, $S.D.$ 13.6) for the engineering students; and 40 - 93 mins. (M = 65.0, $S.D.$ = 11.9) for the rest of the subjects. Following the CBT lesson the subjects were required to fill in the Evaluation Booklet. This process took approximately 60 mins. to complete. The subjects were encouraged to fill this in immediately after the hands-on session, and to be as critical of the user interface (if necessary.) Spaces for written comments were provided beside each checklist question.

3.2.3 Data Collection and Analysis

Two types of data were collected. Firstly, the grading of the checklist questions, which was in the form of a [3] in the appropriate box which best describes the subject's answer to each question, or 'N/A' if the question was not appropriate to the courseware. Secondly, the subject may comment on any issue relating to each specific question in the appropriate column. The objectives of the data analysis were threefold:

Firstly, to assess the usability of the prototype application. To achieve this, global scores were calculated for each criteria question from the sample responses. A correct response was defined as either a [3], 'N/A', or **'don't know'** in one of the appropriate columns on the checklist grid. If a checklist question was left blank, or two responses given, this was defined as a missing value. In the data analysis using SPSS, these values were eliminated, thus reducing the sample size ([SPSS'90]).

Secondly, to (a) identify problem areas and weaknesses within the prototype application user interface; and (b) make recommendations to enhance a multimedia UID for CBT courseware.

Thirdly, using a factor analysis statistical technique, to identify key variables and subsequently design an Evaluation Booklet to assist CBT courseware designers in assessing usability of a UID for their end-users at the prototype stage of development. An explanation of the analytical technique - Principal Components Analysis is contained in ([Patterson'92]).

4 Results from the Evaluation Procedure

4.1 The User Interface of the Prototype Application

A full description of the overall ratings for the Evaluation Booklet are presented in ([Patterson'92]).

The results lead us to conclude that the design of the interface for the Braking System module provided a very satisfactory environment for learning.

The lowest rating scores were identified in Section 10. In this category, User Guidance and Support, only 85 subjects completed this section. The reasons for this can be identified by examining the questions presented in the Evaluation Booklet Section 10. The only user support provided in the courseware was audio and visual feedback if incorrect answers were given by the subjects to the questions.

There was *no* Help menu integrated into the braking system to provide on-line assistance for the aircraft terminology or hardcopy output to supplement the CBT material. The subjects did not have a copy of the training manual to complement the CBT instruction. The data from this section supports these claims. The booklet used in the evaluation process is a generic document for UID evaluation and thus by including options which were not included in the prototype design, can be remedied at the implementation stage of development.

The use of a multimedia platform proved a very successful user environment for learning. 63% of the subjects commented on the effective use of multimedia to present the training material, with a further 10% supporting the specific use of graphics and animation. The lack of an on-line Help facility is also noted as one of the worst features of the system. 33% included comments, specifically mentioning the lack of feedback from the system. A further 24% commented on a lack of explanation of the direction icons. In the written comments, the subjects however noted that once they became familiar with their functionality, they did not pose a problem. It is very encouraging to note that in general terms some 63.5% of all subjects had no difficulty in either understanding the system or in finding any irritating system problems. In recommendations suggested by the subjects for improvement, only 23.3% included the inclusion of a Help facility. Over 55% concluded that the CBT courseware represented a good prototype application. A further 10% suggested that the provision of moving-video illustrations would have enhanced the learning environment.

No evidence existed to suggest that the different subject groups found the user interface environment more complex to use or the training material any more difficult to understand. One reason for this is that no assumed knowledge was required for an understanding of the braking system. The pilots commented on the effective use of multimedia in designing a realistic training environment. In the past, this had only been available when the pilots progressed from the classroom instruction to the Flight Training Devices, and even then this was a static environment. Only when the pilots progressed to training in the Full Flight Simulator was interactivity a part of the learning experience.

4.2 The Revised Evaluation Booklet

The Revised Evaluation Booklet has been designed to assist designers and end-users in assessing the usability of a UID at the prototype stage of development. The questions included in each section are identified from the analysis of performing PCA on the subjects data ([Patterson'92]).

5 Conclusion

It is clear that CBT is now a well proven training tool with a host of successful applications on a world-wide basis. The two most significant factors driving the CBT industry are Open Systems and the developments within the multimedia forum. The issues presented in this paper have embraced both these issues. It is accepted that the design of the user interface accounts for at least fifty per cent of the overall development costs and time in the production of courseware, so it is vital that User Interface Design (UID) principles be established to guide the developers and designers.

The past twenty years have seen both successes and failures in the development of CBT courseware. Several reasons can be established for the failure. These include firstly, a misconceived view of the end-user and inadequate liasion between developer and trainer resulting in poor quality courseware. Secondly, courseware was very often designed and developed by computer science specialists following a software engineering design life cycle.

The framework of MIDAS developed a methodology for successful multimedia CBT production. Built on a froundation of principles of learning and cognitive psychology, a re-examination of the tasks involved in each of the design, implementation and evaluation stages highlighted necessary changes in the development process, ([Patterson'92]).

The objectives of this paper were to assess the usability of a user interface for multimedia CBT courseware and to design an abbreviated evaluation booklet to be used in training environments. An evaluation booklet developed within the MIDAS framework was used for this purpose. The data analysed provided overwhelming support for the use of multimedia as the delivery platform for presenting CBT courseware. The data also identified areas of weakness and problems within the UID. Within the prototype application reviewed by the subjects, the absence of an on-line Help facility was identified. PCA was used to identify the key variables within each evaluation criterion. The revised evaluation booklet designed for use by designers and end-users of multimedia CBT courseware in training environments is presented. The data analysed provides overwhelming support for the use of multimedia as a delivery platform for presenting CBT courseware.

It is believed that the MIDAS model will provide a framework for producing cost effective multimedia CBT courseware for industrial and institutional learning environments throughout the 1990s and well into the next century.

References

Christie, B. and Gardiner, M. M.: "Evaluation of the human-computer interface", Evaluation of human work: a practical ergonomics methodology, pp. 271-320, Taylor and Francis, London, 1990

Clegg, C. W., Warr, P. B. and Green, T. R. G. et al: People and computers - how to evaluate your company's new technology, Ellis Horwood, Chichester, UK, 1988

Gardner, M. M. and Christie, B. (Editors): Applying cognitive psychology to user-interface design, Wiley & Sons, Chichester, UK, 1987

Karat, J.: "Software evaluation methodologies", in Handbook of Human-Computer Interaction, edited by M. Helander, Elsevier Science (North-Holland), Amsterdam,,1988

Maguire, M. and Sweeney, M.: "System monitoring: garbage generator or basis for comprehensive evaluation system?" in People and Computer V, edited by A Sutcliffe and L. Macaulay, Cambridge University Press, Cambridge, UK, 1989

Oppenheim, A. N.: Questionaire Design and Attitude Measurement, Heinemann, London, 1979

Patterson, G.: A Design Model for Multimedia Computer-Based Training, D.Phil Thesis, Faculty of Informatics, University of Ulster, Jordanstown, Northern Ireland, 1992

Patterson, G.; Anderson, T. J. and Monds, F. C.: "A Design Model for Computer-Based Training", in Human-Computer Interaction 19B, edited by G. Salvendy and M. Smith, Elsevier Science (North-Holland), Amsterdam, 1993

Ravden, S. and Johnson, G.: Evaluating Usability of Human-Computer Interfaces - A Practical Method, Wiley & Sons, Chichester, UK, 1989

Senach, B.: Evaluation ergonomique des interfaces homme-machine: une revue de la littérature (English translation), Institut National de Recherche en Informatique et an Automatique, Rocquencourt, France, 1990

Shneiderman, B.: Designing the User Interface: Strategies for Effective Human-Computer Interaction, Addison-Wesley, Reading, MA, 1987

Smith, S. L. and Mosier, J. N.: Guidelines for designing user interface software, Report No. MTR-100090; ESD-TR-86-278, The Mitre Corporation, Bedford, MA, 1986

[SPSS'90]: SPSS Inc., SPSS Base System User's Guide, SPSS, Chicago, 1990

A Visual Display System for the Teaching of Intonation to Deaf Persons: An Explorative Study

Gerard W.G. Spaai[1,2], Esther S. Derksen[2] and Paul A.P. Kaufholz[1,2]

[1]Institute for Perception Research/IPO, Eindhoven, The Netherlands
[2]Institute for the Deaf/IvD, Sint-Michielsgestel, The Netherlands

Abstract. To help profoundly deaf speakers improve their intonation, a system which displays intonation visually is being developed. In this system, the Intonation Meter, visual feedback of intonation is given as a continuous representation of the pitch contour containing only the perceptually relevant aspects of the pattern of intonation. An explorative study was carried out to determine the usability of the Intonation Meter for teaching intonation to prelingually, profoundly deaf children. Preliminary data, collected with a small number of children, indicate that the system can be an important instructional tool for teaching intonation. Suggestions for increasing the usability of the system are given.

Keywords. Speech-training devices, visual feedback of intonation, GUI

1 Introduction

Many investigators have reported on the problems that prelingually, profoundly deaf speakers have with pitch control (Osberger & McGarr, 1982). The characteristic difficulties include abnormally high pitch with respect to age and gender (Stathopoulos, Duchan, Sonnenmeier & Bruce, 1986), excessive phoneme-related variations in pitch (Bush, 1981) and a lack of linguistically relevant pitch variations. Better production of pitch in the speech of deaf persons is important because it contributes to speech quality and speech intelligibility, especially when the segmental aspects of speech are produced fairly well (Metz, Schiavetti, Samar & Sitler, 1990).

It is difficult for deaf speakers to learn to control the pitch of speech because: 1) they may not have sufficient residual hearing to perceive the auditory cues necessary for the control of pitch; 2) tactile and proprioceptive feedback play only a minor role in pitch control (Ladefoged, 1967); 3) the major variations in pitch are determined by the action of the cricothyroid muscle (Collier, 1975), which means that it is impossible to give visual cues on the *control* of pitch. Therefore, to help deaf speakers acquire better pitch control, various researchers have developed sensory aids that extract the pitch from speech and display it visually. The main reason for developing such aids is that they are capable of providing objective and immediate feedback on pitch.

Little is known about the effectiveness of systems for the visual display of intonation in teaching intonation to profoundly deaf persons. Evaluations of these systems (Friedman, 1985) are often based on case studies which were descriptive and not experimental in nature, thereby only allowing for restricted statements concerning effectiveness. Other studies (e.g. McGarr, Youdelman & Head, 1989) incorporated the use of a system for displaying intonation visually into an experimental program for speech training. The effects of this experimental condition were then compared with a control condition in which a regular speech-training program had been used. Practice conditions then differed in more than one respect, making it difficult to determine the effectiveness of the visual display system. Finally, the usability of these systems was often determined with students who had severe hearing losses (e.g. Youdelman, MacEachron & Behrman, 1988). It is unknown, however, whether the findings of these studies are generalizable to profoundly deaf persons.

To summarize, the usability of visual display systems in teaching intonation to persons who are profoundly deaf is still to be fully explored. This may have contributed to the lack of widespread use of these systems in schools. Another factor that may have contributed to this is that in these systems pitch was measured and fed back directly to the deaf speaker without post-processing the pitch contour. Two difficulties arise when speakers receive the unprocessed pitch contour.

The first problem arises from the fact that the interpretation of the displayed pitch contour is hampered by the interruptions during unvoiced parts which are at variance with the continuously perceived contour of pitch. The second problem relates to the presence of many perceptually irrelevant pitch variations (the micro-intonation) in pitch contours that are unprocessed, which may distract attention from the perceptually relevant pitch variations. Micro-intonation can be very conspicuous, especially at transitions between consonants and vowels. It can barely be perceived, if at all, by persons with normal hearing, let alone be imitated. In order to solve these problems, a system has been developed, the Intonation Meter (Spaai, 1993; Spaai, Storm & Hermes, 1993), that gives visual feedback of intonation as a continuous representation containing only the perceptually relevant pitch variations. The course of the pitch contour is approximated by a small number of straight lines, resulting in a stylized pitch contour. This representation of the pitch contour is intended to facilitate the interpretation of the visual feedback of the intonation contour. An example is shown in Fig. 1 for the Dutch sentence, 'Op een dag kwam een vreemdeling het dorp binnenwand'len,' (One day a stranger came walking into the village). The separate dots show the unprocessed pitch measurements and the continuous straight lines show the stylized pitch contour.

The following section presents an experiment that was carried out to find out whether the Intonation Meter can be helpful in teaching intonation to children who are profoundly deaf. In the final section suggestions for increasing the usability of the system are given in terms of the development of a graphical user interface.

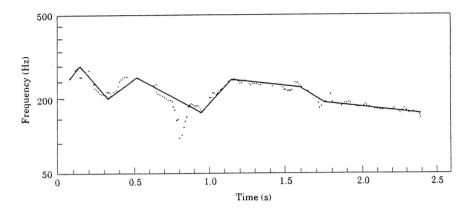

Fig. 1. Display of the unprocessed pitch measurements and the stylized pitch contour for the Dutch sentence. 'Op een dag kwam een vreemdeling het dorp binnenwand'len,' (One day a stranger came walking into the village).

2 The Experiment

2.1 Design and Procedure

Two groups of profoundly deaf students practised intonation. The first group, the *control group*, practised intonation with the help of regular means. This group received speech training using mainly auditory input via personal hearing aids. In addition, information on pitch was, for instance, presented via some visual activity of the speech therapist or via a representation on paper. No visual or tactile sensory aid was used with this group. The second group, the *experimental group*, received speech training using auditory input and the Intonation Meter to provide visual feedback on pitch. Typically, when a student was working with the system, an example of a pitch contour was produced by the speech therapist and displayed on the upper part of the screen of the Intonation Meter and then had to be imitated on the lower part. While imitating, direct unprocessed feedback is given by means of real-time pitch measurements. After the conclusion of the whole utterance, the stylized contour was displayed too. Progress in learning of both groups was compared with a third group, the *test group*, which did not receive any extra practice on intonation.

Progress in learning was measured as differences in an intonation test that was conducted prior to training and also at the end of the training period. This test was based on the Fundamental Speech Skills Test (Levitt, Youdelman,& Head, 1990).

The intonation test was conducted without sensory aids except for the students' personal hearing aids. The students' productions were tape-recorded and a speech therapist who was experienced in listening to and evaluating the speech of deaf children rated the recordings. For this explorative study, results are reported for:

1) the production of appropriate average pitch in words and sentences; 2) the production of pitch variations in long vowels and syllables.

2.2 Training Sessions

The experimental group and the control group practised intonation three times a week, each session lasting about 15 minutes. This was done over a four-month period. Thus, in all, each student in the control condition and each in the experimental condition received about eight hours of training.

Generally speaking, speech training focused on the remediation of an inappropriate average pitch and, to a lesser extent, on the production of variations of pitch in vowels and syllables. Practice consisted of four groups of activities: pitch-awareness training, auditory discrimination and identification of pitch contours, imitation of pitch contours, and production of pitch contours without the benefit of the teacher's model. The four groups of activities were not necessarily hierarchical and training was generally performed in several of these areas simultaneously, as recommended by McGarr, Youdelman and Head (1992). Subjects were trained to produce pitch contours while uttering sustained vowels, syllables and words.

2.3 Subjects

Twelve prelingually, profoundly deaf, students from a secondary school for special education at the Institute for the Deaf in Sint-Michielsgestel, The Netherlands, participated in the experiment. All students received speech training prior to the experiment. They had been educated according to the 'oral reflective method' (Van Uden, 1977). The age of the subjects ranged from 14 to 20 years. They had no motor or intellectual handicaps. All students had hearing losses greater than 90 dB ISO bilaterally. They used acoustic hearing aids binaurally and produced pitch contours that were perceived by their speech therapists to be 'relatively flat', reflecting a monotonous voice. Also, in some cases, their pitch appeared to be too high with respect to age and sex. Subjects were matched in groups of three as closely as possible according to their age, residual hearing, academic performance and speech skills. After the subjects had been divided into three groups, one subject dropped out. The numbers of children participating in the control condition, the experimental condition and the test condition were three, four and four, respectively.

2.4 Results

Average Pitch. Fig. 2 shows the percentages of acceptable ratings in the pretest and the posttest for the average pitch in isolated words (22 items) and sentences (12). The data are presented for the experimental group (4 subjects x 34 ratings = 136 judgments), the control group (3 subjects x 34 ratings = 102 judgments) and the test group (4 subjects x 34 ratings = 136 judgments). Improvement was measured by a shift from an unacceptable rating in the pretest to an acceptable rating in the posttest. The percentage of acceptable judgments for average pitch increased for all groups. However, it is immediately apparent that the experimental group made more progress than the test group and the control group. Furthermore, the control group performed better than the test group.

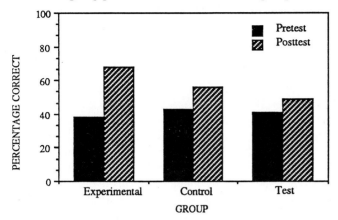

Fig. 2. Average ratings of the mean pitch. Percentages of acceptable judgments are plotted for the experimental group, the control group and the test group. The appropriateness of average pitch in isolated words (22) and sentences (12) has been rated. The data are presented for the pretest (dark bars) and the posttest (light bars).

Pitch Variations in Vowels and Syllables. Fig. 3 shows the percentages of acceptable ratings in the pretest and the posttest for the production of variations in pitch in long vowels (135) and syllables (18).

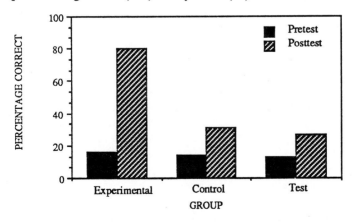

Fig. 3. Average ratings of the production of pitch variations in vowels (135) and syllables (18). Percentages of acceptable judgments are plotted for the experimental group, the control group and the test group. The data are presented for the pretest (dark bars) and the posttest (light bars).

The data are presented for the experimental group (4 subjects x 153 ratings = 612 judgments), the control group (3 subjects x 153 ratings = 459 judgments) and the test group (4 subjects x 153 ratings = 612 judgments). The results clearly show that the experimental group made most progress (64%). The control group and the test group also showed progress but the magnitude of improvement was not as large: the percentage of acceptable judgments increased by about 17%.

2.4 Discussion

The results of this explorative study showed that profoundly deaf students who receive intonation training that incorporates the use of the Intonation Meter show greater progress in the production of appropriate average pitch and the production of pitch variations in vowels and syllables than a control group who received regular training. Although these results were gathered with a small number of children, which may make it difficult to generalize, they are very promising, especially since training time was limited. Also, the children participating in this study could be characterized as having more impervious phonatory problems owing to their age. Therefore, research is in progress to find out whether speech training that incorporates the use of the Intonation Meter can be more effective with young children. Long-term research is necessary to determine whether the intensive use of this system can result in improved control of intonation in connected discourse.

3 Future Developments

3.1 Graphical User Interface

The Intonation Meter is meant to be used for teaching intonation to deaf children aged 4 to 20 years. Since the students and the teachers are not expected to have any computer experience, ease of use is extremely important. A future version of the Intonation Meter should support two modes, a *Teacher mode* and a *Student mode*. In the Teacher mode a speech therapist monitors the deaf student. Here, the speech therapist can adjust parameters specific to an individual student, select exercises and give instructions. In the Student mode, the student practises intonation without the presence of a speech therapist. By merely entering his or her name, a student can start a training session. All system parameters are set up automatically and the student is guided by the Intonation Meter. Parameter settings and selection functions are not accessible to the student. Records of performance are kept for each individual student to provide computerized guidance.

To meet these requirements, two parts of the data presentation in the user interface have to be designed carefully, namely the measured data as represented in the so-called Views, and the organization of functions and features, kept in the Dialogue structure. The interpretation of the display depends on the attributes of the graphical representations of the measured speech characteristics, e.g., line thickness for amplitude. These graphical representations must be clear and easy to interpret. In addition to these graphical representations, fast feedback of measured data is essential. The dialogue structure implies the organization of the functions and features in dialogue boxes. The two parts of data presentation are shown in Fig. 4.

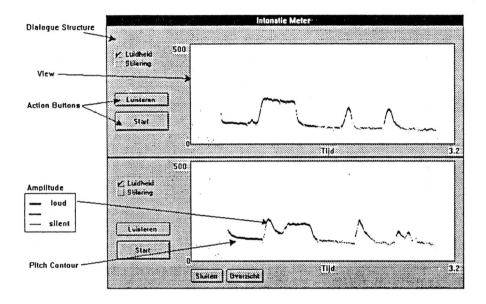

Fig. 4. A possible future implementation of the user-interface of the Intonation Meter. The data is represented in the Views. The Dialogue structure contains the action buttons for the most important functions. The pitch contour and the amplitude of an example and an imitation utterance are displayed.

3.2 The Prototype

The user interface of the current version of the Intonation Meter, running under MS-DOS, has been developed from a developer's point of view. The user interface and the presentation of information were primarily meant for experimental purposes and to facilitate the further development of the system. No special attention was paid to its usability in classroom situations or for students practising independently.

The Intonation Meter is currently being transferred to the MS-Windows environment. MS-Windows is becoming a standard environment for interactive applications for MS-DOS machines, especially in educational settings. Programming in MS-Windows facilitates the development of a user-friendly interface with the use of graphics. The prototype version presented here intends to meet the objectives described above. In Fig. 4 a possible future implementation of the interface of the Intonation Meter is presented. Here, a limited number of functions are accessible to avoid confusion. It should be emphasized that the interface is still under development. The design presented here may change in the near future, based on further evaluations.

The prototype will be tested in regular speech training sessions. During these sessions feedback from the pupils and the teacher will lead to modifications of the prototype. For the new prototype the same procedure will then be followed. The input of the users of the system will help to modify and improve the usability of the Intonation Meter, which may contribute to its use in speech training by making it possible to adapt the system to a variety of teaching techniques and conditions encountered in practice.

Acknowledgment

The authors would like to express their gratitude to the principals, staff and students of the School voor VSO (IvD, Sint-Michielsgestel, The Netherlands).

References

Bush, M. (1981) Vowel articulation and laryngeal control in speech of the deaf. Ph.D. dissertation, Massachusetts Institute of Technology.

Collier, R. (1975) Physiological correlates of intonation patterns. J. Acoust. Soc. Am. 58, 249-255.

Friedman, M. (1985) Remediation of intonation contours of hearing-impaired students. J. Commun. Disord. 18, 259-272.

Ladefoged, P. (1967) Three areas of experimental phonetics. London: University Press.

Levitt, H., Youdelman, K. & Head, J. (1990) Fundamental Speech Skills Test (FSST). Colorado: Resource Point Incorporation.

McGarr, N. & Osberger, M. (1978) Pitch deviancy and the intelligibility of deaf children's speech. J. Commun. Disord. 11, 237-247.

McGarr, N.S., Youdelman, K. & Head, J. (1989) Remediation of phonation problems in hearing-impaired children: Speech training and sensory aids. Volta Rev. 91, 7-17.

McGarr, N.S., Youdelman, K. & Head, J. (1992) Guidebook for voice pitch remediation in hearing-impaired speakers. Colorado: Resource Point Incorporation.

Metz, D.E., Schiavetti, N., Samar, V.J. & Sitler, R.W. (1990) Acoustic dimensions of hearing-impaired speakers' intelligibility: segmental and suprasegmental characteristics. J. Speech Hear. Res. 33, 467-488.

Spaai, G.W.G. (1993) Teaching intonation to deaf persons through visual displays. In: B.A.G. Elsendoorn, F. Coninx (eds.) Interactive learning technology for the deaf. NATO ASI Series F, Vol. 113, pp. 151-163. Berlin: Springer-Verlag.

Spaai, G.W.G., Storm, A. & Hermes, D.J. (1993) A visual display system for the teaching of intonation to deaf persons: Some preliminary findings. J. Microcomp. Appl., 16, 277-286.

Stathopoulos, E.T., Duchan, J.F., Sonnenmeier, R.M. & Bruce, N.V. (1986) Intonation and pausing in deaf speech. Folia Phoniatr. 38, 1-12.

Van Uden, A.M.J. (1977) A world of language for deaf children. Lisse: Swets & Zeitlinger.

Youdelman, K., MacEachron, M. & Behrman, A.M. (1988) Visual and tactile sensory aids: Integration into an on-going speech training program. Volta Rev. 90, 197-207.

XProcSim: An X Window Based GUI for the Dynamic Simulation of the Chemical Recovery Cycle of a Paper Pulp Mill

Fátima Pais[1], B. Gay[2] and A. Portugal[1]

[1]Department of Chemical Engineering, University of Coimbra, Largo Marquês de Pombal, 3000-Coimbra, Portugal [2]Department of Computer Science and Applied Mathematics, Aston University, Birmingham B4 7ET, U.K.

Abstract. An interactive software system (XProcSim) that offers easy and efficient analysis of the transient state of the chemical recovery cycle of a pulp mill is described. It is formed by two independent but coordinated components: a graphical user interface (GUI), and a set of simulation modules. Process representation, control of the integration performed by the simulation programs, inputs of data and perturbations and graphical representation of results are controlled by a mouse/menu driven interface. Significant differences between other existing systems and the software described here are XProcSim's use of the X Window system for the development of the GUI, which ensures portability to a number of hardware platforms. Remote, networked X-based display systems can be used, and it is also possible to run the simulation program on a remote machine. The distributed structure makes it possible to utilize the most powerful features of various machines.

Keywords. Graphical user interface (GUI), distributed systems, process simulation, chemical recovery cycle, pulp mill

1 Introduction

Process simulation is one of the most widely used tools for the design, optimization or simply the study of industrial units in steady or transient states. If the analysis of the dynamics under conditions of start-up, grade changes, emergency outages and shutdowns is desired, then dynamic simulators are necessary (Schewk and others 1991). The goal of this work was to develop a package for computerized simulation of the transient state of the chemical recovery cycle of a paper pulp mill. Simulation of the detailed behaviour of each unit led, in some cases, to complex mathematical models of large dimension which were difficult to solve and time consuming to simulate. In order to manage the amount of data involved and the results produced, and easily define or alter all the simulation parameters and impose the desired perturbations, it soon became apparent that a powerful interface was needed. The development of a GUI, which would allow the graphical display of the results of the simulation, was therefore a very important feature for the ease of use of the programs. Based on investigations of software ergonomics, the conclusion that graphical interfaces are the interactive man-machine communication of the future is now widely accepted, as considerable increases in both productivity and accuracy of completed work are achieved using GUI's (Peddie 1992). There is, however, a lack of standardization and the number of existing systems is high. Examples are X Window for UNIX workstations, MS Windows and Presentation Manager for IBM Personal Computers, the MacIntosh software for Apple computers, GEM for the Atari and Intuition for the Amiga (Pangalos 1992). In the UNIX-based world the *de facto* standard, developed by MIT (Scheifler and Gettys 1986), is usually known as X Window. X can display output windows from several applications at once in one screen, and these programs can run simultaneously on different machines. The machines do not have to be the same type or run the same operating system, as long as they support multitasking and interprocess communication (Moore 1990). X relies, in practical terms, on the development of graphical user interface toolkits — sets of widgets, or building blocks, such as menus, buttons, scrollbars, etc. — to assist the developer of applications. In this work, a colour UNIX Sun SPARCstation2 + graphics accelerator workstation was used. Sun's XView toolkit, together with the Open Look interface and window manager as developed by Sun and AT&T, were also used. A toolkit is an indispensable tool for saving time, since it avoids lengthy sets of low level intructions to create a simple object and guarantees consistency across all objects — that is, the same look and feel. To simplify developing applications, X toolkits employ concepts used in object-oriented programming. This is noteworthy inasmuch as the toolkit is written in and for the C language, which does not directly support objects (Miller 1990).

2 Basic Features of XProcSim

XProcSim's interface was designed from scratch so a number of ways of achieving the desired objectives was usually available. Although "design is a creative process and hence there are few absolutes that must be adhered to" (Rubin 1988) consideration was given at every stage to the human factors guidelines which play an important role in the new science of designing user interfaces. Two important characteristics of the interface are the fact it is menu-based and that it is, primarily, a colour application. The advantages of menu-based interfaces over those using command language are well known (Kantorowitz and Sudarsky 1989): there is no need to learn the command language which allows for productivity in a very short time, there is the possibility of exploring the operations provided by simply browsing through the menus and, if an adequate help system is installed, no need for a manual in most cases.

On the other hand, although colour is an excellent means of improving the comprehensibility of displays such as pie and bar charts (Rubin 1988), the use of colour must be judicious to avoid visual interaction that results in communication-damaging noise and that can produce strong after-effects. According to cartographic principles, background dull colours are more effective, allowing the smaller, bright areas to stand out with greater vividness (Tufte 1992). Rubin (1988) also states that the use of colour in a man-machine interface should be as consistent as possible with everyday usage. These basic principles were followed by XProcSim, where the default background colour is consistent through all the windows (light grey). Wherever possible, colour is used to convey information about the physical system itself. Units where green liquor is processed are coded green, units where lime is the main reactant are coded yellow, and so forth. In the lime kiln diagram, for example, colour goes from yellow to red as temperature increases. However, a package should never be totally dependent on the use of colour since potential users would be significantly restricted and compatibility of the interface with monochrome displays is now under development. Another basic feature of XProcSim is the fact that all its windows are scalable by the user. No limitation has been imposed on the maximum number of windows that can be displayed simultaneously. Windows can at any time be reduced to their iconic state — icons have been attributed to all of them — so that avoidance of a cluttered screen is left to the user.

The structure of the interface is presented in Fig.1.

Basically, the objectives aimed at were:

• Graphical representation of the process and individual units;

• Organization and easy access to simulation data;

• Graphical representation of results;

• Possibility of executing the simulation program on remote machines and full control of its execution status;

• Easy access to integration data;

• On-line help system;

• Error warning and recovery;

• Possibility of executing a selected set of UNIX commands through menu options provided by the interface.

2.1 Graphical Representation of the Process

A very simplified flowsheet of the process, in the form of a block diagram, is displayed on request and gives access to all of the data for all units. This diagram is formed by unit and stream type elements. Selecting one of these will display a pop-up menu containing all of information available for that unit or stream. These include schematic representations of all units, possibility of displaying instant internal profiles, design characteristics of the units, physico-chemical properties, and others.

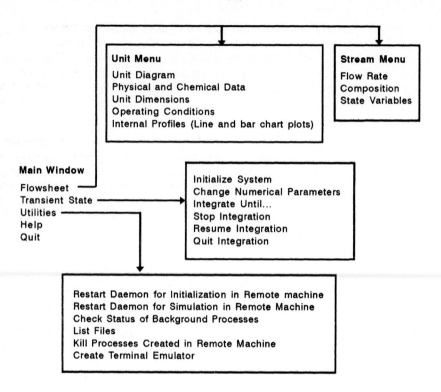

Fig. 1. Main options available through the interface.

2.2 Organization and Easy Access to Simulation Data

No commercial database of physical properties was used. However, all of the values used in the simulation of a unit, initially stored in files, are available and can be changed through the interface using data panels. Among these data are the already-referenced dimensions of the unit and physico-chemical parameters such as heat transfer coefficients, activation energies and Arrhenius constants for the chemical reactions.

2.3 Graphical Representation of Results

Two interactive modules, one for line charts and one for bar charts, have been developed to perform the final task of creating a visual image on the screen. The line chart is used to represent either profiles in space for a given time or variation of a variable with time. Because it would be impossible to prepare charts with all possible combinations of variables, only a limited number have been selected and are automatically prepared for graphical display. However, both the line and bar chart modules can load data files so the more experienced user can generate his own data files corresponding to whatever variables are required to be represented graphically. Both modules present a range of options to the user such as colour of all the elements, text font size, line width, colour and style (for the line chart), bar colour and fill pattern (for the bar chart) and automatic or manual selection of axis range.

2.4 Running the Simulation Program on a Remote Machine

The simulation program is at present being executed in a Sequent Symmetry UNIX machine, so execution times can reach critical values. Communication of the interface with the remote simulation program is done in two ways:

Successful RPC Calls Whenever possible, direct transfer of parameters is employed. The RPC (Remote Procedure Call) package is used to link the local C interface routines to a remote C routine which in turn calls the remote FORTRAN77 routine (see Fig.2). For this purpose a C/FORTRAN77 interface was developed.

Local Machine

Sun Sparc2gx Model 4/75
1- Interface Modules
2- Programming Language: C
3- C Compiler
   XWindow and XView Libraries

Remote Machine

Sequent Symmetry
1- C/Fortran77 Interface Modules
   Fortran77 Modules
2- Programming Languages:
   C and Fortran77
3- C and Fortran77 Compilers

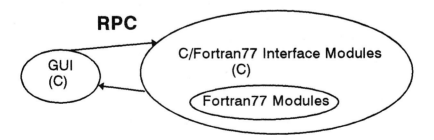

Fig. 2. C/FORTRAN77 structure.

Current parameters are transferred as arguments to the remote C routine using the UDP transfer mechanism. This made it necessary to develop XDR (EXternal Data Representation) routines which transform data particular to a specific machine into a machine-independent format.

Signal Handling Routines Initialization (reading all the default parameters) is done via an RPC call that will in principle have a successful return; sending the simulation parameters to the simulation program is done in the same way. However, execution time of the simulation program can be quite long and is usually unpredictable. In order to avoid blocking the interface until the remote routine returns, a short timeout for the RPC call is specified. An unsuccessful return occurs and is ignored, while execution continues in the remote machine. To compensate for the loss of the initial client/server link, flags are written to a log file whenever a change occurs in the execution status of the simulation program. This change can be the availability of new results or events such as abnormal termination (e.g., due to arithmetic exceptions) of the simulation programs. This led to the installation of a series of system signal handling routines, which catch signals generated by the system and write the appropriate flag to the log file. The interface possesses a routine that periodically checks the log file and takes apropriate action according to the flag value, such as displaying a dialog box to alert the user to the crash of the simulation programs. This methodology makes it possible to know what is happening to the simulation programs while the interface remains free for the analysis of results produced so far. System signals can be generated either by the system — and intercepted and handled by the signal handling routines — or by the user (e.g., to stop, pause or resume the integration) and sent to the remote program.

2.5   Easy Access to Integration Data

Data panels relative to the integration process have been provided. The consist of all the parameters needed by the LSODI integrator (Hindmarsh 1980). In case a different integrator is used, the corresponding data panel must be changed as well.

2.6   Implementation of an Effective On Line Help System

Any kind of help can bring a dramatic improvement in user performance. Giving users the option to make help requests is better in terms of speed of task and error frequency (Rubin 1988). Context-sensitive help (i.e., help information that is related to the particular point the user has reached) has been selected. Although it is quite simple to create a help button in every window which, on pressing, causes a text read-only window to be displayed, the optimal structure of such a help system has to be seriously thought through and is still under study.

2.7 Error Warning and Recovery

In the case of errors being made by the user on the interface side, error detection is simple and performed by checking the value returned by the function. If an error value is returned, a dialog box is displayed.

In the case of errors occurring on the simulation side, the strategy described in section 2.4.2 is employed. Dialog boxes are displayed in any case.

2.8 Possibility of Executing a Selected Set of UNIX Commands Through Menu Options

Including some UNIX commands as menu options was thought to be a convenient feature. The aim was to provide a very simple interface to the operating system in order to perform operations such as listing files or checking the processes currently being executed. All the already referenced commands to be sent to remote programs such as halting execution or resuming it are also UNIX commands, in the form of system calls. Lastly, if the user wants direct access to the operating system, a terminal emulator window can be created by the interface. This can be useful if a more experienced user wants to have full and unrestricted access to the operating system. The keyboard will then of course be used to input commands as with any command tool.

3 Conclusions

XView together with the X Window libraries have been shown to provide a wide range of graphics capabilities and a useful set of general purpose widgets. XProcSim is a GUI for the graphical representation and management of data pertaining to a specific set of simulation programs. Its future development is to create a front end for process flowsheeting and/or dynamic simulation programs in general.

The general guideline, as far as GUI's are concerned, seems to be that there are no strict guidelines. It is however generally accepted that, to be fully effective, a GUI must be consistent, easy to learn for the novice user, must provide shortcuts for the experienced user, obey ergonomic and human factors (such as adequate width and depth of menus) and even satisfy aesthetic considerations. At this point of the work, it is obvious that feedback from users is deeply needed in order to refine the prototype. This kind of practical information is probably, apart from theoretical considerations, the ultimate assessment of interface utility.

4 Acknowledgments

We are grateful to the Commission of the European Communities, under the Science Program grant contract No.B-SC1/900596, for the financial support that made this work possible.

Telephone Information Systems: Dialogue Specification Language

Andrés Santos, José Colás and Juan Lestani

Dpto. Ingeniería Electrónica - E.T.S.I.Telecomunicación, Univ. Politécnica Madrid
Spain. E-mail: andres@die.upm.es

Abstract. The success of automatic systems in providing information over the telephone relies heavily on the power and flexibility of the dialogue it is able to maintain. In this paper a language to define the dialogue scripts is presented. An environment for parsing, compiling and simulating applications has also been developed. It allows the designer to study the user's reactions to the system and to analyze its operation.

Keywords. Speech technology, dialogue definition, information systems, human-computer communication

1 Introduction

Speech technology can be applied in services that provide information through the telephone without the intervention of a human operator. The systems that are available today, however, provide limited information and they need touch-tone telephones. These systems have at least two basic faults: users can only access the information in a restricted and artificial way (menu-driven with codified commands) [1-3] and they have to use touch-tone telephones that are not universally available. (In some countries, like Spain, touch-tone telephones account for only 5 % of the terminals).

The success of automatic information systems depends highly on the use of speech technologies. Speech is the natural way to communicate among people of every culture. Any useful system needs speech recognition and speech production capabilities to operate through a telephone line. Furthermore, it has to control the dialogue flow so that the user gets the information, i.e., it needs a *dialogue manager* [4-6]. This dialogue manager receives requests from the user, decides whether more specific data from the user are needed, gives the information if available, etc.. To perform these tasks, it has to interact with the application, using some access functions.

Considering man-machine communication, there are two main restrictions: one is due to the capacities of the speech recognizer; the other to the possibilities of the system to *understand* and *generate* speech:

a) There are several kinds of recognizers categorized according to their vocabulary and complexity, from the simplest that can only recognize isolated digits to more complex systems that recognize continuous speech with large vocabularies. Obviously these differences have a big impact on the performance of the whole system [7, 8].

b) Depending on the system's ability to understand the user's speech, the dialogue can be menu-driven or unrestricted. In the first case, the user can only give answers included in a menu; the dialogue is then very limited as the user cannot give any unsolicited data. In the second one, the dialogue is much more flexible as the system can accept any answer; if it finds that more specifications are needed to provide the information solicited, it asks for such data [9, 10].

In this paper we will consider first different kinds of information systems with different complexities. In the following section the basic modules and tasks that are included in a general system will be presented. Next, a high-level language to define the dialogue and the operation of the system is described. Finally the application generator tool and its possibilities are considered.

2 Scenarios and Strategies of Dialogue

Dialogue can be thought as a sequence of communicative acts between the user and the information system. The behaviour of this system should have the objective of providing the information sought by the user (it has to be *successful*), but two subobjectives can be defined: minimizing the number of interactions in the dialogue (*effectiveness*) and achieving dialogues which are similar to human dialogues (*naturalness*).

With these objectives in mind, different models of system behaviour (different scenarios) can be defined. In each scenario the user has different degrees of flexibility to convey information to the system. The vocabulary and the linguistic contents that can be used are defined. So are the quantity and the kind of information that are interchanged in each dialogue intervention.

The system should transmit to the user these restrictions imposed on his/her answer. They define a *dialogue strategy*. Possible strategies are the following ones:

- **Menu-Driven:**

    a) Isolated Digits
    b) Isolated Words
    c) Digit spotting
    d) Word spotting

- **Unrestricted Speech (Natural-Language):**

    e) Multiple keyword spotting (island-driven)
    f) NL without dialogue history (semantically complete sentences)
    g) NL with dialogue history (including sentences with ellipsis or references to previous questions).

In the first two strategies, a and b, the system has to ask very restricted (and artificial) questions to constrict the user's answer (see the scenario in figure 1). Strategies c and d allow more natural questions and the user's answer is not so limited (figure 2).

<u>System</u>: Hello, this is Sports Information Service. Please, speak carefully, one word at a time. Is this the first time you have used this system, yes or no?
<u>User</u>: No.
<u>S</u>: You said no. Please, say <u>one</u> if you want <u>football</u>, say <u>two</u> if your choice is <u>basketball</u> or say <u>three</u> if you want <u>tennis</u>.
<u>U</u>: Two.
<u>S</u>: You said two. Information about basketball. The last results in the European Cup are...

Fig. 1. Example of dialogue using an isolated-digit recognizer

---

<u>System</u>: Hello, this is the train information system. Please, answer the questions speaking carefully. At any point, you can say <u>help</u> to obtain more information about this system or <u>operator</u> to speak to a human operator.
<u>S</u>: Where do you want to leave from?
<u>U</u>: From Madrid.
<u>S</u>: Where do you want to go?
<u>U</u>: To Valencia.
<u>S</u>: At what time?
<u>U</u>: Well... around 3 p.m.
<u>S</u>: So, you want to go from <u>Madrid</u> to <u>Valencia</u> approximately at <u>3 in the afternoon</u>. Is that right?
<u>U</u>: Yes.
<u>S</u>: There is a train at 3.15 ...

Fig. 2. Example of dialogue using a word-spotting recognizer.

Strategies e, f and g impose much more requirements on the module that processes the user inputs. The questions are more natural and the human answer is not so restricted (see scenario in figure 3).

S: Hello, this is the automatic train information system.
U: I want some information about trains to Valencia.
S: From where do you want to go to Valencia?
U: From Barcelona.
S: At what time?
U: In the afternoon.
S: So, you want to go from Barcelona to Valencia in the afternoon. Is that right?
U: No, sorry. I want to go in the morning.
S: O.K. You want to go from Barcelona to Valencia in the morning. Is that right?
U: Yes. In the morning.
S: Well. You have an Intercity at 8 o'clock...

Fig. 3. Example of unrestricted dialogue

3 Basic Architecture of a Dialogue System

The general structure of an information system is shown in figure 4 [11, 12]. Depending on the scenario, these modules have different degrees of complexity. In the following paragraphs, they will be commented.

3.1 Input Manager

This module is part of the user's interface. It provides the dialogue manager with the inputs from the user. For more complex tasks it can be divided into two different modules:

a) **Speech recognizer:** this is the acoustic module that tries to recognize the speech produced by the user and to give the corresponding sequence of words (text). It uses a specific vocabulary (not being able to recognize any word not included in this vocabulary), which may be different in each phase of the dialogue.

The recognizer could make some *errors*: part of the input could be misrecognized.

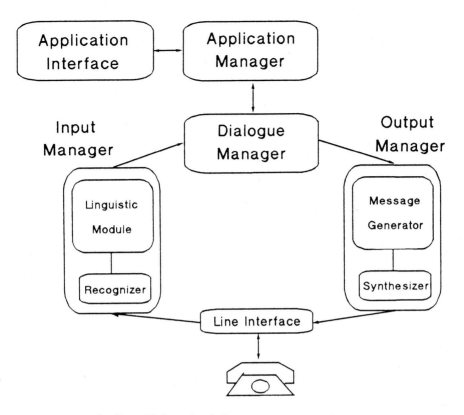

Fig. 4. Modules of a General Information System

b) **Linguistic module**: This works at the syntactic and semantic levels. Its objective is to produce a semantic representation of the user's input. It has linguistic information that could be a grammar, semantic rules, statistical data, etc.. In some systems, as in menu-driven dialogues, this module is very simple or does not exist at all.

Its *errors* are semantic: in the formalism used, it would not be possible to represent the input text or an incorrect representation may be found.

3.2 Output Manager

a) **Synthesizer**: The speech can be produced either with a text-to-speech converter (unrestricted vocabulary) or storing fixed messages. The first method gives much more flexibility to provide information, but its quality is usually lower.

b) **Message generator or selector**: Depending on the method used to produce speech, this module could just select one of the predefined messages, or it could produce the text to be sent to the synthesizer. Some techniques to generate natural language could be used in the most flexible scenario.

The messages produced by the system can be classified into four groups:

- Information requests: to complete or to define the user's demand.
- Confirmation of inputs.
- Answers - Information requested.
- Error Messages.

3.3 Application Manager

This is the only application specific module [13]. It translates the *application functions* used by the Dialogue Manager into commands and functions needed by the application. This module allows the rest of the system to be independent of the specific application.

3.4 Dialogue Manager

This is the main module that controls the dialogue. It works at the semantic level and interacts with the input and output managers and with the application manager.

The dialogue manager can be considered a finite automaton. The transition between states is determined by the input module. Each state can activate two kinds of functions:

- application functions: generally queries of a data base; they interact with the application manager to obtain the requested information if available.

- internal functions: to maintain the history of the dialogue to solve further ellipsis and ambiguous queries. They also provide some help to the user, call a human operator, etc.

This finite automaton can be studied in two different scenarios:

In <u>Menu-driven</u> applications the sequence of states that control the evolution of the dialogue seeks to obtain a complete query to access the data base. The user goes through a path of dialogue interactions until his/her request is fully defined.

In <u>Natural-Language</u> applications the dialogue manager builds a data structure that contains the information needed to produce a query in the formalism defined by the application manager. This dialogue manager should identify the missing information in the request made by the user and ask the corresponding question to obtain it.

In each case, the dialogue manager has two additional tasks:

Error handling: the manager has to identify the errors that may be produced in the other modules and take the corresponding action (it usually generates an error message).

Dialogue history: it has to maintain an internal data structure to keep track of the valid data in the previous dialogue interactions. This structure will allow the completion of further questions.

A dialogue state can be defined. In menu-driven systems it will be the state of the automaton. In natural-language applications it will be associated with the main data structure. In each case, the dialogue state will include:

- a set of current possible interactions with the application
- a linguistic sub-dialogue database: it could be the vocabulary available to the speech recognizer, the set of messages to be produced, etc.
- a set of possible errors and their handling procedures.
- a set of linguistic rules (grammar rules) to define the syntactic structure of the valid sentences at that point in the dialogue.

4 Dialogue Definition Language (DDL).

As seen in the previous section, the architecture required to build an application is complex, especially if we want a flexible and in some way intelligent dialogue. To build commercially viable applications, we should provide the *application developer* [14] with a standard architecture and a tool with which it can be edited. We expect the application developer to concentrate on designing a well structured dialogue, but he/she will not have a thorough knowledge of the internal operations of the system nor of the speech synthesizer/recognizer. Therefore, a high level language to describe the dialogue has been defined. It is called Dialogue Description Language (DDL) [15, 16].

DDL is a formal language to describe the operation of the whole system as a finite state machine. To define an application using DDL, the following elements have to be defined:

a) A set of dialogue states, each with a data structure and a history.
b) The transitions between states.
c) Functions, divided into three classes: I/O, control and application functions.
d) A subset of the language (vocabulary plus messages) active in each state.
e) A set of error handling procedures.

The following types of functions have been defined:

- I/O instructions:
    * Line Control: wait_for_call, answer_phone, hang up, ...
    * Speech output functions: synthesize, send_message (pre-recorded), record, ...
    * Speech input functions: recognize_vocabulary[1], recognize_digit_string, ...
    * Error handling: send_error_message, call_to_operator, ...

- Control instructions:
    * Flow control (transitions between states): goto, subroutine call, etc..
    * History keeping functions: store data, etc..

- Application Functions:
    * Search Functions

5 A Menu-Driven Application Generator with a Wizard-of-Oz Module Incorporated

Once the application designer has described the dialogue using DDL, he/she needs to test the description and to obtain user's reactions. The application generator is the tool that allows him/her to define and simulate the communication between the user and the application using DDL.

The application generator has the following functions:

* Editor (textual or graphical) to describe the application in DDL.
* Parser to detect errors in the description.
* Compiler to translate the application into the architecture, customizing the modules and the internal data structures.
* Help messages for the designer: about system characteristics, language functions and syntax, etc.
* Tools to edit the interface to the speech generator.
* Application Simulator: The system can be debugged simulating the

---

[1] The function that calls the recognizer deals with certain errors: no word recognized, timeout, too many errors, the user hangs up, etc.

interactions between the application and the users. The speech recognition module can be replaced by a human operator who listens to the dialogue and simulates the recognizer. In that way, the system goes from one state to the other, following the designed automaton. This method is known as the *wizard-of-oz* [6].

Figure 5 shows a block diagram of the whole tool.

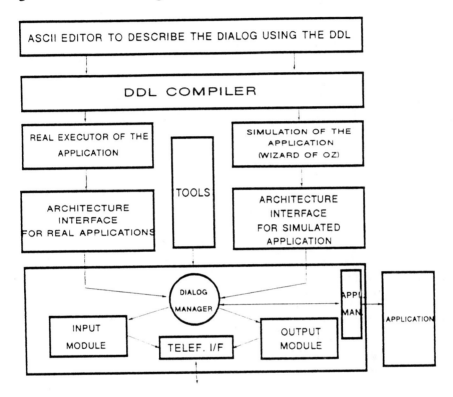

Fig. 5. Block Diagram of the Application Generator

6 Conclusions

A general model for automatic information systems has been presented. The structure has to be easy to customize and modify. So a Dialogue Definition Language (DDL) has been defined. It is fully adequate for menu-driven applications. For unrestricted speech, the general structure seems adequate, but further research is needed to translate the speech produced by the user into a data structure to guide the dialogue and the access to the application.

Acknowledgements

The authors wish to thank Juan Manuel Montero for his suggestions to improve this paper and Francisco Javier de Pedro for his contributions to the definition of DDL. This project has been supported by Comunidad de Madrid (C065/91).

References

1. Springer, S., Basson, S., Spitz, J. (1992) Identification of Principal Ergonomic Requirements for Interactive Spoken Language Systems. Proc. ICSLP 92, Canada, pp. 1395-1398.
2. Siles, J.A. (1990) Telephone Speech Input/Output Applications in Spain. SPEECH TECH '90.
3. Gagnoulet, C., Damay, J. (1990) MARIEVOX: A Speech-Activated Voice Information System. CNET, rapport de stage; Lannion, 1.990, pp. 569-572.
4. Guyomard, M., Siroux, J., Cozannet, A. (1989) The Role of Dialogue in Speech Recognition. The Case of the Yellow Pages System. Proc. EUROSPEECH 89, Paris, pp. 1051-1054.
5. Young, S.J., Proctor, C. (1989) The Design and Implementation of Dialogue Control in Voice Operated Database Inquiry Systems. Computer, Speech and Language 3, 329-353.
6. Jack, M.A., Foster, J.C., Steinford, F.W. (1992) Intelligent Dialogues in Automated Telephone Services. Proc. ICSLP 92, Canada, pp. 715-718.
7. Rosenbeck, P., Baungaard, B. (1992) Experiences from a Real-World Telephone Application: teleDialogue. Proc. ICSLP 92, Canada, pp. 1585-1588.
8. Riccio, A., Carraro, F., Mumolo, E. (1989) Voice Based Remote Data Base Access. Proc. EUROSPEECH 89, Paris, pp. 561-564.
9. Mast, M., Kompe, R., Kummert, F., Niemann, H., Nöth, E. (1992) The Dialog Module of the Speech Recognition and Dialog System EVAR. Proc. ICSLP 92, Canada, pp. 1573-1576.
10. Pozas, M.J., Mateos, J.F., Siles, J.A. (1990) Audiotext with Speech Recognition and Text to Speech Conversion for the Spanish Telephone Network. Voice System Worldwide 1990.
11. Noll, A., Bergmann, H., Hamer, H.H., Paeseler, A., Tomaschewski, H. (1992) Architecture of a Configurable Application Interface for Speech Recognition Systems. Proc. ICSLP 92, Canada, pp. 1539-1542.
12. Morin, P., Junqua, J.C., Pierrel, J.M. (1992) A Flexible Multimodal Dialogue Architecture Independent of the Application. Proc. ICSLP 92, Canada, pp. 939-942.
13. Haberbeck, R. (1989) The Communication Interface - A Management System for Advanced User Interfaces. Proc. EUROSPEECH 89, Paris, pp. 573-576.
14. Lofgren, D. (1988) A specialized language for voice response applications. Proc. Speech Tech '88, vol. 2, 1, 93-94, Media Dimensions Inc., New York.
15. Boogers, W. (1989) Dialogue Construction by Compilation. Proc. EUROSPEECH 89, Paris, pp. 853-856.
16. Nielsen, P.B., Baekgaara, A. (1992) Experience with a Dialogue Description Formalism for Realistic Applications. Proc. ICSLP 92, Canada, pp. 719-722.

Improving Functional Programming Environments for Education

J. Ángel Velázquez-Iturbide

Dpto. de Lenguajes y Sistemas Informáticos e Ingeniería de Software,
Facultad de Informática, Universidad Politécnica de Madrid,
Campus de Montegancedo s/n, Boadilla del Monte, 28660 Madrid, Spain

Abstract. Most functional programming environments are currently inadequate for educational purposes. A proposal of the minimum requirements these environments should satisfy to be successful is included; emphasis is put on the integration of tools and the existence of syntax and semantic-based tools. Early efforts to develop a prototype of an environment (named HIPE) along these lines are also described.

Keywords. Functional programming, integrated programming environments, expression evaluation, tracing, syntax-directed tools, editors, user interface

1 Introduction

Functional programming languages have experienced a great advance in the eighties, evolving from dialects of Lisp to modern functional languages [3]. The syntactic and semantic improvements of the later languages and the simplicity of the functional paradigm has promoted functional programming as an increasingly frequent subject matter in computer science education [6]. In particular, functional programming is very adequate for teaching some complex concepts of programming (e.g. recursion, data types), and for rapid prototyping.

Surprisingly, programming environments for modern functional languages are usually very crude. Even worse, most implementations are commonly not available for personal computers, machines very common in software laboratories. This is a consequence of the fact that functional programming is still in an experimental phase. The lack of environments adequate for educational use is an important tie for the expansion of this paradigm. However, the syntactic and semantic simplicity of functional languages allows us to hypothesize that building such environments will not be too costly, compared to the potential profit.

The paper describes the minimum requirements a functional programming environment should fulfil to be successful in educational use and the author's experience in building a prototype along these lines for the functional programming language Hope$^+$. The paper is structured as follows. Sect. 2 describes the requirements we identify for educational environments for functional programming, including desirable features and tools. The third section describes the prototype mentioned above, named HIPE. In Sect. 4 we describe some of the improvements we plan for the prototype and our experience with the environment.

Familiarity of the reader with functional programming [3] is assumed in the paper; the interested reader should refer to [2, 4] for more information about the language Hope⁺, [6] for a design of a modern course on functional programming, [9] for a detailed description of HIPE, including a comparison with related environments, and [10] for details of the implementation of HIPE.

2 Requirements for an Educational Environment for Functional Programming

Programming has been recognized as a task hard enough to deserve the best software tools. Ideally, a programming environment would carry out all the tedious and repetitive tasks, and would aid the programmer in the more creative tasks. The user interface would be friendly to reduce the user's cognitive load for these tasks.

Requirements for a programming environment to teach functional programming can be better identified after considering current context:

- Existing environments for functional programming, based on either Lisp or other functional language. It is remarkable that most environments for the latter languages are just a set of tools, with emphasis on interpreter efficiency.
- Current hardware and software technology. The scenario described in the first paragraph only seems to be realistic if programming environments make exhaustive use of current technology. In this regard, three developments are especially influential: personal computers, friendly user interfaces, and integrated programming environments and syntax-directed tools.
- Educational purpose. A comprehensive education in computer science must include and bring together theoretical and experimental aspects [8]. Programming environments contain the tools used for programming experimentation, so they should be designed to relate practice to theory.

We think that, given this context, a programming environment suitable for the teaching of functional programming must fulfil the following requirements:

- It must be an integrated programming environment.
- It must include a small and powerful set of tools, that reflect and exploit the syntax and semantics of the language.

Let us analyze and elaborate on these requirements in detail.

2.1 Integrated Programming Environments

A programming environment contains a set of *tools* and *utilities* that help the programmer to develop programs: editors, compilers, etc. Their usage is facilitated if the programming environment is *integrated* [1]. The integration of tools can be achieved with respect to several criteria [7]:

- Presentation. Minimize the cognitive load the user suffers when she interacts with the tools. This property is usually achieved when user interfaces have similar appearance, behaviour and interaction. The user interface of current functional programming environments is commonly very rudimentary.
- Data. The information (i.e. programs) contained in the environment is managed as a consistent and nonredundant whole.
- Control. The user must be able to use flexibly the tools in the environment.
- Process. Support effectively the programming part of the software process [1]. Usually, functional programming environments include a compiler or interpreter and some additional utilities (e.g. tracing). However, they are not integrated environments since they do not provide other tools necessary to support a simple programming process (e.g. an editor and some book-keeping facilities).

As a consequence, an integrated environment to teach functional programming should provide at least the following elements:

- A friendly user interface, with similar appearance, behaviour and interaction for the different tools of the environment.
- A consistent and nonredundant management of the user's programs.
- A set of tools that permit the easy development of functional programs: an editor, a compiler or interpreter with tracing facilities, and a set of utilities necessary to carry out mundane tasks, such as handling of files and programs.

2.2 Tools Based on Operational Semantics

Functional languages have a very simple operational semantics, where functional expressions are evaluated according to a system of rewriting rules and a strategy of application. Tools and utilities related to the execution of functional programs should be based on this semantics, rather than on other *ad hoc* views (e.g. function calls). The following utilities can be identified as relevant for educational use:

- Freedom to *choose the evaluation strategy*, at least the eager and lazy strategies. In this way, algorithmic techniques based on lazy evaluation can be explored [2]. In the rest of the paper, use of eager evaluation is assumed.
- Flexible control of the number of rewriting steps applied to a given expression during evaluation. In this way the programmer can *trace* any intermediate expression, what can be used, depending on the case, either to *understand* the execution of programs or to *debug* programs.

    One way of controlling easily the number of rewriting steps is to give the user several kinds of advance, that she may select and combine. At least three kinds of advance can be identified:

a) Step-by-step: The expression is rewritten only for the first step.

b) Break-point: The expression is rewritten until a break point is reached. Functions can be arbitrarily marked as break functions. A break point appears when the next rewriting step is the application of a break function.

c) Complete: The expression is completely evaluated. The resulting final expression is the value of the original expression.

An example can illustrate these ideas further. Suppose we have the following program that determines whether an element is contained in a list:

```
infix or : 4 ;
dec or : truval # truval -> truval ;
--- true   or _ <= true ;
--- false or b̄ <= b ;

dec member : alpha # list(alpha) -> truval ;
--- member (_,nil ) <= false ;
--- member (x,y::l) <= (x=y) or member (x,l) ;
```

An example of complete evaluation of an expression is as follows:

```
member (4,[4,5])
↓
true : truval
```

Step-by-step advance would provide a sequence of intermediate expressions:

```
member (4,[4,5])
↓
(4 = 4) or member (4,[5])
↓
true or member (4,[5])
↓
true or ((4 = 5) or member (4,nil))
↓
true or (false or member (4,nil))
↓
true or (false or false)
↓
true or false
↓
true : truval
```

If advance proceeds through successive break-points produced by function member, a shorter sequence that only shows expressions with recursive applications of member is obtained:

```
member (4,[4,5])
↓
true or member (4,[5])
↓
true or (false or member (4,nil))
↓
true : truval
```

Notice the difference between this way of watching intermediate expressions and usual tracing utilities. Our proposal shows complete expressions during the evaluation, while usual tracing only shows selected parts of the expression (e.g. function applications), out from the context where they emerge.

2.3 Tools Based on Syntax and Static Semantics

Functional languages have a simple syntax and static semantics, making feasible the embedding of syntax and static semantics in several tools:

- *Syntax-directed editor.* Syntax-based editors [5] alleviate the programmer from typing whole programs, but produce these programs under guidance of the programmer. This kind of interaction guarantees secure hand-typing, and is useful when the effort necessary to press the appropriate keys is less than that necessary to type the corresponding text. This effort is worthwhile for expressions with a fixed format (typically containing reserved words), but not for arbitrary expressions. As a consequence, a mixed text and syntax directed editor is more appropriate for functional programs; functional expressions would be typed by the programmer and other parts would be produced *via* commands.
   For instance, the initial state of the editor would be:

```
<declaration>
```

where the user could select to expand this prompt with a declaration of a function. The previous declaration would be converted into:

```
dec <function identifier> : <data type> ;
<equation>
```

Now the programmer could write the identifier and the data type of the function `member`. She could also expand or write, where appropriate, the equations of `member` until the whole function declaration was developed.
   An attractive feature of syntax-directed editors is the possibility of coping with *static semantic*, e.g. to check whether an identifier has been declared previously. In effect, syntax-directed editors can manage internally a representation of the syntax of the program, augmented with static semantic information. As a consequence, semantic information can be easily propagated.
   For instance, let the current state of the editing of `member` be the following:

```
dec member : alpha # list(alpha) -> truval ;
<equation>
```

The programmer can choose an option to expand the equation. The resulting equation will contain the name of the function, since it is known, producing:

```
dec member : alpha # list(alpha) -> truval ;
--- member <pattern> <= <functional expression> ;
<equation>
```

The most interesting checks of semantics in functional programs are *data type checks*. Well-typing of expressions, as well as pattern completeness and consistency could be interactively checked.

For instance, during the previous editing session, the editor should report on an overlapping between the patterns of the next two equations:

```
--- member (_,nil) <= false ;
--- member (x,1) <= <functional expression> ;
```

and the user would modify appropriately the second pattern, if desired.

- *Syntax-directed tracing.* We saw in last subsection that tracing utilities based on operational semantics show clearly the process of evaluation, but the user can get lost when expressions are very large. One solution is to have the possibility of browsing through expressions under syntax support. In this way, a large expression obtained during the evaluation process could be easily examined using common facilities in a syntax-directed editor, such as *ellipsis* [5], i.e. reducing irrelevant parts of an expression with suspension points.

For instance, if advance with break-points was performed keeping anything but recursive calls under ellipsis, the resulting trace would be:

```
member (4,[4,5])
↓
   ... member (4,[5])
↓
   ... member (4,nil)
↓
true : truval
```

where the sequence of recursive calls is easily appreciated. At each step, the programmer should be able to view an expression in different ways. For instance, three different views of the last intermediate expression are:

```
... member (4,nil)
true or (false or (member (4,nil)))
true or ...
```

3 HIPE: Hope⁺ Integrated Programming Environment

An environment prototype based on the previous ideas has been developed. The environment is called HIPE (for *Hope⁺ Integrated Programming Environment*), in a trial to find a name similar to the name of the language.

The environment is integrated with respect to the aspects detailed in Sect. 2.1. For instance, data integration is achieved by keeping a unique representation of programs in the environment, stored in an internal form, appropriate for efficient evaluation of expressions. However, the user views programs as text. Translation between both representations is made when necessary, e.g. to edit a program.

3.1 User Interface

HIPE has an homogenous user interface that provides presentation integration. The screen is divided into three parts: a top line with a menu bar, a bottom line for informative messages, and the rest as working area.

The dialog is based on *text menus* and *text editors*. Menus are used to select operations of the environment (e.g. evaluating a given expression), and editors are used to introduce data. There is a line editor to introduce strings of characters (e.g. a file name), and three screen editors to introduce larger amount of data, namely a file editor, a program editor and an expression editor.

The use of menus prevents the user both from learning a command language to handle the environment and from making input mistakes that would occur if she had to write what she wants, instead of choosing it. The selected menu format is usual in many commercial products: hierarchical menu structure, a main menu bar, secondary pulldown menus, navigation through the options with the cursor, etc.

One important consequence of adopting consistently this style of interaction is a change in the way of evaluating expressions. Traditional environments are based in the so-called *read-eval-write loop*, i.e. the user writes an expression, the environment evaluates it and finally its value is presented to the user. Users of HIPE edit expressions, which later are selected for evaluation with a menu option.

3.2 Utilities and Tools

The utilities and tools of the environment can be classified into four groups:

- *Interaction with the operating system.* The environment has the usual options for this task: change the active unit or directory, consult the file contents of the active directory, load the program contained in a file, store a program to a file, and terminate the environment execution. The menu also contains a file editor facility that can be used to edit text files (e.g. to determine whether a program is appropriate to be loaded, or to examine an evaluation of an expression).
- *Editing Hope* programs.* The user can edit functional programs with a program editor. For the sake of flexibility, there are two editing modes: the user can edit the whole program or a single declaration.
- *Evaluation of functional expressions.* Functional expressions can be edited and evaluated. The environment keeps a list of expressions, so that the programmer can edit a new expression, or modify or select an existing one. The user can also select the evaluation strategy, and mark or unmark existing functions as break-functions. Finally, the user can control the advance of evaluation of the selected expression, choosing and combining the three advances identified in Sect. 2.2. A completed evaluation can be saved in a file if desired.
- *Book-keeping of the environment.* A set of utilities allows the user to handle easily the declarations stored in the environment. Thus, the set of program

identifiers can be looked up under their syntactic category (e.g. data type). The declaration of a selected identifier can be examined or deleted, and its identifier can be renamed. The same operations can also be done on identifiers of modules. Finally, it is possible to clear the environment of declarations.

4 Future Developments and Experience

HIPE is a first step towards the fulfilment of the requirements described in Sect. 2. We think that integration features described in Sect. 2.1 have been mostly achieved. Likewise, we have developed tools described in Sect. 2.2, but tools described in Sect. 2.3 still have to be developed.

Independently from further improvements, the prototype system is nearly ready to be tested by students in their functional programming course. We plan to use HIPE experimentally during the next school year with a group of students, so that in the subsequent year it can be used by all the students with confidence.

Acknowledgements

This work was supported by the Universidad Politécnica de Madrid under contract A-9333, and by the Comisión Interministerial de Ciencia y Tecnología under contract TIC91-0111.

References

1. Dart, S.A., Ellison, R.J., Feiler, P.H., Habermann, A.N.: Software development environments. Computer 20, 11, 18-28 (1987)
2. Field, A.J., Harrison, P.E.: Functional programming. Reading: Addison-Wesley 1988
3. Hudak, P.: Conception, evolution and application of functional programming languages. ACM Computing Surveys 21, 3, 354-411 (1989)
4. Perry, N.: Hope⁺. Technical report IC/FPR/LANG/2.5.1/7, Dept. of Computing, Imperial College, University of London, 1989
5. Reps, T., Teitelbaum, T.: Language processing in program editors. Computer 20, 11, 29-40 (1987)
6. Sánchez-Calle, A., Velázquez-Iturbide, J.A.: Fun, rigour and pragmatism in functional programming. SIGCSE Bulletin 23, 3, 11-16 (1991)
7. Thomas, I., Nejmeh, B.A.: Definitions of tool integration for environments. IEEE Software 9, 2, 29-35 (1992)
8. Tucker, A.: Computing curricula 1991. Communications of the ACM 34, 6, 68-84 (1991)
9. Velázquez-Iturbide, J.A., Belmonte-Artero, M., Castillo-Sánchez, J.A.: An integrated programming environment for the functional language Hope⁺. In: XVIII Conferencia Latinoamericana de Informática. Proceedings, 1218-1226, Las Palmas de Gran Canaria 1992. (In Spanish)
10 Velázquez-Iturbide, J.A., Belmonte-Artero, M., Castillo-Sánchez, J.A.: Architecture of an integrated environment for functional programming. In: Primer Congreso Nacional de Programación Declarativa. Proceedings, 345-348, Madrid 1992. (In Spanish)

Designing an Intelligent Interface for an Advice-Giving System

Ivan Alexandrov and Mariofanna Milanova

Technical University of Sofia
kv. "Strelbishte" bl. 25, ap. 20, Sofia-1404, Bulgaria

Abstract. The techniques for man-machine communication are applied to the development of a CAM (Computer-Aided Manufacturing) system which automatically generates a program for CNC (Computer Numeric Control) machines in order to produce a given detail in manufacturing. The CAM system generates CNC programs for the following types of detail manufacture: 2-D and 3-D milling, turning, pocketing, drilling and wire EDM machining. It also includes an advice-giving module which determines the sequence of tools that can be used for manufacture of a given detail and the regimes of processing. The interface between man and computer is organized using different types of man-machine communication: menus, y/n questions, requests with syntax for response, commands. This system has been adopted in different Bulgarian and Russian enterprises.

Keywords. CAM system, CNC machines, man-machine commucation

1 Introduction

The development of computer sytems presently is causing the number of computer users to be sharply incremented. Most of them are not computer specialist and they do not have time to learn much about computers. That is why modern computer systems have to take into consideration the features of the human mind and to help people solve their problems using a minimum of effort. Creators of computer systems should also take into consideration that users have different levels of knowledge about computers, i.e. the systems can be used by beginners, intermediate specialists and experts.

2 Man-Machine Communication

Man-machine communication means the interactive exchange of messages between a user and a computer system in order to solve a certain task. A basic principle of man-machine communication consists of the user's independent choice of input and the system's totally deterministic reaction. Dialog can be considered as a problem-solving method where the user knows the problem and the system is used to solve subproblems [1].

Man-machine communication can be organized in different way, but can be classified by 3 levels of abstraction: basic structure, representation and technical realization. Basic structure includes fundamental features which characterize the dialog. These are the problems about the initiator of the dialog, the way the action influences the reaction, the establishment of the task and so on. Representation includes the description of messages by which action and reaction are represented (vocabulary, inner and outer format, etc.). Technical realization includes the technical media (input and output facilities) by which the messages are realized.

On the basis of the basic structure six types of abstract dialog exist:

--Simple question. This is a question by the system with predetermined input interpretation: the user can only enter objects that will be interpreted. This type is mentioned in connection with data collection;

--Proposal for selection. The user chooses from a set of alternative tasks proposed by the system. Two variants of this dialog type are the menu and the yes/no question;

--Request with syntax for response. This means a system's request on which the user has to react with a syntactically restricted input. A question of the system about the data is a request of this type;

--Request for free response. The system demands from the user a statement in quasi-natural language;

--Command. The user specifies his tasks and objects according to a prescribed syntax;

--Quasi-natural language statement. The user freely chooses a task using a familiar language. This type of dialog imposes the least restrictions on the user.

On the basis of the representation, the dialogues can be classified using the following components: vocabulary, inner and outer format of input, formal input redundancy, output syntax and format, semantic properties and others.

3 Description of the System

Our team has developed a CAM system which can be connected with any other CAD system (for example, AutoCAD by AutoDESK) and which can generate CNC programs for the following types of detail manufacture: 2-D and 3-D milling, turning, pocketing, drilling and wire EDM machining [2-3].

The flowchart of the system is given in Fig. 1. The interface between the user and the computer system is organized using some menus. At first the user has to select the type of operation he wants to use (milling or turning or pocketing or something else). Then he has to choose the tool and its diameter. The tool can be selected from a tool library where tools are presented as icons. The geometry of the detail has already been given in the CAD system so the user has to tell the CAM system where this geometry is stored. He has also to determine some regimes of manufacture such as spindle, feedrate, etc. After that the system determines the tool path and creates the CLDATA file. Using a menu, which contains different types of post-processors, the user can select the suitable post-processor for its CNC machine and as a result a CNC program is generated.

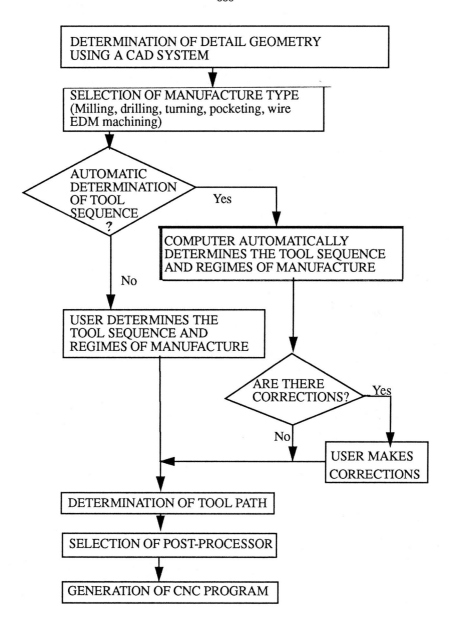

Fig. 1. Flowchart of the System

For some types of manufacture an advice-giving module is developed. This module can determine the sequence of tools that can be used for manufacture of a given detail and the regimes of processing in drilling (more precisely, manufacture of holes) and milling (more precisely, manufacture of channels). The sequence of tools and regimes of manufacture given by the advice-giving module can be used directly by users or can be corrected. This module asks users about the sizes and the locations of the holes and channels to manufacture. In order to determine the tool sequence and the regimes of manufacture the system uses algorithms which are developed on the basis of the knowledge of specialists in this field.

The following types of man-machine communication are used in the system:

-- Menu. In this case the dialog step consists of the display of section possibilities (action) and the indication of the chosen alternative (reaction). The action has the following basic characteristics: vocabulary (natural language words) and output syntax (quasi-natural language sentences). The reaction has the following characteristics: vocabulary (natural language words), inner format (a sentence out of those displayed in the action) and outer format (free, with an input termination symbol at the end);

-- Yes/no question. The characteristics of the action are the same as in the previous point (menu). The characteristics of the reaction are: vocabulary ({yes,no}), inner format (a single word is allowed) and outer format (free);

-- Request with syntax for response. This type is used when the user should determine the sizes of holes and channels;

-- Command. This type is used when the user should determine the location of the holes and channels. He initiates the dialog between himself and the computer system when he tells the system that there is a hole or a channel somewhere.

4 Conclusions

A CAM system was developed. This system gives users the possibility of generating CNC programs for detail manufacture. The man-machine communication in this system is developed on the basis of modern techniques. That is why the system is user-friendly so people can work easily with it.

References

1. Dehning W., Essig H., Maass S.: The adaptation of virtual Man-Computer Interfaces to User Requirements in Dialogs, Lecture Notes in Computer Science, 110. Berlin: Springer-Verlag 1981
2. Pavlidis T.: Algorithms for graphics and image processing, Computer Science Press, 1982
3. Choi, Lee, Hwang, Jun: Compound surface modelling and machining, CAD, 1988.
4. Kim, Biegel: A path generation method for sculptured surface manufacture, Computer Engineering, 1988

List of Participants

Ivan Alexandrov
Technical University of Sofia
kv. "Strelbishte" bl. 25 ap 20
Sofia 1404, Bulgaria

Antonella de Angeli
University of Trieste
Via dell'Universita N. 7
I-34123 Trieste, Italy

Lisette Appelo
Institute for Perception Research/IPO
P.O. Box 513
NL-5600 MB Eindhoven, The Netherlands

Philip Barker
University of Teesside
School of Computing and Mathematics
Borough Road
Middlesborough, Cleveland TS1 3BA, United Kingdom

Dominique Béroule
LIMSI-CNRS
BP 30
91406 Orsay Cedex, France

Robbert-Jan Beun
Institute for Perception Research/IPO
P.O. Box 513
NL-5600 MB Eindhoven, The Netherlands

Tom Bösser
ACit - Advance Concepts for interactive technology GmbH
Spiekerhof 6-8
D-48143 Münster, Germany

Don Bouwhuis
Institute for Perception Research/IPO
P.O. Box 513
NL-5600 MB Eindhoven, The Netherlands

Sviatoslav Brainov
Bulgarian Academy of Sciences
Institute of Mathematics
Acad. G., Bonchev str. bl. 8
Sofia 1113, Bulgaria

Eric Brok
Open University
Faculty of Engineering
P.O. Box 2960
NL-6401 DL Heerlen, The Netherlands

Maddy D. Brouwer-Janse
Institute for Perception Research/IPO
P.O. Box 513
NL-5600 MB Eindhoven, The Netherlands

Shari Campbell
Department of Speech and Hearing Sciences
University of Washington
Seattle, WA 98195, USA

Igor Chmyr
Institute of Low Temperature
Engineering and Energetics
1/3 Petra Velikogo St.,
Odessa 270100, CIS, Ukraine

David Connah
Institute for Perception Research/IPO
P.O. Box 513
NL-5600 MB Eindhoven, The Netherlands

Mark Cosgrove
University of Technology
Science and Technology Education
P.O. Box 222
Lindfield NSW 2070, Australia

Anita Cremers
Institute for Perception Research/IPO
P.O. Box 513
NL-5600 MB Eindhoven, The Netherlands

Donald Day
Syracuse University
School of Information Studies
4-282 Center of Science and Technology
Syracuse, NY 13244-4100, USA

Berry Eggen
Institute for Perception Research/IPO
P.O. Box 513
NL-5600 MB Eindhoven, The Netherlands

Roger Espinosa
University of Michigan
School of Education
610 East University
Ann Arbor, MI 48109-1259, USA

William Gaver
Rank Xerox Cambridge EuroPARC
61 Regent Street
Cambridge CB2 1AB, United Kingdom

Tedde van Gelderen
Institute for Perception Research/IPO
P.O. Box 513
NL-5600 MB Eindhoven, The Netherlands

Ronny Geluykens
Universitaire Faculteit St. Ignatius Antwerpen
Faculteit Letteren en Wijsbegeerte
Rodestraat 14
B-2000 Antwerpen, Belgium

Tom Harrington
Fast Motion Perception
4715 Mayberry Drive
Reno, NV 89509, USA

Rachelle Heller
George Washington University
Department of Electrical Engineering
and Computer Science
81 22nd Street, NW
Washington DC 20052, USA

Stacie Hibino
University of Michigan
188 Frieze Building
Ann Arbor, MI 48109-1285, USA

Rudy van Hoe
Universiteit Gent
Department of Experimental Psychology
H. Dunantlaan 2
B-9000 Gent, Belgium

Robert J.K. Jacob
Human-Computer Interaction Lab.
Naval Research Laboratory
Washington, DC 20375, USA

James Juola
University of Kansas
Department of Psychology
Fraser Hall
Lawrence, KS 66045, USA

Victor Kaptelinin
Russian Academy of Education
Psychological Institute
9 "V" Mokhovaja Str.,
103009 Moscow, CIS, Russia

Andrzej Kasiński
Department of Control, Robotics and Computer Science
Politechnika Poznańska
60-965 Poznań, Poland

David Keyson
Institute for Perception Research/IPO
P.O. Box 513
NL-5600 MB Eindhoven, The Netherlands

Helen Kommissarova
Psychological Insitute of the Ukraine
2 Pankovskaya
252033 Kiev, CIS, Ukraine

Gilbert Madigan
Tilburg University
Computer Department C220
P.O. Box 90153
NL-5000 LE Tilburg, The Netherlands

Betty Majoor
Institute for Perception Research/IPO
P.O. Box 513
NL-5600 MB Eindhoven, The Netherlands

Judith Masthoff
Institute for Perception Research/IPO
P.O. Box 513
NL-5600 MB Eindhoven, The Netherlands

Teddy McCalley
Institute for Perception Research/IPO
P.O. Box 513
NL-5600 MB Eindhoven, The Netherlands

Britta Meurers
Universität Gesamthochschule Kassel (Fachbereich 03)
Holländische Strasse 36-38
D-34127 Kassel, Germany

Michael Miettinen
University of Helsinki
Department of Psychology
FIN-00014 University of Helsinki, Finland

Peter Mikulecký
Department of Computer Science
Institute of Management and Information Technology
501 91 Hradec Králové, Czech Republic

Mariofanna Milanova
Technical University of Sofia
kv. "Strelbishte" bl. 25 ap 20
Sofia 1404, Bulgaria

Paul Munro
Department of Information Science
University of Pittsburgh
3939 O'Hara Street
Pittsburgh, PA 15260, USA

Floris van Nes
Institute for Perception Research/IPO
P.O. Box 513
NL-5600 MB Eindhoven, The Netherlands

Mike Oaksford
University of Wales
Department of Psychology
Bangor, Gwynedd LL57 2DG, United Kingdom

Margriet Offereins
Twente University
Department of Computer Science
P.O. Box 217
NL-7500 AE Enschede, The Netherlands

Fátima Pais
Universidade de Coimbra
Engenharia Quimica
Largo Marquês de Pombal
P-3000 Coimbra, Portugal

Garry Patterson
University of Ulster
Department of Information Systems
Co. Antrim BT37 0QB, Jordanstown, United Kingdom

Oleg Pilipenko
Odessa State University
2 Petra Velikogo St.,
Odessa 270100, CIS, Ukraine

Octav Popescu
Research Institute for Informatics
8-10 Averescu Boulevard
71316 Bucharest 1, Romania

Eva Ragnemalm
University of Linköping
Department of Computer Science
S-581 83 Linköping, Sweden

Amadeu L. Rodrigues
New University of Lisbon FCT/UNL
P-2825 Monte de Caparica, Portugal

Andrés Santos
Universidad Politécnica Madrid
E.T.S.I. Telecomunicación
Ciudad Universitaria
Dr. Federico Rubio 100
E-28040 Madrid, Spain

Alma Schaafstal
IZF-TNO
P.O. Box 23
NL-3769 ZG Soesterberg, The Netherlands

Benjamin Singer
Laboratoire Aramiihs
31, Rue des Cosmonautes
F-31077 Toulouse Cedex, France

Olga Soler
Universitat Autònoma de Barcelona
Departament de Psicologia de l'Educació
Apartat postal 29
08193 Bellaterra (Barcelona), Spain

Gerard Spaai
Institute for Perception Research/IPO
P.O. Box 513
NL-5600 MB Eindhoven, The Netherlands

Marc Swerts
Universitaire Instelling Antwerpen
Departement Germaanse Filologie
Universiteitsplein 1
B-2610 Wilrijk, Belgium

Alp Tiritoglu
University of Kansas
Department of Design
Fraser Hall
Lawrence, KS 66045, USA

Dan Tufis
Center for Research on Machine Learning and Language
Processing
Romanian Academy
Calea Victoriei 125
Ro 71102, Bucharest 1, Romania

J. Ángel Velázquez-Iturbide
Universidad Politecnica de Madrid
Facultad de Informática
Campus de Montegancedo, s/n,
Boadilla del Monte
E-28660 Madrid, Spain

Ellen Verheijen
Institute for Perception Research/IPO
P.O. Box 513
NL-5600 MB Eindhoven, The Netherlands

Remko Westrik
Institute for Perception Research/IPO
P.O. Box 513
NL-5600 MB Eindhoven, The Netherlands

Subject Index

NATO ASI Series F

Including Special Programmes on Sensory Systems for Robotic Control (ROB) and on Advanced Educational Technology (AET)

NATO ASI Series F

Including Special Programmes on Sensory Systems for Robotic Control (ROB) and on Advanced Educational Technology (AET)

NATO ASI Series F

NATO ASI Series F

Including Special Programmes on Sensory Systems for Robotic Control (ROB) and on Advanced Educational Technology (AET)

NATO ASI Series F

Including Special Programmes on Sensory Systems for Robotic Control (ROB) and on Advanced Educational Technology (AET)

NATO ASI Series F

Springer-Verlag
and the Environment

We at Springer-Verlag firmly believe that an international science publisher has a special obligation to the environment, and our corporate policies consistently reflect this conviction.

We also expect our business partners – paper mills, printers, packaging manufacturers, etc. – to commit themselves to using environmentally friendly materials and production processes.

The paper in this book is made from low- or no-chlorine pulp and is acid free, in conformance with international standards for paper permanency.